# WOMEN'S AMERICAN FOOTBALL

Breaking Barriers
On and Off
the Gridiron

**RUSS CRAWFORD**

University of Nebraska Press   Lincoln

Acknowledgments for the use of previously
published material appear on page ix, which
constitutes an extension of the copyright page.

The University of Nebraska Press is part of a land-
grant institution with campuses and programs on the
past, present, and future homelands of the Pawnee,
Ponca, Otoe-Missouria, Omaha, Dakota, Lakota, Kaw,
Cheyenne, and Arapaho Peoples, as well as those of the
relocated Ho-Chunk, Sac and Fox, and Iowa Peoples.

Publication of this volume was assisted
by the Getty College of Arts and Sciences
at Ohio Northern University.

Library of Congress Cataloging-in-Publication Data
Names: Crawford, Russ, author.
Title: Women's American football: breaking
barriers on and off the gridiron / Russ Crawford.
Description: Lincoln: University of Nebraska Press,
[2022] | Includes bibliographical references and index.
Identifiers: LCCN 2022002169
ISBN 9781496233332 (Hardback: acid-free paper)
ISBN 9781496233813 (ePub)
ISBN 9781496233820 (PDF)
Subjects: LCSH: National Women's Football League
(U.S.)—History. | Women football players—United
States—History. | Football—United States—
History. | BISAC: SPORTS & RECREATION /
Football | SOCIAL SCIENCE / Women's Studies
Classification: LCC GV955.5.N37 C73 2022 |
DDC 796.330820973—dc23/eng/20220604
LC record available at https://lccn.loc.gov/2022002169

Set in Lyon Text by Mikala R. Kolander.
Designed by L. Auten.

# Contents

# Acknowledgments

Any author depends on the help of a number of people to create a manuscript. I have been fortunate to have the help of more than 240 women and several men from the United States and around the world who have told me their football stories. Thank you to each and every one. I did not quote each of you in the pages that follow, but you all helped me understand the motivation and struggles of women playing American football.

I would particularly like to thank Louise Bean for serving as something of a research assistant by putting me in touch with several of her teammates and opponents. Likewise, Crys Sacco helped me get several interviews with players from the Utah Girls Football League. Carolyn O'Leary, of the Columbus Comets, surprised me at the New Orleans Saints' practice facility when she recognized my voice from previous interviews she had listened to. Then she invited me to a Comets practice session for more interviews. Diane Beruldsen not only gave me several interviews, most of which do not appear in this book, but she also talked to my students and welcomed me to her P-Town Classic flag football tournament and the Kelly McGillis Classic tournament.

Oscar Lopez and Michael Burmy are the strongest voices for women's football online. Lopez's *Gridiron Beauties* podcast runs weekly with news from all women's leagues around the world. Burmy's Hometown Women's Football Facebook site also carries all the news that is news on women's football in the United States. Both men agreed to do interviews with me, and Lopez had me on his program several times.

This book would have been very difficult without Neal Rozendaal's *Encyclopedia of Women's Football*, and I was happy that Frankie de la Cretaz and Lyndsey D'Arcangelo's *Hail Mary: The Rise and Fall of the National Women's Football League* was published in time for me to read before editing this.

Book projects also often cost a considerable amount to research, and my university, Ohio Northern University, along with ONU's Getty College of Arts and Sciences, has allowed me to travel to many locations to conduct interviews. Thank you also to my wife, Sophie, who encouraged my travels and even went to some football games with me. Thanks also to Jean-Marc Burtscher, who took me to my first women's game. Just another step in our Mission for Football!

Roger Kelly of *American Football International* has smoothed the way by providing me with press credentials that have given me access to various events. I suppose that I should also thank Dr. Jennifer Welter, the head coach of the Australian National Team, for making me feel like an actual reporter by sending an assistant coach to ask me to leave her team's practice. Jason Aikens, the archivist of the Pro Football Hall of Fame in Canton, helped me access their Women's Football file.

Oral history does not end when one turns off the recording device, and a truly awful part of the process is transcribing. So thank you to all of my student research assistants who worked for me, or students in my various courses who earned extra credit by helping me out. In particular, I would like to thank Emily Hughes, Ryan Oberlin, Nate Bracy, Katie Hauter, Jennifer Ulmer, and Cassie Krencisz.

I also had help arranging and translating interviews. Christian and Genevieve Mercadier, my French father and mother, helped me with some of the French interviews, as did my wife, Sophie. Michael and Desy Loughlin helped out with Spanish. Dr. Ekaterina Isaeva, a Russian colleague from Perm State University, found Mariia Kalina and Alex Hatsekelevich, two of her students, to help me.

Finally, I want to make sure that I thank Rob Taylor, along with everyone else at the University of Nebraska Press. I am glad they believed in this project and helped me put the manuscript in publishable form.

I apologize to anyone that I have forgotten, and there are likely many who helped make this project a reality. Even if I have not mentioned you by name, you have my gratitude.

Portions of this book previously appeared in:

*Le Football: The History of American Football in France* (Lincoln: University of Nebraska Press, 2016).

"The 'Sun of Austerlitz' Shone for the Molosses," *Sport in American History*, 21 July 2016.

"Brits Upset Finns in 2017 IFAF Women's World Championships Opener," *American Football International*, 26 June 2017.

"United States Beats Team Canada, Captures Gold at Women's World Championship," *American Football International*, 2 July 2017.

"Canada v. USA in Historic Girl's 'Battle of the Border' Club Team Challenge—Part 2," *American Football International*, 29 November 2017.

"Women's Football Arrives at Super Bowl LIII," *American Football International*, 6 February 2019.

"ESPN's Born to Play a Groundbreaking Documentary on Women's Football," *American Football International*, 14 July 2020.

"Women's Football Alliance Crowns Three National Champions," *American Football International*, 27 July 2021.

# Introduction FREE TO PLAY

Once the blinders fall away, women playing football can be seen everywhere.

Women and girls on more than 150 teams play tackle football in around ten leagues in the United States, and there are also hundreds of flag football leagues for females of various ages across the country. When Canadian and Mexican teams and leagues are added to the North American mix, another two hundred teams and approximately fifteen leagues get added to the total. Outside of North America, women tackle the sport, and each other, in nearly thirty nations from Europe, Asia, Africa, Australia, Central America, and South America.[1]

Those blinders, created by a culture that views tackle football as a man's game, are difficult to remove. They have been created by our history, our popular culture, and our sporting press, not to mention society's long-held views on proper gender roles in sport.

Historically, women have played football here and there since 1896, but never in large numbers. Those female athletes who did play likewise have not received a great deal of attention for their efforts. When they did manage to enter the gridiron, they were primarily seen as a novelty. The tradition of the powder-puff football game, an occasional exception to the male-only custom, was designed for amusement, which proved the rule that this was a man's game.

Although football does not have a film library devoted to the sport as large as baseball's, what films that do exist primarily depict large and violent men playing the game. There have been a few exceptions, and they are perhaps becoming more common, but the gridiron is still largely depicted as a man's world. However, women in the United States began enjoying increased societal freedom in the latter half of the twentieth century. Some women used that freedom to join their male counterparts by playing the most popular sport in the nation.

This was not always easy. School-aged girls, in particular, faced opposition from coaches and other officials, concerned that football was too dangerous for them to play with the boys. As we will see, however, if the girls had the support to challenge their exclusion, courts often sided with them, indicating that the law recognized a girl's right to put her safety at risk.

Women faced criticism in the press, when they were mentioned, and also sometimes had to deal with derogatory comments from family, from friends, and occasionally from passersby. But if the women wanted to play badly enough, the freedom was there. In the United States, there was no national football association that prohibited women from participating, as had been the case with women's soccer in other nations.[2] That freedom to play meant increased opportunities from the 1960s to the 1980s, and hundreds of women took advantage. After a nearly two-decade hiatus, thousands of women began taking their place on the field starting in 1999.

During the twenty-first century, there has been a proliferation of media outlets, primarily online, that have grown with the goal of covering women's sport. The casual reader who often peruses those sites might occasionally learn about a few girls who are playing on mostly male football teams, but their blinders are quite likely to remain in place concerning women playing other women at a high level. Even American sites that are dedicated to women's sport, that cover the latest news on women curlers, for instance, largely ignore the thousands of women who play the most popular sport in the nation.

Our view of the proper role for the female athlete has evolved greatly since the U.S. Congress passed Title IX in 1972, and the courts have interpreted that law to require that women be provided with roughly equal opportunities in sport. However, as women have moved into areas that were once male only, with a great deal of fanfare and media coverage, some areas such as women's professional tackle football have seemingly been excluded from those celebrations of this new equality. Perhaps this is because a counternarrative, created by many in the commentariat, along with much of the academy, depicts football as being too violent, as being the certain road to permanent mental impairment, or as a reflection of the "worst dimensions of our national character."[3] This counternarrative may well cause those who believe it to ignore a large group of women whose love for the sport is proudly worn on their jersey sleeves.

That being said, once those blinders that society has placed over our eyes fall, it is not difficult to discover that a whole new world exists: where women run down the field with reckless abandon and with no thought for their personal safety to cheerfully collide with other women; where young girls sprint around other girls joyfully striving for the end zone; and where female athletes who share the common language of football have created a global sisterhood of tough, aggressive players bound by a love for the exhilarating and violent sport.

The first women's game that I attended while considering this project was in Asnières-sur-Seine, a northwestern suburb of Paris. It was the final of the second Challénge Féminin, the championship of women's football in France sponsored by the Fédération Française de Football Américain in 2016. The Molosses d'Asnières-sur-Seine were playing the Argocanes, a team made up of players from Aix-en-Provence, Montpellier, and Marseille. The two teams had played each other in the final the previous year, and the Argocanes were hoping to avenge the 14–6 loss that the Molosses had handed them in 2015. They would be disappointed, and the home team once again defeated their southern challengers, this time by a score of 24–0.[4]

The Molosses are a team that grew out of the Sparkles de Villeneuve St. Georges, the first women's football team in France. Sarah Charbonneau created the Sparkles in the southeastern suburb of Paris in 2012, after watching her cousins play and deciding that the game would be fun.[5] Christelle Harnais, a player who started on the Sparkles, remembered that the team wanted better coaching and reached out to the staff of the Molosses, at that time an all-male team. The Molosses sent coaches, and eventually some of the players migrated to Asnières.[6] Since the change, the Molosses have dominated the Challénge Féminin, defeating the Argocanes twice and beating the Bordeaux Lions 34–14 in 2017.

In addition to succeeding on the field, the team has also achieved a modicum of fame in the film world. At the start of *Bande de Filles*, a 2014 movie released under the title *Girlhood* in the United States, a group of players with "Molosses" clearly displayed on their home and away uniforms ran onto the field and began running, blocking, and tackling. After hitting each other for a while, they removed their helmets to reveal that not only were they playing what is an obscure game in France but that they were also "Black teenage girls and young women" playing the typically masculine game.[7] Christine N. Ziemba, writing for *Paste Music*, acknowledged the "disorienting" nature of American football being part of a French film, but argued that the scene "brings gender issues front and center." Apart from the opening scene, *football américain* disappears from the movie, but Ziemba opined, "Symbolically, however, the mix of competition and camaraderie exhibited on the gridiron is representative of the rest of [director Céline] Sciamma's film," which followed the life trajectory of the character Marieme, as she struggled against the strictures of being a Black, working-class woman in France.[8]

Harnais, who works as a nurse in a hospital a short distance outside of Paris, plays running back for the Molosses and said that she likes the "running," and the "contact" of playing football. Unlike the fictional Marieme, Harnais, who is also young and Black, has found focus in the sport, reporting that her team is a "tight" group. She also credited the sport with making her calmer, even at her job. Playing has also broadened her horizons, taking her to Spain and Poland to play matches against teams there. She was "thrilled" and "excited" to play in her first ever game against the Spanish National Team in 2012. It has not always been easy—the Molosses took a twenty-hour bus ride to Poland, arriving just in time to play, but they defeated the Warsaw Sirens 20-0, and she scored "one or two" touchdowns. Like many other women around the world, she has also visited the United

States to attend the Women's World Games (WWG) and is now a part of the global sisterhood of football. She and some of her Molosses teammates went to the 2017 WWG in Orlando, and she described the "great thrill" of being in the home of football.[9]

That first match between the Molosses and Argocanes, along with the interviews with Harnais, Elisa De Santis (quarterback), Soraya Gharreb (tight end), and Sarah Viola (wide receiver) of the Molosses, suggest several themes that will be a part of this work.

The Molosses versus Argocanes game was interrupted several times by injury timeouts, particularly for the Argocanes, who did not appear to be as physically ready to play as the Molosses. Football is a difficult physical sport, even for the young, and when athletes in their twenties and thirties play, the toll on bodies that might not be in peak playing shape can be severe. Officials called the game in the middle of the fourth quarter, and some players had to be helped onto the field for the trophy ceremony at the end.[10]

Those in charge of women's football teams are hungry for their sport to be recognized in the press. When my friend Jean-Marc Burtscher and I arrived at the game, we bought our tickets and were climbing to the stands when the director of the Molosses offered us press passes for the game. Jean-Marc is a photography enthusiast, and that day he was carrying a camera with a large telephoto lens. Presumably that made him a member of the press in the eyes of the director (I must have been taken for a reporter), and if the game did not make media outlets such as *Le Monde*, *Figaro*, or even *L'Equipe*—the primary French sporting newspaper—then at least the teams received a write-up in *Sport in American History*, a blog for sport historians in the United States.[11]

Women playing football are often a part of what might be termed the "Sisterhood of the Traveling Shoulder Pads." The Sparkles played in Spain before they had a match with another French team, and several of the Molosses players have been to the WWG. Elisa De Santis, the quarterback of the Molosses, has played flag football in a number of countries, including playing on the French National Flag Team in the European Championships in Italy and Finland and the World Championships in Korea, Canada, Sweden, and the United States. She also played for a flag team in Italy and on a men's team, but that is a story for later. When I spoke to De Santis, she was interested in going to Boston to try to play for a women's team there.[12] Sarah Viola, the wide receiver, is from Belgium and began playing for a men's team. After that introduction to football, she broke a path for De Santis and took her game to the United States, where she played with the Boston Renegades of the Women's Football Alliance. When she returned to Europe, she began playing with the Molosses.[13]

Since my interviews with De Santis and Viola, I have talked with Americans who have played in Europe and Europeans who have played in European nations outside their own and in the United States. In a recent online conversation with Louise Bean, a former quarterback of the Utah Falconz, she told me that her former team had four international players (from Mexico, Samoa, Tonga, and Japan) playing for them in 2018.[14]

Women are playing on nearly every continent. This work seeks to tell the story of women playing in the United States, using what documents exist, but particularly reporting the words of the athletes themselves. More than 240 women, and a few men, contributed their stories through interviews for this project. These range from my first interview with Leah Hinkle of the Portland Fighting Shockwave, to Natalie Hacksell of the Gothenburg (Sweden) Marvels, who, at the time of her interview at the 2018 Women's World Games, had not yet played in her first game, to Melissa Bedwell of the Tampa Bay Inferno, who began playing in 1998 with the Lake Michigan Minx.[15]

I consider girls and women playing tackle football in various leagues, at various ages. This includes stories of the first women's professional football players and leagues and proceeds to cover the top women's leagues of the current day. These included, when I began this project, the Independent Women's Football League (defunct), the Women's Football Alliance, the Women's National Football Conference, the United States Women's Football League, and the Legends Football League (now the EXTFL or X League). Whether they play fully dressed or scantily clad, this is the story of women who gladly put in hours of practice to then risk life and limb on the gridiron. Their stories are fascinating, and well worth reading.

The first chapter examines the beginning of women's professional football in the United States, when teams such as the Toledo Troopers and players such as Linda Jefferson received enough attention for their exploits on the field to be profiled in the press and to be invited on the *Network Battle of the Sexes* program in the 1970s. As with the National Football League in its first decades, the early leagues rose and fell, and after the Women's Professional Football League (WPFL) and successor leagues folded, nearly twenty years passed before adult women once again had the chance to knock each other around on the gridiron.

That rebirth of women's professional football began with the Minnesota Vixen and the Lake Michigan Minx, who were formed to play a barnstorming series in 1998. The explosion of women's leagues and teams is the topic for chapter 2. The WPFL grew out of those two teams, and various leagues came and went before the situation stabilized, at least for the past decade.

That stability was provided, in part, by the Independent Women's Football League (IWFL), founded in 2000. For a time it was the largest women's football league, and during that period the IWFL was an organization that helped women's professional football grow. It was under its auspices that the first national team went out to compete against the rest of the world. How that happened, and how the league has ebbed, flowed, and finally died, are considered in chapter 3.

Today's largest league for American women playing football is the Women's Football Alliance (WFA), which had sixty-five teams for the 2018 season and expects at least sixty-three for 2022. Jeff and Lisa King created the league in 2008, and play began in 2009. In 2017 the WFA supplied forty-two (of forty-five) players for the American National Team for the Women's World Championship and twelve for Canada's.[16] How the WFA split from the IWFL and grew into the largest league for women is the topic of chapter 4.

The majority of women around the world play in uniforms indistinguishable from their male counterparts, but starting in 2009, Mitchell

Mortaza established a niche during the Super Bowl halftime for women playing football wearing very little. This novelty pay-per-view program evolved into the Lingerie Football League (LFL), which rebranded as the Legends Football League in 2013 and became the X League, which, after the COVID shutdowns, will resume play in 2022. The most visible of the women's football leagues, the LFL is also the most controversial. The league briefly expanded to Canada in 2012 and to Australia in 2013. Those international attempts to expand the LFL brand influenced Mexican entrepreneurs, who have formed several bikini football leagues. This controversial version of women's football is covered in chapter 5.

Women's football leagues come and go with alarming regularity. When teams from the IWFL grew discontented with the way the league was operated in 2018, the Texas Elite Spartans, Utah Falconz, San Diego Surge, and Seattle Majestics decided to break away. After a successful Best of the West Women's Football Championship in Las Vegas that year, the four teams formed the core of the new Women's National Football Conference that debuted in 2019. The new league's brief history is explored in chapter 6.

Chapter 7 briefly discusses girls who played the sport on male teams after Congress passed Title IX in 1972, and then looks at those who have been attracting media attention for their abilities on the field in the new century. Consideration continues through the formation of all-girls leagues in Canada and the United States. In recent decades a few women have managed to play at the university level, and in 2018 two women were offered scholarships to play with men's teams. There are still only a handful of women who have competed at that level, so they are included with their grade school and high school sisters. The perceived dangers of football are also considered in light of the expansion in the number of girls and young women playing the game.

Many women have had the chance to do something that many of their male counterparts cannot claim—play for an official world championship. The International Federation of American Football (IFAF), along with the national federations in sixteen countries, has sponsored the Women's World Championship (WWC) in 2010, 2013, and 2017.

Team USA has won all three WWC competitions, but their margin of victory has been declining. International competition sponsored by IFAF is the focus of chapter 8.

A postscript explores the increasing visibility of women's football. Girls and women have appeared in commercials with more frequency. Sam Gordon (see chapter 7) was named as an NFL Game Changer during the festivities that accompanied Super Bowl LII and was part of an NFL commercial during Super Bowl LIII. During the lockdowns that accompanied the coronavirus pandemic in 2020, the Entertainment and Sports Network (ESPN) aired a documentary by Viridiana Lieberman about the Boston Renegades women's football team. This documentary and its reach are a primary topic for the postscript.

Interspersed with the histories of the various American leagues, I also include stories of my personal experiences covering several events around the world, such as the story above of the final of the Challénge Féminin. Since beginning this project, I have attended the following games:

The International Federation of American Football's (IFAF) Women's World Championship that was held in Langley, British Columbia, from 24 to 30 June 2017. I interviewed nineteen players from Finland, Mexico, the United Kingdom, and Canada over the course of the championship.

The Battle of the Borders, two games between teams from the Manitoba Girls Football Association (MGFA) and the Indiana Girls Tackle Football League (IGTFL) held on 18 and 21 November 2017 in Mooresville, Indiana. These were the first international matches held between teams of middle and high school girls. Six athletes from the MGFA and six from the IGTFL spoke with me about their experiences.

The fifth Women's World Games, sponsored by USA Football at the New Orleans Saints' practice facility from 21 to 25 February 2018. Eighty-two women from sixteen countries, including the United States, gathered in New Orleans to learn the finer points of playing tackle football. I managed to pack thirty interviews with women from several countries into the four days of the WWG.

On 10 March 2017, I went to a Columbus Comets practice and interviewed six players, including the team's general manager and the head coach of the team that plays in the Women's Football Alliance.

On 13–14 April 2018 I immersed myself, and my wife, Sophie, into the world of Salt Lake City girls and women's football. We met with coaches, officials, and players from the Utah Falconz and Seattle Majestics on Friday. Saturday morning I watched games of the Utah Girls Football League (UGFL) and interviewed nine players. That afternoon we watched the Falconz and Majestics play, and afterward I interviewed three more players.

The Best of the West Women's Football Championship, from 20 to 23 July 2018 in Las Vegas, Nevada. The Texas Elite Spartans, Utah Falconz, Seattle Majestics, and San Diego Surge played for the championship won by Texas.

On 11 August 2018 Sophie and I, along with our French friends Jean-Marc and Agnes Burtscher, attended our first Legends Football League (LFL) game in Chicago between the Bliss and the Omaha Heart.

From 2017 to 2021 I attended games by the Comets, Thee Toledo Reign, the Tampa Bay Inferno, the Cincinnati Sizzle, the Detroit Dark Angels, the Cleveland Fusion, the Minnesota Vixen, the Orlando Anarchy, the Maine Mayhem, the Music City Mizfits, the Chicago Bliss (LFL), the Utah Falconz, the Texas Elite Spartans, and the Nebraska Nite Hawks.

On 23–24 July 2021 I attended the WFA's National Championship that was held at Tom Benson Hall of Fame Stadium in Canton, Ohio.

On 17–20 September 2021 and 24–30 January 2022 the International Women's Flag Football Association held tournaments at Provincetown, Massachusetts, and Key West, Florida, respectively. Though flag tournaments, there were several tackle players using the events as off-season training, including members of the Pittsburgh Passion and the Boston Renegades.

At most of these games, I conducted postgame interviews with the players and sometimes with coaches or team officials.

This is a work that suffers somewhat from tunnel vision. It leans heavily on the interviews that I have done with more than two hundred girls and women and with a small number of men. My goal is to explore the world of women playing tackle football using their own words, wherever possible. Not much has been written about women's tackle football, at least academically, although that is beginning to change. Therefore, my descriptions of this history are sometimes brief considerations of the sweep of that history until it leads into the oral histories I have done with respondents who have generously taken the time to tell me their stories.

# Women's Professional Football Begins

Girls and women had played football for decades but had not been associated with professional teams until 1926, when the Frankford Yellow Jackets and the Chicago Cardinals met for a game. A team of women played against two men as halftime entertainment during their game. The 7 November 1926 *Philadelphia Public Ledger* carried a story about the event, and its coverage indicated that this was most likely a stunt, rather than an opportunity for women to demonstrate they could play the game. The paper described the players as the "prettiest football team Frankford has ever seen," and called them "female gridiron invaders."[1] This may have been a onetime contest sponsored by the Yellow Jackets, who later became the Philadelphia Eagles, but some authors have indicated there may have been other National Football League (NFL) teams that held similar events.[2]

During the 1920s women did have increased freedom to take advantage of sporting opportunities, and that included "invading" fields that had previously been reserved primarily for men. The 1922 Thanksgiving edition of *Flapper* magazine, for instance, featured a woman dressed in a football uniform crouched in a four-point stance, and although this may have merely been a provocative image, it still demonstrated that some were imagining the possibility of women playing.[3] In 1933 sportswriter Grantland Rice filmed Babe Didrickson dressed in a football uniform, punting and catching punts.[4] Though the *Flapper* cover was likely a conceptual cover photo designed to create cognitive dissonance in the viewer (the "Old Fogies" that the cover proclaimed the magazine was not for), and Didrickson's football exploits were designed to demonstrate that the Babe could do any sport, there were women such as the Frankford players who were entering the gridiron.

Ohio was the site where the NFL began, and it can also make a strong claim to being the foundational home to women's professional football. In 1930 Herman Metzger and Dick Lazette, two Toledo businessmen, recruited and coached two women's football teams that played a series of barnstorming games. They dressed their players in uniforms borrowed from a local youth league, and according to Metzger, "We played exhibition games wherever we could book them." The games made money, but soon the pair ran into opposition.[5]

Even though some women had experienced a new freedom in the 1920s, the Great Depression that began in 1929 served to reverse many of those gains. Metzger mentioned that the teams had to cancel a game scheduled for the University of Detroit when university officials withdrew permission to use the site after they decided that football was not a proper sport for women. They even received pressure from the highest quarters. Lou Henry Hoover, wife of President Herbert Hoover, wrote them a letter asserting that the promoters were "exploiting womanhood."[6]

Although the First Lady was herself a football fan, she apparently felt that making money off of women playing the game crossed the line.[7] It is difficult to discern exactly what she meant from the brief mention in one newspaper article, but she may have had a point. It was suggestive that the athletes were able to fit into the uniforms worn by youth league players, so the women must have all been relatively petite and might therefore have been chosen for qualities other than athletic ability. Perhaps, therefore, the games were designed to exploit the women. Given the paucity of information about the teams or their games, it is impossible to come to any hard conclusions. The one certainty, however, was that at least twenty-two women who were playing football, and perhaps making money doing so, lost that opportunity when pressure from various quarters ended their careers.

The experiences of the Toledo women would be replayed in a multitude of locations across the nation as professional physical educators began asserting their control over women's athletics. These women and men asserted that sports were dangerous for female athletes. Female athletes might lose their "womanly qualities" by engaging in competitive sports.[8] Some argued that female athletes might harm their reproductive health, while others feared sports might produce "muscle molls," or "mannish" women.[9] The physical education professionals maintained their grip on the mainstream of women's sports for much of the mid-twentieth century. Only after the passage of Title IX of the Education Amendments in 1972 did their influence mostly disappear.

There were still women athletes during the period when women's physical educators held sway. Mrs. Hoover was back in public life and so had lost some of her social clout, which perhaps took some of the pressure off of women who wanted to play football. British Pathé films provided other scattered examples of women playing the game during the 1930s. In a short film from 1932, titled *Uncle Sam's Feminine Football Fans*, viewers saw two women's teams playing a game in what appears to be a professional stadium, perhaps the Los Angeles Coliseum. The visuals showed the women playing the game in a fairly standard manner, but the editors added some slighting touches to remind viewers that these were, after all, women. An opening panel asserted "Now we know where the bargain counter hands train for the sales!" The film opened with players passing in front of a mirror to place their helmets perfectly over their hair and checking their makeup. The football action appeared little different than films of that era that showed men playing. There were runs into the line, long passes for touchdowns, and an interception returned for a score. The athletes did not move as fast as their male counterparts, but the intensity seemed largely the same.[10]

British Pathé must have been impressed, for they came back for more in 1934. This time the *Pathé Gazette* produced *Women Battle on the Gridiron: Fair Sex Show Much Promise in Keen Rugby Game*. Once again the action on the field was framed in a condescending manner. During the kickoff, the narrator mentioned that "Martha kicks off, and the ball is taken by Hazel. She's had her hair waved for this match and looks just too stunning." After a quarterback threw an interception, the defensive player was tackled out of bounds. The narrator intoned, "No touchdown, but just to wind up, a little touchup," as the scene shifted to an attractive young player wearing lipstick and powdering her nose with the help of a hand mirror.[11]

Pathé was not the only media outlet that featured women's football. Fox *Movietone News* and other newsreel producers, magazines such as the Hearst's *American Weekly*, and various newspapers had films or stories about the "powder bowls." The tone of the various stories was typically the same; coverage of the game, heavily leavened with the narrative that these were the equivalent of a carnival sideshow, if not actually calling the games freak shows.[12]

Perhaps the players that Pathé filmed were from the Los Angeles-based Marshall-Clampett Amazons. Athletes from that team were featured in *Life* magazine and *Click* in the 1930s. Members of the team not only played football but also were players on a top softball team at the time. Softball came first for them, and football was merely a way to keep some money coming in during the offseason. According to an article in *Smithsonian* magazine, the experiment with football succeeded and drew crowds of more than three thousand. Even though they, like the Toledo teams, had financial success, they also faced criticism from those who thought football was not a sport for women. The *Smithsonian* article by Erica Westly mentioned that "a newswire article [in] November 1939 described them as an invasion 'of one of the last strongholds of masculinity.'" *Life*'s article also asserted that football was "too dangerous for women, warning that 'a blow either on the breasts or in the abdominal region may result in cancer or internal injury.'" The league did not last long, and Westly reasoned that it likely folded because softball "offered considerably more opportunities than football did." Westly found evidence of another league, also made up of softball players in their offseason, in Chicago, but that one only played a few games.[13]

Some women obviously enjoyed the freedom to play football, but while there were no overarching bodies, such as the British Football

Association, that banned women from playing, American society did not provide much support. That would begin to change in the 1960s and 1970s. In an interview Diane Beruldsen of the International Women's Flag Football Association told me that she believed that one of the impetuses for women playing flag football was the remarkable success and notoriety of the NFL's new Super Bowl, which began in 1967. She also connected the dots further and claimed that many of the athletes on early tackle football teams came from the flag world.[14] The connections still exist, as players such as quarterback Lisa Horton and linewoman Kaitlan Niedermeyer of the Pittsburgh Passion played in an IWFFA tournament in Provincetown, and Erin Diette, a defensive linewoman for the WFA 2021 Champion Boston Renegades, played in the 2022 Kelly McGillis tournament in Key West.

In subsequent interviews others gave Beruldsen's assertion additional credence. I talked with Anna "Tonka" Tate and Andra Douglas of the New York Sharks. They had begun playing flag in the New York City area, and played with Beruldsen. After the Sharks had won a tournament in Key West, promoters working on creating the Women's Professional Football League (WPFL) got in touch with them and offered the team a chance to play tackle football against a combined team made up of players from the Minnesota Vixen and the Lake Michigan Minx. At least in one case, therefore, Beruldsen's suggestion that flag players formed some early tackle teams was correct. In the case of the Sharks, they would form a team in the late 1990s and are discussed later.[15]

After a more than thirty-year absence, women's professional football returned to Ohio when another entrepreneur decided that the market was ready for the women's game. Sid Friedman, a talent agent from Cleveland, wanted to stage a "gimmick," and so he created the Cleveland Daredevils, who were alternatively known as the USA Daredevils. Friedman received some initial positive press coverage by hiring former Cleveland Browns standout Marion Motley to coach the team. Motley had been a star in both the All American Football Conference and the NFL, and part of his agreement with Friedman was that he would "be allowed to coach the team like true professionals." The Daredevils played against men's teams, losing all three, but reportedly held their own. They also played a game against the Detroit All Stars, another women's team, and defeated them. This convinced Friedman to focus on starting a league made up of only women's teams for 1968, and he marketed this as the Women's Professional Football League. After an initial struggle to find teams, the league finally had four teams in 1971: the Daredevils, the Pittsburgh Hurricanes, the Buffalo All-Stars, and the Toledo Troopers.[16]

There is some dispute as to which Ohio city should be given the title of "the birthplace of women's professional football." The website of the current Thee Toledo Reign team uses the initial Toledo teams in the 1930s to argue for that city being the birthplace of women's professional football. Mitchi Collette, the Reign's owner, WPFL historian, and a former player on the Troopers, argued that professional women's football began in Toledo. In an interview Collette spoke of the 1930s team and told me: "It [women's professional football] kind of got played around with in the mid-sixties by a talent scout named Sid Friedman out of Cleveland. It didn't go well at that time but he started it up again about 1971 where he ended up going to get a team out of Toledo and a team out of Cleveland, and do an exhibition game. Well, Toledo went to that exhibition game in Cleveland and lost, but again as like that guy in 1930, Sid Friedman made a lot of money out of it, so he ended up getting a lot of other teams: Buffalo, Pittsburgh, Detroit, Columbus. All these teams around this area in the Midwest and Northeast, if you will, and had a schedule, and we all played each other. Well, the Toledo Troopers coming out of Toledo, they never lost another game after that exhibition game, not until 1976 in Oklahoma City to the Oklahoma City Dolls."[17] Collette argued that since the 1930s barnstorming tour began in Toledo, and the inclusion of the Troopers in 1971 arguably marked the true beginning of the WPFL, Toledo should therefore be seen as the birthplace of the professional sport for women.

Neal Rozendaal, the author of *The Women's Football Encyclopedia* (2016), disagreed: "That's a suspect claim, at best. It's impossible to tell how organized these teams were and how serious the attempt at launching women's football in Toledo in the 1930s was. In any event, we know that the women's football movement in Toledo in the 1930s never attracted major press or got past the barnstorming stage; the effort lacked staying power and quickly dissipated."[18]

Whichever city is credited with being the birthplace, it is clear that the professional game for women began in Ohio. The halftime show by the Yellow Jackets was apparently a onetime thing, and the same was seemingly true of any other NFL teams that held games, if any did. Collette's argument for Toledo as the birthplace is compelling. Regardless of how well organized the Toledo teams were, they were playing "professional" football and might have continued, absent the intervention of First Lady Hoover and other critics.[19] The WPFL and later the National Women's Football League did not really begin to be something more than a novelty until the Troopers joined. I confess that I may be biased—I have interviewed Collette and have seen her Reign team play several games, so the reader can factor that into the argument.

Friedman's search for teams for the WPFL also led him north of the border, and the Canadian Belles became the first women's team outside of the United States. In *The Girl and the Game: A History of Women's Sports in Canada* (2016), Canadian historian M. Ann Hall wrote that the Belles were "rough and tough ladies," but that is about all of the information available on the team.[20] There were mentions of the Canadian team in a 1969 blurb in *Sports Illustrated*, and Rozendaal also mentioned the team in passing.[21] "Shaping and Being Shaped: Examining Women's Tackle Football in Canada," a 2014 master's thesis written by Katrina Kawec at the University of Windsor, did not even mention the team.[22] In *Hail Mary: The Rise and Fall of the National Women's Football League* (2021), authors Frankie de la Cretaz and Lyndsey D'Arcangelo do provide more detail to the story, including discussion of how Friedman and former Canadian Football League player Fred Robinson worked to interest Canadian women in the sport.[23]

Despite de la Cretaz and D'Arcangelo's recent work, a few mentions here and there were precious little fanfare for the first attempt at internationalizing America's game for women. This is not unusual for women's sports in general and women's football in particular. Very little that happened, and continues to happen, on the female side of football is ever noticed by the press. Had social media existed at the time, there would likely have been more information, but if ifs and buts were candy and nuts, we'd all have a merry Christmas.

In what would become a common theme in women's professional football, Friedman and the WPFL soon faced competing leagues. The Alliance debuted in 1972 with four teams: the Pittsburgh Powderkegs, the Detroit Fillies, the New York Fillies, and the Midwest Cowgirls. The Alliance received much needed help when the Toledo Troopers, the WPFL's marquee team, left the league to join the Alliance.[24]

Bill Stout became the first, and only, head coach of the Troopers in 1971. In a 16 June 2013 *Toledo Blade* article that reported on a possible film about the Troopers, Tom Henry wrote that when Friedman started moving in the direction of making women's football more like sexualized spectacles such as mud wrestling, he and the league owner began to diverge in their goals for the women's sport. According to Henry, Stout believed the Troopers should "be a legitimate team."[25] De la Cretaz and D'Arcangelo added that they had been told that Friedman also suggested that the Troopers "throw a game or two, because their continued domination wasn't good for him."[26] Neither suggestion set well with Stout or his athletes and led to the breakup.

The *Blade* story also quoted Stout from a 10 November 1974 article in the *Toledo Blade*, in which the coach and team owner told *Blade* reporter Tom Lorenz: "A lot of people come out to laugh. They think it's a joke or something. But when the game starts and they see these girls play, they realize it's a football game. These girls play great football." Lorenz was a fine writer and wrote a compelling game story that contained a great deal of insight into the players and coaches. Perhaps he just couldn't resist the opportunity to remind readers that even though the Troopers were rough and tough football players, they were still women, subject to the slighting narratives that the 1970s placed upon them. Lorenz reported that in the midst of the pregame preparation, a commotion erupted in one corner of the locker room, caused by the athletes being scared by a spider. "Sure enough, right in the middle of a pro football briefing session, a spider no bigger than a match head has come down from the ceiling, dangling there timidly on its invisible thread, thereby clearing out one whole side of the Troopers' defensive line."[27]

Despite a few digressions such as that, the tone of the article was very positive about the team and its members. By the end it was clear that the blinders had fallen from the writer's eyes. Lorenz was a freelance writer from Bowling Green, and he confessed to the magazine's editor that he had been nervous about the assignment. "I knew the Troopers were good but I had no idea what they would be like as people. Considering the silent treatment they've gotten so far in the Toledo area, I expected them to be abrupt and maybe even hostile, and I wondered if I could get out of there if they decided to rush me. Instead, I found them to be warm and articulate and extremely cooperative, with a kind of adventurous spirit that completely won me over. They made the story a pleasure to do."[28]

It was informative that the editors of the Blade had to reach out to a freelance writer to do this article. They had a sports section with several writers, but perhaps the regulars were the cause of the "silent treatment" that the Troopers had suffered through previously. After winning all but one game in their history since 1971, that they had to wait four years before having their accomplishments recognized by their hometown newspaper would be par for the course in women's football. According to the Troopers' Sue Crawford, who was quoted in the article, "The worst high school team in Cleveland gets more coverage than the Troopers."[29]

Gary Kiefer, in an opinion piece titled "A Woman's Place Is in the Game," argued, "A large part of the problem is traceable to local media, controlled, for the most part, by middle-aged males who seem to think that a woman's place at a football game is on the sidelines leading cheers." He further told readers that the Troopers had moved up their start times by a half hour on Saturday nights because the Blade's "traditional-minded sports editor has contended that late games and early deadlines have been responsible for abbreviated stories in the past."[30]

Lorenz closed his article with an interesting question. Given that the Troopers played mostly teams from Columbus and Detroit that gave them no real problems, how good were they really? The story quoted coach Bill Stout as saying, "At this point we really don't know." Lorenz theorized, "Chances are, nobody will know, at least until the Troopers can find somebody—the Los Angeles Dandelions perhaps, or maybe the [NFL] Rams—who can give them a football game."[31] The Troopers would finally find a suitable foe in the Oklahoma City Dolls, but decades later, a similar question would be asked and answered about the 2018 Utah Falconz, but more on that later.

In 1973 the Troopers joined a new league, the National Women's Football League (NWFL). The new league was formed by "groups of men and women with ideas for the future [who were] trying to solidify football league competition for women." In an article in the November 1973 edition of *Ebony*, the unattributed author perhaps felt the need to reassure readers about the purpose of the new league: "'We are forming this league,' emphasized people like Joyce Hogan, an owner of the Los Angeles Dandelions, 'not to compete with men but because there are women who can play this game.'"[32]

The league marketed itself as women's "professional" football, but the players rarely received any compensation. According to the *Ebony* article, the Troopers players did not sign contracts, "to protect their amateur status." They were paid mileage to get to and from practice, but Carl Hamilton, one of the Toledo coaches, asserted, "Most of them don't care about the money anyway. . . . All they want to do is play football." Words to warm any team owner's heart, and perhaps it was true—Linda Jefferson reportedly wanted to compete in the Olympics, and in 1975 she turned down a free car that was part of her prize for winning Woman Athlete of the Year from *WomenSports Magazine*.[33]

However, most people, including women football players, generally would not turn down money when offered. The Dallas Bluebonnets, another team in the league, did pay their players $25 per game, and the disparity between teams in their compensation schemes demonstrated that the NWFL was more of an alliance of independent teams rather than a true league.[34]

At the time of the *Ebony* article, the league consisted of eight teams, but before it folded in 1985, it would contain a high of thirteen teams located around the Midwest, the South, and on the West Coast. The WPFL had folded in 1978, and when the Troopers followed them in 1980, some of their proven star power (primarily Jefferson) left the league.[35]

As mentioned above, the pattern for women's professional football has been that new leagues came and went with regularity. Often a personal dispute, such as the one between Friedman and Stout, led to a team or teams leaving their previous league and forming a new one. Since there was no powerful league that provided benefits that were too good to give up, there was little motivation for disgruntled owners to stay. Over time, this has weakened the ability of women's football to break into the consciousness of the national press and, via it, the public. Instead of one strong voice seeking recognition, there have generally been several small voices raising a small hubbub. For a time, however, some of the league's voices were heard, and such was the case of Toledo and the NWFL.

The Troopers, led by Stout and all-star running back Linda Jefferson, became a legitimate team as the coach had wished. Between 1971 and 1977, the Troopers became the centerpiece of the NWFL. Over that span they won seven consecutive league championships. Jefferson became something of a media star, appearing on numerous media and entertainment outlets.[36]

By the time Jefferson had become a star for the Troopers, she was already an accomplished athlete used to success. She was the Toledo summer recreation league champion in the long jump from 1966 through 1968, and her 220 relay team had won the city championship in 1966, when she was only eleven years old. In high school she was all-city in basketball for three years and continued to win on the track and on the softball diamond.[37]

After graduation from Libbey High School, she continued to play softball and basketball; then one day she learned of the Troopers from one of her friends and decided to give the team a try. The first hurdle that she had to overcome was her mother, who was opposed to her daughter playing a man's sport. Jefferson told Chris Schmidbauer of the *Toledo Free Press*, "My mom told me that there was no way that I was going to play football, so I had to sneak around to practice without her finding out." She finally let her mother know that she would be playing for the Troopers by coming home one day with her football uniform.[38]

Fortunately, Jefferson managed to convince her mother that she should play. Initially she was a receiver, "so I would be away from all the roughness in the line," but her coaches quickly realized how fast she was.[39] Speaking with Tom Melody of the *Akron Beacon Journal* in 1978, she reported, "I can run the 40 in 4.7. Maybe faster—depending on who's chasing me."[40] Once Stout saw that, she was moved to running back. In her first season for the Troopers, she justified her coach's judgment by gaining 1,338 yards and scoring 32 touchdowns.[41] According to a press release on Troopers letterhead, during her career Jefferson gained 8,027 yards, which placed her fifth in total rushing yards for professional football players at the time, behind Jim Brown, O. J. Simpson, Joe Perry, and Jim Taylor. She scored 140 touchdowns—fourteen more than NFL Hall of Fame running back Jim Brown, who held that league's record.[42]

On 28 November 1978 Jefferson did make it into the Professional Football Hall of Fame, as a speaker. She had been scheduled to appear two weeks earlier, but faulty directions had sent her to Minerva, Ohio, which was nearly twenty miles from her intended destination. Once she arrived at the proper location, she got laughs from the Hall of Fame luncheon club by repeating what must have been her stock line about running a 4.7 40-yard dash, or faster, depending on who was chasing her. She also fielded questions about the Troopers' decision to allow male reporters into their locker room after games. She joked there too, telling the crowd of "over 200 members" that "I didn't mind at all. I wanted them to stick around and wash my back but they said they had other things to do."[43]

On a more serious note, Jefferson told the attendees that she did not agree with a federal court ruling that allowed high school girls to compete in contact sports. "The only way a girl can play football with men is to start the training very young along with the boys. By the time they reach high school they could be in the shape as the boys and be able to compete. Where the girls are right now, playing on a boy's team is just crazy." She also anticipated Sam Gordon's call for high schools to sponsor what the Trooper star called "powder-puff" football, and noted that the Troopers had trouble recruiting just-graduated athletes, since they tended to "get scholarships and go to college after high school."[44]

Jefferson was inducted into the Semi-Pro Football Hall of Fame in 2002, the first African American woman inducted there, and one of only four women in the now apparently defunct hall of fame.[45] As mentioned in chapter 7, she and the Troopers were also inducted as the first class of the Women's Football Federation (WFF) Hall of Fame in 2014.[46] Perhaps one day football's major hall of fame in Canton will ask her to attend once again, this time to take her spot among the great players in professional football, which would be fitting.

Although her exploits received only sporadic attention in the local press, others noticed, and her ability on the field catapulted Jefferson to fame. As mentioned above, she was named as the first Woman Athlete of the Year by *WomenSports Magazine*, a publication copublished by tennis star Billie Jean King. She was also named the NWFL Player of the Year for 1976, 1977, and 1978 and was the Most Valuable Player for the league's first two championship games in 1976 and 1977. The media, outside of Toledo, also noticed her, and she appeared on several high profile programs of the time. Among those were television talk shows hosted by Phil Donahue and Dinah Shore, and she also appeared on ABC's *Good Morning America*. Perhaps the pinnacle of her fame occurred when she earned fourth place in the *Women's Superstars* competition televised by ABC in 1976.[47] Jefferson was the second women's football player to take part in the televised competition, following Barbara O'Brien, the quarterback of the Dallas Bluebonnets, who finished in seventh place in 1975.[48]

Her success was not without cost, and as her career wound down, she suffered from nagging injuries, sometimes as a result of being targeted by competitors. She told Tom Melody of the *Akron Beacon Journal* that "some of those girls are out there to kill me—and I mean that literally." She recalled that in the 1978 championship game against

Oklahoma City, "three defensive players were assigned to me—and never was I hit by fewer than five." At the time of her interview, she was still trying to overcome an ankle injury that resulted from a "cheap shot" in a 1976 game, and she also had a hyperextended knee suffered in the first game of the 1978 season.[49]

Such injuries, whether incurred on clean or dirty plays, are the life of a football player, and at the time Jefferson seemed good to go for the next season, but the Troopers' time as champions had come to an end. In the 1978 NWFL championship game, the Dolls' tactic of assigning three players to Jefferson paid off, and Oklahoma City handed the Troopers their first shutout, defeating them 8–0. The Toledo team played one more season, but in 1979 the Troopers managed only two nonforfeit wins and lost in the playoffs to the Columbus Pacesetters. Without Toledo in the championship game, interest declined, and the final never took place.[50]

Though their championship run ended in 1977, the Troopers had dominated the NWFL, winning seven straight championships between 1971 and 1977. That period was a highlight in the lives of many of the athletes who wore the yellow and green, and many are still close to one another. They had a reunion of sorts at their induction into the WFF Hall of Fame in 2014, where they interacted with girls from the Manitoba Girls Football Association, accentuating the theme that the Troopers were the past, and the MGFA team the future of women's football.

They have also had other gatherings, including a 2016 Women's History Month panel at Bowling Green State University (BGSU), where six former Troopers told a crowd of around seventy-five about their experiences as pioneers in the sport. In addition to the six presenters, several more former Troopers, along with some of the current Thee Toledo Reign players, were scattered in the audience. The WFF's executive director, Tamara Jarrett, moderated the panel and testified that Jefferson and the Troopers had inspired her as a girl to play football. "Because you played, I played. You carved a path for us. . . . I don't know if you'll ever understand the gratefulness I feel." Eunice White, who played defensive end for the team, summed up the feeling that the former athletes shared when she told Tom Henry of the *Blade*, "We'll always have each other's backs until we die."[51]

Some of the Troopers who remain in the Toledo area still attend the Reign's games when they can. The Reign played the Columbus Comets on 21 April 2018, and the cold weather kept many fans at home. It was not cold enough to deter Iris Smith though, and at halftime of the game, she took some time to remember her days as a defensive tackle/middle guard for the team. She answered a newspaper advertisement recruiting players for the Troopers and played for the Troopers from 1973 to 1979. The first year, she remembered, there were initially only sixteen players, but that grew to twenty-three during the season. For most of her time on the team, the players were not paid a salary, but they did get their expenses and medical insurance paid. She remembered that one season, perhaps in 1976, they were paid $25 a week, but for only two weeks. At one point Stout, the owner/coach, gave the athletes an option, disband the team or play for free.[52]

Smith recalled, "We all stuck in there as a team. We all stayed. No one left. We were having so much fun!" She, like many other ex-athletes, did not survive her sporting experience without some physical consequences. Smith told me that she had two rotator cuff surgeries while playing and had problems with osteoarthritis in her knee, which may have been related to playing football. Despite that, Smith reveled in her glory days as a Trooper. The players mostly had day jobs, then "we practiced for two hours a day, five days a week, and then played on Saturdays." Their practice field was whatever they could find, and generally was in poor shape. They also faced critics who did not think that women should be playing football, but Smith said she "overlooked them because we weren't playing for that reason [public approval]; we were playing because we wanted to play the sport. We enjoyed it, and we had this opportunity to be able to do something like this instead of that flag and tag football." Smith had lost contact with most of her teammates, but the reunions got her back in touch with them, and now she maintains contact with many of them. Summing up her feelings about her experiences, she said, "I love it. I love football, and I love watching these girls [the Reign] play. I never really thought we would make it this far."[53]

When the Reign played the Pittsburgh Passion, it was a warmer but stormy night on 19 May 2018, when Eunice White shared her experiences. During a weather delay because of lightning, Smith told me that she joined the team while studying physical education at the University of Toledo. "I was playing in a traveling softball league, and one of the teams we played against had a player that played for the Troopers, and she asked me about coming out for the team. Basically I told her she was crazy." The friend persisted though, and White eventually went to a practice and was hooked. "She kept bugging me, and bugging me, every time she saw me. Well, then one of the days she brought out Jim Wright, who was the offensive line coach, with her to a game. And they just kept wanting me and kept wanting me, and finally they said, 'Well, just come out and watch a practice.' So, to get them off my back, I said, 'Okay, I'll come out and watch a practice.' So I did, and in a few minutes they brought me all this stuff over, some of which I knew what to do with, most of which I did not know what to do with—all this equipment. And before the end of that practice, which was on a Wednesday night, I was practicing with them, and I played a game on Saturday."

Like Smith, White played for the team from 1973 to 1979, and they lost only one game during that time. She remembered some of the opposition to women playing football did not last long. "Especially young men came to Toledo Trooper games to make fun of the football team." White said the young men would think, "'Hey, it's Saturday night and there's nothing to do—oh let's go make fun of those girls.' But they didn't leave that way. They would leave fans, and that's how we'd build our fan base. Come out and watch, and see if you think it's a sideshow, or if you think it's a football game. Well they found out it was a football game." White credited playing for the Troopers with teaching her much needed life lessons. "I was going into teaching and coaching, and some of the need for discipline to be successful was taught to me through football; the need to practice hard. So, practice was harder than games. Practice is not supposed to be fun, games is [*sic*] supposed to be fun. Games are only fun if you win. And it taught me that you could be big and strong, but you don't have to be mean. You can be big and strong and do your job, but you don't have to be mean and nasty. And that was a lesson I needed to learn, because the big people that'd been around me before were mean and nasty. So I learned that you could be big and strong and a leader, but you didn't need to be nasty. And that was important personally in my life, for me."[54]

White expanded on the remarks she made at BGSU by telling me: "What I'd like to tell the young people today is, the last year the Troopers played was 1979. Next year, that's forty years. And almost every Trooper has memorabilia. And lots of Troopers have lots of memorabilia. Forty years later. So it was important to them. And when I played, in the early seventies, you gotta remember what the seventies were like. There was racial issues going on, there was a lot of unrest, and the Troopers had whites, had Blacks, had Chicanos, we had married people, we had straight people, we had gay people, and it didn't matter. You were a Trooper; you were a tight-knit group. You might agree or disagree with how they live outside the football field, but you had their back outside the field, and you had their back on the field. And that's a lesson that we still need to learn as a country today. You don't have to agree with everybody to get along and have each other's backs."

In between interviews with Smith and White, Mitchi Collette, who owns and helps coach the Reign, took some time before the team's practice to provide her memories of the Troopers. Collette also started playing for the team in 1973 and played linebacker during their championship years. She remembered that despite the lack of press coverage in the *Blade*, the Troopers were still very famous in the city, which sometimes led to interesting situations. "Sometimes it got a little hairy, because I remember driving down the street, and there was a cruiser right behind me with his lights on and he pulled me over, and I couldn't understand why he pulled me over, and so when he pulled me over and I rolled my window down and he goes, 'Do you play for the Troopers?' because I had a sticker on the back of my car, and I go, 'Yes sir, what did you stop me for?' and he says, 'You ran a red light,' and I didn't run a red light, but he stopped me and he goes, 'Oh and I know this one,' and he starts naming some of my teammates, and he let me go." Fame also meant that going out in public was sometimes problematical. Collette said, "I remember when Linda Jefferson and I went to—we were good buddies—we went to Burger King one time, and we couldn't even eat. We sat down and started eating and people wouldn't leave us alone. There was a lot of good press out there, you know, we had a lot of people. We probably had about a hundred, in between, give or take twenty, people coming and literally watching our practices every practice. We filled up the stadium to standing room only; it was phenomenal back then."

Before instant replay become pervasive, arguments about disputed plays could last for decades with no resolution, and no backing down from either party involved. Nebraska Cornhusker fans, for instance, still argue that officials blew two calls that allowed Penn State to score a winning touchdown against them in 1982, and that argument will likely only end when there is nobody left to argue.[55]

The Troopers and the Dolls were involved in one such controversy. Collette remembered: "They had this great running back, and still a good friend of mine today, Frankie Neal, number 45. She was a beast of a running back, and we were not expecting that at all, so they beat us on a flea-flicker, and devastation grew in Toledo, and we ended up having to play them for the Championship in 1976 at the Glassbowl in Toledo. It was 11 December, and it was 19 degrees, and there was snow on each side of the field. It was fourth quarter, and we were beating them 13–12, because they had just scored, so they needed to kick that point after. I was a linebacker at the time, and I watched the kick—the upright was right behind my back, and I turned and watched the ball, and what it did was it was right above the upright, but just outside. We had an official right underneath the upright and he sees it, and he saw they didn't make it, which means that we won, and we're all jumping around and everything like that. Well, it ended up they were swearing up and down that they made it. For three months they swore up and down they made it, and it got to the point where our coach and owner [Bill Stout] said, 'Okay, it was a tie.' [Be]cause it had gotten that bad. According to me, it's not a tie, because I watched the football go just outside that goalpost."[56]

Having instant replay might bring resolution, but it also precludes what often becomes a hobby for those interested in arguing their points. When asked if she and Neal ever discussed the event, Collette replied, "We might have talked about it twice. The first time, she says, 'You know, I think you're right.' That's all she said. The second time she said, 'I don't want to talk about it, [be]cause I know you're right.' She was the running back at the time. I don't think she was a holder, but she was in the backfield for the kick, she saw it. She was on the same side I was. So she saw it, she knew. Every time we went to Oklahoma City the whole team hated us, except Frankie Neal. Frankie Neal filled up her whole car with Toledo Troopers, and we went out bar hopping and everything like that, and we come back to the hotel, and we had at that time Coors Beer in our bathtubs. They'd fill up our bathtubs with all this beer, at this time it wasn't past the Mississippi. It was over in Oklahoma City. You never saw it over on this side. So of course I'm gonna say it now: we did bootleg some Coors back over to this side of the Mississippi."[57]

As had Jefferson, Collette had thought of trying to make the Olympics throwing the shot, but after her male coach told her to play for the Troopers, she started playing, and women's football has been a significant part of her life ever since. Like Smith, she has not escaped unscathed. When asked if she ever had an injury, she replied, "Actually, yes. I had a major injury. I was a linebacker, and the team that we were playing, they were going to my left, and I went to go tackle their right tackle, who was on my side of the field. Their right tackle went and tackled me, but what she did is she put her shoulder pads right underneath my knee and hyperextended my knee the other direction. It was devastating. So when I got to the hospital and ER, they said that I hyperextended my knee. Well, twenty-six years later I was playing football, and it was for Thee Toledo Reign, and I got hit by the Wisconsin team—they're my friends now—but I got hit, and for some reason, my knee—the swelling never went down. So I ended up having to go to the doctor, and he said that I had a trauma well over ten years before, and I said, 'Well, yeah, that was September of '77,' and they said that I had no ligaments whatsoever. I never knew this. I went through army basic training, I did 5ks, ran 10ks, ran marathons, I mean, I went through the army obstacle courses and won, and all this stuff, and never knew that I didn't have any ligaments. I knew my knee was a little loose, but to me it was a little football injury, so I ended up getting a cadaver [the transplanted ligament came from an organ donor], and it's been okay ever since."[58]

The Troopers' players might still be carrying not-so-pleasant reminders of their playing days, but none of those who provided interviews seemed to mind. They had been football players, and football players sometimes get hurt. This was a price they had been, and still were, willing to play.

The Troopers' major rival, the Oklahoma City Dolls, had little time to enjoy their accomplishment in replacing the Toledo team as NWFL champions, but they made the most of it. The Dolls were created by Hal and Mike Reynolds in 1976. Mike Reynolds read an article about the Troopers game against the Dallas Shamrocks and called his older brother Hal to suggest that they should start a team in Oklahoma City. They recruited former college athletes such as fullback Frankie Neal, who held the Oklahoma state record in the shot put, and quarterback Kathy Gerenda, a former track athlete at the University of Oklahoma.[59] Quarterback Jan Hines was a two sport letterwoman at the University of Oklahoma, and Glenda Cameron was an All-American basketball player at Phillips University.[60]

Athletes they were, but the women had never played football. In an interview with reporter Lacy Lett of KFOR television news in Oklahoma City, Jean Derry, the middle linebacker, remembered, "We had to learn everything. I mean, yes, we know what most of the basic positions were." Derry added, however, "I don't think most of us knew the difference between a guard and a tackle." The Reynolds brothers brought in another pair of brothers, named Selmon (Lee Roy and Dewey), who had starred in football at the University of Oklahoma, to help teach the finer points of the game. Derry did learn these finer points, and also the thrill of victory and the adulation of an enthusiastic fan base. "The best part of the game was after the game. All the little girls would come screaming down to the field: 'I want your autograph."[61]

The Dolls were only in existence for four years, from 1976 to 1979, but they compiled an impressive 32-6-1 record, losing only to the Troopers once (officially) and once to the Dallas Bluebonnets. They won or shared the NWFL championship twice in their short life, only losing the title to the Troopers in 1977. Money doomed the team, according to Mike Reynolds in a 1991 interview. "There were a lot of expenses involved. . . . It wasn't easy flying a bunch of girls all over the country to play football. . . . A lot of cities began having problems, too, and before long you were hearing bankrupt, bankrupt, bankrupt. We were one of the last teams to go."[62]

The Reynolds brothers did have an impressive run, and their success did not go without drawing notice. Little girls were not the only ones impressed by the Dolls, and in 1981 representatives of the American Broadcasting Company (ABC) approached the brothers with the idea of producing a television movie about the now-defunct team. Mike Reynolds remembered, "We used to get some national clips on TV, you know, like on NFL today on Sundays. . . . I guess somebody in California saw us and thought it was a good idea to do a movie."[63]

In her book *Wallowing in Sex: The New Sexual Culture of 1970s American Television* (2007), Elana Levine situated the resulting *The Oklahoma City Dolls* (1981) among ABC's efforts to sell "jiggle television" under the leadership of Fred Silverman, the president of the network's entertainment division. According to Levine, Paul Klein, a National Broadcasting Corporation (NBC) executive, coined the term to describe programming such as ABC's *Charlie's Angels* that featured "a young, attractive television personality running at top speed wearing a limited amount of underwear."[64]

The movie certainly contained elements of that genre, with a couple of locker-room scenes that displayed the female athletes in suggestive, but somewhat tasteful, states of undress. However, it also seemed to suffer from some plotline schizophrenia. The story veered from *Charlie's Angels* to *Maude* (a sitcom about a vocal feminist) with a little of the pro-union *Norma Rae* (1979) thrown in for good measure.

In short, it is a typical "based-on-a-true-story" treatment from the film industry. The true-story part—a team of women played football in

Oklahoma City—was the canvas upon which the filmmakers painted their plotlines of bosses versus workers and women versus the patriarchy. ABC's production team ignored the entire NWFL, and overlooked that the Dolls were a late addition to that league. Instead, they imagined that the team came about as a result of unequal treatment of female workers at an industrial plant.

In his interview with KFOR, Mike Reynolds stated, "It didn't have a lot of truth as far as our team was, but that was okay with us. Just the fact that they had the movie and named it the 'Oklahoma City Dolls.'"[65] ABC flew the Reynolds brothers and some of the team members to Los Angeles to provide ideas for the filming. When "60 stuntwomen failed at throwing a forceful, perfect spiral," Mike Reynolds was given a wig, and he remembered that "I threw all the passes but one in the movie."[66] Jan Hines, the Dolls' quarterback, who demonstrably could throw a forceful and perfect spiral,[67] was unfortunately "not built like [Susan] Blakely," and so she couldn't fill in for the actress convincingly. Hal Reynolds also quipped, "Yeah, I was the first coach of the Dolls, but nobody had to bail me out of jail to coach like they did Eddie Albert."[68] If they raised any objections at the time, perhaps someone from ABC paraphrased the oft-used message from veteran athletes to newcomers and told the Oklahomans, "Welcome to Hollywood, rookies."

As the movie opened, production line worker Sally Jo Purkey (Susan Blakely) was initially angry with plant management for forcing the female workers to pick up the slack for male workers who were given time off to practice for the plant football team. When she complained, she received support from John Miller (Robert Hooks), a federal government Equal Employment Opportunity Commission (EEOC) bureaucrat who forced J. D. Hines (David Huddelston), the plant manager, to allow the women to form a team. The plant manager attempted to hinder the women's ability to play, and nearly succeeded, but Miller appeared just in time to require that the Dolls be able to play a game. Miller reminded Hines that the parent company was in line for a federal contract, and if they did not allow the women to play, the contract would be in jeopardy. Another women's team from Minnesota, the Minneapolis Maids (a minor character described the Maids' players as "a women's team, if you want to call them that—women"), was quickly located, and the big game was set. After the Dolls were mauled by the large mannish-appearing women from the visiting team during the first half, Homer Sixx (Eddie Albert), the Dolls' alcoholic coach, wanted to call the game off to spare his players, but Purkey convinced him they should play. In fine made-for-television fashion, the heroines came back to defeat the villainous Maids and won the game. Tying up loose plot strings, Valene Burns (Ronee Blakely), a wide receiver whose husband abused her, caught the final scoring pass from Purkey. The victorious quarterback took back her less-than-supportive boyfriend Wayne Doak (country music star Waylon Jennings), and all presumably lived happily ever after.[69]

*New York Times* television critic John J. O'Connor wrote a generally favorable review of the movie, declaring: "'The Oklahoma City Dolls' sets out to say something about women and, whatever its flaws, it does. Like Sally Jo's man friend, most male viewers are likely to wind up admitting, 'I love a quarterback.'" He conceded, "Much of the 'Oklahoma City Dolls' is not subtle," which is something of an understatement. Although O'Connor's review was generally positive, he demonstrated some of the bias that women athletes have faced, and still face, when he described the Dolls' on-screen opponents the Maids as appearing to be "formidable lesbians."[70]

Peter J. Boyer, the television writer for the Associated Press (AP), on the other hand, declared that the movie was "as complete a compendium of irritating TV-movie themes as I've ever seen." He took the film to task for trying to mix "jiggle, a la 'Dallas Cowboys Cheerleaders,' with feminist consciousness raising. Really." His scathing review savagely criticized what he saw as the production's shortcomings. "There's a lot of bad grammar, faked Southwestern accents and male pigs spewing outdated clichés about a woman's place and such. There's also sexual reference and bouncing flesh. It's a ridiculous, trite and most of all, crashingly tedious piece of insignificance."[71]

As the movie has aged, new audiences have found that the dramatized story fits with narratives about the past that they have internalized. Paul Mavis, posting on the *DVD Talk* site, wrote: "Beckett lays out a convincing case for the difficulties faced by women in a late 70s American society that claimed to be equal by this point in our history . . . but wasn't (the games manager Huddleston plays to keep the women workers down aren't at all far-fetched in their company-approved childishness)."[72]

Another contemporary poster, Louis Fowler, wrote: "It's weird to think that there was a time when men were so afraid of women taking their place that they'd harass and threaten them just because they wanted equal pay, equal breaks, and equal extracurricular recreation time—especially when it came down to playing on a company football team." Fowler interpreted the movie as being "about the brave group of women who challenged the patriarchy, started a football team and helped move the women's-rights movement a little bit forward, at least in Oklahoma."[73] The movie must have struck some sort of a chord with Fowler, since he posted another review more than a year later, claiming that the football action was "interspersed with Diet Coke first-wave feminist rhetoric that is toned down enough so dad wouldn't change the channel."[74]

The question of what role feminism played in women's early attempts to break into what was considered a man's game motivated Andrew Linden to interview several players from those early teams and ask them for their opinions. Linden published a 2015 article with his findings in the *International Journal of the History of Sport*. After interviewing thirteen former players from the Troopers, Dolls, and Columbus Pacesetters, Linden concluded: "Most women athletes, and women footballers in particular, articulated little connection between taking the field and the larger feminist campaigns for corporeal autonomy and equality. Some went so far as to pronounce a distinctly antifeminist identity." Linden did find a few players such as former Trooper Julie Sherwood, who told him that "I saw myself as a feminist. . . . I don't see that as something to be ashamed of." The afore-quoted Mitchi Collette, however, argued that there was "'absolutely not' a connection between the 1970s women's movement and her football career."[75]

Likewise, in an AP article, the Troopers' Jefferson maintained unliberatedly that marriage "should be an ultimate goal in a woman's life."

She also reportedly "doesn't equate female sports competition with the women's movement."[76] Clementine Bloomingdale, writing for *Playgirl* magazine, found the same. Bloomingdale watched the LA Dandelions play against the Detroit Demons and wrote: "Women's football is in its infancy, and these teams are pioneers. They state that they do not think of themselves as part of any women's movement—that they are interested in football as a sport, not as a political statement."[77]

Linden did argue persuasively that although very few of the athletes he interviewed claimed to be feminists, their actions "made radical statements about the social world in which they lived. They challenged conventional ideas about gender. And their actions are no less important than what other women fought for during feminism's second wave."[78]

Likewise, de la Cretaz and D'Arcangelo also noted the lack of overtly feminist sentiments exhibited by the NWFL players and also argued, "But you don't have to think of yourself as a feminist in order to be one." Those authors also analyzed that for women who had spent their lives "breaking stereotypes by sheer will and determination, it was easier to distance themselves from the larger women's movement than it was to align with women who seemed so different than they were."[79]

Although not using the term, Linden, de la Cretaz, and D'Arcangelo seem to be arguing for the idea that the women football players he interviewed were exhibiting the "practical feminism," to use the term coined by Jean Williams, in *A Contemporary History of Women's Sports* (2014), to describe women involved in sport for the experience, rather than as a chance to strike an overt blow to the patriarchy.[80] A major goal of the women's movement was to give women freedom to control their bodies. For theoretical feminists, a large part of this has involved questions of reproductive rights.[81] For practical feminists, as described by Williams, this might encompass reproductive rights, depending on their political affiliations or religious values, but it also includes the freedom to launch their bodies at their fellow women on the football field. The women who played football for the Dolls, the Troopers, and other teams were using the freedom that resulted from the women's movement to take part in a sport that interested them, despite what the "patriarchy" might think about them playing a traditional male sport.

The Reynolds brothers might have been copacetic with what Hollywood made of *The Oklahoma City Dolls* story, but the movie's dramatization of events did a disservice to the team and its story. The history of the team was impressive enough without making the movie a vehicle for (theoretical) feminism and union activism, and a subtle reminder that the federal government was a force for progress. The athletes who played for the Dolls and the Reynolds brothers who started the team did something amazing, as did the other women who played for the less well-known teams in the NWFL.

The league had been facing difficulties for some time, and after the NWFL limited play between divisions, several western teams broke away in 1978 to form the Western States Women's Professional Football League (WSWPFL). The Los Angeles Dandelions, Hollywood Stars, Mesa (AZ) American Girls, Phoenix Cowgirls, Tucson Wild Kittens, Long Beach Queens, and Southland (CA) Cowgirls were the teams that left the league.[82] The ease with which this happened illustrated the difficulties that have always plagued women's football; it is just too easy to leave established leagues. This happened when some NWFL teams left the WPFL, and again with the schism of the NWFL. This continued to be a challenge for women's football during the 2018 season, but more on that later.

The NWFL, now devoid of its star teams, still limped along and continued to serve as an organization for women's football in Ohio and Michigan until 1985. They finally managed to hold championship games from 1983 to 1985. The championship trophy, if one existed, returned to Ohio for the first two of those. The Cleveland Brewers won the title by defeating the Columbus Pacesetters in 1983. A fusion of Trooper veterans and newcomers named the Toledo Furies brought Toledo its last title in 1984, when they defeated the Brewers. The league held one more championship, won by the Grand Rapids Carpenters, and then essentially folded.[83]

During the summer of 1980, Kasey Carter was taking continuing education credits for certification as a music teacher in graduate school in Wisconsin. Her goal upon return to Ohio was to play for the Troopers, but by the time she got back, the team had ceased operation. She described herself as "the official Toledo Trooper wannabe." When some of the Trooper veterans were forming the Furies, Carter joined that team. The team was to be somewhat unusual, for the time, in that the players banded together to form a group named Women in Team Sports that would make up the ownership of the team. Carter remembered that "sometimes we'd have practice and afterwards have to go to somebody's house for a business meeting. And we had to raise, I think it was $20,000, and so we had lift-a-thons, and candy sales, whatever we had to do we did. And we dug into our own pockets as well." The Furies, in short, existed under what is the contemporary pay-to-play model of women's football. "You know, we owned ourselves, and we have tremendous respect for the Troopers, [but] everything was provided for the Troopers. All of their equipment, their uniforms, their transportation everywhere. The Furies, we had to provide that for ourselves. Or we had to do fundraisers or whatever we had to do, that's what we did."[84]

In a sport where many women, out of necessity, play nearly every position at some point, Carter was an unusual specialist. "We fielded the team in 1983. And the core of the team was the former Troopers. I was place kicker—kickoffs and extra points." Carter echoed the women quoted above on women's liberation not playing a role in their decision to play football and on their love for the game. "Well, I just thought it was cool. I had played other things, mostly softball, and I really wanted to play football. It looked like a lot of fun. It was never about women's liberation, Title IX—all that. It was never about that. It was just about having watched the game of football, watching men play football, and wanting an opportunity to play on the women's team. I was absolutely thrilled when the Furies came along. To this day, and I'm sixty-five years old, if anyone ever said, 'What's the neatest thing you ever did?' [I'd say] I played football."[85]

Many of the women who played football between 1968 and 1985 had an experience that defined their lives. They forged friendships that will last as long as they live, and they created memories that still thrill them. Their example also inspires a new generation of girls who want to play football, at least when they become aware of it.

They also made enemies. The Pro Football Hall of Fame's "Women in Football" file contained an unsourced article that quoted two male coaches named Edwards and Orr who told a reporter that "the women have exhibited more enthusiasm for playing the game and yet less of the 'killer instinct' than their male counterparts. . . . But noticeably, the girls don't seem to have that will to hurt or maim an opponent. They enjoy beating an opponent on the scoreboard or being more skillful, but not hurting."[86] That would have been news to the Troopers' Jefferson, and also to Joan Williams of the Dolls. Middle linebacker Williams remembered that in one game, "when I got down in the stance, I heard a girl say 'Take her out now,' so a six-foot, 230 pound girl stood me up, and another ran her helmet plumb though my knee and broke it from side to side and that kind of ended my career."[87]

If Beruldsen's analysis mentioned above was correct, the Super Bowl captured the imagination of Americans and gave many women and girls a new dream—playing football. Entrepreneurs such as Friedman, along with Stout and the Reynolds brothers, thought they might make some money by offering women and girls a chance to do so. In *Hail Mary* de la Cretaz and D'Arcangelo criticized Friedman and other owners who were mainly concerned with making money, but without a financial incentive, it is likely that the women's game would not have existed in the 1970s.[88]

There does not seem to be much evidence that the women's liberation movement had much to do with this phenomenon, but the narrative that women should be able to do what they wished had gained momentum and quite possibly helped females dare to dream about participating in sports once considered to be male only, and then to translate those dreams into reality. When the WPFL began, and was almost immediately followed by the NWFL, Title IX was not yet law, and even afterward girls often had to bring lawsuits to be able to play. Therefore it played no role in the creation of women's football. In the absence of any direct evidence, Beruldsen's Super Bowl thesis is likely a good explanation for the numbers of women who seemingly sprang up from nowhere to stock the teams and leagues created closely in the wake of the new football spectacular.

It is unclear from extant sources, but perhaps Friedman sought to cash in on the football craze that had gripped the country. Whatever his motivation, for nearly two decades several hundred women had a blast interacting violently with their peers. Many still carry the scars, but I have found none who had regrets that they played. Most are quite aware that they did something unique, and they revel in that knowledge.

After the demise of the NWFL, it seemed that there would be only one generation of women's football. Many women, including players from the Cleveland Brewers and the Columbus Pacesetters, continued to play flag football.[89] The memories of those adventurous days on the gridiron faded over time and were limited to dusty newspaper archives and to the fading memories of those women who had, for a brief time, been football heroines. For those who were not directly involved, the blinders remained firmly in place, waiting for a new generation who would once again attempt to remove them.

# Women's Football Roars Back

After the NWFL collapsed in 1985, fourteen years passed before women returned to the gridiron. In 1999 Terry Sullivan and Carter Turner, with a reported investment of "more than $40,000 from Ernest Delanghe," created a company named World Wide Sports. Sullivan and Carter reportedly sought to capitalize on the buzz surrounding the birth of the Women's National Basketball Association and the American victory in the 1999 FIFA Women's World Cup by founding a women's professional football league.[1]

They advertised nationwide in newspapers, and "about 360 women showed up" to try out for a place on one of the proposed two teams in various locations, including Minneapolis, Miami, and Daytona Beach. The 90 women that made the cut were split into the Minnesota Vixens and the Lake Michigan Minx. The first game set the tone for the tour, when the Minx defeated the Vixens 33–6.[2] The Minx went on to win all six of the matches.[3]

The No Limits barnstorming tour included games in Minneapolis, St. Paul, Green Bay, Chicago, New York, and Miami. The NFL also invited the two teams to take part in the NFL Experience as part of Super Bowl XXXV.[4] There seemed to be some success for the tour, and plans for a new women's football league continued despite concerns over the finances of the original tour. How many tickets were sold for the entire tour is difficult to determine, but the first game held at Midway Stadium in St. Paul drew around 2,400 curiosity seekers, along with the players' family members. Tickets reportedly cost $20 apiece, so after the cost of renting the stadium was deducted, there may not have been much profit to go around.[5]

In November of that first year, George Dohrmann and Jim Caple of the *St. Paul Pioneer Press* published a lengthy article that provided background information on Sullivan and Turner. Sullivan had a long background of shady financial dealings, and Turner had a rap sheet that included convictions for various felonies including assault and burglary. The report called into question Sullivan and Turner's plans for launching their Women's Professional Football League (WPFL) in 2000. The tour promoters reportedly planned to charge a $50,000 franchise fee for new teams, along with an additional $15,000 required for "equipment and an organizational plan."[6]

Despite the shaky financial footing of the new venture, women's football did receive considerable publicity. According to Laura Billings of the *Pioneer Press*, reporters from *Sports Illustrated* and ESPN attended the first game, which caused some consternation among the players, who were not used to being in the spotlight. Billings, rare for a reporter, seemed to have some grasp of history. While challenging the notion that the game was "history making," she did note, "In fact, two other pro women's football teams have failed already." She may have committed a typo there by writing "teams" when she meant "leagues," or she may not have had that much of a sense of history that preceded the first game of the No Limits tour.[7] In either case, a reporter being at least somewhat aware of the past is unusual enough to justify comment.

The Minx and Vixens were also the subject of a documentary, titled *True Hearted Vixens* (2001), directed by Mylene Moreno for the Public Broadcasting Service's POV program. Moreno decided to focus on one player from each team. From the Minx, she chose linebacker Jane Brolin, who commented, "I always prided myself on the fact that, hey, I play sports, I'm pretty good, and I'm not a dyke," perhaps the most memorable line from the documentary. The other focal player, Kertria "Moochie" Lofton of the Vixens, was a wide receiver whose goal was to play in the Women's National Basketball Association. Moreno followed the two as they struggled to learn the game and deal with off-the-field issues surrounding their personal lives and the financial situation of the tour. Lofton struggled with having her daughter accompany her and was therefore unable to travel to New York for a game that pitted a team combined from Minx and Vixen players against the New York Sharks, a team that had only played flag until 1999. Sullivan used his appearance in the documentary to accuse the *Pioneer Press* reporters of being biased against women's football. "The only reason they could be writing this story is to go after women's sports and say 'We don't want women playing tackle football.'" Ultimately, Lofton departed the Vixens, and Brolin revealed that despite her assertion otherwise, she had become involved with one of the Vixens, and Sullivan "decides that his days as a football promoter were over."[8]

*True Hearted Vixens*, despite being bogged down in personal stories that took away from the action on the field, did demonstrate that women were willing to make often significant sacrifices in order to play football. The documentary received generally positive reviews by academics such as Susan Cahn and from more general writers, although Robert Koehler of *Variety* criticized Moreno for her failure to "trace extensive connections to other sports (such as boxing, basketball and soccer) where women are attempting to establish durable pro businesses."[9]

Sullivan may have left the sport promotion business, but Turner continued to work on creating the new professional league. Despite their success, the Minx did not become a part of the WPFL, but the Vixen, now without the *s*, continued to compete. After more than twenty years they are still going strong—they lost to the Boston Renegades in the WFA championship game in 2021. As an illustration of the somewhat chaotic nature of women's football, during that time span, the Vixen played under the auspices of four different leagues.[10]

On 18 February 2018 Michele Braun, one of the original Vixens, told me about that first year and her subsequent twenty-year career in women's professional football. She remembered that her football journey began when she read "a little one inch by one inch ad in the *Minneapolis Star Tribune* back in 1998." She continued: "That was the original barnstorming tour year 1999. Between the Minnesota

Vixen and the Lake Michigan Minx, which were actually two teams that were created to play each other on this barnstorming tour to get interest into women's football. So actually it was eighty players, and we were separated into two teams: the Lake Michigan Minx and the Minnesota Vixens, and we played each other on a six-game tour of kind of the Midwest to gain interest, to see if women's football could catch on."[11]

Braun played her entire career for the Vixen(s), but Melissa "Missy" Bedwell, one of the original Minx, had to play on seven different teams to put in her twenty years. We talked at the New Orleans Saints' practice facility on 22 February 2018 when she was participating in the Women's World Football Games. As with Braun, Bedwell saw the small advertisement that Sullivan and Turner had placed in papers nationwide. "I was living in Miami at the time, and I saw an article in the newspaper, 'Try out for women's professional football.' So, I drove to Daytona that weekend and tried out, and they invited me to Minnesota to play. There were two teams at that time, Lake Michigan Minx and Minnesota Vixens, and they were doing a barnstorming tour. They chose eighty girls from across the country to be on those teams, and I was lucky enough to be one of those chosen."[12]

Braun also considered herself lucky to have made the team, given the level of competition that the athletes faced. "We had a lot of coaches who had NFL experience, and we just met. We had, I think, in the first initial tryout, I think we had over four hundred women trying out. I was lucky to make one of the spots. It was quite interesting to see. We had women from Canada, we had women from all over the United States. We had Wendy Brown, who was an Olympic decathlete from California. We had people from Florida. We had people from the East Coast. It was quite a diverse mix of women and very, very talented athletic women too. We had a lot of local people from the Twin Cities area, obviously, that made the team. I would say the percentage of people that were outside the state of Minnesota were pretty close, I would say, to at least a third, that were outside the state of Minnesota that made the team. We had a woman who was an astronaut for NASA. Like I said, we had a lot of diverse people with a lot of cool backgrounds."[13]

Not being one of the athletes from Minnesota, Bedwell had to find a place to live. The tour organizers did not do anything to help their players find work, so she initially tried to live on the cheap. "Actually, I quit my job in Florida and moved to Minnesota. I was trying to rough it—brought a tent with me. I was camping in a national forest up there. One of the girls on the team was looking for a roommate, and I ended up moving in with her—renting a room from her. Luckily, I was in the military, so I get a check every month, and I could live off of that for a little while until the season was in, and that helped. I just up and decided that football was gonna be my life, and that is what drove me."[14]

Bedwell had to hustle to find teams to play for during her career. She started with the Minx, then transferred to the Vixen for one season. When she moved to Virginia, she traveled to practice and games with the Carolina Cougars, and then she was with the Philadelphia Phoenix for three years. She relocated briefly back to Florida, where she played for three years with the West Palm Beach Punishers. Her longest stint was with the D.C. Divas, where she played for "six or seven years." During her tenure with the Divas, she also experienced her most successful years in football, as her D.C. team won back-to-back Women's Football Federation championships in 2015 and 2016. The next year she changed teams and was back in Florida. She returned to the championships with her current team, the Tampa Bay Inferno, who lost to the St. Louis Slam in the 2017 WFA championship game. The Inferno made the playoffs in 2018 but lost in the semifinals to the eventual champion, the New York Sharks.[15]

If movies such as *The Oklahoma City Dolls* (1981), discussed in the previous chapter, are to be believed, then those early players should have faced a great deal of opposition to playing—not only from the public but also from friends and family. Both Braun and Bedwell maintained that this narrative did not apply in their case. Braun told me, "My father had passed away by then, but my mother was very proud of me. My mother, up until her death in 2010, attended every home game. I think she missed one home game due to illness. But she had come to every single one of my games. She passed away just into our 2010 season. She had been to my last game. We played against Iowa at a home game, and then she died about four or five days later, very suddenly. So my oldest brother, up until his death in 2015, had been to every single one of my home games. I think my brother had missed just once. I had a lot of great support from my mother and my brother as far as that. I think in this sport to survive you have to have a good family base and have a good family foundation to have that support. It's very hard to do this without support at home or with a spouse/partner/whatever. You know, to have that support and say, 'We understand and we're rooting for you. We think what you are doing is great. We just want you to be happy and safe, obviously,' because football is a tough sport."[16]

Bedwell agreed: "I've been lucky that my family supports me, my mother has told me ever since I was little you can do anything you want. 'You can be anyone you want to be. Never let anyone tell you, you can't.' She's always had my back. She supported me—she may not have liked it, and was always worried, but she always supported me. My dad came to a lot of games, and wasn't in my life a lot when I was younger, but now that I'm older we've worked together, and things like that, so he's been a part of my life in football because he wasn't in high school when I was in softball, volleyball, and basketball. So he supported me, my brother supports, my whole entire family, and it's an amazing thing."[17]

Both players have benefited from a strong support structure among their family and friends, but playing football for twenty years has not been without a price. According to Braun: "I've been pretty much blessed in this sport to be relatively healthy. Through my twenty-year career, I think I've sprained an ankle, broken a finger, tore a shoulder muscle, I had a [torn] meniscus in my right knee, I sprained an MCL, and four concussions. You know, for the most part, I think twenty years, I'd take that in a heartbeat."[18]

Bedwell added: "I'm so lucky to still be playing after twenty seasons, you know. I've had six or seven surgeries. I've had injuries. I've lost jobs. Family members have been, like, 'Why aren't you coming to see me at Easter?' 'Aren't you gonna come to my wedding?' 'I have a game.' This has become part of who I am. Everyone knows from

April to August you can find me every Saturday on the football field. This is my football schedule—if you want to see me, come see me. It may be for a different team, but I'm still going be playing this time every season."[19]

It was obvious that both women felt that they had come out ahead on their bargain with football. When I talked to Braun, she was getting ready for her twentieth and last season with the Vixen. In her retirement announcement on Facebook, Braun listed some of her career highlights:

Well . . . every athlete knows when its time to retire . . . and its mine. For 20 years, I have been fortunate to play one of the greatest sports ever . . . Football. Trying out all those years ago with over 400 talented women, making one of 80 spots . . . creating History. Being a Minnesota Vixen has been a great accomplishment in my life. Being a Captain, Leader, All Star. Traveling all over the USA, playing in the Metrodome & Orange Bowl in Miami! Gonna miss the playing & being with teammates as a player . . . but hope to continue on our storied tradition as a coach . . . and bring this team a championship! Thank you to all who have lived this ride with me & supported me through it! I could not have done it without you![20]

To put an exclamation point at the end of her career, Braun was named to the Women's Football Hall of Fame. In her introduction the presenter mentioned some of her impressive accomplishments: "Michelle has played in every game the Minnesota Vixen have ever played but one, being the longest existing continually operating Women's tackle Football team in the Nation! Over 160 games played . . . Michele played thru injuries & played for the desire of a dream of football. She has been a 3 time All Star, and named Team Captain 14 times. Probably her most impressive stat is that she started at Center in a playoff game in 2017 at age 50 years old!"[21]

Bedwell was hooked from the start, and that sustained her career as a nomadic player. I met her at the 2018 Women's World Games sponsored by USA Football, and after nineteen years, she was still working to improve. She told me that her fondest memory was one of her first. "The very first game, October 6th or 7th, back in '99, standing on the sideline and listening to the National Anthem at that first game, still gives me chills. I remember standing there thinking I'm playing women's professional football, and I just started crying. It still gives me goose bumps. Standing there listening. Just this amazing feeling knowing that you're playing. Don't get me wrong, winning my first Super Bowl [the 2015 Diva championship] was amazing too, but that feeling of just being on the field for the very first time, listening to the national anthem, knowing what that sport had brought to me—the purpose that it had given me, just being out of the Marine Corps. It was amazing for me."[22]

For women such as Braun and Bedwell, football provided a focus for their lives. The Minnesota Vixen, along with several other teams for Bedwell, gave them a team on which to play. At first, the WPFL organized those teams into something larger. The new league would not be the only game in town for long though, and through a combination of their own self-inflicted troubles, along with a surge in interest among women who wanted to play football, the number of leagues and teams mushroomed in the early years of the new century.

The WPFL kicked off the 2000 season but immediately faced problems. William Dean Hinton, writing for the *Orlando Weekly*, captured some of the chaos of those first years in a 2001 article. He opened with the story of the Orlando Lightning playing the Miami Fury. The home team reportedly was completely outclassed by the Fury (a team that still exists), and matters only worsened after the game when co-owners Marsha Beatty and Cassandra Miller, who Hinton informed readers were "lovers off the field," got into a shoving match over a dispute about ownership of a water cooler. The Lightning were already the result of a dispute between owners of the Orlando Fire. The teams split when some of the team's management group suggested that "several owners wanted to receive a paycheck before players."[23]

Hinton used the Lightning's issues to segue into a generalization about the state of women's football in 2001. "Such is the world of women's professional tackle football, a sport with a short history that is laced more with off-field controversy than on-field heroics. Not just teams, but entire women's tackle leagues have sprung up only to crash and burn without completing a season." The reporter had done his homework and referenced not only the Toledo Troopers and the NWFL but also the failed 1920s experiment; he also noted the women's sport was spreading to Germany. The article was largely critical of the chances of a women's football league succeeding, but subsequent history bore out his contentions concerning the successors to those early efforts that started at the beginning of the twenty-first century.[24]

The WPFL started off with considerable promise, boasting that eleven teams would play in the league's first season. Andra Douglas, in *Black and Blue: Love, Sports, and the Art of Empowerment* (2019), summed up the motivation for the women who flocked to these teams when she wrote: "Thousands of females who heard about the Women's Professional Football Association wanted a hit of the football drug, and we made it clear that we would do anything, pay any price, cross any line, do whatever it took to suit up and get onto the field. We were desperate for a fix."[25]

The early promise collapsed, however, when Carter Turner and his management group "greatly overestimated their revenues" and could not pay their bills.[26] Turner blamed "fraudulent investors" for the WPFL's problems. "The funny thing about women's football is that it's attracted about 99 percent really good people, but it has attracted some people who think they can make fast, easy money off of women and football, and that's what happened with the WPFL."[27]

Hinton wrote that *Sports Illustrated for Women* had reported the WPFL was $100,000 in debt after the first season. He also mentioned that the league promised players $100 per game, which never happened, and that "several lawsuits reportedly have been filed over the league's breakup." Turner told Hinton, "We had some investors who borrowed some money in the name of the league and we never saw them again. . . . They were in it for an easy buck."[28] The league did manage to hold a hastily arranged championship game, and the Houston Energy (another still-existing team) defeated the now-defunct New England Storm 39–7.[29]

After that first chaotic season, several league owners worked together to restructure the league. Concerning those early struggles, Dawn Berndt, who served as executive director of the league and also as the owner of the Dallas Diamonds, contacted me out of the blue on Facebook Messenger. Her 5 August 2018 message asked about my project, and then, when I told her that I was unsure of what I would write about the WPFL, she told me that it would not be a true history of women's football if I did not include the role of the league. She argued, "There would be no stories [I told her that I would include oral history interviews] if not for the WPFL." She added, "If the 4 founding mothers of the sport hadn't given what they had, there would not be a sport." I searched for founding mothers of the WPFL in various ways, but the only mention I found was while writing this chapter. The Wikipedia page on the league mentioned that Melissa Korpacz of the New England Storm, Robin Howington of the Houston Energy, and Donna Roebuck and Dee Kennamer of the Austin Rage were the owners who reworked the league and created the structure that lasted until 2007.[30]

Although I may be consigned to the historians' hell for citing Wikipedia, the information there has proven correct, as far as I can determine. Korpacz owned the New England Storm and was the WPFL executive director prior to Berndt. Chris Shott, the sports editor of the *Cranston Herald* in Warwick, Rhode Island, wrote a laudatory 2002 article about her role in the league. He opened by asserting that Korpacz "is aiming to become the Robert Kraft and/or Paul Tagliabue of women's professional football." That was hyperbole, but Korpacz was one the first owners to forge a "working relationship" with the New England Patriots of the NFL. Korpacz was optimistic that other WPFL teams would do the same. "I think it's just a matter of time before the NFL picks us up," she said. "Ideally, I expect it to happen within the next three years." That did not happen, but at the time of the article, Korpacz, who "earned a law degree from Suffolk University in Boston," was optimistic, and the league was growing. In 2002 the WPFL had ten teams split into two conferences with teams scattered across the country from Los Angeles to Medford, Massachusetts, where the Storm were located. She anticipated further expansion in 2003 and told Shott that "representatives of over 20 additional teams have queried the league on its entrance requirements."[31] Some of her optimism was justified, and the WPFL added seven teams and increased to four divisions for 2003, but the increase was short-lived.

Texas teams dominated the WPFL for its first six years, winning four league titles and finishing second once. The Houston Energy won championships in 2001 and 2002 and finished second in 2006 and 2008. The Dallas Diamonds added another two championships in 2004 and 2005, and the Austin Rage finished second in 2001. The Florida Stingrays also won two championships and were joined by the Northern Ice (2003), the New York Dazzles (2007), and the SoCal Scorpions (2008), which also won championships before the league folded. Melissa "Missi" Korpacz's Storm managed to finish as runners-up three times (2000, 2002, and 2003) before they were expelled.[32]

The league lost teams in 2004, before stabilizing at fifteen or sixteen teams per year until 2007, when their remaining teams left for either the National Women's Football Association (NWFA) or the Independent Women's Football League (IWFL).[33] One of the teams that left the WPFL in 2004 was Korpacz's Storm. She and her team were expelled from the league "after officers had determined they had violated WPFL bylaws." That last was from *Korpacz v. Women's Professional Football League*, a 2006 lawsuit that Korpacz brought against the league. Also released was the statement that "some of these statements are formal notices issued by the WPFL Commissioner to the WPFL League Office, concerning various disciplinary complaints by and against plaintiffs, while some are emails among WPFL members raising concerns about plaintiff Korpacz's conduct in league related business." Other than these statements, the record of what the disputes actually were is not contained in the judges' decision. In her lawsuit the former Storm owner charged the league with seven torts, but the presiding judge in the U.S. District Court of Massachusetts issued a summary judgment against her, finding that none of the charges were actionable.[34] Thus for one of the four founding mothers, the situation changed drastically, and chaos such as this would be recapitulated in a variety of women's football leagues, up to and including the present day.

Robin Howington of the Houston Energy was also one of the women who helped turn around the WPFL, but progress was difficult. In a December 2001 article by Wendy Grossman of the *Houston Press*, Howington listed the team's problems, which included declining spectator support—from the nearly 1,700 fans who saw their first game, ticket sales declined to "between 500 and 800." Howington remarked: "It got worse and worse. If we don't get corporate sponsors, there won't be a Houston Energy. We're not going to make it." The owner pointed to not having much funding for advertising, which hurt her efforts to promote the team. Her pessimism was as justified in 2001 as Korpacz's optimism was in 2002. After beginning with eleven teams in 2000, by 2001 there were only four teams left. Howington struggled to find a coach for the team who would work with her. NFL veteran Haywood Jeffries, their first head coach, did not see eye to eye with her and quit the team for "unspecified reasons" after their third game. That situation stabilized after Robin Henry, a former assistant coach at a local high school, took over. Mentioning the difficulty in coaching women who had never played the game, Henry told Grossman, "We are straight, basic, old-fashioned football." He continued: "I've seen everybody trying to get too fancy. Most of these girls, all they know of football is what they've seen on TV. Even though they know what to do in a complex offense or defense, they really don't understand why they're doing it."[35]

Despite Howington's concerns, the one problem she and her team did not have was winning. The Energy won the first hastily organized WPFL championship and then dominated the league for the next two years, winning the 2001 and 2002 titles.[36] Her assertion that the team could not last without sponsors also turned out to be an incorrect prediction. Either that, or the team found those sponsors, for the Houston Energy still exists and finished the 2018 season as the champion of IWFL after defeating the Nevada Storm 34–0.[37]

Demonstrating the difficulty that women's football has getting press coverage, much of a 2018 article on the championship in the *Alvin (TX) Sun* dealt with the team's cheerleading squad, made up "almost entirely of girls from Alvin ranging in age from 7 to 15."[38] The Energy then also kept the chaos rolling that is a mark of women's football when they followed up their championship by jumping from the IWFL to the WFA for the 2019 season.[39]

Like the Vixens and Minx before them, Rage owner Dee Kennamer also attracted documentary makers. Sean Pamphilon, who later became notable for his role in releasing audio interviews that helped fuel the New Orleans Saints' Bountygate scandal, produced *Playing with Rage* (2006) about the team and about larger issues such as gender-based violence that women face.[40] The trailer for the film began with a clip of veteran sports reporter and commentator Bob Costas, who somewhat ironically intoned: "Who says success is measured by how many television cameras there are? Maybe success is just in doing it." The scene cut to what was presumably the Rage locker room, where Austin head coach and offensive coordinator Kennamer told her team: "I want every single one of you to live out your dream of playing football, and I'll tell you why. It was my dream too." As The Who's "Baba O'Riley" (1971) played in the background, a quote by Michael Silver of *Sports Illustrated* ("It's 'Rocky' for women") flashed across the screen, and Kennamer's pregame speech continued. She told her players, "When you walk out that tunnel right there, you get the attitude that you're the best that's ever played this game." The question of safety was raised by displaying scenes of players crashing into one another, including some apparently badly injured, while other athletes downplayed the risk. The theme of domestic violence was raised, at least on the trailer, by Kennamer, who stated, "Women are hit every day." But she added, "If the home is not safe, then by God, we'll make the football field safe for them."

The project appeared to be a fascinating exploration of women's football. In addition to Costas, Julie Foudy, a former member of the women's national soccer team and later a broadcaster, Steve Sabol of NFL Films, ESPN reporter Suzy Kolber, and then NFL running back Ricky Williams added their voices to the project.[41]

What they might have said appears to have been lost, since other than the trailer posted on YouTube by executive producer Royce Toni and a brief summary written by Pamphilon for the Internet Movie

Database (IMDb), the film has disappeared. The producer's IMDb blurb promised that the film "tackles the issues of domestic violence, gender roles . . . and the current sad state of the sports media and the abnormal amount of importance that is placed on today's professional male athletes and the games they play." Unlike *True Hearted Vixens*, there is no record of the documentary on WorldCat or anywhere else that I could find, other than on social media. Sandy Glossenger, who, along with her husband, Dale, promotes all-star women's games throughout the Americas, posted that she had watched the documentary on 25 July 2019, apparently in a live screening that included Pamphilon, but she did not mention how she found the film.[42]

"Playing with RAGE," a Facebook group dedicated to the project, includes footage of an interview that might have been in the documentary.[43] In it, a player named Tiffany, identified as a safety and as a grade school teacher, told Pamphilon about her abusive husband. Tiffany related how playing football gave her the strength, both mental and physical, to turn the tables on her abuser.[44] Kennemar, in a 25 November 2018 interview with me, confirmed that the "further you drill down, the more stories you'll find, and we had a couple of abuse cases on our team, and after the women learn that they could really pack a punch, they took up for themselves and beat the crap out of their abusive husbands. I don't mean to be so crass about it, but after years of abuse they finally were able to stand up for themselves."[45] A request for more information about the film on the Facebook group never received a reply.

It is a shame that the full version of the documentary is unavailable, and it would be fascinating to learn the story of why it is not accessible. *True Hearted Vixens* was not hard to locate and acquire through interlibrary loan. *The Oklahoma City Dolls* full movie discussed in chapter 1 is available on YouTube. *First Down*, a documentary about the New York Sharks' first season in the WPFL, can be accessed through Vimeo.[46] *Tackle the World—Tough Game, Tougher Women*, a short documentary made about the 2013 International Federation of American Football's Women's World Championship that is discussed in chapter 8, is also readily available. Perhaps Pamphilon, who has written, directed, and produced several documentaries, holds the rights too closely for the film to be readily available, although there are no sites offering it for sale either. Kennamer asserted that there were "copies still floating around," but for now at least, the fate of *Playing with Rage* remains a mystery.[47]

The bulk of my interview with Kennemar dealt with the Rage and its short career in the WPFL. When prompted to talk about the fascinating times in which she took part, the former coach replied, "It was a fun time. It was exciting to do something that was different." That surely was an understatement. Women such as Kennemar were involved in an effort to create something radically new for the time. In 1998 there were no women's professional football teams or leagues. By 2001 Pamphilon asserted on his IMDb page for *Playing with Rage*, "There are over 100 teams of women in America who play professional football." That was an overstatement in 2001, but there were at least 72 teams competing by 2015.[48] Something revolutionary was happening during those years. The teams and leagues that exploded onto the scene after the 1999 barnstorming tour were evidence that women had the freedom and were willing to play football, given the chance.

The WPFL initially created a team in Austin, called the Rose. Apparently the players did not like that name, and Chennell Brooks came up with the new name, the Rage. When asked if the players had some rage issues, as many football players seem to, Kennamer once again used what must have been an understatement. "Yeah, well, you know, twenty years ago it was a little bit different for women trying to play tackle football."

According to Kennamer, "Something happened between the head coach and the WPFL people, and so they were going to shut the team down." Rather than do that though, the WPFL contacted Kennamer, who was well known in the flag football world in Austin, and asked her to take over the franchise. She and her partner, Donna Roebuck, bought the franchise, and Kennamer became the head coach/offensive coordinator. She referenced the initial chaos that hindered the league and said: "Well, the whole thing was pretty chaotic, and as you might well guess, the biggest problem was underfunding, and the business plan was weak. Because the business plan—it wasn't a really good concept of how it was going to be put together, and so there was a lot of dissatisfaction. Not only with the fans but [also with] the players. But they did get to play football—that was the main objective, and that part did occur."[49]

She also downplayed the difficulty that her athletes faced in learning a new sport. "There was definitely a learning curve, but most of the players, a good percentage of the players have played tackle football, only with no pads, so getting hit and throwing somebody on the ground was nothing new. All these people grew up playing football in their backyard." When I mentioned that might be a function of growing up in Texas, Kennamer replied: "Yeah, it's Texas. So I can't speak for all of the states. I've lived in Alabama and Texas. And in Alabama and Texas the girls know football and they play football, so, of course, there was a learning curve for adjusting from playing flag to playing tackle football in pads. Playing in pads is different, and so, of course, there was a learning curve, but they took to it like ducks to water. After about the third year you saw the speed of playing increase."[50]

When the Rage began practices, they had no shortage of players. Kennamer remembered that there were "about eighty [at] the first tryout that I had." She also had helped the Energy's Howington with her tryouts and stated that their cross-state rivals had around 350 athletes at their tryout. Early on, the Austin coach was not too selective. "You know, most of the tryouts, because the equipment wasn't available yet, at the tryouts people were just trying out in shorts and T-shirts. They were not in full pads, so [at] the tryouts you didn't even have the ability to look at someone in full tackle scenario. You don't get to see that. You were looking at people that had speed and had hand-eye coordination. That could kick and could throw—things like that. But you weren't looking at anybody tackling anybody. In my case if you could walk and talk, I kept the players." They had sixty players to start the season and suited fifty-three for games, "just like in the NFL."[51]

During the 2001 season, their second year in existence, the Rage had some success on the field. They played the Energy for the WPFL championship but lost 47–14.[52] That, however, turned out to be their last season. The bleachers at Del Valle High School's stadium, where they played in 2000 and 2001, failed an engineering inspection and were declared unsafe, and the engineers also declared that "there was not appropriate access to the facilities for persons with disabilities." Kennamer was unable to locate another field. Athletic directors gave various reasons, such as not wanting "too much traffic on their fields" or they "did not want to staff another event." Some venues wanted "a ridiculous amount of rent," while others complained that they no longer rented to outside groups after their field had been damaged. According to a post on the Visit Wimberley, Texas website, the Rage was scheduled to play on their field in 2002, but something happened, and that plan fell through.[53]

Kennamer reported that the Rage could have found a venue for the 2003 season, but the WPFL stepped in and fined her and the team $15,000 for not playing. Her memory of the event provided a fascinating window into the world of team ownership and relations with the league. "Yeah, we got fined $15,000 for pulling out of the league, because we couldn't turn a facility. And that's what killed us, because we could have come back the next year. But we had that $15,000 fine over our head, and no way. You know, when you sell four hundred tickets at a game for $10 apiece, that's $4,000. The field costs a thousand bucks, right, and paying the people to operate the concession stands, that's another couple of hundred dollars. I mean, the expenses were way in excess of the revenue. It was just ridiculous. So my team actually accused me and Donna of stealing money from the team—when it cost us nearly a quarter of a million dollars over three years to keep the thing running. It was ridiculous. So the only reason we had a team was because Donna and I were writing checks. We lost our tails. The WPFL contacted me initially about the Houston franchise, and I didn't think that it was marketable, so I said—no, let's wait a few years. Robin [Howington] bought the franchise, and then, when I saw it going in, they called me back about the Austin franchise; then I decided to go ahead and do it. I was right initially. It wasn't marketable. We didn't make any money. We lost a lot of money, and so did Houston. I think New England probably made some money because she (Korpacz) did a really good job with the franchise."[54]

On her dealings with the league, Kennamer remembered: "There was a lot of misinformation flying around at the beginning. There were a lot of personalities, and my personal take on it was that there were some people that were more ego driven, like, this is about me, blah blah blah, instead of let's get this done. There was a lot of fighting going on between different teams—people getting their feelings hurt because somebody said something about this and that they didn't like, and it's just, you know, let's fine this team for doing this. Hey, you can't fine somebody $15,000 when they're barely making it financially. That's just stupid." On the WPFL expelling the Korpacz and the Storm, she specified, "I believe it was the same year that we withdrew from the league, and we're talking twenty years ago so my memory might be a little foggy." She did remember that "Well, there were a lot of people who didn't like some of the ways that Missy went about doing things, but my dealings with her were always square up."[55]

Andra Douglas, another player who stepped up to buy a team, also struggled with the finances and her players. In *Black and Blue: Love, Sports, and the Art of Empowerment*, a fictionalized account of her life as a player and owner of the New York Sharks, Douglas wrote that WPFL officials contacted her to buy the team. She negotiated the price down from the $50,000 asking price to $20,000, but she also faced accusations from her players that she was misusing their player fees.[56]

Douglas dealt with that much in the way Kennamer did, by informing the players that she consistently lost money by owning the team.[57] Like Korpacz, Douglas and the Sharks also formed a relationship with an NFL team, the New York Giants in her case. In a 2020 interview, Douglas told me that her Sharks had the chance to play a halftime exhibition during a game between the Giants and the Dallas Cowboys game on 2 January 2005. In both her memoir and in our interview, Douglas also mentioned the lack of support, and sometimes interference, by the WPFL, which caused the Sharks to play as an independent team for one year in 2002, before they joined the IWFL.[58]

The WPFL began with chaos, and that continued. After four seasons, three of the so-called founding mothers of the league had been forced out, and Douglas had left. Whatever role women such as Korpacz,

Kennamer, and Roebuck might have played in keeping the league alive was lost in a storm of internal politics. That storm did not abate. In 2006, according to Michael Weinreb of the *New York Times*, the New York Dazzles were "embroiled in a lawsuit with their league and may not play this season."[59] The author did not specify what the legal action concerned, but while the players were not making any money from football, the lawyers seemed to be doing well.

After showing signs of weakness that first season, the WPFL immediately faced several challenges from rival leagues. One challenge came from Carter Turner, who left the league as it foundered and formed the Women's American Football League (WAFL), which began play with sixteen teams in 2001. Turner told King Kaufman, a reporter for *Salon*, that his new league addressed the problems of the WPFL by replacing the one league investor model and instead allowed member teams to be more autonomous, with individual teams being "responsible for their own outfitting, upkeep and travel, and keeping any profits."[60] Lisa Davis of *SF Weekly* reported that WAFL franchises cost "about $20,000, but realistically, owners estimate that it costs about $100,000 to get through the first year."[61] According to Hinton, the WAFL, to separate its brand from its competitors, also billed itself as the "'ethical' and 'credible' professional women's league and has mandated that its teams open their books to players."[62]

While Carter Turner and the new organization thought they had addressed a significant weakness that plagued the WPFL, they could not remove the chaos that sometimes afflicted individual teams. Davis's 2002 article described the problems that beset the San Francisco Tsunamis. Besides suffering through a winless season, to that point, the team had not been able to draw any attendance from the Bay Area. The game that Davis attended had around seventy fans. That was a minor point, however, and a significant portion of the article examined the dysfunction that existed between team owner/wide receiver Wendy Brown and head coach Alonzo Carter. When asked how the owner got along with her coach, Davis quoted Brown as saying, "We have no relationship. He's the coach of my team, and I don't like him." Carter was hired only two weeks before the season began, and some of the players, along with the owner, did not like his old-school style. While admitting that he was likely part of the problem with the team, Carter defended his methods, asserting: "You can't be sensitive and play football. It don't mix. If a male is sensitive and tries to play football, it won't work." Matters came to a head after the loss described in the article, and less than a week later Carter, along with his offensive and defensive coordinators, quit the team. Davis reported that the Tsunamis lost their next game as well, and during that 1-point loss, "at least one San Francisco player was injured during a bench-clearing fight."[63]

Some teams such as the San Diego Sunfire had crowds of around five thousand, at least according to Turner, but the chaos must have reached further than the Tsunamis. By the end of the year, the nine remaining teams had either folded or had defected to the IWFL.[64] The same fate would befall many of the other leagues that sprang up in the early twenty-first century.

Another new league also calved off of the WPFL. Catherine Masters, who initially consulted for Turner on the league's start-up, apparently grew weary of working with him. She decided to replicate the barnstorming tour that had launched the WPFL with the intention of creating a "well organized and professional run league." Her National Women's Football League, which changed its name in 2002 to the National Women's Football Association after the NFL protested that their name was too close to the more established brand, started with the Nashville Dream playing a series of games against the Alabama Renegades.[65] According to the still extant NWFA website, the tour succeeded, and the league added eight more teams in 2001, eleven teams in 2002, eight in 2003, and another eight in 2004, to total, as of that year, thirty-seven teams.[66] Neal Rozendaal, in his *The Women's Football Encyclopedia*, counted only thirty-four teams in the 2004 NWFA, but it increased to its peak of thirty-nine teams in 2005. After that the league began losing teams until 2008, when they were "racked by the loss of their last six league champions," and teams began to abandon the league. The NWFA finished the 2008 season, but eighteen teams defected to the new Women's Football Alliance in 2009.[67]

During its run, however, the NWFA was for a time the strongest of the leagues, and Masters was able to garner considerable attention for the league. She broke from the WPFL model by scheduling games in the spring, rather than the fall, which has become the norm for women's football in the United States. Initially, there was the promise of having the NWFA games on the Football Network, but the new network never materialized. Masters set the price for new teams joining the league at $35,000, which was the highest for all of the various leagues. Other innovations included events designed to raise the profile of the league such as the *Whammys*, an award show for women football players, although whether that ever actually happened is unclear.[68] Perhaps one of the most significant accomplishments of the NWFA was that Las Vegas noticed women's football for the first time and published a betting line for the 2002 SupHer Bowl (another term that the NFL disagreed with, and that the NWFA subsequently dropped). They did so again in 2003, but after that the oddsmakers must have lost interest.[69]

Masters did have a media success with *The Gender Bowl*, a made-for-television reality program that pitted a team of older male football players against an all-star team made up of players from the D.C. Divas and the Pittsburgh Passion. The teams played their game in the Los Angeles Coliseum, and Dish Network broadcast the event on 8 December 2005. According to Donna Wilkinson, a running back for the Divas, the game was exciting, with the women tying the game with a touchdown in the last minute, but the men's team scored on a long touchdown run to win. Wilkinson challenged that victory and asserted that the referees missed the men's player stepping out of bounds before he scored.[70] How many people were aware of this reality show, or watched it, is unknown. No reviews of the program are readily accessible, and although Jacqueline McDowell and Spencer Shaffner of the University of Illinois at Urbana-Champaign published a 2011 article about the game in *Discourse and Society*, their effort tracked the pregame insults used in the game. The authors neglected to include the final score, and there was no mention of audience size.[71]

Masters was one of the first women inducted into the American Football Association's Hall of Fame in 2006. The AFA, an organization "dedicated to the advancement of semi-pro/minor league football through the United States," stated in its announcement for her induction that not only had Masters built the NWFA into the "premier league for women's full tackle football," but she had also "signed a motion picture development deal . . . to produce a film about women's football and the NWFA." The announcement went on to note that the league had been "featured in more than 250 major publications."[72] Those articles and other media mentions have seemingly been deposited in the dustbin of history, or at least they are not readily available online.

Another website, the Sports Critics, did expand on the AFA's mention that a movie about women's football was in the works. The press release posted there announced that Masters had signed a deal with Ithaka Entertainment, and Paul Cuschieri, a screenwriter, had been assigned to the project. Both parties were enthusiastic about the production. Cuschieri stated, "The world of professional women's football is extremely rich from a storytelling perspective, and I feel fortunate to partner with Catherine Masters and the National Women's Football Association to bring their sport to the big screen." Masters added: "The last great movie about women's sports was a 'League of Their Own,' and we feel we have an equally great story to tell. With the right studio, producer and companies behind this project, we are confident it will be a big movie. Building women's pro football is an outstanding story that needs to be told."[73] As with the film project about the Toledo Troopers, expectations were high that women's football would get the same sort of exposure that came to the All American Girls Professional Baseball League after *A League of Their Own* (1992), but those expectations came to nothing.

Douglas told me that she was also trying to find a movie deal to bring *Black and Blue* to the big screen. At the 2021 WFA championships, during Douglas's WFA "Breaking Barriers" award introduction, actress and producer Julie Bowen announced that, with Douglas, her production company was developing a project for television based on *Black and Blue*.[74] Perhaps she will be successful in developing a better made-for-television fare than *The Oklahoma City Dolls*.

Masters had big plans, and the ability to negotiate deals with television and Hollywood, but once matters left her hands, her negotiating partners lacked sufficient force to push the various projects to fruition. The movie did not get made, the Football Network died before it was born, and eventually the league folded. Rozendaal argued that one of the reasons that the league failed was that owners were frustrated by Masters's "autocratic leadership."[75]

In the interview with Weinreb, the reporter wrote, "She also maintains autonomy over the league's operations, to the point that she does not mind being labeled a dictator." Masters added, "I actually make all the decisions. I don't feel it's in the league's best interest to let other owners make policy. I have no problems making decisions for the betterment of everybody."[76] Perhaps she was autocratic and a dictator, but her leadership seemed to be working. The other owners apparently did not see it that way, however, and Masters was forced out of the league.

The NWFA had one of the best teams of the time. From 2002 to 2005, the Detroit Demolition won four league championships and won another with the IWFL after they switched leagues. The Detroit team originally played under the name of the Danger, and in 2002 the ownership ran an advertisement on *Monday Night Football* announcing tryouts. According to her web page, Kim Grodus was one potential player who saw that ad and attended the tryout, "among several hundred other women."[77] Grodus became the team's first and most successful quarterback. With five national championships, she was arguably one of the best quarterbacks to have played women's football.[78] Grodus's page contained some of the highlights of the Danger/Demolition program. The team, coached by former Michigan Wolverine defensive back Joel "Tony" Blankenship, won the NWFL's first championship in 2002 and then changed owners and names, along with the league changing to the NWFA. The Demolition continued winning, and in 2003 they defeated the Pensacola Power 28–21 for their second consecutive title.[79] According to Grodus, they played the game in Nashville, Tennessee, at Vanderbilt University's stadium in front of "over 7,000 fans in attendance." She asserted that the crowd was "the largest" and that this was the "most well attended game in the history of women's full contact football," and she was likely correct. She also mentioned the NWFA's media reach and that the team's record, when she posted, was 45-1.[80] That must have been in 2006, just before the Demolition joined the IWFL, since a press release from that year has the same won/loss record.[81]

It is interesting, and perhaps illuminating of the problems that women's football faced, that two of the leagues that formed during the initial boom period of the early 2000s promised to be ethical and credible, or at least well organized and professional. Those phrases must have been attempts to set themselves apart from their competitors and spoke to the problems that women's football had in reestablishing itself as a sport. It is also informative that when individual owners or league directors made significant gains, whether it was partnering with the Patriots or getting players on television, other owners joined forces against them and forced them out.

In addition to the WPFL, the WAFL, and the NWFA, there were several other leagues that did not have as many teams. Information about them is even scarcer than for the big three. Therefore, their impact on women's football did not seem to warrant more research or mention, other than to list those leagues. The best source for this proliferation of leagues is Neal Rozendaal's *Women's Football Encyclopedia*. He reported that in 2002 there were "*nine* [italics in original] documented women's football leagues split between the spring and fall." In addition to the three largest leagues, there were also the Women's Spring Football League (WSFL) with four teams in the Pacific Northwest, the United Women's Football League (UWFL) with seven teams located primarily in Colorado, the Women's Football League (WFL) with three teams in the Southeast, and the IWFL with sixteen teams. These leagues played in the spring and summer, as did the NWFA. Playing in the fall, along with the WPFL and the WAFL-WFA, were the Women's Affiliated Football Conference (WAFC), with nine teams mostly from California or the Southwest, and the American Football Women's League (AFWL), with five teams from California. There were a total of eighty-four teams playing in those nine leagues.[82] If those teams averaged 40 players, that would mean that nearly 3,500 women were playing football in 2002, up from zero in 1998.

So what was going on? According to an unnamed woman featured in the trailer for *Playing with Rage*, "It was never about the interest. It was about the opportunity."[83] Her statement was confirmed by actual events. Women had the freedom, and given the opportunity, a relatively large number of women decided to don pads and play America's most popular, and most violent, sport. Kendra Nordin, the author of a 24 November 2000 article in the *Christian Science Monitor*, put it this way: "The athletes tell reporters how they'd dreamed of becoming football stars when they played backyard games with brothers and neighborhood boys. And here they are, making history, by exchanging the Velcro belts of flag football for the real thing—helmets and pads."[84] The teams that they played for and the leagues in which those teams competed rose and fell with some regularity, and so, to the outside observer, chaos seemed to be the order of the day. However, as Kennamer told me, thousands of women did have the chance to play a sport that might have seemed out of their reach only a few years before.[85]

As previously mentioned, neither feminism nor ideas of gender equality motivated the players, at least in the small sample asked about it. While I did not ask that question, none of the current or former players volunteered that as a reason for playing. Although the women who played and are currently playing may not be doing so because they identify as feminists, they are and were, I have argued, exhibiting a practical feminism. They may or may not agree with the politics of contemporary feminism, but they are doing what they want.

However they feel about feminism as a political position, many of the current player cohort and their predecessors demonstrated a commitment to this practical feminism. Now and then they mentioned that they were conscious that their efforts had the potential to offer a better future to young girls who dared to dream of one day playing any sport, regardless of whether it was considered appropriate for females.

Houston's Howington told a CBS reporter in 2001, "I think this is a huge step for women. I get 50 or 60 e-mails a day from young 13-, 14-year-old girls, saying, 'Thank you for doing this.'"[86] In *Atta Girl: A Celebration of Women in Sport* (2003), Alexandra Powe Allred stated, "No one wants the success of the WPFL more than Coach Dee Kennamer and her Austin Players because they feel very strongly about showing little girls they do, in fact, have something to dream about."[87] Laurie Frederick, who helped found the IWFL, commented in a 2014 interview, "We all know the story of the one girl who joins the boys to play football. . . . It's our opinion that there's probably another 30 to 40 girls behind her who'd want to play if it were all girls." The article went on to assert, "It's that belief that keeps Frederick going as she continues to grow the IWFL and builds a foundation that encourages girls who dream of carrying a football instead of pom-poms."[88]

This is still a strong current among contemporary players, teams, and leagues. To highlight two such efforts, the Maine Mayhem and team owner Alicia Jeffords have been using the team's Facebook page to feature "The Girls of Fall," which includes profiles of young girls who are playing at various levels from youth leagues to high school.[89] Another is the Gridiron Queendom site begun by Adrienne Smith. The site has numerous posts about girls who play youth or high school football, such as Alexa Karsel, a sixteen-year-old kicker from Colorado.[90] Allowing girls and women to freely play any sport they want is certainly a principal of historical feminism. It does seem, however, that this goal has become more of a practical focus that diverges from the theoretical feminism that seems to dominate today.

So what motivated these women? Many of the athletes I interviewed pointed to the team nature of the sport and indicated that they had found something of a sporting family by playing. Several indicated that they were looking for something more than the usual recreation league softball games that required little dedication on the athlete's part. Many who were former collegiate athletes wanted a sport that would challenge them, and they found that in football. When asked about this, Bedwell told me, "I've loved football since I was little, and so when I saw it, I said, 'I'm ready to try something new.' So, it inspired me to go and try something else. I was always a team player, I always loved to bond with people and have that opportunity to be something with someone on a field, and so that's what I wanted to do."[91]

Most of those I interviewed grew up loving football, and when the chance came that allowed them to play, they jumped at it. Some women such as Tiffany might have been looking for a way out of an abusive relationship, or to connect with women who might help them feel less isolated. For whatever reason, the women who began playing football at the turn of the twenty-first century found a sporting opportunity that filled a need, athletic or personal, in their lives, along with the freedom to play, and many embraced it.

Those opportunities exploded in the first years of the twenty-first century but were sometimes limited due to the lack of revenue teams could generate. Kennamer declared that she and Roebuck spent in the neighborhood of $250,000 over three years, and they had, in her words, "lost our tails."[92] In a 10 November 2003 interview, Howington told Kendra Nordin of the *Christian Science Monitor* that she had "spent $35,000 to $40,000 a year of her own money just so women could run, pass, and tackle." Nordin reported that the 2003 championship game won by the Northern Ice 53–12 over the Florida Sting Rays had only drawn "about 2,000" spectators, and that the league had averaged "about 1,500 spectators a game." The lack of paying clientele meant that, according to Howington, "We don't have advertisement dollars. The media doesn't give us much attention at all. There's no exposure, so there's no sponsors. Sponsors want [fan] numbers, we can't go get the numbers without money for advertising."[93] When I asked Douglas if there were any years when she came close to breaking even financially, she told me, "Yeah, I think there were one or two years, it never happened, but it was close. Maybe five or ten thousand short of breaking even. Hey! That's a year to celebrate!"[94]

The two largest factors in creating stability in women's football were unfortunately out of the hands of the owners or league organizers. In order to escape their dependency on gate receipts, they needed to either form financial relationships with the NFL or at least with individual professional teams. If that did not happen, they needed revenue from a television contract. In the heady early days of league formation and team expansion, many of the leaders of the various leagues were certain that it would be "just a matter of time before the NFL picks us up," according to the WPFL's Korpacz in 2002. The Storm owner did negotiate a working relationship with the Patriots, and many others shared her optimism. She also negotiated a television contract, but the network never launched.[95]

It is likely that the explosion in the number of teams and leagues worked against efforts to entice the NFL into relationships with women's teams. Many in women's football wanted to replicate the example of the Women's National Basketball Association, whose teams were created with the support of the NBA.[96] However, the WNBA was created by the men's league and has remained largely under their control. It was not selected from among a group of competing leagues, each headed by individuals, both male and female, with strong egos and thoughts about what form a women's football league should take.

The question of with whom the NFL should deal was also complicated by the internal politics of the various leagues, as we have seen. Korpacz and Masters seemed to be moving their leagues in positive directions but were forced out by other owners who disagreed with their actions, or perhaps their personalities. Then NFL commissioner Paul Tagliabue had enough problems dealing with owners such as Al Davis and may not have wanted to add any more challenges, such as what teams or what leagues should be supported.

In the mid-2000s the women's football scene began to shed some of the chaos. The IWFL had replaced the WAFL as one of the top three leagues and began picking up the champions of the NWFA as the Demolition left for the greener pastures of the IWFL in 2005 and was followed by the D.C. Divas and Pittsburgh Passion, winners of the league title in 2006 and 2007, respectively. When the smoke cleared in 2008, the IWFL alone remained and was acknowledged as the premier women's football league with forty teams.[97]

# The Independent Women's Football League   3

More than a thousand fans gathered at Cottonwood High School to see how good the Utah Falconz would be in 2018. The Falconz had dominated the Independent Women's Football League (IWFL) since their inaugural season in 2015. They lost 41–37 to the Pittsburgh Passion in the IWFL final that first year but then won the next two championships. In 2016 they routed the Minnesota Vixen 49–6, and in 2017 they defeated the Austin Yellow Jackets 35–18.

But this was a new year, and the Falconz were dealing with the semi-retirement of Louise Matthews Bean, their longtime quarterback. Their opponent for the day, the Seattle Majestics, had just rejoined the IWFL after having successfully competed in the Women's Football Alliance (WFA) since 2013, forging a 36-4 record there. The Falconz and Majestics had played only one previous game, which the Falconz won, but the visitors had been playing in a more competitive league, so there was a great deal of anticipatory buzz around the game. Falconz head coach Rick Rasmussen did not display any uncertainty, and at a lunch the day before the game he told me in a matter-of-fact voice, "We are better than them."

After watching Utah Girls Football League (UGFL) games on Saturday morning, my wife, Sophie, and I went to see if Rasmussen's confidence was justified. After several WFA games and even a French championship, this would be my first IWFL match. The game was scheduled to begin at 3 p.m., and the day was a bit cool, but the sun was shining, so it was a perfect day for football. The Falconz put on a good show, and the atmosphere surrounding the game was equivalent to a typical small college game. During warm-ups, Coach Rasmussen, with an eye on the future, invited young girls from the stands to come down to take part in the festivities. The two Falconz mascots, Felix and Flex, arrived at the stadium riding motorcycles and then added to the festivities by interacting with the crowd and the little girls. Several of the players from the Bingham Bone Crushers of the UGFL were introduced, and halftime entertainment included an exhibition between the Canyons Lethal Angels and the West Granite Quake, two other UGFL teams.

The Falconz coach's confidence proved to be more than mere bravado, and his team jumped out to a 13–0 lead at the end of the first quarter. The Utahans, with more than fifty players on their team, managed to play each of their three platoons. Bean, who had moved to Montana before the season, returned to keep her hand in the game and played a few series at quarterback. The Falconz increased their lead to 27–0 by halftime and increased it to 33–0 by the end of the third quarter. The Majestics finally scored in the fourth quarter, and the game ended with the Falconz defeating the Majestics 33–7.

Following the game, players and coaches from the two teams met at a nearby barbecue restaurant. Seattle head coach Scott McCarron and a handful of his players attended, but it was largely a Falconz affair. This postgame gathering and the previous day's lunch were apparently a routine part of the process for home games in Salt Lake City, and part of the Falconz Way.

That "way" began in 2014, when a group of players from the Utah Jynx became dissatisfied with how they were being treated by their owner and coach. Led by Rasmussen, who had been an assistant coach for the Jynx, Hiroko Jolley, who became the Falconz' owner, and several Jynx players broke away to create a new team.

Rasmussen graduated from the Air Force Academy and flew for the U.S. Air Force. After his retirement from active duty, he worked for the Federal Bureau of Investigation and also coached high school football. Assistant coach Marc "Hutch" Hunter remembered that when Rasmussen took over coaching duties for the new team, he called the men he had coached with previously and told them, "It's time to get the band back together." As with many men who have ended up coaching women's football, Hunter thought that his friend was pulling a prank on him, but he was finally convinced that women's football was a real thing.[1]

Rasmussen brought with him definite ideas on how to run a football team, and Falconz owner Jolley provided the freedom to bring the ideas to fruition. He told me that his practices last "two hours, no more."[2] Bean remembered that her previous Jynx coach once at the end of practice had his players run twenty 100-yard sprints and refused to let them drink any water.[3] Rasmussen ended those open-ended exercises in sadism and ran a team that became a well-oiled machine. The coach was by no means easy going, and if a player did something that displeased him, he would let her know in no uncertain terms. According to team president Samantha Smith-Meek, "Yeah, well, you can't compare coaching staff, but I think we have the best coaching staff out there. Our defensive coordinator, Jody Thompson, and Rick Rasmussen, they are just great men. You really can't compliment them enough. I mean they are a bit hard on us as coaches, but there's no coaches out there that cares [sic] more about their players."[4]

The Falconz Way produced results, and they became the marquee team for the IWFL, until they dropped out of the league late in the 2018 season. Chaos reigned during that season, which started with great promise, but the league suffered from numerous teams canceling their schedules. The difficulty that the Falconz and other teams had in securing opponents, along with a general imbalance in opponent strength, led them to leave the league. Joining them in leaving the IWFL were the Majestics and the San Diego Surge, a team that had just jumped to the league after playing for the WFA for six seasons. Rounding out the teams that would label themselves "The Best of the West," was the Texas Elite Spartans, which was a new team but contained many of the players that had won the WFA championship as the Dallas Elite in 2017. These breakaway teams grew dissatisfied with the IWFL and were hoping to find greener pastures elsewhere. Chapter 6 looks at the Best of the West alliance, which has morphed into the National Women's Football Conference, along with what that might mean for the future of women's football.

The IWFL ironically was once the greenest of pastures, or gridirons. It emerged from the chaotic period that ushered in the return of women's professional football discussed in chapter 2. The period between 1999 and 2009 saw at least nine leagues come and go. The IWFL briefly became the league with the most teams and the only organization that sent women to the International Federation of American Football Women's World Championship in 2010, which is discussed in chapter 8.

The IWFL was organized by Laurie Frederick. According to a lengthy 14 May 2014 article by Cassandra Negley in the *Sporting News*, Frederick began the league in 2000, after playing for a team in another, unspecified, league. The author stated that Frederick "felt the men who started that league 'were not in it for the best reasons,' adding that it 'felt like a bit of a scam.'" The allusion to the "men who started the league" suggested that she likely started out in the WPFL.[5] Rozendaal asserted that the IWFL's first season was "an exhibition season in 2001and expanded to a full season the following year."[6] On the beginning of the league, whenever that happened, Frederick told the *Sporting News*, "We had the football bug bite us and wanted to play. . . . It was definitely a grassroots start. Several teams found each other, and we made a loose league." Negley's article also quoted Ebony Kimbrough, the "owner/coach/manager/player" for the Carolina Queens. She provided some additional insights into the finances of women's football. She reportedly contributed "several thousand dollars out-of-pocket each year to keep her team going." Rookie players were charged $1,000 for equipment, while veterans paid only $150 per year. Frederick dodged the question Negley posed about the league's finances and replied that it was "'hard to say' what the league's finances looks like, but that it breaks even.'" Negley added that this was "likely because there's little money involved. No one with the IWFL is paid—everyone running the national sports league is a volunteer." Frederick echoed that, saying, "Some people watch TV in their spare time. People in our league office do this."[7]

The IWFL reached their apex in 2010, with forty-seven teams in two divisions.[8] The dream of forging a relationship with the NFL was apparently dead at that point. When queried if the league had any plans to support women's football, Brian McCarthy, the NFL's vice president of corporate communications in 2014, replied, "We don't currently have plans (for a women's league)."[9] They did partner with USA Football to send the first ever women's national team to the IFAF Women's World Championship in Stockholm, Sweden.[10] As discussed in more detail in chapter 8, Team USA dominated the games, outscoring their opponents (Austria, Finland, and Canada) 242–7. Kimbrough told Negley, "I'm not patting ourselves on the back, but we literally destroyed every team we played."[11]

The league had little time to revel in being at the top of women's football. In a 2010 interview, when Frederick was asked, "What is the most rewarding aspect of your job?" she replied, "Strangely enough it's the unknown. When you are in a growth mode such as this, your path often requires you to zig when you expect to zag all along. We have to react to what we see happening in our sport and think outside the box. For example, as we grew we saw it was necessary to split the IWFL into essentially two leagues to accommodate the interest we had from minor markets as well as major markets As far as I know, no other pro league has done that before. It's exciting to innovate in ways such as that."[12] Frederick would encounter the unknown soon enough, as several of the top IWFL teams deserted en masse for the rival Women's Football Alliance at the end of the 2010 season.

The IWFL also had to face a different kind of competition beginning in 2009. The Lingerie Football League (LFL) began playing an indoor version of football that featured women in scanty uniforms. That league, which is discussed in chapter 5, immediately caught the attention, usually negative, of the media. After that, articles about women who played in full uniform would often include a line affirming, "We don't play in lingerie."[13] The LFL, which changed its name to the Legends Football League in 2013 (and the X League in 2020), would prove to be a challenge to all full-kitted women's teams, but the timing came just as the IWFL had taken over as the premier league for women's football in 2010.

Up to that point, the league had been adding additional teams, but they were not free from the chaos that had troubled their competitors. According to Alecia Sweeny, a former Demolition player and then the owner of the successor Detroit Dark Angels, the Demolition had jumped from the NWFA "looking for better competition."[14] They found that competition, winning only one championship in three years, but they also found their eventual dissolution.

During the 2009 season, the Demolition, which had won its first and only league championship in 2007, had their owner and general manager suspended by the league. According to Marvin Goodwin, writing for the *Oakland (MI) Press*, owner Al Seder and general manager Kevin Kramis had received an email from Frederick informing them that they had been suspended. One of the charges against the Demolition's management was that they "had no ambulance at another game despite our lenient ruling on this noncompliance issue in the past.... Nor have we received payment for the services we have delivered all season." This proved to be the end of the Detroit team that had won five championships in eight seasons. Coach Blankenship and his staff retired from coaching women's football. "I enjoy the coaching part, [but] I'm not interested in being a part of a situation of things not being done the right way."[15]

In this case, the league seemingly acted correctly. Seder had not fulfilled his responsibilities to the IWFL and to his players. Still, it indicated the difficulties of running a league that depended on independent owners doing things the right way.

Another 2007 issue was more closely related to how Laurie Frederick and Kezia Disney operated the league, particularly when dealing with the "unknown." The Kansas City Storm and the Demolition were scheduled to meet in a playoff game, but the Storm decided to forfeit their chance at a national title.[16] The 6-2 Storm had lost their previous contest against the Demolition 63-0.[17] They must have decided that the Demolition would likely repeat the drubbing, and that they would have the added burden of traveling to Detroit to accept the beating.

According to IWFL rules, Detroit was allowed to "accept a forfeit or demand that [the] league take all possible action to provide a suitable replacement game." The league had pressured the Demolition to play a game against the Portland Fighting Shockwave, but Detroit decided to accept the easy win. Disney told Cosmo, a blogger who wrote about women's football, that the rules allowed the Demolition to take the forfeit. "In setting the rules, she said, it never occurred to any of the team owners that there would be a forfeit in a playoff game. It has happened only once before. In 2003 the Miami Fury forfeited a first round game to the Boston Rampage (then the Bay State Warriors)." Disney also told Cosmo that "no one [in the IWFL] is taking the situation lightly. It's a big deal. Kansas City will be penalized." Cosmo went on to quote an unnamed team official who said, "I've lost all respect for Detroit and am embarrassed that the league doesn't have the power to force Detroit to play someone, anyone." The unnamed official added his contention that Detroit was "desperate to win the IWFL championship this season," even though they were a team that was weakening, compared to the rest of the league.[18]

That may have been a correct assessment. The Demolition lost the 2006 title to the Atlanta Xplosion 21–14 but managed to win their only IWFL championship 17–7 over the Xplosion in 2007.[19] After that, Detroit fortunes declined until their owner and general manager were suspended. Although Seder vowed that the Demolition would continue despite the setback, the team never played again.[20] Providing some continuity, Jeffords was, at the time I wrote this, the general manager of the Detroit Dark Angels.

What penalty the league leveled on the Storm was not clear, but it was, in any case, irrelevant. At the end of the season, the KC team merely transferred to the NWFA. Having teams forfeit out of the playoffs indicated a lack of seriousness that some teams in the league demonstrated. The Storm was acting logically in its self-interest, but that interest clashed with the league's interest in forming an entity that fans, and sponsors, could respect. Enforcing any sort of rules against an offending team was also problematical, if not impossible, when the offending organization could easily jump to a competing league.

A somewhat strange, and uncorroborated, report concerning another 2007 incident depicted Frederick and Kezia Disney, the league's chief operating officer, in a more negative light. According to Merle Exit, a former New York Sharks player, she had convinced Lon Smith, the curator of the Museum of World Treasures in Wichita, Kansas, to host an exhibit on women's football. Smith agreed, and the museum received "owner and former quarterback Andra Douglas' retired jersey, [a] photo of her accepting an award from the Women's Sports Foundation, [a] football signed by the team, and a group of several photos depicting the history of the longest (since 1999) and winning team." Still according to Exit, when the exhibit was set to expand into a celebration of the IWFL, Frederick and Disney were late to the opening, apparently due to the pair picking up a stray dog. Exit also complained that the two wore "totally inappropriate clothing." To add insult to Exit's and Smith's aggravation, Frederick and Disney reportedly never apologized and even took credit for the IWFL Hall of Fame on their website. Exit claimed she contacted the IWFL executives about this but never heard back from them. Exit concluded, "With enough problems just getting the word out there about women playing tackle football, it only makes it worse when you have women not only being unsupportive but taking credit where credit is certainly not due."[21]

I hesitated to include this story, but it fits in with a pattern that others have reported about Frederick and Disney, including Rozendaal and Oscar Lopez, who operates a podcast on women's football. In our October 2020 interview, Andra Douglas confirmed the substance of the report, although she added, "Laurie Frederick and Kez Disney, they really did a good job running that league in the early years. It was very well done and a lot of fun."[22] And perhaps the attitudes alluded to there helped cause some of the issues that arose after the 2010 season.

The playoffs seemed to have been a difficulty for the league and for women's football in general. In 2016 the Houston Wildcats and the Austin Yellow Jackets had a repeat match postponed because of weather. Rather than reschedule the game, the league canceled the makeup game. The Austin-Houston match had playoff implications, since Austin had defeated Houston 22–12, but if Houston could win the rematch, they could have made the playoffs by strength of head-to-head play. According to Rozendaal, Disney told the Wildcats that whoever had the most points in the two games would advance to the playoffs, but then she changed her story to indicate that total points allowed was the tie breaker, which heavily favored the Yellow Jackets. The league justified their decision to cancel the rematch by saying that the game was not necessary, since Houston could not make up enough ground in the tiebreaker. As a result of the seeming league confusion, the Wildcats were denied an opportunity to play for the national championship. At the same time, the league also canceled a game between the Rocky Mountain Thunderkatz and the Nebraska Stampede, which would have been a forfeit in favor of the Stampede, in any case. As a result of their forfeit, the Thunderkatz were reportedly banished from the league. In the same post Rozendaal indicated this was the latest in a three-year string of playoff controversies the league had to deal with.[23]

Any sport organization will face occasional difficulties. The WFA, discussed in the next chapter, has also had issues with the playoffs. The NFL has had difficulties in the past, and likely will again. However, the NFL is an established league and brings in billions of dollars each year for their owners. They can weather some problems. The IWFL in 2010 had problems that were difficult for a relatively new league that was still operating on a shoestring budget.

At the end of that season, the IWFL suffered a major defection of teams to the WFA. Fourteen teams switched leagues that year, and included among that group were the league champion Boston Militia and most of the rest of the tier-one winning teams.[24] Who the first defector was is difficult to tell from the available sources.

In the D.C. Divas 2014 media guide, the team asserted their move to the IWFL was to "search for stronger competition." They had won an NWFA title in 2006 and continued to win in the IWFL, but they never won the league championship. They finished second to the Kansas City Tribe in 2009, losing 21–18 in what the site termed as an "upset." Although there was no explicit reasoning for their decision to move to the WFA, it seemed to be motivated by the same desire to continue playing against high-level competitors. With most of the rest of the IWFL's power teams relocating to the WFA, they did the same.[25]

The Kansas City Tribe, the team that had replaced the Storm in the IWFL, went so far as to bring a lawsuit against the IWFL to be able to leave the league. Their disagreement with the league apparently stemmed from their championship win over the Divas. The KC team alleged that "the IWFL failed to successfully market and promote the team." In what "was supposed to be the IWFL's marquee event," the game in Round Rock, Texas, had "only 500 fans." The lawsuit also sought to free the Tribe from paying the IWFL $50,000, which resulted from a noncompetition clause that fined teams if they moved to another league. The team's owners, reportedly law school classmates, countered that they had never signed the agreement.[26]

Linda Bache, the owner and general manager of the Chicago Force, provided the most detailed rationale for switching leagues. She told Ross Forman of the *Windy City Times*, "We want to challenge ourselves by playing against the highest level of competition, which is no longer the IWFL." The Force joined the Divas, the Tribe, the Dallas Diamonds, the San Diego Surge, the New York Sharks, and the Pittsburgh Passion in relocating to the WFA. Bache continued to tell Forman, "All of these teams are leaving in an effort to advance women's football, create more opportunities, and have a greater voice in their team and league operations. We will have a much more competitive regular season schedule [in 2011] than was possible in our previous league. We'd also be facing the absolute best teams in women's football in the playoffs. It's a huge challenge and a great opportunity." The plan for 2011, according to Bache, was for the former IWFL power teams to be "a separate entity," not officially part of the WFA. That apparently did not last long, as the teams are now mostly still part of the WFA. Later in the interview, she returned to what must have been dissatisfaction with the IWFL leadership. "We left [the IWFL] to pursue a situation that would allow for a more democratic approach to league operations, an improved level of competition, reduced travel costs and greater marketing opportunities. [It] became an easy decision as most of the power teams left the IWFL. We want to play tough teams and challenge ourselves, so we need to go where the tough teams are." She also added that this might be something revolutionary for women's football. "We are developing an affiliation with the WFA that would involve their top teams joining ours to create a top division of women's football teams. It will be a separate entity that is an affiliate of the WFA. For the sport to truly advance, we need the leagues to begin working together. If we're successful, this could be the beginning of that unification."[27]

Aside from the Tribe there were no other reports about noncompetition agreements that have been uncovered from any of the other teams that left the IWFL in 2010. Perhaps the Tribe was the first to leave and paved the way for the others. Perhaps the noncompetition threat was a league bluff to keep their teams. Whatever might have been the case, league efforts failed, and the teams jumped to the WFA.

Despite the departure of the majority of its best teams, the IWFL continued, now as the second league in terms of team numbers. In 2011, the IWFL had thirty teams, compared to the WFA's fifty-nine.[28] They were the first women's football league, however, to have a championship team that played outside the United States. The Montreal Blitz, after winning its first league title in the IWFL's Tier II in 2008, repeated as champion of the lower division in 2010. With the consolidation of the two tiers, the Canadian team won the IWFL title in 2012.[29]

The league still contained talented teams, including the Passion, which returned to their original league for the 2014 and 2015 seasons. The Pittsburgh team won the league championship both of those years. Perhaps their leadership decided that they would rather be champions of a weaker league. Their website had a press release announcing their return to the WFA for the 2016 season, but there was no equivalent release explaining their move to IWFL in 2013 or 2014. The communiqué stated that the Passion had "22 consecutive victories and won back-to-back IWFL championships," so perhaps after finding that they could dominate the smaller league, they decided to return to the more competitive league.[30]

The Passion defeated the up-and-coming Falconz in the 2015 championship game. That close 41–37 loss, which was also their only setback in 2015, would be the last that the Falconz would suffer until the Dallas

Elite Spartans defeated them in the Best of the West championship in July 2018. The Falconz recovered and dominated the IWFL the next three seasons. With the Passion gone, the Falconz blew out the Minnesota Vixen 49–6 in 2016 and bested the Austin Yellow Jackets 35–18 in 2017. They were undefeated and seemingly headed toward a third straight championship in 2018. When problems with scheduling games and other issues arose with the IWFL, they decided to leave the league and contend for the Best of the West, which evolved into the WNFC.

The idea for the Falconz arose out of issues that a group of players and coaches had with the Utah Jynx of the WFA. In addition to the grueling practices mentioned above, there were also financial issues. Both Bean and Rasmussen were somewhat hesitant to go into specifics when I talked with them, but Matt Gephardt, an investigative reporter for KUTV in Salt Lake City, interviewed some of the players, and his reports provided more detail. According to a 4 March 2014 report that featured interviews with some of the players, including Bean, Gephardt looked into the team's finances and found several issues. Bean told the reporter, "We all paid $1,150 in fees." That was not the end of financial requests from Greg Cover, who was the team's owner and head coach. According to Gina Mondragon, another of the interviewed players, Cover would "ask for money before we even left or during our travel like, we need twenty bucks from each player for gas." Kelly Colobella told the reporter, "All we hear about was money all the time." Gephardt investigated their claims and found that Cover owed more than $1,000 each to a local printing firm and to the Granite School District that rented out their field to the team. When Gephardt contacted the coach, he told the reporter that the complaining players were "facing charges" for various offenses including "slander, defamation of character, and torturous interference with a business." Gephardt investigated that and other claims Cover made to him and found that the owner/coach was not being factual. As a result of "numerous complaints," the WFA had decided not to continue to include the team in their league. Gephardt quoted Lisa King, the founder and president of the league, as saying, "We just don't want this type of person or this type of team in our league anymore."[31]

*Get Gephardt*, as the KUTV segment was billed, was back on the hunt a few months later, when Chelsie Bell reported she had bought cookie dough during a team fundraiser and had never received the product. This time Gephardt found that the team had stopped competing "about halfway through the season" (it had joined the IWFL) but was still raising funds. A player whom Gephardt contacted on Facebook told the reporter that Cover had "told the team that the cookie dough money had been spent 'on a game.' The player added that if customers were going to get the cookie dough for which they have paid, team members 'needed to do more car washes to get that money back to buy it.'"[32]

Although Rasmussen was not mentioned in the story, Bean told me, "He was able to instruct us with his professional background. He didn't do it, per se, but he just taught us girls how to do it, and how you deal with criminals." The coach was also one of the group of eight players and coaches that left the Jynx in 2014. According to Bean, "One of the players at the time and her husband had started successful businesses, so Rick Rasmussen said, 'Hey, you know what, we can do this better. Let's do it.' There were eight of us that got together, and this was at the same time the end of the other season was still going on, just kind of started throwing out the ideas of, 'Hey, what if we were going to do this?' and it just kind of went from there. Most of the players from the Jynx remained on the team, because they wanted to finish the season. They came over to the Falconz the next year, and Hiroko Jolley was a player that decided to be the owner and take on the financial burden and responsibility of that. Rick Rasmussen became the head coach, and several of the coaches came, and the two of them set a standard for leadership and organization and how a successful organization should be run."[33]

In an 18 September 2015 interview with Amy Donaldson of the *Deseret News*, Jolley added that she and her breakaway teammates also had problems with how Cover coached and ran the team. "A lot of technique wasn't being taught." This, along with the financial issues, led her to imagine a different possibility. "I just kept thinking, 'If they had the right conditions, under good ownership, under a good coaching staff, it could be a team that would be unstoppable,' she said. 'I would come home upset, and (Troy [her husband]) would say, 'Just quit.' I said, 'I can't quit. We have all of these other women, and we're all just there for each other.'" Jolley's husband suggested that she start her own team, and when she decided to do so, her "first phone call" was to Rasmussen, who was the offensive coordinator for the Jynx. Donaldson quoted Jolley as saying, "I wouldn't have done this without Rick as my head coach. He's a great leader, and he teaches great leadership skills to the women." Jolley and her husband started the team in 2013, using "$40,000 of their own money."[34]

Originally Jolley began the team as a Limited Liability Corporation but later created Women's Excellence 4 Life (WE4L), a nonprofit organization, to administer the team.[35] She told Donaldson that the team was interested in more than just winning games. "We wanted to build something good in the community. I've seen this [football] change a lot of lives."[36] Of course, they also won, which is always nice.

Coach Marc "Hutch" Hunter echoed that sentiment in a 14 March 2018 interview. When he considered retiring from coaching the Falconz, his wife talked him out of it. Not because of the football, but because of the influence he had on the team's athletes. Hunter told me, "There are some women on the team who come from a very, very tough background. Some of the women who come to us have never had a positive male role model in their life. Abusive husbands . . . dads who never knew them when they were kids, possibly alcoholic dads. My wife just said to me, you're a positive role model for these women, so just give them one more year, and it has been a positive thing. It's like these women are all my daughters."[37]

Assistant coach Hunter, who handled the offensive line for the Falconz, also added an interesting perspective that could apply to any women's football team. "The fifty-five women on our team, if it weren't for football, have no business being together. This football team binds them together, and I'm telling you what, it is a cohesive unit. And when you're a Falcon, and you put on those Falcon colors, the number fifty-five is just as important as the number one person on our team."[38]

His point that the women who play the sport come from a wide variety of economic, social, racial, and educational backgrounds but bond as teammates is an important one. In the normal course of life, molecular biologists such as Samantha Smith-Meek would likely have limited social interaction with bakery owner and powerlifter Kelly Colobella.[39] As members of the Falconz, however, they spend several hours per week together, they endure the drudgery of practice together, and they share the common goal of working toward victory. This practical application of *e pluribus unum* (out of many, one) is true of any women's football team in the United States.

Defensive coordinator Jody Thompson also spent time during his interview telling me about the effect playing for the Falconz has had on the athletes. "I could pull up text after text after text on my phone of touching stories of how these women didn't have a strong male figure, you know, that encouraged them, that was positive with them, that didn't beat them. How they are appreciative of that and how we've changed their lives. How we have supported them, and how they've seen how relationships really should be and how they can be, you know, of the life lessons that we've taught, and really that's one of the main reasons I coached football." As with Hunter, Thompson had to be chivied into coaching. Jolley got his name as a possible coach and contacted him. He was "hesitant" but attended a 7 a.m. Saturday morning practice, and when he saw the "thirty-five or forty women in full pads out practicing," his attitude began to change. When he saw quarterback Bean "take a snap, and she's got a three-step drop, and just rifled a bullet down the sideline . . . and a receiver just caught that. I thought that's got to be a mistake, so I sat there and watched play after play of these ladies, these *athletes*, going at it, and I thought, 'Wow, this is pretty interesting.'" One more practice, then he began coaching the team, and his life changed as well.[40]

Smith-Meek, who succeeded Jolley as the head of the foundation and team president, also gave the rationale of helping women as one of the reasons that she was willing to take on the responsibilities of running the organization. "It's a fun job to help women. I don't know if you know that we're a 501(c)(3) organization called Women's Excellence

4 Life that the Falconz are funded through. Basically, what it is, is an organization that helps use football to help them in their lives. So, we give people a job to do, that they can turn around and use it on their résumés and things like that. And then teach them certain aspects of life; what you learn from football. You learn discipline and all that, and how to apply that in their actual everyday life, rather than just on the field. That part I kind of love. I like being about helping people get on their feet."[41]

There are other advantages to setting up a nonprofit organization to administer the team and the foundation that seeks to teach "life skills to women—who then inspire those in their scope of influence to take responsibility, and commit to each other. WE4L connects women, provides direction, discipline, and a sense of family." In early 2018 Jolley decided to relinquish ownership of the team and foundation, and she turned over direction of the nonprofit to Smith-Meek. The team name, since the team was part of the foundation, remained the same.[42]

This had not been the case for several of the best teams in women's football history. When Linda Bache, the owner of the Chicago Force, decided to discontinue her role, the team name left with her. The Force had won "10 division titles, 3 conference titles and a national championship" during their fifteen years playing in various leagues.[43] The team, and its history, disappeared when the owner decided to call it quits. The same fate befell the New York Sharks, who played their first tackle game against a team made up of players from the Vixen and Minx in 1999. When Sharks owner Andra Douglas sold her historic team, the name did not transfer.[44] Bache offered no reason for her decision to retire the team name, but Douglas told me that she retained ownership of the Sharks name, and therefore its brand, to be able to entice filmmakers to make a movie out of her *Black and Blue* book (see chapter 2).[45]

The Falconz began their first season in 2014 and played as an independent team. According to Bean, "We were independent that first year, because, now they just seem to take teams right and left, but at the time they wanted us to prove our validity, so we did. We played a schedule with WFA and IWFL teams and went undefeated but didn't go to playoffs because there were no playoffs. Then, the next year, we were all set to join the WFA. Then, right at the end, some things happened that caused us to not be admitted to the WFA. So we switched to IWFL at the beginning of the season and have been IWFL ever since."[46]

Since that first season as an independent team, the Falconz created a winning tradition by doing things their own way. Rasmussen explained the Falconz Way to me, which included using a platoon system to make sure that all of his players get meaningful time on the field, a focus on winning, and the triple option offense. He explained his and the team's philosophy on ensuring that all fifty-five (in 2018) players were involved. "If I'm paying $1,000 and you're paying $1,000, or you're paying $5 and I'm paying $5, we both should get the same, or a similar experience. We have our one common theme from our team: we believe our fifty-fifth player is more important than your number one player. We make sure our fifty-fifth player believes that, knows that, and is treated that way. That develops this camaraderie, this cohesiveness wherein somebody is not the star of the Utah Falconz."[47]

His team has bought into working for victory, rather than simply existing as a social and recreational experience. "Now, the first time we meet as a team, which occurred on the day after Valentine's day this year, the question was posed: "Are we here to make sure everyone plays the same number of reps, or are we here to win?" Unanimously, the team votes to win. So, the understanding is, if it's a dogfight, we are going with our twenty-two best pilots, that's what we are going to do. But if it's not a dogfight, I'm not going to leave Keeshya in so she can get eighty-four touchdowns, so she can compete with some player on a team with twenty-seven players who has to play the whole game because they don't have the personnel. I'm a firm believer that you don't win on Saturdays based on anything other than your preparation during the week. That means your scout team has to be pretty good. If your scout team isn't very good, your performance on Saturday is not going to be pretty good. So, that's the way we do it. We have some incredible athletes with some incredible stats over the last four years, but that's not what we celebrate. We celebrate our scout team. We celebrate our kickoff team. We celebrate our kick-return team or third platoon. That's where the team really takes pride is the starters are expected to get on the field, do their job, and get off the field and let the other players get their experience because, unlike some teams, our team plays the same."[48]

Running three platoons ensured that every player participates to achieve victory, and it also helped with recruiting from the Salt Lake City area, which, at that time, had two other semipro women's teams. Rasmussen added, "When a good player in the area has the choice between a rec [recreational league] experience or a competitive experience, the good athletes are going to generally come to the good-quality football, even if they know, as a platoon, they are not going to be playing every play of the game." He gave an example using Bean as his illustration. "Two seasons ago, the person with the least number of reps was our starting quarterback, because she got three series a game and that was it. She was done and standing on the sidelines."[49]

Rasmussen was an option quarterback during his high school days in Los Angeles. He did not play football at the Air Force Academy, other than for his "squadron," which must be the academy's version of intramurals. "I attempted to play my freshman year. My academic standing was found to be wanting," he told me. He enjoyed playing the option, since it allowed smaller and faster players to excel. "My team here, although there are a lot of us, we are not a gorilla, we are more like an ant build. There's a lot of us, we are persistent, and we are gonna put the leaf on our back and carry it to the hole. That's pretty much our theory of playing the sport."[50]

Bean admitted that it took some time for her to feel comfortable with running the option as a quarterback. "For me, triple option is great. I loved it. I fell in love with it. I think it is super demanding on the quarterback, which I loved. We had so much decision-making. It doesn't mean I haven't had my frustrating moments, and it doesn't mean I haven't messed up, and it doesn't mean there isn't a lot at play. . . . I remember the point to where it was just a field, and not just thinking. I feel like [it took] a couple years, where you can just feel and sense what those defenders are going to do, and you control them and they don't control you. It's a very powerful feeling. I would say it's very empowering." She backed up Rasmussen's analysis of how the option worked for the Falconz. "We never have been very big, and that was why it was a good system for us, because we had a lot of speed but weren't very big. But our athletes are just very smart. They're taught to be very smart, very technical, and they're taught to be precise, and that's just coupled with great speed. We knew that was going to be very beneficial for us."[51]

When she and her family moved to Montana in 2018, the quarterback still kept her hand in the game. She had to improvise to stay sharp, and that included finding receivers so she could practice her passing. She became the scout team quarterback for Great Falls Central High School. The team played eight-man football, and won the 2018 state championship, with some help from their scout team quarterback. She also commuted between Montana and Utah for some practices and games.[52] She played in the game against the Majestics and came back for another big match against the San Diego Surge on 19 May 2018.

The Surge, like the Majestics, were new to the IWFL. They had spent their entire history in the WFA and have been one of the most successful teams in women's football. Their win-loss record since 2011 has been 64-12, and they won the WFA national championship in 2012, when they went 12-0 for the season.[53]

The game proved to be one of the most competitive in the 2018 IWFL season. In a game at Cottonwood High School, the visitors scored first when Surge quarterback Melissa Gallegos hit Deana Guidry for a 54-yard touchdown. After the extra point failed, the Falconz came back and scored a touchdown on an option pitch from quarterback Elizabeth Lane to Keeshya Cox. Guidry scored again on a jet sweep to put the Surge back in front, and when Gallegos found Kaycee Clark for a 13-yard score, San Diego went up 18–7, where the score stood at the end of the first quarter. The Falconz' offense sputtered, but in the second quarter Rasmussen sent in Bean, now the third-string quarterback, and she immediately ignited the offense. She completed her first pass and then pitched the ball to Cox, who ran the rest of the way for a 62-yard touchdown. On the next possession, Bean took a one-step drop and hit Lexie Floor for a 52-yard touchdown pass, and the Falconz took their first lead of the game at 19–18. The Surge came back and drove to the Utah 5-yard line, before turning the ball over on downs. On the Falconz' first play after the stand, Bean handed off to Tina Tela, who ran 95 yards for another score.[54]

The Falconz led 25–18 at half, and the halftime entertainment included a scrimmage between UGFL teams, with help from the Falconz' mascots Felix and Flex. Tasha Aiono returned the second half kick to the 24-yard line, and the Falconz struck immediately when Bean handed off to Cox on an inside trap, and she took it all the way for a 76-yard score. With a 14-point lead, Rasmussen put Lane back in to direct the offense, and she marched the Falconz down the field on a scoring drive that culminated in a 14-yard touchdown from the option. The defense stepped up, and Aiono intercepted a Gallegos pass at the Falconz' 27-yard line and ran it back 73 yards to add another score. Up 45–18, with 3:44 left in the third quarter, the Falconz lost some focus. The offense began turning the ball over, and the defense started allowing the Surge offense to get on track. Guidry scored on a 40-yard jet sweep, Courtney Rosado scored on a 4-yard run, and Gallegos hit Guidry for the 2-point conversion to make the score 45–34 Falconz. The Gallegos-to-Guidry express clicked again, this time from 23 yards, and they connected again for the 2-point conversion to make the score 45–42, but only four seconds remained in the game. The Surge recovered the ensuing onside kick at the Falconz' 32 with two seconds left, but the San Diego attempt at a hook-and-ladder play failed, and the home team held on for the win.[55]

This was a game between two of the top teams in women's football, and it was professionally streamed so that distant fans of the sport could watch. Rasmussen called the Surge one of the "Blueblood teams" in the sport. On his team's five fumbles, he told me, "We had already begun to rotate our players. We had pulled it out of afterburners and quickly had to jam it back into afterburners, which is never a good place to be as a team. Thank God there weren't another two minutes in the game; because they were on a roll. . . . It was quite a game. I would like to tell you it was fun. I thought the first quarter was fun. I thought the second and third quarters were a whole lot of fun, and I don't ever want to have a fourth quarter like we had."[56]

Rasmussen, Bean, and the Falconz would have another tough game, this one a loss, to close out the 2018 season, which dropped their record to 49-2 overall. Close games and the occasional loss by top teams, however, are what women's football needs for the sport to gain any attention. The same holds true of the ability to stream games, either live or on YouTube. Fans of the sport should be able to watch the big games in the various leagues to spread excitement for the sport. Unfortunately, blowouts, forfeits, teams suspending or ceasing competition, and only local fans being able to see the game were the main components of the IWFL's schedule in 2018.

The Falconz Way proved successful against the other teams in the IWFL, and while it might be trite, the old saw that "nothing succeeds like success" has been effectively illustrated in Salt Lake City. After losing only one game in three years, and winning their first league championship, the team was awarded the right to host the 2017 IWFL championship weekend. Bean told me that her husband, Don Bean, knew Wayne Niederhauser, the president of the Utah Senate, and had sent him news of the team from time to time. The Falconz' success must have intrigued Niederhauser, who suggested that the state should "bring the championship to Utah." In addition to expressions of interest, Niederhauser and the Utah Sports Commission also provided a grant to fund the event. Having the event in their hometown put some pressure on the team. According to Bean, "Now our big goal, of course, was that we wanted to host the game, but [we] didn't want to not be in it. It was a big deal for us." The team responded by again winning all their games and then cruising through the playoffs. For the championship final, Gary Hebert, the governor of Utah, flipped the coin to start the game. Again, according to Bean, they had a crowd of "just under three thousand" on hand to watch the Falconz defeat the Austin Yellow Jackets 35-18. The quarterback estimated that their usual crowd size was "five hundred to six hundred," and so the crowd at the final was "pretty good for a female sport in Utah."[57]

The team worked to provide the pageantry around the championship game that was akin to the events at a major sporting event. Rebecca Olson, a singer and actress, headlined the event that also included a children's choir and a Polynesian dance company, along with various country and rock groups. The weekend included a press conference, social gatherings for the athletes, coaches, and owners, and an all-star game.[58] The Founders Bowl, a game for third place, was canceled, but the weekend was an overall success for the Falconz and the IWFL.

The success continued into the 2018 season, and the state of Utah once again backed up their admiration for the hometown team by providing a yearly grant of $30,000 to help with operating expenses. On the *Gridiron Beauties Blitz Radio* program, Bean told host Oscar Lopez that the "every-year grant" would cover the team's expenses for attending the league championship. In order to continue receiving the money, the team must show continued "viability, and if the team is honorable." Lopez asserted that "excellence deserves recognition" and offered his hopes that official recognition such as this "bodes well for the team, but it also bodes well for women's sports in general to have a team recognized, especially in a sport like women's football that gets probably little to no press, so it's nice that the state recognizes that excellence."[59]

As with many of the top women's football teams, from the Troopers to the Falconz, when people happened to show up to a game, they left impressed. According to Smith-Meek, the chief executive of the state had the same "aha" moment when his blinders came off during the championship game. "The governor out there, just grinning ear to ear, watching us. He was shocked, I think, at what he saw. Most people, when they come watch us, are shocked the first time the see us because they expect it to be some sort of side show because its women playing football. They don't expect it to actually be football."[60]

State support freed up some funds, and the organization took a step forward in strengthening local recognition by leasing a billboard on one of the major routes through the city. The billboard featured Smith-Meek, flanked by wide receiver/defensive back Elisa Salazar and defensive end/tackle AJ Roby, along with the team logo.

In an informal survey, conducted with the various Uber and shuttle drivers who conveyed us to the various sites my wife and I visited, only one of six or so had heard of the Falconz or women's football. That one was a hotel shuttle driver who was a family friend of Kase Tukutau, one of the Majestics who were also staying at our hotel. Aside from the small-world effect, the two-time champions had seemingly struggled to make an impression on the people who might be counted on to be aware of local organizations, so the billboard will perhaps be money well spent.

After I interviewed Bean, the quarterback became an informal research assistant and helped me line up several interviews with other Falconz players and coaches. She was the first IWFL player that I interviewed, and she also reached out to a number of players on other teams in the league.

Sara Galica, who plays defensive back, quarterback, and wide receiver, was one of those helped by the Falconz' foundation. While working on her degree in professional sales and human performance management, she arranged an internship with the team, which helped her build her skills. "I would consider myself a late bloomer in regards to my athletic ability. I wasn't really skilled in high school, I didn't really play sports my senior year. I have all of the heart but not really any of the physical capabilities. My body and mind were not working together. Football has been really where I've been able to step up and find that true calling, where I can be an asset to something bigger than just myself. So it's just definitely changed my life for the better. And when I say to something bigger than myself, I've actually been able to explore some of these skill sets. I did an internship, part of my collegiate degree, with the Utah Falconz. I was afforded the opportunity to do the things for the team organizationally that I probably wouldn't have had the opportunity [to do] elsewhere. I approached them about it, and they let me have a position doing tasks here and there, and one of the tasks that has actually stuck with me is that I am the video/stats coordinator. So that is kind of how I contribute to the team off the field. I do all of our game day stats, get all of our video uploaded, [and] share it with other teams. That's what is cool about the Falconz; we are more than just a football team. We are actually like an ecosystem where people can help out and use their skill set for the team to really make it flourish."[61]

Galica has also worked to pass along the lessons she has learned on and off the field for the Falconz. She coached the girls' basketball team at DaVinci Academy, a charter school in Ogden, which is just north of Salt Lake City. In 2018 her Dragons team finished in third place at the Utah State Championship Playoffs.[62] Galica spreads the Falconz Way, modified for basketball, to her athletes. "I always talk about how football and basketball, regardless of the differences—the similarity is that they teach life skills. It is more than just being a player out there on the field or the court."[63]

BreAnn Cintron, who plays guard and linebacker and also authored articles about her team for the *Deseret News*, testified to the benefits of the Falconz' efforts to use football to better the lives of their athletes off the field. In her pre-football life, she told me, she had been "quiet and shy." She credited the sport with helping her "break out of my shell a little bit." To illustrate her growth in confidence, she told me a story about a conversation she had with a coworker, who knocked on her office door and told Cintron, "'Hey, I just heard that you play football, and my boss told me that you could probably beat me up.' I was like, well, that's an interesting conversation that they had, and I kind of laughed and said, 'Oh no, there's no probably about it.' I kind of laughed, and I said, 'Well, let's just say there are not a lot of people that I'm afraid of right now.'" She added, "I would say I am a lot more confident. You know, if I were to walk alone in an empty parking lot—I mean my attitude before would be to be scared, and I think now I probably would be like, 'Just try. Just try to attack me, and I'll show you!' But yeah, I'm a lot more confident in who I am and what I'm capable of, and I think it's great that it has helped me break out of my shell."[64]

Although that may sound like bravado, Tiffany, the Rage player discussed in chapter 2, essentially did show her husband what she could do when he attempted to continue his abuse. A large percentage of the women I interviewed asserted that football had changed their lives for the better, and many credited their participation in the sport with helping raise their confidence level.

It was Cintron who first mentioned the idea of blinders coming off of the eyes, as mentioned in the introduction. "It was almost like taking the blinders off and seeing . . . that it was kind of a hidden world out there. I had no idea that there were teams all over the country. There are teams all over the world. I had no idea that women were kind of stepping up and saying, 'We want to play football too,' and, 'Let's make this a reality.' It's so great to see. It's kind of a movement that's starting to gain speed all over the world, and it's empowering to see women step up and say, 'Yeah, it's a male-dominated sport, but just go ahead and watch me.'"[65]

For Maira Alcala, playing for the Falconz filled a need in her life that had been missing. An army veteran whose current career was with the U.S. Army National Guard, she didn't lack confidence. She told me, "I'm like super competitive from the get-go, you know, from when I was born I was super competitive." When she moved to Salt Lake City, she missed competition, and football gave her an outlet. "When I when I first moved to Salt Lake before the season actually started, I guess I just miss the competition. So any kind of competition is really good for me. If I'm not competing in something then I start to go downhill, I guess you could say. It's something to look forward to. Something to occupy my time besides, you know, having the normal schedule of just waking up, going to work, coming home, and doing home stuff. It has definitely been really good for me. Not only as a player but also building up my leadership as well, as far as that goes, on both the military side and the civilian side as well."[66]

Tasha Aiono, who played cornerback, running back, quarterback, and kick returner, learned of the Falconz when she was playing flag football. Bean and other Falconz players competed against her in a flag football league, and after the game they recruited her. One of sixteen siblings, eight of whom were at the Majestics game, the third-year player had bought into the Falconz Way. It took some convincing, but when she finally attended a practice, she was hooked. "You show up, and it's so organized. It's so disciplined, and I miss that college team aspect, you know. I was afraid that it'd be like a rec thing, you know, unorganized, kind of sloppy. But, you know, you show up and the coaches are intense and legit. You can tell it's a real team thing, so I just bought in. It was awesome. I was right back in it." She also endorsed the idea that football teaches lessons outside of the gridiron. "Coach Rick and Jody [Thompson, the defensive coordinator] and all the coaches, I think they—they connect football to life so well. I think I've become a more disciplined person, a better person. I think that I've learned more life lessons in football than any other sport I've played. It's definitely . . . I don't know if it's the awesome teammates and the great coaches, but it's completely, you know, given me a different outlook on a lot of things I've done. It's been really awesome." When I asked her if the Falconz would win their third championship in a row, she answered me in the manner that a veteran coach such as Rasmussen would have if asked by a reporter. "Oh, man. That's the plan. Obviously we would love to do that. That's the end game, but I think we're all, you know, right now we're looking to our next game. I mean, right now, our focus is Tuesday [the next practice]. And then it's the next game. And that's just how we kind of run things, you know? We don't like to look too far ahead, because we gotta get through Tuesday's practice first. As a team we gotta learn Tuesday, we gotta learn Thursday, and then the next game."[67]

As Hunter mentioned, the Falconz are a diverse group, as is the case for most, if not all, women's football teams. In a Facebook Messenger conversation, Bean told me that they stretched their net internationally to find players, or at least to find international athletes living in Salt Lake City. According to her, they have had players from Japan, Tonga, Samoa, and Mexico.[68]

The team also has had women from a wide range of sporting backgrounds join them. Rookie wingback and linebacker Chanel Johnstun first played football with the Oklahoma City Lady Force that played under the banner of the Xtreme Football League, an eight-on-eight women's football league located in Oklahoma and Kansas. The Lady Force was similar to the Falconz in that they had won multiple back-to-back championships. For the Oklahomans, as of the 2018 season, they had yet to lose a game and had won the league championship four years in a row.[69] When I interviewed Johnstun, she was recuperating from a rib injury, but that had not dimmed her enthusiasm for the sport. "I got hit in the ribs—I was running too high, so hopefully I learned that lesson for the next time."[70]

They have had some players who had football experience before joining the team. Alcala played football in seventh grade, before her mother decided that was enough. Rather than facing opposition from male players, the boys that she had been playing baseball with encouraged her to go out for football. "I was talking to some of the guys that I was playing with, and they were like, 'Hey, you should totally try out for the football team.' At first, I didn't really think too much about it. But then after thinking about it, I was like, 'Man, I should probably do that.' So I asked my mom and my dad, they didn't really seem to care. So I did. I signed up that summer, and I started playing football with them." She played defensive back, but when the boys had the growth spurt that often hits between seventh and eighth grade, her mother grew concerned and told her, "You probably shouldn't play anymore."[71]

Nor did Jasmine Teeters, an offensive tackle for the Falconz, face the male opposition that our popular culture teaches us to expect when females take on nontraditional roles. She started playing in the sixth grade and continued through high school. "I didn't have any problems with the guys. I felt like I was part of the team for the most part. Also, my high school coach would make the guys condition extra if they went easy on me. So I always felt like I was part of the team and was just working as hard as everyone else." She explained that rather than encouraging her to quit, her coach's threat of punishment was designed to provide her with the "same experience" as her teammates and to help her elevate her game. She went on to play four years with the Portland Fighting Fillies, then played for the Falconz for two years, spent another year with the Portland Fighting Shockwave, and finally played during the 2017 and 2018 seasons for the Falconz.[72]

In 2017 several of the Falconz played in an all-star game in Las Vegas. Some of their teammates played for the Majestics, and the two groups made some interleague friendships. The Majestics, after finishing 7-1 in the WFA, did not make the playoffs, and this perhaps helped them decide to switch to the IWFL for 2018. Bean helped me line up interviews with some of the Seattle players. Since they were in the IWFL from 2003 to 2012 and rejoined the league, briefly, in 2018, their stories are included here.

The Majestics began play in 2002 as the Tacoma Majestics in the Women's Spring Football League. They joined the IWFL the next season, and until 2005 they won twenty-four games and only lost two, including a Western Conference Championship in 2005. The next year, they combined with the Seattle Warbirds to take on their current name. Between 2006 and 2011, they won forty-nine games and lost only fifteen, and one of those wins was an IWFL Tier II national championship.[73]

After the original ownership left, and the team appeared "headed for a quick and quiet death," players Camille Head, Heather Gallemore, and Michel Rene Volk stepped in to fund the team, which included paying the "$4,500 franchise fee" to the IWFL. In 2008, the team budget was "about $80,000," and players paid $750 fees, plus furnishing "their own equipment and some travel."[74]

In 2013 the Majestics joined the WFA and were a member of that league until their 2018 jump to the IWFL. They continued to be successful in their new league and won thirty-eight games and lost only seven over that time. During three of those years (2013, 2016, and 2017), the Majestics were 8-1, 6-2, and 7-1, respectively, but did not make the playoffs.[75] Since its inception, the team has won more than one hundred games, but during their five years in the WFA, despite posting an 84 percent winning percentage, they had only made the playoffs twice.

I first met McKenzie Tolliver at the IFAF Women's World Championship, but we did not find time for an interview until the following year. Tolliver had been a competitive swimmer in college and had tried out for the Junior Olympic Team, but when her athletic career at Washington State University ended, it left a void. "When I was in college, I was just finishing up college swimming, and that had been so much of my life since I was ten or eleven, I started traveling around the country.

I kind of had an identity crisis. I didn't know what to do in the world without sports." As with many women football players, Tolliver's road to joining a team started online. She found information about the Dallas Diamonds and considered moving there, but by then she was married and had children. "When we moved out to Seattle, I needed that competition in my life. I got on Google and saw that there was a Seattle team. I emailed the coach (Scott McCarron) and haven't looked back since." Since that beginning, she has become a member of the board that oversees the Majestics and played on the U.S. National Team. She has also had injury issues. When asked about how her parents had reacted to her new football career, she told me, "It surprised pretty much no one in my life. I've always been rough and tough, playing with the guys. I am super competitive with everything that I do, whether it is a spelling bee, or if I am drinking a glass of water with someone, I'll still try to beat them. It didn't surprise them. They were like, 'Welp, don't get injured,' which I have managed to do every season." When I talked with her, she was recovering from a spinal surgery, and at the time of the world championship, she was "only about eleven weeks out of spine surgery when I went for the games. I got a doctor's clearance, but yeah, that's a very, very, intense injury." Just after our interview, she injured her knee, but at the Falconz game she played through the pain.[76]

Like Tolliver, Majestics linebacker Holly Custis has had to return from injury to play. Custis started playing for the Eugene Edge while studying history at the University of Oregon. After the Edge folded, she played three years for the Corvallis Pride and four more for the Portland Fighting Phillies. She had played for the Majestics for the last four seasons when I interviewed her. During the 2021 season, Custis moved on to play for the Falconz.

Just after returning from the Women's World Games in Orlando, Custis was running a simple pass pattern in practice when her knee failed. She would face surgery and rehabilitation before she could play again. Custis wrote about the injury on her *Relentless21: A Gridiron Mindset* blog and about the recovery process that followed.[77]

On her injury and rehabilitation, Custis told me, "My knee injury has been a huge process, and it's only been about two years, actually just over two years [from] the date that I had my surgery, and it's only now that I finally feel kind of normal. So it's been a long time, but because of that process it's taught me a lot about endurance and about pushing your way through things that are difficult. Because of that, I kind of feel a little bit renewed, and so I'm going to take it year by year as I go forward. But I think, because I've gotten through this injury, I feel like I could go another few years here, if I'm lucky enough to do so. I mean this is an injury that it took me—I basically had to relearn how to walk. It took me three months to relearn how to walk, another three months to get to the point where I was kind of jogging, then like every couple months I would be having to force my way through a plateau basically. Having football really helped me persevere through it."[78]

She had been happy to join the successful Majestics. "So in 2015 I moved up to Seattle. I got a new job. Seattle was a team that I had played against for so many years, and they had always been a really strong team. If they weren't the best team in the Northwest, then they were always competing for that. They were always a team that would go far into the playoffs, and I was really excited to play in the bigger market on the team that was established and had a lot of tradition. So my first year was in 2015. That went really well, and we went to the playoffs. I think we lost in the second round in San Diego."[79]

By the time I interviewed Custis, she was back on the field and had several tackles against the Falconz, playing the game she loves. When asked what football has meant to her life, she asserted, "It has made a lot of difference. I think it's something that, ever since I started playing, it has been an outlet for me. So whenever I've had issues going on in my personal life it has been like a safe haven for me. It has been therapeutic. If you have a bad day at work, you can go on the field, get the pads on, and get that frustration out. On top of that, because of all the relationships. . . . It's basically a fraternity, and your team becomes your second family. I think it's by the very nature of the sport because it's so physical, number one, and number two, it's the most team sport out there—you need all eleven people out there to move the ball, and all of the people to stop it. No matter how good of a running back you have, you need the rest of the people to block.

Otherwise it's one versus eleven, and you're not going to move the ball. Because of the very nature of the game, you need every single person, and everybody has a job to do, and you all do it together. Because of that it builds a level of trust and a level of family that I haven't had in any other sport that I played."[80]

The reasons the linebacker gave for playing were echoed by a large percentage of the women I interviewed. Most of them, like Custis, had to wait until they were beyond college age, or older, before they had the opportunity to play the game. Some very few were able to play on boys' teams during their formative years, but those were few and far between. A consequence of that is that as one ages, one is more prone to injury in high-impact sports. Perhaps a benefit of being an older athlete is that adults are free to decide to come back, even from serious injuries, if they are so inclined.

Kase Tukutau played defensive tackle for the Majestics and was another athlete who had played football in high school. As with Jasmine Teeters, her high school experience was positive, and her coaches "pushed the guys to go a little harder because they noticed 'there's a girl on the team who's running faster than you and hitting harder than you, and you guys got to pick it up,' and things like that. So, I think I held my own for the longest and that's probably what kept me afloat a lot." At times, she did more than hold her own. She remembered at one practice the team went through a hitting drill called "King of the Hill," and she was lined up against a "really big" senior. "I hit him so hard that he had a concussion, and he had to sit out the rest of the practice. Everyone at practice was just, you know, jumping up and down and just going crazy. At the school the next day, everyone's talking about it. So that's fun." Unlike Teeters, Tukutau played quite a bit in high school. She started on the freshman team and played all four years. She also played on the varsity basketball team and on the softball team. Her participation in athletics gave her a positive high school experience: "If I could go back and do it again, I would." Tukutau told me that it was not until she played with the Majestics that she began understanding the game. "What's crazy is when I played football in high school; I really didn't know what I was doing. The language to me was completely different."[81]

Tukutau continued: "So when I came to play for the Majestics they kind of started speaking in the language that I can understand more. So in high school, I didn't really understand the game of football, and I was still learning but still didn't comprehend, fully. So when I played for the Majestics, that's when everything started to click." It clicked well enough for her to be among the top tacklers on her team during her rookie season, which she credited to her experience playing rugby. She also gained notice from the WFA and was named the league's 2014 Rookie of the Year.[82]

Another Majestics athlete that had extensive experience in contact sports was wide receiver Julia McComas, who had played rugby for over a decade. She experienced some cognitive dissonance in making the transition from the fluid sport of rugby to the more static game of football. "So, I came into football with almost a false expectation of being a huge asset to the team because I had that rugby background, and came in thinking, 'Okay, I'm going to come in and ball out because I'm a rugby player, I got this.' [But] football is just such a different game than rugby. Rugby is just—you don't really have to think much. It's not a mental game. It's just punch down the field and out-athlete; move and run. Football is very mental. So, there's a huge learning curve for the first one to two years. The third year, everything starts to click; it's a lot like learning a new language." McComas, similar to most women who end up on the gridiron, "had no idea that women's football even existed." Some of her friends did know, and they convinced her to try out for the Majestics. She checked the team out online, and what she found piqued her interest. "I went and checked them out and I was like, 'This is awesome, these guys are great.' It's highly competitive, there's such a production value with the game. So you go out there and hear your name on the loudspeaker, and there's just so much hype surrounding the moment that it's not just like you're out at a random field and maybe your mom and your uncle are on the sideline. But there's stands full of people, and they all know your name, and it's cool. It's really fun." McComas echoed Custis in describing what football had meant to her. "Football is amazing. I can't even imagine my life without it. It's the perfect life-work balance, and it gives me something to be dedicated to and gives me something to work toward. It gives me a slight sense of purpose in the sense that my free time is put toward an actual, tangible goal. And then it helps me not get burnt out in my work world, too, because work is extremely taxing. So if all I had going for me in my life was work, and then just relaxing from work, and work again, I don't know that I would feel fully fulfilled in my life. I'm really glad I have the outlet of football to use sort of as the balancing force. When I have to retire from football, I'm hoping to coach on a team, do something in the world so I can still really be fully involved."[83]

Tolliver put me in touch with Cyndi Butz-Houghton, a former player, Majestics coach, and team chief executive officer. She began playing for the New York Sharks in their first full season in 2000 and then transferred to the Philadelphia Liberty Belles, before landing with the Seattle Majestics. During her time in Philadelphia, the Liberty Belles won an NWFL national championship in 2001. Butz-Houghton told me that who would go to the championship came down to which team, her Liberty Belles or Boston (Massachusetts Mutiny), could score the most points in their final game. "We had flown somebody to Boston, so they could text us the game score, while we were playing our game, so we could decide, oh, do we have to run up the score on the Connecticut Crush to win this game, or can we just relax and play this game. We had to run our score up into the eighties."[84] Rozendaal has the score against the Mutiny listed as 74–0, but whatever the outcome, Butz-Houghton and her Liberty Belles earned the right to play against the Pensacola Power, whom they defeated 40–7.[85]

Butz-Houghton also gave me the rationale of why the Majestics had decided to leave the WFA. "We just felt like our goals, as far as our team, and how we ran our team, and where we wanted to go in the future, where we wanted to take a sport, was just not aligning with the WFA anymore. A lot of their so-called transparencies of how they run the organization weren't as transparent as people believed. We went to the last owners' meeting, and we asked some questions that weren't getting answers, and made the owners of the WFA very uncomfortable. I think what it comes down to—when you don't know what you're getting from an organization that you're putting into, it makes it very hard to run your organization. The thing that I love about the IWFL is, right off the bat, you have one team that has one delegate. So I'm the delegate for our team in the league. Every team that is putting into this league has a say—you're in the know with everything that they're doing. I just felt like there was so much going on with the WFA that none of the teams knew about, and you couldn't really get any answers. I just didn't feel comfortable with that. They weren't really running the organization that we want our organization to be tied to. So in the end, we had to make that move. They have, I want to call it a board . . . with maybe nine members, and I'm not even sure how the people got on the board. It's made up of the members of other teams, but I'm not even sure how the people get on the board. When we were sitting at the table at the owners' meeting, Scott McCarran, the head coach of the Majestics, who was, supposedly, one of those members—they were passing out a list of new members to vote on. He didn't even know what was happening. He wasn't even on the list. Nobody understood who these people were. That's just the kind of stuff that made us really uncomfortable. We don't even know who these people are, and that we're changing representation, but you want us to give to your league and trust that you're going to take care of our team. It just didn't feel right."[86]

She also provided an alternative view of why the IWFL had lost so many teams and had become the second largest league. "It (the IWFL) is smaller. They started bigger, years ago, but they ran into a lot of problems. They grew way too fast. We were a member, and then we left them to go to the WFA. And then they said, 'Okay, we're not doing this right. Let's regroup, and let's do this right.' They went down in size, which I think was so smart, because you need to focus on a good handful of teams, and getting it right before you start to grow. You can't just let people into a league because, 'Oh, I have a few thousand dollars and I have thirteen women who want to play football.' 'Okay, you can have a team.' I don't think it can be that way. So them going smaller made a lot of sense."[87]

On why leagues come and go, and teams switch leagues with such frequency, Butz-Houghton told me, "You know what, unfortunately,

I have been around for a while, and I've seen so many trends. Somebody thinks they can do it better. That's really all it is, and because we're not million- and billion-dollar teams, it's easy enough to just say: 'Hey, why don't you come on over here with my league?' Or: 'Why don't you come join my team? That team's not doing it right.' So many players leave teams to start their own team because they think they can do it better, and I think it's exactly what happened with the leagues. Someone thought they could do it better, and they just decided to go with it. They're not really thinking about the well-being of the players, or the well-being of the sport, and that's the hard part. We are confusing everybody with all the leagues and all the teams all over the country. It's hard to be a fan, if you don't even know what team you're rooting for. So I just think it's as simple as that when it comes to women's football—somebody thinks they can do it better, and they just go off and try."[88]

Butz-Houghton's description seems correct, if not a little ironic. After I spoke with her, the Majestics, which had just returned to the IWFL, jumped to the new NWFC. Teams, and individuals, make decisions that they feel will benefit themselves, and the lack of monetary motivations inherent in women's football provides a kind of freedom that leads to the rapid reshuffling of the women's football world. The Majestics made the decision that conditions in the IWFL would benefit them, so they switched leagues. When their calculations did not match the reality of the situation, they followed their perceived self-interest and moved again. The fallout from those decisions, however, is the confusion that fans, and likely potential sponsors, find when they consider women's football.

Erin Miller, who when we spoke was planning to play for the Eugene LadyHawks, once she too recovered from a knee injury, indicated that the Falconz Way may be spreading beyond Utah. Miller played defensive back for the Jynx for two years and two more for the Falconz, before moving on to the Portland Fighting Phillies. When head coach Calvin Griggs moved from Portland to Eugene to coach the first-year (in 2018) LadyHawks, Miller followed him. "Coach Griggs reminds me of Coach Rick [Rasmussen], like pretty much down to the core. So I wasn't getting what I was getting from Portland because 'I feel like I'm playing for a recreational team,' just because the coaches didn't put a lot into it. It was just that type of coaching that was more lackadaisical, and I [would be thinking], 'We have a game in a week, we should be preparing differently.'" Of her experience with the Falconz, Miller told me, "As soon as you are in the system, and you see how the system is working, and you see the byproduct of it. If you put in the system, what you are going to get [is] the output. The output is you are going to get a championship team. If you keep gaining fans, and you keep getting more eyes on the team, and you get more women committed, and you get them buying into the system, everything else works itself out. So I would love to try and bring what I was taught with the Utah culture up here. I tried doing it here in Portland, but unfortunately that just didn't work out. Not the right people saw my vision. So I don't know. It seems like Eugene is really going." When the Eugene team was considering which league to join, the WFA had some concerns about existing teams losing players to the startup. According to Miller, Jolley reached out and "basically invited us to be part of the IWFL."[89]

In addition to recovering from her injury, Miller, who served in the U.S. Army and now works for a veterans' crisis line, had higher goals. "Women's football [has] given me the platform that, you know, someday I wish that I will be able to coach girls' football up here just like what is happening down in Utah with Crys [Sacco], with Sam Gordon, with that league. What they are doing is just amazing. So I hope that one day I'll be able to use my talents, and use my knowledge, so I can pass it along to future generations. I've made some amazing connections with some great, great, strong, powerful women that if it wasn't for football, I would have never met. [Football] gave me the chance to travel—trying out for Team USA. I went there, I tried that. I was in Pittsburgh for the All-American game. I was in Las Vegas, where I was injured. I was able to reconnect with my old coach, Rick, and my old teammates, and my old battle buddies that I served in the military with. So, football, it's just beautiful, and it's just great for women that didn't have the sport when I was a kid, and that they will be able to really be who they want to be."[90]

The LadyHawks finished with a 1-5 record in 2018, only winning when the Rogue Valley Elements forfeited the last game.[91] After losing 78-6 to the Falconz, Griggs gave Austin Meek, a reporter for the *Eugene Register-Guard*, what was likely a summary for their entire first season. "We're going to take our bumps and bruises, and that's OK." Meek's article mentioned that the LadyHawks were the fifth attempt to create a women's football team in the area. When asked why she started the team, LadyHawks owner Naomi Hunkin told him, "Too many people said it couldn't be done. . . . When you tell a woman that she can't do something, there's going to be something in them that's going to want to prove you wrong." Meek made it back to the team's last home game and noticed that the LadyHawks had made strides toward improvement, and that "their first brush with tackle football hasn't dampened their enthusiasm for the game." Beth Horner, the quarterback, told him, "I'm so excited for next year . . . I'm hooked." Whether Horner's enthusiasm, Miller's hope for the future, and Griggs patience would result in a positive output would have to wait for next year.[92]

The Los Angeles Bobcats also had a difficult year in 2018. Although the players I talked to were positive about the season, injuries or other calamities struck, and after playing three games, they had to forfeit the remainder of the season.[93] That season was only their third as a team, and they had success in the past. In 2016 they had an undefeated regular season before losing in the playoffs.[94] However, in 2017, when they played the Falconz, they only had twelve players, according to quarterback Jane Brinkman. On a more positive note, she added that they had still managed to score a touchdown against the eventual champions.[95] The team planned to be back for 2019. The Bobcats' Facebook page announced that Tim Holmes, formerly of the IWFL's Carolina Phoenix, would coach the team in 2019 and also posted information about tryouts in December. Demetrea Hardiman, the team's co-owner, attended the Best of the West championship, and the team was set to play in the WNFC next year.[96] As of 2022, the team was no longer active, although the Los Angles Legends of the WNFC seems to be the successor team since the Bobcats' Facebook page redirects to the Legends'.

The Bobcats did gain some unusual publicity when an NFL commercial commemorating its one hundredth season featured some of the players. The commercial showed various athletes in the Los Angeles area working out or performing. One segment featured the Bobcats marching into a stadium; another showed them in their pregame ritual.[97] They were on the leading edge of an increased presence of females in commercials.

The first Bobcat player that I interviewed was Sybil Gonzales. We spoke when she was in Langley, British Columbia, and playing for the Mexican National Team. Gonzales credited playing with the then Carson Bobcats with helping her prepare to play in the Women's World Championship. "It was a learning experience for me, because, if you can see the average of the Mexican girls—the height and the weight—it's really different as American girls. For me, it was a really good experience to match the girls that I was going to play against here in this tournament. I could match them and see how I could adjust my blocking and things like that." The Mexican teams also play "eight-a-side," so the experience of playing eleven on eleven also helped her. Unfortunately for her and the Bobcats, she was in Canada when the Bobcats were in the playoffs, and they lost their game.[98]

Her Bobcats teammate Olivia Morgan, another player that Bean steered me to, had played for the Nevada Storm before she moved to Los Angeles. A sprinter on her track team in college, Morgan found football when she was looking for something to keep her mind and body active after graduation. When she moved to LA, she tried out for a team in the WFA, but since the Storm played in the IWFL, she wanted to stay in the league where many of her friends played. "I tried out for another team that was out here, but I decided to go with the Bobcats. . . . I definitely want to stay with the IWFL, so it was an easy choice. I have a lot of friends that still play in the IWFL. It's always fun to see them and play against them. Since I started off in the IWFL, I just felt that it was right to stay in there. I didn't feel like I needed to make the switch anytime soon, to the WFA."[99]

After we discussed her career, I asked Morgan if there was anything else that she wanted to tell me about playing football, and she replied:

"I just want to reiterate how important it is to me for women's football to get their name out there. I know there have been articles that ESPN has put out over Sam Gordon. I think it's important that women's football gets the recognition that they deserve, especially now, because we are trailblazing for the younger generation." When asked what the Bobcats were doing to make this a reality, she told me, "We're trying to put together a camp, so we can bring the younger generation on— get them involved with football, or just with any aspect of the game. I think that's going to be our biggest victory, if we can put that camp together, and get women and teenagers to understand the game. I think that is going to be a huge accomplishment."[100]

Morgan also expressed her conviction that football is for all women. "We have a player that is deaf, and so we never want anyone to feel like women's football is excluding anybody. Because we will support people with disabilities to get awards and to get a chance to play these games that they've always wanted to do. It's important for everybody all around. So I think the Bobcats are doing a great job blazing a trail for people from all backgrounds."[101]

The IWFL had faced controversy over inclusion, and that was most likely what led to their ultimate dissolution. In 2018 Christina Ginther, a transgender woman, won a state court decision against the IWFL and the Minnesota Vixen. Ginther tried out for the Vixen in 2017, but when the team discovered that Ginther had been born a male, they cited league rules that "a player may not play in the IWFL, unless they are now, and always have been, legally and medically a female, as determined by their birth certificate and driver's license."[102] Ginther recalled that the Vixen had told her that the IWFL "didn't allow players who were born biologically male because of safety reasons."[103] Ginther sued the defendants for violating Minnesota's Human Rights Act, and in December 2018 a state court awarded the former player (for the Minnesota Machine) $10,000 for emotional distress and another $10,000 in punitive damages.[104]

The Vixen posted an update on their Facebook page on 28 December 2018, asserting that they had tried to change the IWFL policy but were bound by it when Ginther attempted to join the team. According to their post, "Disgusted by the IWFL's policies and refusal to change to be more inviting, within weeks and well before Ms. Ginther filed her lawsuit, MN Vixen left the IWFL for the Women's Football Alliance, which allows transgender athletes to participate. The MN Vixen have proudly had transgender athletes on their team ever since." The jury in the trial found the IWFL, but not the Vixen, liable for the $20,000 in damages, and the team also posted that they were "now attempting to recover its attorneys' fees and costs from the IWFL."[105]

Given the financial structure of women's football, the necessity of paying lawyers and finding $20,000 to pay for the jury award will not likely be easy. Had the Vixen been found liable, it might have spelled the end for the team. With fewer than twenty teams and if the team fee of $4,500 that the Majestics reportedly paid in 2008 remains the same, the league must have been hard pressed to find that amount lying around unused. As it turned out, the league ceased operation soon after the decision, so coupled with the defection of their top teams, that judgment seemingly spelled the end for the league.

Women's football certainly does not discriminate against women engaged in same-sex relationships. More than a few of the players I interviewed told me that they met their spouses on their football teams. In her interview with the *Deseret News*, Hiroko Jolley estimated that "70 percent of her teammates are lesbian, and there are couples within the team."[106] The Cleveland Fusion was featured in a 2004 article by Rebecca Meiser for *Scene Magazine*. The story was purportedly about the Cleveland Fusion playing the Columbus Comets in the first NWFA game in an NFL stadium. However, the author spent a fairly large part of her article discussing the sexual orientations of some of the players and the reactions of some of the straight players to their teammates' public displays of affection on the team bus after the Fusion's first game with the Comets.[107] There are also articles and podcasts, such as *My Gay Life*, co-hosted by Butz-Houghton, which celebrates the women's game for being open to lesbian players.[108]

In my interviews I did not ask about sexual orientation, but some players such as Jane Brinkman volunteered, "My wife gets tired of football." Brinkman came to football after having played professional basketball for the Women's National Basketball Association's Phoenix Mercury. Some of my interview subjects told me that football had saved their lives, but perhaps they didn't mean that in the same sense as Brinkman. She started playing after her second bout of chemotherapy and radiation treatment for cancer. "I had just finished chemotherapy for the second time, and a friend of mine—I was complaining about not being in shape—and she's like, 'Well I'm going to try out for this team, you should come with me.' So I did, and I made it. I've been playing ever since. Yeah, it kind of changed everything. When I started, my blood counts were pretty low, and I had to get permission from my oncologist. Then the next thing I know, when I went back a couple weeks after I had started playing for the San Diego Sting, my blood counts and everything improved tremendously. So my oncologist said, 'I don't know what you're doing but just keep doing it,' so I've been playing ever since. My doctor and my surgeon both thought I was crazy at first, but I mean mentally and physically, I've been an athlete my whole life, and it's been my savior in a lot of areas."[109]

Brinkman was another athlete who was not totally new to football. Her father coached the sport when she was growing up, and she played for him during junior high. She attempted to continue playing in high school, but after someone lodged a complaint with the Wyoming State Athletic Association, she was forced to leave the team. Association leaders argued this was for her safety, which is the primary rationale that has traditionally been used to exclude women from many sports, but particularly contact sports.[110]

After she moved away from San Diego and the Sting, Brinkman found the Bobcats. The team has had its ups and downs—trying to play the league's top team with only twelve players, for instance. Brinkman acknowledged that her team has struggled to find athletes that were willing to furnish the commitment to build a winning program. She used the example of the Utah team to provide a contrast to what the Bobcats faced. "I mean they run sixty-five deep, and in some people's eyes, they are unbeatable. They just have a fine-tuned engine with the coaching staff—all the way down. It appears that they never struggle with some of the things that the other teams struggle with, like commitment or, you know, roster. They never struggle with numbers." She continued to analyze what is necessary for a team to reach that top level. "It's commitment. It's getting in shape, and most teams, they practice twice or three times a week. When you are successful at something, in my experience, you have to work out on a daily basis—not only physically but mentally. Football is a mental game, and you have to think about it, you have to be smart, and that takes time outside of being on the field. The biggest problem that I have encountered over the years that I have played is that a lot of women don't get it, or they're not interested, or they're afraid. So it's difficult to get people to commit to something on top of the fact that it is pretty pricey, because we pay to play. So a lot of people don't have the luxury of being able to have a hobby, if you will, like this. In my eyes there are a lot of obstacles that the league and the sport for women have to overcome. Somehow, some way, Utah has successfully overcome that."[111]

Brinkman compared women's football with the WNBA. "They're almost identical. I mean, my experience is almost identical. The only difference is that when the WNBA came to fruition there was a salary offer for women. It wasn't very much—it was like twenty-eight grand, if you made the cut. . . . It's funny, because actually women's semipro football, from what I understand, has been around a lot longer than the WNBA. It's parallel in my eyes. Even the WNBA, you go to a game, and maybe a quarter of the seats are filled. It's a dream of a lot of women to go into the WNBA and to play for the USA team, and all of that stuff. But 80 percent of the women in the WNBA are realistic that this is not going to be a profitable career." She contrasted that with men's teams, where even awful teams still make a profit. She did see women's sports making strides—the women's national soccer team, for instance—but the general outlook for women was unequal. As with Linden's interview subjects, Brinkman distanced herself from feminism, even while making a feminist argument. "I'm not a feminist by any means. I try to stay out of that kind of stuff. If you look at any sport, male professionals make more money, and actually have a career afterwards—for women, not so much."[112]

Melissa Korpacz had begun working on a relationship with the Patriots, and with two NFL teams struggling for attention in Los Angeles, it would seem that one would take an interest in women's football. Brinkman told me, "I suggested the Rams and the Chargers, and trying to get meetings with the right people." She credited the Bobcats' owners with working hard to find potential sponsors and to get the word out about the team, but she acknowledged that the process was difficult. "Kris [Bannon] and 'Beast' [Demetrea Hardiman], the owners of our team, they have done an excellent job of reaching out to the councilmen, and that kind of stuff, but again, it's trying to get somebody to take you seriously. It's difficult. It's marketing. It's selling. If you can't sell the concept or if the people that are writing the checks don't believe in it, they're not going to write you a check, and a lot of people don't understand, nor do they believe, that women should play football."[113]

Following the 2018 season, when four of the top teams still remaining in the league left to form the nucleus of the WNFC, the future of the IWFL was in question. Michael Burmy, who maintains "Hometown Women's Football," a Facebook page devoted to the sport, was considering writing a eulogy for the IWFL. In a 10 October 2018 post, Burmy wrote, "The Houston Energy Football have an EXTREMELY unique distinction: first WPFL World Champions (2000, then '01 and '02) and probably the final IWFL National Champions (2018)." *Gridiron Beauties'* Oscar Lopez warned Burmy not to be too quick to declare the league dead though: "I don't know if the IWFL is no longer. They still claim independent status. So maybe wait for Spring before the eulogy. Justsaying [*sic*]."[114] Along with Rozendaal, Burmy and Lopez follow women's football as closely as anyone, so if they were unsure, then their concern for the league's future turned out to be well founded.

According to Lopez, there were signs of weakness before the season began. Perhaps motivated by the confusion surrounding the 2017 playoffs, the league had made changes, but they did not seem effective. Butz-Houghton had mentioned that each IWFL team sent a representative to league meetings, but problems grew as the date for the season arrived. Lopez addressed this on his podcast.

When Bean, who regularly appears on the *Gridiron Beauties Blitz Radio* podcast, mentioned that the "Austin [Yellow Jackets] got lucky this year, because they have eight games, and most of the other either IWFL teams don't have eight games, but they're able to." Lopez responded by going on what he termed a "rant" and said: "I'm totally disappointed with IWFL leadership. All this hype in the offseason. All these changes, everybody coming on board the council and everything, and we can't even get a website updated to hype up the season, to get a schedule set. Odessa [Jenkins], Holly [Custis], everybody out there involved in the IWFL—somebody needs to wake up because you guys are on the snooze button right now. This is just not good, and all the hype that was presented. . . . This is not good for this league! They gave us the perception that this was going to be a better product, with a better upgrade, and it's starting to look very foolish. If you can't even get an updated website hyping your [league] either on Facebook, or even on Twitter, somebody needs to get somebody that loves social media and get it up there. To me, it's kind of frustrating as a fan, because we are fans, of the sport, that this league continuously disappoints. You would think you would be able to get the schedule out by what, mid-February at least—the latest by the first week of March. Now you're expecting fans to go watch your games when you can't even get a schedule up. You can't even get access to the games!" Bean, who was enjoying Lopez's rant, responded by saying, "Oh, keep going, because, believe me, I have plenty of people who are not happy with how things are shaking out."[115]

As the season turned out, the Yellow Jackets, who finished second to the Falconz in 2017, did not play a single game in 2018. They won their first game when the West Texas Lady Hurricanes forfeited to them, but the next two games were Austin forfeits, and that was all that was listed on the IWFL page.[116] The Nevada Storm had the most games in the 2017 IWFL season with nine (5-4), and the Tulsa Threat were second with eight (3-5). The eventual champion, the Houston Energy, finished at 4-1, according to the league website. They defeated the Storm to win the IWFL championship. The Falconz were 6-0, with one forfeit, but joined the 3-0 Texas Elite Spartans, the 5-1 Majestics, and the 4-1 San Diego Surge and left the league to play in the Best of the West tournament in Las Vegas.[117]

As of 8 March 2019, the IWFL website has gone dead. According to Ashly Edmiston on her 3 March 2018 *Four Point Stance* podcast, "The IWFL is essentially gone."[118] Most likely, although this is speculation, the challenge of coming up with $20,000 proved to be too much for the league.

The Force's Linda Bache was full of hope for a brighter future in 2010, when so many of the best teams in the IWFL defected to the WFA. She optimistically posited the possibility that this signaled a move toward the unification of leagues that would help the sport advance. Her hopes and rationale were not all that different from the press release by the Women's National Football Conference in 2018 that is discussed in chapter 6.[119]

The issues surrounding women's football, therefore, have not changed all that much since the resumption of play in 1999. There was a great deal of anticipation that the WFA would be the answer, but the expansion and contraction of leagues continues. The WFA, however, remained in its position atop the women's football league structure as the 2022 season approached. To discover more about how they started and fought their way to the top, turn the page.

# The Women's Football Alliance

TOLEDO, OHIO, 21 APRIL 2018

Carrie Hall rushed for 139 yards on twenty-five carries, and Amanda
Herbst completed eight of thirteen passes for 156 yards, including
a 68-yard touchdown pass to Deasha Talley, to lead the Columbus
(Ohio) Comets to a 22–8 victory over the Toledo Reign.[1] It was a relatively cold evening that kept many of the Reign's fans at home, but
perhaps one hundred of them and a handful of Comets fans were on
hand at Rogers High School to watch the teams play the third game
of the season for each.

The Comets came in with a 1-1 record. They lost their first game to
the Detroit Dark Angels 22–28 and defeated the Columbus (Indiana)
Vanguards 22–12 in week 2. The Reign had won both of their previous
games, defeating the Grand Rapids (Michigan) Tidal Waves 32–0 and
then drubbing the Flint City (Michigan) Riveters 69–0.[2]

The game matched two teams that have been active for fifteen years.
The Comets, formed as the Flames in 2003, changed their name to the
Comets in 2004 and had a record of 96-56. Over their sixteen years,
they have qualified for the playoffs eleven times.[3] They reached the
WFA final in 2010 but lost to the Lone Star Mustangs of Texas 12–16.[4]
The team began in the National Women's Football Association and
transitioned into the Women's Football Alliance (WFA) when most of
the NWFA teams joined the WFA in 2009.[5]

The Reign also began in 2003. They were founded by Mitchi Collette and Beth Razzoog. They played in the WPFL from 2003 to 2007, suspended operation in 2008, played with the WFA from 2009 to 2014, joined the IWFL in 2015, and rejoined the WFA in 2016. They struggled in their first decade, but beginning in 2012, they began to have more success, qualifying for the playoffs in five of the seven seasons since then.[6] The team's official name is Thee Toledo Reign. Collette told me that the "Thee" in the title originated from a dispute with the owner of the Toledo Spitfire. Collette, who played with the Troopers, had been with the Spitfire team, but she and the team's owner had different ideas. Collette left the team "with the offensive coordinator, the marketing person, and nineteen other players, because it just didn't mix." When she and the defectors from the Spitfire started the process of joining the WPFL, the Spitfire owner heard about it and took measures to thwart them. According to Collette, "What she did was go to the computer and buy every which way you could have Toledo Reign: Toledo Reign Football, Toledo Reign, all of this, except for Thee. A funny thing happened. I was taking a shower the next morning, and I guess it does work in the shower. I'm thinking, 'Did she buy "Thee"?' I get out of the shower, put a towel on, and go over to the computer. We're checking: 'No, she didn't.' So it became Thee Toledo Reign."[7]

The Comets and the Reign were evenly matched, with around twenty-three players. The game was close until the second half, when Herbst hit Talley for the long score, which gave momentum to the visitors. They added a late touchdown to ice the game, but both teams had played well, particularly on defense. The Reign made a couple of mistakes, and that was the margin in the game.

Both teams went on to the playoffs in their respective divisions. The Comets defeated the Philadelphia Phantomz 22–14 in the first round of the Division II playoffs but lost to the eventual champion New York Sharks 36–55 in the second round. The Reign defeated their cross-state rivals the Cincinnati Sizzle 28–8 in the Division III first round but also lost in the second round 6–12 to the Richmond (Virginia) Black Widows.[8]

Ohio was arguably where women's football began. The state, as of 2018, had four teams—the Comets, the Reign, the Sizzle, and the Cleveland Fusion. During the 2018 season, all of the teams played in the WFA. The Comets and Fusion play in the league's Division II, and the Reign and Sizzle are in Division III. With the exception of Cincinnati, the other sites had been hosting women's football since the original WPFL in the 1970s. The Comets, Reign, and Fusion followed in the footsteps of the Columbus Pacesetters, the Toledo Troopers, the Cleveland Daredevils, and other Buckeye state teams. Therefore, Ohio, if not the original place for women's football, certainly has a long pedigree there.[9]

Since they were close to my home, the Comets and the Reign were the teams I got to know best. The first women's game that I saw in the United States was a match between the Comets and the Derby City Dynamite from Louisville, Kentucky. If the Falconz versus the Surge, or the Elite Spartans, represented women's football at its best, then the 8 April 2017 game between the Comets and the Dynamite demonstrated the game at its worst. The Dynamite had a small team with very few backups, and they were totally outclassed by the Comets, who easily won 59–6.[10] The strain of playing both ways took its toll on the Kentuckians, and just prior to halftime a Dynamite player was seriously injured. There was a long wait before an ambulance arrived. The game started at 7:00 p.m., and by the time the first half ended, it was nearly 10:00. I had an hour-and-a-half drive to get home, so I left seriously unimpressed. The crowd of perhaps two hundred fans did not seem perturbed, but they had, no doubt, seen games like this before. The one unique thing I remember from that game was that after the first touchdown, Herbst, I presume, went out to hold for the point after. When she was down on one knee to hold for the try, she vomited onto the field. I had seen that in football before, but never during an extra point try. So, my first experience watching women playing football was not very satisfactory.

During the next year, I fortunately had the chance to watch more women's football at a higher level of play than in that first game. I also had the chance to interview several of the Comets, along with Hank

Patterson, their head coach, and Lorrain Harris, the general manager. Ironically, the first Comet I interviewed was Carolyn O'Leary, whom I met in New Orleans at the Women's World Games. I also watched them play against better competition, including the game against the Reign. Although they had a rough 2017, the Dynamite came back in 2018 to make the playoffs.

I also had the chance to watch the Reign play several more games, including two playoff matches in 2017 and another in 2018. After the Columbus game, I had the chance to interview several players, and I later talked with Collette. Women's football in Toledo had a long history, as evidenced in chapter 1, and the Reign had direct connections to the Troopers (1971–79) and the Furies (1983–84). Even though the city in northwest Ohio is relatively small, with fewer than three hundred thousand in population, it has been able to support various teams in a succession of leagues. The team's present home is in the WFA, which currently houses the largest number of teams in women's football. As discussed in the previous chapter, the WFA emerged and evolved into the premier women's football league during the explosion of leagues in the first decade of the twenty-first century.

As was the norm, the WFA joined the competing women's football organizations when someone decided they had a better idea of how to run a league and acted upon it. In the case of the WFA, it was Lisa and Jeff King who believed that they had a better idea. The Kings were both experienced at playing football. Lisa King played for the Los Angeles Amazons of the NWFA and IWFL for two years.[11] Jeff King played in high school and college and then played and coached semiprofessionally in the United States and in Europe. He had also made an attempt to organize men's semiprofessional football teams into the Minor League Football Association (MLFA).[12]

In a 2016 article for Yahoo! Finance, Mandi Woodruff-Santos put forth that "disenchantment with the way teams were managed in the IWFL" was the Kings' motivation for beginning the new league. Lisa King told the author, "We wanted to make it more affordable for these teams to compete." King went on to tell the reporter that "she thought the IWFL was making it more expensive than necessary for players to form new teams." According to numbers quoted in the article, the WFA charged $2,000 for league fees, while the IWFL required a fee of between $2,000 and $6,700 annually. Woodruff-Santos went on to mention that since the WFA had become the largest league, the IWFL had dropped their prices. A key feature of the new league that would allow them to function at a more affordable price was their organization as a nonprofit entity.[13]

Woodruff-Santos wrote her Yahoo! Finance article some eight years after the WFA began. Jeff King provided a more contemporary account in a 2008 interview on the *Women's Football Talk* podcast hosted on *Blog Talk Radio*. In the interview with program host Barbara Coletta, Jeff King expanded on how the WFA would save owners and players money. On their motivation for forming the league, King stated, "We are opening up the doors to help the teams. They get 100 percent of what they can bring in and what they do. We don't have a franchise fee. We have a lower yearly league fee. We're promoting this thing for it to grow for our owners. We're not saying we don't want our owners to make money. We just want this thing to be affordable and more feasible." He expanded on that, saying, "If an owner owns a football team and they are pressured with twenty-five players, they can't really do what they want to do. They can't market it the way they want to do. They're behind the gun, so to speak. We are hoping that with our marketing efforts, and with our connections, and with our years involved with football, we can help these owners build their teams to a point where they have forty-five to fifty girls out in order to be a real situation. We believe that this is a good concept. It's a good idea, and once we start building it regionally, we can tie it together with other regions. It'll make travel a lot cheaper for teams. Because we are doing this at the nonprofit level, the whole overall picture is cheaper for teams. We really don't have it. When you want to build a football team in the WFA, we help you build a football team. We have all the same type of marketing packages, coaching packages, everything like that, but we don't charge a franchise fee. We charge a yearly league fee to be in, and this covers [the teams] 100 percent. Our owners are able to have tryouts when they want to have tryouts. They are able to structure a player fee where they want it to be. Maybe they want to charge their players, or maybe they want to act professional and have no charge at all. So I think it would be an owner's dream, and a player's dream, because it really lowers the cost, and I think that will up the level of participation."[14]

King also used his connections with the MLFA to encourage teams to join his new league. He told Coletta, "Say a team in New Mexico comes into the WFA. We [the MLFA] have fourteen teams throughout the state of New Mexico, so we can help in their efforts to find a stadium. We can help in their efforts to find a coach. So, I think the concept is great. I think it is awesome."[15]

At the time, the nonprofit status of the league did set the nascent WFA apart from its competitors. The Kings were on solid ground promoting that idea. In a larger sense, however, they were walking down a well-traveled path that other league owners had already been down. Each new league promised to fix the errors of the past and promised a bright new future. The Kings' statements followed the format of announcements made by Carter Turner of the AWFL, Catherine Masters of the NWFA, the Founding Mothers of the WPFL, and Laurie Frederick and Kezia Disney of the IWFL, who broke away from the existing structure to form new leagues. They saw an issue with an existing league and then created something new that addressed at least some of those problems. Optimism was the order of the day, and as exiting teams bought into that potentially bright future, they jumped from one league to another.

The Kings' vision was not confined to just the game in the United States. Jeff King also held out the possibility of an international component to the new league. "I was blessed to be on a few football teams that had their stuff together so well in Europe that they had women's football teams. In Austria I wasn't on a team that had a woman's team, but there were two really good teams that were in close proximity to where I lived, so I've actually got some experience being around the women's game. I think, just like the men, the women could actually get coaching jobs in Europe and get playing jobs in Europe. I've seen professional women being recruited for volleyball, for basketball, for handball from the States, so I really think that there's an avenue also for some of the European women to come to the States to play, and for some of the experienced women from the U.S. to go over and play in Europe also." He also posited the possibility that WFA champions might be able to play champions from the European leagues. "We just want to have as many opportunities as possible, and I think that'd be awesome, a great reward for our champions to play a champion from another country—that would be a huge media thing. And then, you never know, some of those coaches might get jobs. There could be players that want to come for a year or two, and relationships can be developed that can last a lifetime and just grow and help women's football grow even more."[16]

Much of what King envisioned became reality. During the league's first year in 2009, the New Orleans Blaze played a match against the Aguilas Regias of Monterrey, Mexico. The Blaze began play in the NWFA in 2002, under the name of the Spice, and had been among the teams from that defunct league that had jumped to the WFA in 2009. The Aguilas Regias, an American football team for women in Mexico, had only begun in 2007. The difference in experience did not translate into a lopsided score. The hometown Blaze won, but only by 12–0. As with the debut of the Mexican national team in Langley, Mexican athleticism helped make up for their lack of experience (see chapter 8). Fernanda Valdez, a safety for the Monterrey team, described the Mexicans' trepidation at playing the Americans. "We were the first team to go out to play in the United States. We were very nervous because they [were] a team that has been playing for years. They were much bigger, and they were also better trained than us." Despite the loss, Valdez saw the 15 August 2009 match as "something unique, a life experience that definitely marked the history of this sport in our country." The Aguilas Regias were slated to join the WFA, but as with many American teams, disputes between players and owners soured the relationship, and the team folded.[17]

There have also been North American players, including athletes from the WFA, who have traveled to Europe to play on teams there. During the summer of 2016, Lea Kaszas of the Indy Crash played with the Turku Trojans of the Suomen Amerikkalaisen Jalkapallon Liitto Ry (SAJL), the women's football federation in Finland. While she was there, her Trojans played the Hameenlinna Huskies, a team that included Tee Sanders and Courtney Powell, Kaszas's teammates from the Crash. Kaszas had a good season in Turku, leading the team to the championships, where they lost to the perennial powerhouse Helsinki Roosters.[18] Though Kaszas, in the second interview I did for this project, told me that she had "the best experience playing football of my life," the chance came with a cost. She had taught in the Indianapolis Public Schools (IPS) but had to give up her job to play in Finland. "I actually had to quit for going to Finland because I was leaving early and coming back too late. IPS starts really early, so I wouldn't have been able to play my last four games. So I sacrificed my job for football." When I talked with her, she had been planning to go back and play with the Roosters, but an Achilles injury prevented that.[19]

Today, there is something of a sisterhood of traveling shoulder pads that now exists globally. A good deal of the traveling involves European athletes playing across the borderless Eurozone, but quite a few Europeans have also come to the United States to play for teams in the various leagues, but mainly in the WFA. Teams have also started organizing international games, and Andrea Tooley, an American coach, was hired to coach the women's team of the Flash de La Courneuve in France.[20]

The final part of King's prediction came true in 2018, when the WFA DII champion New York Sharks played an international tournament in Great Britain. The first ever, and so far the only, Transatlantic Trophy tournament pitted the Sharks against the Birmingham Lions and the Helsinki Wolverines.[21]

Jeff King reached out to me via email on 16 February 2021 to mention that the league had formed an International Division. He wrote, "We are trying to help develop football around the world starting with camps and games played by the WFA Team United. We are also offering our platform to teams, leagues, and federations for support. Whatever gives more opportunities for women to play tackle football."[22]

As of March 2022 the WFA website has a WFA International page that has some of that information. It also includes a Player Exchange program and plans for a WFA International Bowl to be held at the Hall of Fame village in Canton during Championship Weekend.[23]

According to the WFA Facebook page, the league plans to send their Team United to play the champion of the Mexican Liga Femenil Football Americano Equipado on 17 September 2022 in Mexico City. Many of these plans had to be put on hold during the COVID pandemic, but the world seems to be opening up once again, and sisterhood may be back on the road.[24]

But let us return to the WFA's first season and their incredible growth. The league debuted with thirty-one teams in 2009. Eighteen of those teams had departed the failed NWFA, and they joined thirteen new teams to fill out the league roster. Team numbers climbed to fifty-nine for 2011 and then slipped back to forty during the 2015 season.[25] The league added two more teams in 2016, but during the off-season, they experienced another major growth spurt and added twenty-seven teams. Of those, eight were new teams, and four had returned from sojourns in the IWFL. Another ten long-time IWFL teams that had never played in the WFA also switched leagues. Rounding out the roster were three teams that came from the United States Women's Football League (USWFL), one team from the Ladies American Football League (LAFL), and one team from the New Mexico American Football League (NAMFL).[26] Teams come and go, and the league contracted to sixty-two teams in 2018 but saw an uptick to sixty-nine teams signed up for the 2019 season.[27]

Since 2016, the league adopted a divisional structure similar to the tier system that the IWFL used in its heyday.[28] In 2022 the WFA's Pro division included eleven teams, with three teams, the three-time WFA champion (2018, 2019, 2021) Boston Renegades, the Tampa Bay Inferno, and two-time champion D.C. Divas (2015, 2016), on the East Coast. There were two teams, the Arlington Impact and the 2017 champion Dallas Elite Mustangs (not to be confused with the Texas Elite Spartans of the WNFC), in Texas. Two more, the Cali War and the Portland Fighting Shockwave, were located on the West Coast. The

Midwest was represented by the Kansas City Titans, the Minnesota Vixen, the Pittsburgh Passion, and the St. Louis Slam. The Nevada Storm, two-time champions (2019 DIII and 2021 DII), also joined the top division. Division II was made up of thirteen teams spread from Miami to Seattle. Division III was the largest with twenty-nine teams representing most regions of the nation.[29] Following the COVID shake-out, the league has added a nine-team Developmental division that includes some new teams such as the Sioux Falls Snow Leopards, but also teams such as the Cincinnati Sizzle that were unable to play during the pandemic shutdowns.

Boston has dominated the top division, with five championships. After winning an IWFL title in 2010, the Boston team moved to the WFA, and the first two championships were won by the team under the name of the Boston Militia. They were the first team to win two WFA titles, the first in 2011 and the second in 2014.[30] The Renegades then had a short drought but have won the three championships from 2018 to 2021 (due to COVID, the league did not hold their 2019 season or championship). The Militia, which had also won an IWFL championship in 2010, was the descendent of the Massachusetts Mutiny and the Boston Rage that had joined to form the Militia in 2007.[31]

Team owner Ernie Boch Jr. took over the team then, and the billion-aire car dealership owner pumped money into it. He hired coaches and once even flew the team to the championship game on a private jet. Militia player Vicky Eddy told a reporter in 2015, "It was probably the closest that any of us got to feeling like a professional athlete."[32]

Though they had won the 2014 championship, Boch had grown disenchanted with the league, and reportedly some in the league were dissatisfied with him as well. His financial support caused "grumblings throughout the league that the Militia had bought their championships." Boch's concern was that the WFA was not scheduling enough games for his team. He told Sam Goresh, a reporter for the *Somerville Journal*, "They [the WFA] couldn't provide a schedule for me. They said, 'Hey Ernie, these teams aren't going to travel four–five hours and have their asses kicked by 50 points and then go home. They don't want to play you.'" Bloch told Goresh, "I said to myself that I have a decision—I can go on with the team and play at a lower level, or I can just call it a day. Leave on top and hope that someday they'll combine the leagues, and I'll be able to play at the level I want."[33]

When Bloch dropped out, the players were unsure that they would be able to continue. Eddy led the way and contacted former player Molly Goodwin, who brought in Erin Baumgartner and Mia Brickhouse to help organize the team. When Bloch departed, the Militia name went with him, so the players decided to call themselves the Renegades. According to Goodwin, some people from whom they sought help were concerned that they were trying to create a team brand too quickly. "The one thing I think they didn't understand was the girls don't care about the name, they don't care about the logo, they don't care about the rollout. All they want to do is play football."[34]

That was no doubt true, but when teams and leagues are desirous of forming some sort of a relationship with the NFL, the example of the Renegades might not be the way to go. Korpacz and the New England Storm did have something of a relationship with the New England Patriots, but then she and her team were expelled from the WPFL. The Mutiny and the Rage combined to form the Militia, which in turn folded after seven years but became the Renegades. Some players such as quarterback Allison Cahill, for instance, played for the Storm, Mutiny, Militia, and Renegades, so some of the players were the same, but the team for which she played changed names several times.

The same fluidity in team names, if not necessarily in player personnel, continues. As discussed in the previous chapter, the New York Sharks, a team that played its first game in 1999, changed ownership in 2018 and became the New York Wolves in 2019. The St. Louis Slam won the first WFA championship in 2009, then won two more Division II championships in 2016 and 2017, but did not play in 2018. The team was back for the 2021 season, but the Chicago Force was not—it folded after owner Linda Bache retired the name in 2017, and the second city remains without a team. First division WFL teams such as the Pittsburgh Passion (2003–present) and the D.C. Divas (2001–present) seem to be stable, but both teams have played in three leagues during their history.

The case could be made that the core cast of players remained the same, even though their organization changed, and so women's interest in playing football in New England, or New York, or St. Louis was stable. If the NFL would provide funding, then stability in team names would likely follow. That was what a group of women's football players wearing jerseys from the Divas, Sharks, the Philadelphia Phantomz, and the New York Knockouts argued during the Women's March on 19 January 2019. Around twenty women from those teams gathered outside of NFL headquarters in New York City to demand the creation of a Women's National Football League. Armed with the hash tag #WhenWNFL, the women also organized a Change.org petition that made the following demands:

The NFL form an eight-team WNFL by 2020
The NFL and the NFLPA support the league with a grant of $20 million per year
All NFL teams adopt a women's football team in their area
USA Football pay women on the national team in line with their male counterparts

By March 2022, 2,275 had signed.[35]

If the NFL responded to the press conference that accompanied the demonstration, it was well concealed. Perhaps one quasi response took place during Super Bowl LIII, when a commercial sponsored by the league featured current and retired players raising mayhem when a symbolic football placed atop a cake hit the floor, which triggered the athletes' "Fumble!" response. At the end of the commercial, the ball flew into the air and landed in the hands of Sam Gordon of the Utah Girls Football League. Dressed in a red evening gown, she caught it, and when Richard Sherman (defensive back, San Francisco 49ers) asked her for it, she replied, "You want this? Come and get it!" Then she spun around him and pitched it to Saquon Barkley (running back, New York Giants). The message, according to Brent Gordon, Sam's father, was to "show a century of NFL history, pivoting to the end to,

'What's the future going to be like?'"[36] According to the commercial, at least, the future would include women.

Despite that possible response, which was not actually a response but had been planned for months, no discernable movement by the NFL to accept the demands was evident. The fluid or, less charitably, the chaotic nature of the ownership in women's football was most likely a reason that the league was not rushing to fund a women's league. The WNBA model to which women's football players often point as an example was not really germane. When the NBA created the league, there was only one established women's basketball league, the also newly established American Basketball League, so they did not have to deal with a multitude of team owners or existing teams. The NFL already has sufficient billionaire-owner on billionaire-owner disputes to be unlikely to want to add to their public relations issues by taking over some women's football teams.

Before the 2019 season began, there were somewhere around one hundred women's teams playing in the United States. Which teams would the NFL fund, and who would be left out? If the NFL followed the Change.org petition and created an eight-team WNFL, what would the women who were left out have to say about it? In short, Twitter would explode, as it is in the habit of doing. It is ironic, but the freedom and success that women have had in playing football also probably means that they will have to continue paying for that opportunity.

Elizabeth Jenkins, the chief administrative officer for the Women's National Football Conference and center for the Texas Elite Spartans, had a different view from the protesting players. She told me, "I saw some of the publicity around the protesting, and I'm not going to speak to you-know-who chooses to do that or not do that. I just don't think that's the right way to do it. If you want to go and demand that they give something to women's football. Why? What do you mean you're going to demand? How do you demand? For me that's like that era we're in now—the millennials—where there's this huge entitlement thing. So you're owed something? Nobody's entitled to anything. If you want it, go fucking bust your ass for it, and go get it. I'm not going to go and demand from the NFL that they give 1 percent of their players' salaries and give it to a women's league. Why? For what? What have you proven as a women's league that you can even do? What have you proven? You've proven that you can get eighty teams to sign up? What does that do for the sport? Nothing. So what we are doing is we're putting a product together that we can then go out and we can get buy-in, not demand from the NFL, but we can get buy-in from them one day, and maybe it's three years from now, maybe it's five, maybe it's ten years from now. Maybe they say, 'Wow! We've seen what you guys have really done. You know what? Let's make this thing a WNFL.'"[37]

The NFL's public relations problems concerning treatment of women, which were exacerbated when Patriots owner Robert Kraft was charged with soliciting prostitution in Palm Beach County, Florida, in early 2019, might provide some motivation for the league to make a symbolic move that would benefit women's football.[38] Odessa "OJ" Jenkins, then the owner of the Dallas Elite of the WFA, suggested something similar in a 2017 article about the New York Sharks. *Buzz-Feed*'s Alex Wong wrote:

Odessa Jenkins, the first-year owner of the Dallas Elite of the Women's Football Alliance, believes—especially given the NFL's public perception problem stemming from its mishandling suspensions related to the domestic violence cases of Ray Rice and Greg Hardy—that the league would benefit from partnering with women's football. "We're mothers," she says. "We're sisters. We're the consumers. We buy their apparel, we buy our husbands and sons their NFL tickets. The angle that football empowers girls is undeniable. If the NFL is the key that opens that door to more people, that would say a lot."[39]

Kraft already funds the Kraft Family Football League in Israel, so the idea might not be too far-fetched that he would sponsor a women's football team or league.[40] The Patriots, under previous ownership, had once formed a relationship with the New England Storm. What affect Kraft's legal troubles or the NFL's continuing efforts to counter the narrative that they do not care about women is unclear, but this moment perhaps represents an opening for league support of women's football. Kraft further recognized the Renegades in 2021, when he offered the Patriots' team plane to fly the women's team to Canton for the championships.

The Renegades did get some measure of support from the Patriots during their 2018 championship game against the Los Angeles Warriors, when Donna Wilkinson and Brian Sweeney, the game announcers, mentioned that it had been "confirmed" that the Patriots had tweeted, "Go Renegades!" and so were "on Boston's bandwagon." Sweeney hoped that this presaged some "meaningful relationship" with the NFL team. Wilkinson agreed, saying, "Any meaningful relationship any of our teams can get going with the NFL is going to be important to building the future of this sport."[41] That the game, which the Renegades won 42–18 over the Warriors, was being televised on ESPN3 was a step forward for Lisa King (league/team owner and wide receiver for the Warriors) and the WFA.

They also received recognition from a source that no other women's football team had ever had. According to Adrienne Smith on Gridiron Queendom, her site devoted to women's football, "On November 14–15, 2014, the Boston Militia made history by becoming the first women's football team to receive an invitation to the White House."[42] The YouTube video features footage of the athletes in the capital and contained quotes from several of the players who were active for their championships. Cahill, the team's quarterback, and the first woman quarterback to lead her team to one hundred victories in 2016, focused primarily on that winning, for which they were being honored.[43] She told the videographer, "The goal is always the same, I think. As long as we have this core group, it will be a championship focus. I think we've done a good job. Starting in January, and working on getting better, practice by practice, month by month, and kind of building momentum as we go, and taking it one game at a time. But, again, we all know that the end goal is to win a championship."[44]

Running back Whitney Zelee in 2013 became the second woman to rush for more than 2,000 yards in a season, finishing with 2,832 (first was LaKeisha Johnson of the Pensacola Power, who rushed for 2,725 yards in 2008).[45] She reflected on what it meant that a women's football team had been invited to the White House: "It's just a big deal that our nation's capital, the people in our nation's capital, they recognize the importance of what we do, and they think it is special enough to honor us."[46]

Smith, a Renegades wide receiver, mentioned the athletes' importance as path breakers. "I think as women, we're showing that we are really good role models, and that we're able to accomplish great achievements in what is known as a male-dominated sport. It was awesome to be recognized for that."[47] Smith's Gridiron Queendom organization posted the video, so it is likely that she also put it together, or at least directed the effort. She first thought of that name as the title for a film about Team USA's 2013 victory in the International Federation of American Football Women's World Championship that was held in Vantaa, Finland. She initiated the process of creating the project, but when the name of the film was eventually changed to *Tackle Girls*, Smith took "Gridiron Queendom" as the name of her organization that seeks to promote girls and women playing football.[48] In addition to her other pursuits, Smith also branched out into old-school gaming and created "a football-themed card game" called Blitz Champz.[49]

The Renegades have also been relatively active in the realization of WFA cofounder Jeff King's vision of the global sisterhood of women's football. Sarah Viola, a Belgian woman who played wide receiver for the Molosses de Asnieres-sur-Seine in France, came across the Atlantic and played for the Renegades during their first season under that name in 2015. In her first game against the Central Maryland Seahawks she caught a 38-yard pass at the end of the game but was stopped just short of the goal line.[50]

Viola was no stranger to playing football in the United States. She attended the Women's World Games (WWG) operated by USA Football to teach the finer skills of the game to American and international players. This gave her the idea of attempting to play for an American team. She told me that after attending the WWG she had the dream of playing in the United States. "I was so enthusiastic about playing with women, and in the years after [the WWG] I was, like, I want to play football in the U.S. It was a dream." She contacted Adrienne Smith, who helped her land a spot on the team. She enjoyed her experience: "That was very cool. They were very friendly . . . I'm very thankful about that. They taught me a lot about football."[51]

Noriko Kokura, who played on men's teams in Japan, began playing for the Militia in 2014 and made the transition to the Renegades the next year. From Tottori Prefecture, in a 2011 *Japan Times* article, Kokura told reporter Kaz Nagatsuka that watching Super Bowl XXXII had convinced her not to commit suicide. As a young girl, she had "suffered from multiple diseases" and had decided to end that suffering. But watching Terrell Davis of the Broncos interact with his teammates changed her mind. From that point on, she focused on becoming a professional football player in the United States. She played running back and defensive end on the men's team at Shimane University and then got her chance to play in America.[52] In 2008 she became a Sacramento Raven and played there from 2008 to 2013. In 2014 she joined the Militia and then transitioned to the Renegades for the 2015 season. She had told Nagatsuka that she wanted to win a championship in women's football, and she accomplished this with the Militia during their 2014 championship season.[53]

Elisa De Santis, the quarterback of the Molosses, also attempted to play for the Renegades in 2018, but she was unable to find a way to stay in the United States without being able to work. As mentioned in the introduction, De Santis had some experience playing as an expat. She played for an Italian flag football team as well. She told me that the team paid for her flight to Italy, so in addition to De Santis finding a novel chance to play football, it was perhaps an example of sport tourism.[54]

During the 2019 and 2021 championships, the Renegades had the services of Ruth Matta, a star running back for the Birmingham Lions and the Great Britain Lions national team. In 2019 Matta rushed for 174 yards on thirty-two carries, added another 95 yards on three catches, and scored three touchdowns to earn the Most Valuable Player award. She scored another touchdown while rushing for 80 yards on seventeen carries and caught three passes for 30 yards as she helped Boston finish their three-peat and become the first WFA team to do so.[55]

The Renegades were not the only team to win multiple WFA championships nor the only team to have international players. Until the Renegades won back-to-back championships in 2018 and 2019, the D.C. Divas had been the only team to accomplish that feat, winning the title in 2015 and 2016. They nearly had the chance for a three-peat but lost 27–24 to the Renegades in the second round of the 2017 playoffs. The Divas, who finished the regular season with a 6-4 record, led the 8-0 Renegades at half and maintained that lead until Renegades quarterback Cahill hit Chante Bonds from 25 yards out for the touchdown. The Divas had a chance for a last second field goal, but the attempt failed.[56]

According to the team's "History" page, the Divas began in 2000 and were one of the original teams in Catherine Master's National Women's Football Association. Who owned the team that year is unclear, but during their second season Leah Fahringer and Kelly George took over ownership duties until 2004, when Paul Hamlin bought the franchise. During their six years in the NWFA, the Divas made the playoffs four times, losing to the Detroit Demolition twice. They won their first and only NWFA championship in 2006, when they capped an undefeated 11-0 season by defeating the Oklahoma Lightning 28–7. After their championship, the Divas led the wave of teams leaving the NWFA for the IWFL. In that league the D.C. team qualified for the playoffs in three of the four years they spent there, and appeared in the 2009 final, where they lost to the Kansas City Tribe 18–21. They jumped to the WFA in 2011 and for the next four years lost to the Militia in the playoffs. They turned the tables and defeated the Renegades twice during their 12-0 2015 season and defeated the Dallas Elite 30–26 for their first WFA championship. The Divas lost their first game of the 2016 season to the Elite but came back to qualify for the playoffs, and once again they defeated the Texans in the final 28–26. Over their first eighteen seasons, all under the same name, the Divas won 133 games and lost 43.[57]

The Divas have also imported or welcomed international players. Tea Törmänen began playing football in Helsinki, Finland, and played there for the Helsinki Demons from 2007 to 2009. She also played for the Finnish National Team in the 2010 and 2013 IFAF Women's World Championship. Törmänen, a linebacker, played for the Divas during the 2010 and 2011 seasons. She was on two championship teams with the Demons but was on the Divas teams that lost to the Militia in the playoffs.[58]

After the Divas' 2016 championship, President Obama invited the team to visit the White House to honor their accomplishment. Allyson Hamlin, the longtime quarterback of the Divas and the first woman (or man) in Washington DC football history to throw two hundred touchdown passes, posted on Facebook: "Thirty years ago I was the only girl on every team and dreaming of a moment like this was inconceivable. Yet here we are. President Obama, you gave my team, the 2015 & 2016 WFA National Champion D.C. Divas, a feeling we fight for daily . . . Validation. Validation that a woman's tackle football team is worthy enough to be invited to the White House and honored by the President of the United States."[59]

Divas players might have been part of the demonstration demanding that the NFL sponsor teams, but the league has already brought aboard three of their athletes as coaching interns. Although she only played in two games during the 2017 season with the Divas, Stephanie Jackson parlayed her playing background and her experience at the WWG to earn an internship with the Minnesota Vikings. She told *Sports Illustrated*'s Jenny Vrentas that she had met Samantha Rapaport at the WWG and then again at the Women's Career Forum that the NFL executive had organized for the league. Rapaport, who helped create the WWG while working for USA Football and who is now the director of football development for the NFL, put Jackson in touch with Anne Doepner, the Vikings' director of football administration. Jackson initially interned for Doepner, and then she worked with the team's legal team, before finishing up with the scouting department.[60]

Two other players with longer careers with the Divas became interns with the New York Jets. The team posted on their Facebook page that

Callie Brownson and Rachel Huhn would be scouting interns for the Jets in 2017.[61] Huhn has played in the Divas offensive line since 2008, and wide receiver Brownson joined the team two years later.[62]

The Jets had a long history of hiring women in their scouting department. Connie Carberg began working for the Jets as a secretary and then transitioned into the scouting department, where she worked from 1976 to 1980. The highlight of her career, which she detailed in *X's and O's Don't Mean I Love You*, a 2017 book written about her life with Elizabeth Meinecke, was that she helped convince the Jets to draft defensive lineman Mark Gastineau in 1979.[63]

Brownson, in addition to playing on the two Divas WFA championship teams, also played on the USA National Team in the WWC in 2010 and 2013. Her background playing and serving as an NFL scouting intern also earned her a spot as a coaching intern with Dartmouth College during the 2018 preseason. She performed well enough in that role that the college kept her on as their offensive quality control coach for the regular season.[64] After a coaching internship with the Buffalo Bills in 2019, the Cleveland Browns hired her full-time as the chief of staff for head coach Kevin Stefanski.[65] On 29 November 2020 she became the first female position coach in the NFL, when Stefanski put her in charge of coaching tight ends during the Browns' game against the Jacksonville Jaguars.[66] To commemorate that groundbreaking event, the sideline jacket that Brownson wore that day, along with an autographed game ball, was placed on display at the Pro Football Hall of Fame in Canton, Ohio.[67] In 2022 Brownson also became assistant wide receivers coach.[68]

As discussed in previous chapters, women's football has attracted the attention of documentary makers. The Divas 2015 season was the subject of *Victorious*, a film directed by Robert Mac. The trailer, which was available on Vimeo, showed various scenes from that season, including Hamlin leading a team cheer and several unnamed players talking about the team. There was game action of the Divas playing the Chicago Force, the Columbus Comets, and the Boston Renegades. One of the interview subjects, defensive back Elini Kotsis (presumably, since no names are listed), delivered the pro forma denunciation of the LFL. "I totally believe the Lingerie League is degrading to women. It is basically soft porn on a football field."[69] That quote seemed a bit off topic, but it was likely included since the LFL was the most visible women's football league, and that angers women who play the traditional game.

As is the case with *Playing with Rage*, discussed in chapter 2, *Victorious* seems to be stuck in documentary limbo. A now closed Indiegogo crowd-funding page stated, "This film is not finished!! We need your help. Post production is now required. But if the DC Divas have taught us anything, it's that you play your heart out 'til the very last second of the fourth quarter. So we're taking a page from their playbook and launching another campaign in the hope that you'll be able to help us score one more touchdown and help us finish our documentary." The campaign hoped to raise at least $50,000 to complete "editing, graphics, animation, and final color correction." As of the end of the fundraising campaign, 118 donors had pledged $12,340, which was below their "minimum goal" of $40,000.[70]

The trailer was well done, and the full documentary would have been interesting to see, but it seems that projects such as *Playing with Rage* and *Victorious* suffer from the same problem as women's football—there are just not enough people interested in the films, or the game. This must be supremely difficult for the athletes, who have poured their hearts and souls into the game. It is also likely is one of the reasons that women playing full-kitted football resent the LFL (see chapter 5), a league that has garnered so much attention.

Joining the Renegades and Divas in the WFA championship winner column were the St. Louis Slam (2009), the Lone Star Mustangs (2010), the San Diego Surge (2012), the Chicago Force (2013), and the Dallas Elite (2017). The Slam, as mentioned above, took the 2018 season off but came back to play—and to win another DII championship—in 2019.[71] The Mustangs folded after the 2013 season, but some of their players, such as 2010 WFA MVP Odessa Jenkins, migrated to the Dallas Diamonds and then moved on to the Dallas Elite.

Jenkins, along with many of her teammates, exited the Elite to form the Texas Elite Spartans of the IWFL in 2018, which became the marquee team in the new Women's National Football Conference in 2019, after she was instrumental in forming the league. The Surge ownership contemplated folding in 2018 but decided instead to play in the IWFL. They joined the Elite Spartans and other IWFL teams in leaving the league at midseason and played in the WNFC in 2019 before calling it quits. The Force ceased operations after their semifinal loss in 2017.

At the time, the future for the Slam and the Surge seemed a bit precarious. The Slam had to resume operations after a year's absence; the Surge ownership reportedly considered folding once, and in 2019 they were without the services of their top offensive weapon, Melissa Gallegos, who threw for more than 12,000 yards before retiring after the 2018 season.[72] The Elite were weakened by the schism when Jenkins left the team, and the breakup was fairly messy.[73] They only managed a 4-4 season in 2019.[74] The Mustangs, Surge, and Force are no longer teams, although some of their players are still in the game. The lack of staying power among teams in Division I is certainly a problem for the WFA.

Competitive imbalance is another issue, not only for the WFA but for all of women's football. In 2018 all nine of the Division I teams posted winning records, from the 9-0 Los Angeles Warriors to the 5-3 Dallas Elite.[75] The eventual winner, the Renegades, had a 6-2 regular season record, but they beat the undefeated Warriors in a game that was not as close as the 42–18 score indicated (see more about the 2018 season in the postscript). The quality of athletes and coaching staffs vary considerably across the league. Given the physical distances between the Portland Fighting Shockwave and the Divas, or the Renegades and the Warriors, they do not meet in the regular season. Instead, teams must fill out their schedules with games against Division II and III teams. These teams have fewer players and overall resources. Due to injuries, or the potential for injuries, these smaller teams sometimes must forfeit games.

Don Harrold, who makes football cards for WFA players, did an analysis of the results through the first fifty-four games of the 2018 season. He found that in 61.11 percent of the games, the winning teams scored an average of more than 30 points, while the losers either forfeited or did not score. He argued that this was not good for fans of the losing teams or for the league.[76] He posted his results on Facebook and asked his friends why this was so. The replies boiled down to either forming one super league or not allowing teams with few players and little support to have teams. Neither option seems realistic.

The one league idea is as old as women's football. Oscar Lopez, of *Gridiron Beauties*, posited a league based on the somewhat successful model of the National Women's Hockey League. A question that he left unanswered was what would happen to the other teams that are left out of the super league? When the mass migration of IWFL teams to the WFA happened in 2011, owners such as Chicago's Linda Bache saw it as a first step in forming such a super league, but nothing came of that. The question of who would stop women from forming their own team was also problematical. Given that several leagues exist, if a team could not find a place in one, they could do so in another.

According to the article by Mandi Woodruff-Santos for Yahoo! Finance discussed in chapter 3, talk of a merger between the IWFL and the WFA "briefly gained momentum in 2014 but sputtered when IWFL chief operating officer Keisha Disney declined to move forward." Neither Disney nor Laurie Frederick, who founded the league, replied to interview requests from Woodruff. According to her story, the WFA's Lisa King thought that a merger would a good thing. "It would be a great thing for women's football if it were to happen. It would decrease costs for the teams . . . and it just makes perfect sense." King, however, also admitted, "There's no love lost between the two leagues."[77]

Had the four Best of the West teams that left the IWFL in 2018 joined the WFA, the dream of the one league might have come closer to reality. That did not happen, however, and those teams instead formed the nucleus of the new WNFC. Until someone, or a group of people, comes along with several million dollars, there is simply no reason for the various leagues to merge. They have no financial motivation to do so. Why give up control, as at least one league director must in a merger, if it was not a lucrative proposition?

In Division II there were several teams that have exhibited long-term stability. The Minnesota Vixen has been in existence since women's football reappeared in 1999. They were one of the two teams created to take part in the barnstorming tour, and they have continued to play in a variety of leagues since then. Michele Braun told me that she and the team had played in the "WPFL, the NWFA, the IWFL, and the WFA."[78] Laura Brown and her husband James took over team ownership in 2014. She told me that while she was playing, she wanted to use her business background to help out the team that was owned at that time by former players Jodi Wallin and Monica Castaldi. "At first, I was thinking that I would help out here and there with a fundraiser or alleviate a little bit of pressure, that is, you know, on the current owners. I didn't really know at the time when I approached them, but they had been looking for an exit strategy. They had been running the team for several years, and they themselves were no longer playing."[79] According to Brown, she was "at least the fifth owner" of the Vixen. Carter Turner and Terry Sullivan were the original owners when they created the team as part of the barnstorming tour in 1999.

That the Vixen have continued under their original name is a bit unusual for women's football teams. The norm seems to be that the team name disappears when ownership changes, which was the case with the New York Sharks, whose owner Andra Douglass retired the name when she sold the team. The Sharks, one of the teams the Vixen played during their 1999 season, became the Wolves in 2019.[80]

When asked about retaining their original name, Brown told me, "The Vixen pride themselves on being able to continue the team even with different owners. Besides being one of the original teams it is one of the unique aspects of the team that has made it successful. As the current owner, I know the Vixen will continue on after me."[81] So while teams such as the Renegades have players like Cahill who have played since 2003, she has done so for four teams, three of which were essentially the same team playing under different names.[82]

Stability often resulted in success on the field. The Vixen earned a spot in the playoffs for their various leagues ten times and appeared in the finals twice, losing both. They lost to the Utah Falconz in the 2016 IWFL championship game and to the Sharks in the 2018 WFA championship. There have been tough seasons as well, and the team's win-loss record is only 79-76, but the team has continued under its original name.[83]

Brown told me in 2018: "Currently, we have fifty-eight on our roster. We are pretty successful, for tryouts we usually have between one hundred to two hundred women that come for the tryouts every year. Some of those women are coming because they just want a taste of football. They want to come and see what the tryouts are about. They might not have a strong interest in playing, some of them are curious, just dipping their toes in the water a little bit. Some of them get hooked."[84] Over the years the number of Vixens who have previous football experience has been growing slowly. Brown stated: "My first couple years with the team, I don't know if we had anybody on the team that had played actually during their youth or in high school. But now I would say, off the top of my head, I can probably think of five people that are on our roster that either played in youth and dropped out in high school or actually even played in high school. So we are starting to see a larger number. And in addition to that, up in Minnesota we have a pretty decent flag football program. So we have actually had some women who had some flag football experience." With a 37-11 record since Brown assumed the ownership, the team seemed to be on a good path.[85]

I had the chance to see the Vixen play against a good Detroit Dark Angels team on 28 April 2018 in Detroit. Both teams came into the game undefeated. The Vixen had defeated the Madison Blaze 46-0, the Wisconsin Dragons 40-6, and the Kansas City Titans 33-25. The Dark Angels, who were the descendants of the Demolition, beat the Columbus Comets 28-22 and the Cincinnati Sizzle 34-0. The spring weather was still cool, falling to cold when the sun went down, and so fewer than one hundred fans were scattered across the stands of Southfield Lathrup High School. After a scoreless first quarter, the Vixen scored 22 straight points in the second. Leading rusher Emilie Halle, who also qualified for the Canadian National Team in 2017, was on the injured list for the game, and the Dark Angles offense never clicked. They did manage to score a fourth-quarter touchdown to make the final 22-6 Vixen.

The score was a bit lopsided, and the weather cold, but at no point did I consider leaving early. The teams were evenly matched—both teams had winning records in 2018. The difference between the Dark Angels' 5-3 record and the Vixen's 9-2 was 16 points that night. There were talented players on both sides and few serious injuries. The action on the field was interesting with crisp tackling and flashes of good offense. This was not one of the games that Harrold was decrying, and if 60 percent of the WFA games were like this one, as was the Reign-Comet game that opened the chapter, the league would perhaps garner more favorable attention.

As mentioned above, the Comets have been active since 2003, and since 2004 under the Comets name. They had been another of the stable teams in the WFA. Donna Ford owned the team, at the time named the Flames, but when she sold it after the initial season, new owners Lori Davis and Shirley Miller changed the name to the Comets.

Ironically, the first Comet I interviewed was while I attended the WWG in Louisiana. After hearing me talk to another athlete, Carolyn O'Leary asked me if I was the guy who did interviews of women playing football. At the end of our interview, she invited me to come watch a Comet practice, and I took her up on the offer.

Current owner and head coach Hank Patterson bought the team in 2010 from Davis and Miller. Patterson had coached the team since 2003, but as with many other male coaches of women's teams, it took some pushing to convince him to take the position. Following a 10 March 2018 preseason practice session, Patterson recounted his thoughts when he was contacted to coach the team. He received the call on a Friday night, and when the caller asked, "Hey man, you feel like coaching a women's football team?" he thought that he was being pranked and hung up. He hung up on the second call as well, telling the caller, "Stop calling me at home!" During the third call, before he could hang up again, he was asked to visit the team's website so he would see that women's football was real. It may have been the website of the NWFA, the Comets' first league, since Patterson remembered thinking to himself, "My God! They're in every major city across America." He assembled a coaching group made up of his brother, Mike, and other men with whom he had previously coached. He, like others before him, was hooked when he met the players. He told me that coaching the team has been a learning experience: "The greatest thing I learned was what women deal with in life. I mean, I could tell you, 'Run hard, run fast,' but I started learning other things. A lady going to work with bruising on her arm—you and I go to work with bruising on our arm, 'Hey man, what's happening—Ah, you know.' But if women go there, they think something's happening at home, and I never thought of that. So then my eyes started seeing other things. I've had people on my teams who've had two degrees, working at a menial job. Stuff like that. My passion for the game, and for them, grew even greater, just because of that. I'm seeing their struggle, and they were doing things for me that are not in the norm at the time, so I go, 'Man. I'm going to go with this.'"[86]

The year he assumed the ownership, the Comets went all the way to the WFA championship game, where they lost 12–16 to the Lone Star Mustangs. They had made the playoffs in all but their first season and had earned a championship game appearance, but they lost to Pittsburgh 0–32 in the 2007 NWFA final. Since 2010 they have qualified for the WFA playoffs four times in eight years. During the 2018 postseason, they defeated the Philly Phantomz 22–14 but fell to the eventual champion Sharks 55–36. Their 7-3 record in 2018 was very good, considering that fifteen players had retired after the 2017 season.[87]

I also watched them play the Pittsburgh Passion in 2018. The Passion was the superior team, but the Comets only led 8-7 at the end of the first quarter. The Passion stepped on the gas in the second quarter, scored 22 unanswered points to lead 29-8 at half, and from there cruised to a 56-8 win. The Comets were soundly defeated, but the Passion never did find an answer for the holes that the Columbus team opened for 2016 All-American running back Carrie Hall, who gained 139 yards on thirty-five carries against Pittsburgh. Hall also accounted for all of the Comets' points that night.[88]

The Passion is another of the Division II teams that have been in existence for nearly two decades. They, like the Comets, began play in 2003 with the NWFA and played there until 2007. They went undefeated and beat the Comets to win the 2007 NWFA championship, but they left for the IWFL in 2008. After three seasons with that league, the Passion returned to the WFA for another three-year stint. In 2014 and 2015 the Pittsburgh team bounced back to the IWFL and won the league's national championship both years. The Passion rejoined the WFA in 2016 and has played there since.[89]

Why the team has been so willing to switch leagues is difficult to piece together from the extant records. After the Passion won their 2007 NWFA championship, they switched to the IWFL for the next season. Team co-owner and head coach Teresa Conn told Jody DiPerna of the *Pittsburgh City Paper* that she made the switch in order to play against better competition. "People want to see competitive football. We could have stayed in the NWFA . . . but for us, with the talent in our region, this is a greater challenge. And I believe that is what people want to see."[90] They dominated the IWFL in the 2014 and 2015 seasons, in which they did not lose a single game. The only close games they had over that stretch were two 7-point victories over the New York Sharks in 2015 and a 4-point victory over the Utah Falconz in the 2015 IWFL Championship Game.[91] The rest of the games were largely blowouts, so perhaps finding better competition motivated their return to the WFA. Their win-loss record since 2003 was 117-35, and since returning to the WFA they have faced stiffer competition. They won seven games each season from 2016 to 2018, but lost three games to the Renegades, Divas, and Force in 2016 and 2017. In 2018 they defeated the Divas and the Renegades in the regular season, before losing the rematch against the Renegades in the playoffs.[92]

Conn began playing for the Passion in its first season when she was thirty eight years old. As a player, she had to endure a period during which she broke both ankles, one at a time, and then her shoulder. In 2005 Conn bought the team from the original owner and currently co-owns the team with former Pittsburgh Steelers star running back Franco Harris.[93]

The Passion has had solid backing in football-crazy Pittsburgh. According to their website, their crowds lead the National League of the WFA's Division I in game day attendance, they have been given a permanent display in the Heinz History Center, which is affiliated with the Smithsonian, and they have been awarded a "Key to the City" by the Pittsburgh City Council. Conn was inducted into the Minor Pro Football Hall of Fame, and the team was honored as "Pittsburgh's Best of the Best" in a ceremony that took place at Heinz Field, the home of the Steelers, where the Passion played a 2012 game. They also give back to the community and raise the team's visibility by "serving over 300 charitable events per year." They also have had a documentary made about them by Jennifer Yee.[94] Like many of these films, any extant copies must be in private hands. There is a copy for sale on Amazon.com, but the asking price is $182.47, so it will probably not get many offers.[95] Anecdotally, when I began this project, I asked Caitlin Kegley, a former student who was from Pittsburgh, if she had heard of the Passion, and she told me that she had. It is fairly unusual for anyone who is not a player to have heard of women's football, let alone a specific team, so that is some confirmation of what the team has on their page.[96]

I had the chance to watch the Passion twice in 2018. The first was the game against the Comets discussed above, and the second was a 19 May game against the Toledo Reign. Once again, the Passion was clearly the superior team, and they easily won the game 54-7. The Passion offense, which had been slow to start against the Comets, was hitting on all cylinders. The passing game, with 2017 world champion quarterback Lisa Horton back on the field (she did not play in Columbus), was particularly impressive. The only thing that stood a chance of stopping the Passion that night was a violent thunderstorm that halted play for about an hour.

After the Columbus game, Horton told me about her team. "I am really blessed and fortunate to have the team that we have. It's football, but it's also our best friends. We go to each other's parties and funerals and weddings, and it's really a special group, and it starts with our ownership, Teresa Conn. She just planted the seed that will grow and continue to grow." Though there was some question if the Passion would come back after missing the 2020 and 2021 seasons, the team's social media page has announced 2022 tryouts.[97]

The Passion was not the only team that has had owners or co-owners from the NFL. The Division III Cincinnati Sizzle was originally owned by former Cincinnati Bengals running back Ickey Woods. The Sizzle began play in 2005 with the NWFA and then joined the WFA in 2009. Cincinnati joined the United States Women's Football League (USWFL) in 2015 and remained there for two years, winning the USWFL championship by defeating the New England Nightmare 30-6. After that championship season, the Sizzle returned to the WFA.[98] Woods sold the team in 2018 to Steve Sherman, a local entrepreneur.[99]

Aside from their 2015 championship season, the Sizzle has not typically been a powerful team in the WFA's Division III. They have only won 31 games and lost 68.[100] The team posted a 4-4 regular season record in 2018 but made the playoffs, where they lost to the Toledo Reign 28-8.[101] Their 2018 website page listing the players contained twenty-seven athletes, but at their first game of the 2018 season against the Music City Mizfits (Nashville), they only had eighteen present. They won that game 16-6 with the help of Tamar Fennell's rushing performance. Fennell was a somewhat unique WFA athlete, in that she also played defensive back for the Chicago Bliss of the Legends Football League. Her dual role meant that she could not play every game for both teams, and she missed the Sizzle's second game with the Detroit Dark Angels, in which Cincinnati was shut out.[102]

Rounding out the Ohio teams, the Cleveland Fusion is another fairly stable team. They are the oldest continuously playing team in the state. They began playing in 2002 in the NWFA and were one of several teams that joined the WFA in 2009 when the older league folded after the 2008 season. As of 2018 the Fusion had a 91-61 record. The team qualified for the playoffs four times in the NWFA and six times in the WFA. The 2018 season was a difficult one for the Fusion. They forfeited their first two games with the Passion and the Renegades. They did play against the Comets in their third scheduled game. Coach Patterson of the Comets told me that this was the team he particularly wanted to beat in the "Battle of Ohio," and he accomplished that goal.[103]

The 5 May 2018 game at the Comets' home field at Grove City Christian School was much closer than the Passion game. The Fusion defense would also face problems in containing Carrie Hall, and the visitors lost a close game 6–16. The Fusion lost to the Dark Angels and the Reign before playing the Comets again. In a similar result, the Comets defeated the Fusion 16–0. The Fusion's sole win came in the second game they actually played, when they defeated the Grand Rapids Tidal Waves 42–0. The team had taken care of whatever problems plagued them at the start of the season and did play Pittsburgh in the final game, capping off a 1-7 season losing to the Passion 61–0.[104]

There have obviously been many other teams that have played in the WFA. Some have played for around a decade, and some are relatively recent additions to the league. There is no way that all WFA teams can have their history chronicled in a work such as this, and so teams that have had success have been featured, along with teams whose players I have interviewed.

One of those is the Tampa Bay Inferno, which has been in existence since 2010. The team began as the Tampa Bay Pirates in the WFA and changed its name to the Inferno in 2012. According to Jennifer Moody, a former wide receiver for the Passion and the current Inferno owner, the Pirates were "a very small team. Maybe fifteen or sixteen athletes who were struggling for a little bit of leadership and growth. She [a work friend who had played] found out about the organization I came from and said why don't you become a part of this. I knew my playing days were done, but I felt I could give back in other ways."[105]

At the practice I saw while interviewing players, there was no sign of a very small team struggling for leadership. Around forty athletes were going through drills under the direction of a seven-member coaching staff. Moody brought professional organization such as she had known while playing with the Passion, and it had paid off on the field.

While I was in Tampa reading AP U.S. history exams in 2017 and 2018, I had the chance to see the Division II Inferno play two games. The first was against the Division III Orlando Anarchy on 3 June 2017. Despite Anarchy quarterback Chandice Hunter's accurate passing, the Inferno defense was able to bar the end zone and won the game easily 52–3.

Perhaps the Anarchy, which finished 6–2 and went deep into the playoffs in 2017, had other things on their mind that week, since the team had been dealing with considerable adversity. On 29 May 2017, just days before the 3 June game, fullback and linebacker Jahqui Sevilla had died in a head-on collision.[106] Sevilla had survived the attack on the Pulse nightclub a little over a year before, an attack that killed forty-nine, including Cory Connell, an assistant coach with the Anarchy. Running back Paula Blanco, who dated Connell, was also one of the wounded.[107]

When I interviewed Inferno defensive tackle Ty Baldwin, she spoke about the work that the team did in the community and told me, "We're nurturers." I ironically asked her if she had been "nurturing" the Anarchy players that she had tackled a few days before, and she replied: "Orlando is one of our babies, we love them. We respect them a lot. I mean, they have been through a lot. So at the end of the day, we are all for one common goal, and that is women's football. But you know with them having tragedy back to back to back, we supported them last year with the Pulse. If you notice, some of the older helmets have the Anarchy symbol on it. So we played them that week as well—we all represented their stickers to show our respect for them then. This week we respected their wishes, but we definitely have their back and support anything they could ever need. We would be there for them."[108]

The Anarchy qualified for the playoffs and made it to the final. I watched them defeat the Toledo Reign 27–20 on 8 July 2017, and they went on to lose the championship game 26–42 to the Arkansas Wildcats.[109] The Wildcats were a small team who could. They won the game against the Anarchy with only thirteen active players.[110] The Anarchy came back to the playoffs in 2018; they avenged their loss to the Wildcats by beating them 46–0 and won the championship.[111]

The next year during APUSH (AP U.S. history) reading week, I watched the Inferno play Jacksonville Dixie Blues. This was their second meeting of the year. The Inferno won the first game 41–7 and improved a bit in the second game when they defeated the Dixie Blues 49–9. The Jacksonville team won their first playoff game that season, defeating the Miami Fury 35–14, before they lost their third game against the Fury 7–48.[112]

At the end of both the 2017 and 2018 seasons, the Inferno qualified for the WFA playoffs, as they had since 2016. In 2017 they defeated the Miami Fury 27–6 and the Carolina Phoenix 35–26, before being scheduled to play the Montreal Blitz in Montreal in the third round. When I interviewed Moody, she told me that being in the playoffs had increased their local exposure (a local news crew was at the 2017 game), but that success came with a hefty price tag. "I was doing a little bit of calculation today. Very modestly, not even including flights or anything like that, this would be van trips to all three states. As a group organization we would be looking [at] anywhere between fifty to sixty-five thousand dollars."[113]

The game with the Blitz caused special challenges, since the players would need passports to cross the border. This was an added cost, and since Canada prohibits people with convictions for crimes such as a DUI (driving under the influence) from entering the country, this might also have presented problems.[114] The WFA stepped in and scheduled the game in Plattsburgh, New York. There was no evidence that any Inferno players had any such legal issues, but the league's explanation was that they moved the game "due to concerns about Tampa Bay players having to deal with travel delays while crossing the U.S.-Canadian border."[115] The Inferno still had to travel, but they defeated the Blitz 58–26 to qualify for the final.

The game proved to be a breaking point for Montreal, a team founded in 2001. Under the ownership of Saadia Ashraf, they played in the IWFL for fifteen seasons, and the Blitz won the 2008, 2010, and 2012 championships there. Ashraf, who bought the team from the original owners in 2004, also played quarterback for the Blitz and for Team Canada in 2010 and 2013. In 2015 Ashraf became the Blitz's coach, and in 2017 she was the quarterback coach for Team Canada.[116] Ashraf and the Blitz moved to the WFA for the 2016 season, but when they had to forgo home field advantage, and the revenue of a home game in the playoffs, they decided they would no longer play in the WFA.[117]

After defeating the Blitz, the Inferno earned a berth in the championship game for the second straight year. And, for the second straight year, they lost to the St. Louis Slam. They had been defeated by the Slam 7–38 in 2016 and lost again to the St. Louis team 15–42 in 2018.[118] They must have felt some optimism in 2018, when the Slam decided to take the season off. The path to a championship must have seemed smoother, but unfortunately for the Inferno, they were defeated by the New York Sharks, who were bent on closing out their team's history with a championship.[119]

The St. Louis Slam was another team that had been active since the days of the NWFA. Founded in 2003, they played six seasons in that league before joining the WFA in its inaugural 2009 season. The Slam won the league title that year with 11-0 record and defeated the West Michigan Mayhem 21-14 in the final. They finished 10-1 the next year but lost to the Columbus Comets 14-21. The Slam's victories over the Inferno in 2016 and 2017 marked their return to the championship form. By 2017 the Slam had a win-loss record of 98-35.[120]

The Slam also had the services of an international player. Frenchwoman Laure Gelis-Diaz began playing for the NWFA Slam in 2005, when she was studying in the United States. According to Gelis-Diaz in an interview posted on YouTube in 2009, "I tried out for five different teams in five different states. The St. Louis Slam offered me a two-year contract, and we had a pretty good season. After that, they extended my contract for five years." She remembered she learned that women play football when she was "looking for a soccer ball in Walmart" and ended up with a football instead. She was throwing the ball with a friend in the parking lot, "and an old man came to me and was like, 'You got good hands, so why aren't you playing women's professional football?'" For Gelis-Diaz, football unexpectedly formed the axis around which her life turned. She translated her experience on the field into a business.[121] She formed her own fitness company (Pro-Active On-Site Corporate Fitness) and helped out with The Elite Football Academy, which helps football players from youth to college with skills development.[122] She has been playing since 2005, and her résumé includes playing for the SLAM, the Milwaukee Warriors, the

Indiana Speed, the Green Bay Chill, and the Chicago Bliss. The first three teams were traditional full-kit teams, and the last two were LFL teams, so Gelis-Diaz has experienced football through a number of different styles.

As discussed in the last chapter and again below, who made the playoffs was sometimes controversial. The same problem had beset the WFA. Because of how the postseason was set up, some teams with losing records made the playoffs, while some teams with winning records stayed home.

The Miami Fury was one of the original WPFL teams in 2000 and had a 79-57 record over seventeen seasons. The Fury switched to the Major Independent Women's Football Alliance, a holding league for teams that left the WPFL, in 2001 and played in the IWFL from 2002 to 2010, when they joined the WFA. They have not, however, fielded a team every year since their debut. The team missed the 2004 season, perhaps because they wanted to "restructure the team," which was the explanation that the team gave for taking off the 2016 season.[123] Although the Fury finished the 2018 season with a 2-6 regular season record, all of the teams from their Southeast Region made the playoffs, but they lost to the Jacksonville Dixie Blues 14-35 to end their season.[124]

In 2017 the Division II Seattle Majestics had a 7-1 regular season record but were left out of the WFA playoffs. Their only loss came to the Division I Portland Fighting Shockwave, which also had a 7-1 record. The Majestics had played the Fighting Shockwave twice, winning the first game 24-21 and losing the second game 0-50.[125] The 6-3 Fury, who had won two games by forfeit, made the playoffs.[126] The 7-1 Fighting Shockwave, who played every game, also stayed home.

The WFL employed the Massey ratings to determine playoff qualifiers. That system was developed by Kenneth Massey while he was a student at Bluefield College in 1997. His system was part of a larger mix of statistical measures used by the NCAA to determine bowl game matchups between 1998 and 2013. The system caused some controversy and was eventually replaced.[127]

Neal Rozendaal, the author of the *Women's Football Encyclopedia* and also the vice president of communications for the D.C. Divas,[128] wrote a post on his personal blog that defended the use of the Massey ratings. He explained how win-loss record, strength of schedule, and margin of victory, along with the location and date of the game, determine who qualified for the playoffs. One of his main arguments for the system was that "it rewards teams that play an aggressive schedule of outstanding opponents, and it conversely punishes those that do not." Without such a system, he argued, strong teams would have no incentive to play other strong teams.[129]

Those who argued against the Massey ratings pointed out that the league sets the schedule, so some teams, because of their location, were set up for failure. Ashly Edmiston, on her *Four Point Stance* podcast, complained of the unfairness of a system that seemed to favor teams such as the Central Cal War Angels, which were owned by Lisa and Jeff King, who also directed the WFA. Edmiston, a former player with the Oregon Hawks, went on to assert, "I will go on record and say—the WFA is one of the shadiest leagues we have ever been involved in." As evidence, she asserted that she had "never seen the War Angels travel in a playoff game" and charged that this was because the Kings adjusted the Massey rankings to benefit their team. She called for the Kings to either focus on their team or on the league, but not both.[130]

The use of statistical measures to analyze almost everything represents a growing quantification of American life.[131] When this is applied to sport, one can easily see how this has affected the National Basketball Association, privileging the three-point shot over other play, which has dramatically changed the game. This quantification—allowing mathematicians to exert controlling influence over athletes—can also be seen as something of a real life *Revenge of the Nerds*, but this could be a book in itself.[132]

Statistical measures such as the Massey system are employed to remove subjectivity from the creation of playoff brackets. However, even methods based on computer algorithms can leave good teams sidelined in the postseason. In college football, Boise State University was the poster child for the flaws of the Bowl Championship Series measures. BSU won seventy-six games and lost six between 2006 and

2011 and had three undefeated regular seasons during that time, but the team never had the opportunity to play for a national championship.[133]

As previously mentioned, the Massey ratings left out of the 2017 playoffs teams such as the Portland Fighting Shockwave and the Seattle Majestics, who both had 7-1 records. Providing a bit of anecdotal evidence of Edmiston's charges, the Central Cal War Angels, who also won seven games but did not lose until the playoffs, did make the playoffs that year. Though they might have had weaker schedules, the Fighting Shockwave scored more points than the War Angels, and both Portland and Seattle gave up fewer points than Central Cal.[134]

Controversy over the playoffs once again appeared at the start of the 2019 season. The 2017 Division III playoff featured eight teams contending for the title, which was won by the Arkansas Wildcats.[135] The league increased the number of DIII playoff teams in 2018 to sixteen total teams, and the Anarchy won the championship. In 2019, after the DI Atlanta Phoenix joined the WNFC, the WFA reorganized the elite division by moving the Passion to DII and did not add a team to replace either Pittsburgh or Atlanta. Division II increased from sixteen teams to eighteen with the addition of the Passion and the new Seattle Spartans.[136] The number of DIII teams remained at thirty-nine, but the league halved the number of teams that could qualify for the playoffs. This led to a long Facebook discussion after Michael Burmy linked the postseason format and posted, "I agree with the playoff format in D1 and D2 . . . but I am NOT happy to see the D3 playoff field contracted like this." This led to a conversation that included more than thirty posts, which was large for women's football on Facebook. Although Burmy stated that he "messaged Lisa (King) with my concerns in more detail," none of the comments appeared to be from anyone in an official WFA capacity.[137]

Most sport leagues have had issues surrounding who qualifies for the playoffs and how those playoffs have been operated. From 2009 to 2019, the WFA has had between thirty and seventy teams spread across the country, so even with the help, or hindrance, of the Massey system, problems arose. In both the IWFL and the WFA, those problems have been blamed on the incompetence or even the bad faith of league leadership. Without any concrete evidence, however, those charges of bad faith must be discounted as merely complaints from those left out of the playoffs.

The Majestics reacted to missing the playoffs by joining the IWFL and then leaving that league for the WNFC. This, as previously mentioned, is a weakness of women's football. It is simply too easy for disgruntled teams to find a new league.

Portland chose to remain in the WFA; in 2018 they finished the regular season with a 6-2 record but made the playoffs. Perhaps this was a "makeup call," or the league adjusting the rating system to mollify the Fighting Shockwave. Perhaps the one-season increase in playoff numbers was an attempt to include more teams and decrease the grumbling. Those possibilities are merely conjecture but at least represent plausible guesses, in the absence of any solid information.

Whatever the reason, the 2017 playoff issues did not hurt the league much. That season the WFA solidified its spot on top of women's football leagues by supplying forty-two of the forty-five players on the USA National Team that won their third IFAF Women's World Championship. Not only did the league almost completely stock Team USA, but WFA athletes also played for the Canadians, the Australians, and the British.[138]

For the 2019 season, the league held relatively steady at sixty-four teams. The collapse of the IWFL added several new teams to the WFA roster. According to the WFA "Teams by Division" page, former IWFL teams such as the 2018 champion Houston Energy, runner-up Nevada Storm, Knoxville Lightning, Phoenix Phantomz, and the Tulsa Threat joined the league.[139] Other refugees from the IWFL such as the Iowa Crush took 2019 off, although there was a new Iowa Phoenix in the WFA, and perhaps that included former Crush players.[140] Some athletes might have also joined the Nebraska Night Hawks of the WNFC.

Curiously, the WFA did not issue press releases welcoming the new teams, aside from a Facebook post welcoming the Energy to the league.[141] In previous years the league made announcements on their "News" page whenever a new team joined. In 2018 that included ten teams, each with their own press release.[142] Perhaps after so many years of no love being lost between the two leagues, the Kings and the WFA did not want to be accused of gloating.

The sixty-four teams in the WFA dwarfed their competitor leagues. The United States Women's Football League had twelve teams, and the new WNFC had fourteen.[143] The Bud Light Guam Women's Tackle Football League, formerly associated with the IWFL, added five teams, and the Texas-based Xtreme Female Football League had another seven to bring the total of women's teams in the United States and its environs to over one hundred teams as of 2019.

The WFA's numbers remained stable, but the teams that made up the total change often. We have discussed the Sharks, the Force, and other long-established teams that have recently gone out of existence. Likewise, we have discussed the Boston team that has been the result of the evolution of women's football in New England. In addition, the Los Angeles Warriors, who finished second to the Renegades, apparently changed names. The Warriors name was not on the 2019 WFA schedule, but the Cali War was listed, with players including Lisa King, Angel Smith, and Chantel Wiggins on the rosters of both teams, wearing the same numbers and playing the same positions.[144] A 10 October 2018 post on the WFA's Facebook page provided the only clue as to what happened.

> The Women's Football Alliance is pleased to announce that the Cali War has signed on as a full member for the 2019 season. Based in Los Angeles, California, the War will compete as a member of Division 1. With the Los Angeles Warriors' announcement that they will not be playing in 2019, the War fills the void left by them, with almost the entire Warriors roster (as well as several former Central Cal War Angels players). . . . Most of all, the War looks to keep the D1 American Conference Championship in the City of Angels and to take the next step up by winning the Division 1 National Championship which has long eluded even the Golden State's very best teams.[145]

Why the Warriors decided not to play in 2019, after finishing second in 2018, was not addressed, and no additional information was readily available. Lisa King still played wide receiver, but the Cali War website did not provide information on the coaching staff, so whether Jeff King remained a coach was unclear.[146] Sometimes women's football teams and leagues remind one of Winston Churchill's 1939 comment on the Soviet Union: "a riddle, wrapped in a mystery, inside an enigma."[147]

When it began in 2009, the WFA was one of a number of options for players and teams who wanted to play women's football. During the past ten years, the Kings and their league emerged from the pack, and now are the largest women's football league. However, their success has come along with challenges—not only with scheduling playoff brackets that satisfy everyone, which is the bane of most leagues, but also with addressing much larger issues. Are sixty-four teams too many—should the league restrict membership to elite teams? Should teams that follow a more recreational model be in the same league as those who are trying to raise the level of play in women's football? Should team owners also operate the league? And the perennial question: Should all the competing leagues join together to form one organization that might better attract sponsors such as the NFL?

None of those questions have easy answers, and having created a thriving league, the Kings are likely content to ride the inertia they have created. So women's football will continue as it has for the past twenty years, since no consensus is probable in the foreseeable future. One of the challenges that the WFA has faced since its inception is the competition for public attention that they must wage with the Lingerie Football League (LFL), which began league play the same year as they did. This is a rare subject that has created more of a consensus among women who play full-kit tackle football than any other issue—their opposition to the sexualized football spectacle that is the LFL. The creation of that controversial league is where we next turn our attention.

# The X League

**5**

Now for something completely (?) different . . .

By the time I saw my first live Legends Football League game between the perennial powerhouse Chicago Bliss and the historically hapless Omaha Heart, I had seen quite a few women's football games that featured traditional, and full-kitted, play. Instead of eleven-on-eleven, the LFL games were seven-on-seven. Instead of traditional uniforms and pads, the LFL athletes wore cut-down shoulder pads and hockey-style helmets that kept the player's face visible. They wore uniforms that were little more than bikinis, displaying most of the athlete's body. Instead of a regulation-size field, the game was played inside an arena, and the field measured 50 yards long by 40 yards wide.

There were indeed differences, but there were also similarities. The athletes hit as hard, and the collisions seemed faster and more violent since the play was confined to a narrow space.

My wife, Sophie, and I, along with Agnes Burtscher, her best friend from high school, and Burtscher's husband, Jean-Marc, attended the game in a northern suburb of Chicago. The Burtschers were visiting from France. Jean-Marc and I had collaborated on my book on French football, and we had gone together to the 2016 Molosses versus Argo-canes game that sparked my interest in women's football. We had been going to football games together for quite some time, including an earlier trip that summer to the 2018 NFL Hall of Fame Game in

Canton, Ohio, so this was the latest in a long line of events we had attended. Sophie and Agnes, whose interest in football was nearly nonexistent, sometimes came along to humor us, if they could not find anything better to do.

Being a Nebraska native, I had hoped the Heart would provide some competition for the Bliss, who went on to win the LFL championship later that year. I was to be disappointed as the Bliss crushed the Heart 76-0. We put our heads together afterward and guesstimated that there had perhaps been six to eight hundred fans there. Our tickets cost $18 apiece, almost twice what one paid for WFA games.

I was surprised at the uniforms the players wore. At the end of the 2017 season, the LFL had switched from bikini bottoms to leggings. In a 2017 article on *BroBible*, Douglas Charles quoted LFL media relations director Phillip Darnell, who provided a history of the league's uniform changes and at the end stated: "Fast forward to 2017, the next major evolution of the on-field uniform has arrived, full pants uniforms which will place more of the viewer's attention on the athlete and sport as well as providing greater safety for athletes."[1] However, Esteban, writing for *Total Pro Sports*, found that Darnell's announcement had been removed and that the new uniform pants would only be used in the last game of the 2017 season.[2] The League made the switch official with a 30 January 2018 Facebook post, and of the 189 comments, the vast majority were negative about the change.[3]

Those commenters who argued this move would cost the league fans must have been correct, since when we arrived at the game, the players were back in shorts. The LFL had announced the uniform change in a 21 July 2018 tweet,[4] and on 24 July their Twitter account asked fans, "Do you like the new Shorts Uniform?" Some 385 responded, and 71 percent answered along the lines of, "Yes, Love Them."[5]

Whether the somewhat small crowd we estimated at the Bliss game was indicative of fan dissatisfaction was hard to determine, since the league does not publish attendance figures. However, when the Lingerie Football League merely rebranded to the current Legends Football League, Mark J. Burns of *Forbes* reported, "While league attendance numbers have grown approximately 22 percent each season since 2009, last year's (2013) dropped by 12 percent." Mitchell Mortaza, the owner of the league, told Burns: "The fan reception was not very positive at first, to be very frank. The LFL was viewed as the 'Rock n' Roll Football' brand. . . . Fans thought the league was going in the direction of the NFL. That was the initial knee-jerk reaction of the fans. They were not happy about it."[6]

If fans were upset and voted with their feet when the league made what amounted to a marketing change—the league's motto shifted from "True Fantasy Football" to "Women of the Gridiron"—then a radical change to the uniform likely upset them more.[7] The rebranding to Legends Football League also came with changes to the uniform, but those were relatively minor and largely consisted of removing the lingerie-like garters and bows that supported the "lingerie" theme. One article by Antony Sharwood on the Australian site News.com.au had stated in 2015 that average attendance in "many venues" was "5,000 per game."[8] Spike Rogan of *Bleacher Report* mentioned that at a 2009 game he attended, "I give the [Philadelphia] Passion a VERY GENEROUS [Rogan's capitalization] estimate of 2,800 in attendance."[9] So fans seemed to support teams such as the Bliss in fairly large numbers, at least in the past, but not on that night. I would argue that perhaps another reason for the low turnout then was the lack of a quality opponent—the Heart had lost one of their previous games to the Nashville Knights 0-80.[10]

The 2018 uniform change might have led some fans to abandon the league, and so Mortaza, who controlled all aspects of the league, changed course. However, since 2009, if Americans have considered women's football, they have more than likely thought of the LFL. This causes a great deal of disgust among the women who play full-kit football and is the reason that many of the few articles that do get written about traditional women's football since 2009 began with some variation of "This [the WFA] is not your mother's powder puff gang, and it's light years away from MTV's scantily clad 'Lingerie Football League,'" which specifies that the women they are writing about do not play in bikinis.[11]

The LFL began with Mortaza's idea for an alternative to the 2004 Super Bowl XXXVIII halftime show. Reportedly Mortaza came up with the idea while attending Super Bowl XXXVII in 2003. He "noticed how uninterested fans would leave the stands during halftime to use the restroom and tend to other needs," which gave him the idea that "some people might prefer a raunchier option."[12] In an ESPN interview with Steve Nelson, Mortaza told the reporter: "That mass exodus at halftime. It really made me think, 'Okay. How can we capture this audience that's visibly leaving? If this number of people are leaving their seats in the stadium, what's happening across the world during halftime?'"[13]

With the goal of capturing a portion of that audience, Horizon Productions, Inc., Mortaza's company, created the pay-per-view spectacle. Based on the clips included in a YouTube video posted by a user going by the screen name mustangbarry, the media buzz around the event was largely positive and generally focused on the novelty of the idea. ESPN's Nelson asked actress Angie Everhart, "Why would viewers switch from the Super Bowl at halftime to watch an entirely different football game?" Everhart replied with a chuckle, "We're selling girls playing football. In our underwear." Late night comedians such as Jay Leno, Jimmy Kimmel, and Craig Kilborn gave the spectacle free advertising on their shows, and in addition to ESPN, E Entertainment also publicized the event. Much of the coverage was played for laughs and focused on the sexualized nature of the game, but it still served to extend the reach of the advertising that Horizon Productions paid for, which included images on the sides of buses.[14]

Despite the relatively positive mentions in the media, there was some negative reaction. Mortaza secured a sponsorship from DaimlerChrysler for the first iteration, at least temporarily. The car maker's Dodge division sought to increase its exposure to the "'Dodge brand's core demographic' and help the brand cut through Super Bowl clutter."[15] However, after protests from dealers and "every kind of stakeholder," according to the Chrysler Group's Joe Eberhardt, the car company dropped out. Mortaza labeled the protesters as a "few radical groups" and was able to secure backing from PartyPoker.com, an online gambling site.[16]

During that first year and subsequently, Horizon Productions also secured sponsorship deals from "Vivendi Universal Games, Monster

Energy Drink, and AsomBroso Tequila." Mortaza also secured the services of former NFL players Lawrence Taylor and Eric Dickerson to act as game coaches for the event. Other celebrities such as actress Everhart and *Playboy* model Jenny McCarthy took part in the games.[17]

A highlight video of the original Lingerie Bowl is available on YouTube. It began with a slow motion montage of the players, who were professional models or actresses, going through the motions of getting into their football stances, throwing, catching, and spiking the ball. The emphasis was not on the football, but on the bodies of the women who played the first game. Edited game action from the Los Angeles Memorial Coliseum followed and featured player introductions announced by Michael Buffer, an announcer well known by boxing and professional wrestling fans. Other, less well-known celebrities such as game announcer and actress Amy Weber teamed with Ultimate Fighting Championship announcer Mike Goldberg to call the game action. Former *Baywatch* actress Traci Bingham rounded out the broadcast team as the sideline reporter. Weber attempted to provide some substance to the titillation of the event when she told viewers, "These girls have a ton of pride. They don't want to come out here and look stupid, which is why they've had months of preparation. They've learned the fundamentals of football. They've learned the plays, and they're ready to go."[18]

The actual game had some interesting football. In the first quarter, team Euphoria's quarterback Everhart handed off to her running back Roban Lampkin, who then completed a halfback pass to wide receiver Cassie Moore. During that play all of the offensive line used a run-blocking technique that is generally illegal in football, but the officials called no penalty. Perhaps the rules allowed such play, but that was impossible to determine. Currently the LFL rules seemingly make the center ineligible, but that was not the case in 2009, the first year of the Lingerie Football League.[19] More likely, the officials were told to not call many penalties. At the end of the play, Moore's lingerie-style shorts were pulled down, exposing her thong. Although less revealing than Janet Jackson and Justin Timberlake's "wardrobe malfunction" that took place during the actual Super Bowl halftime show that year, it may have motivated the few hundred fans visible in the stands during the video to cheer harder. It was also less revealing than some of the outfits in the fashion show that preceded the game.

Patrick Hruby, who reviewed the game for ESPN's *Page 2*, gave the football a higher grade than the revealing uniforms. He wrote, "As it turned out, the Lingerie Bowl was about as titillating as tossing a football through a tire hanging from a backyard tree. Surprisingly, the football was almost decent, in a Pop Warner/XFL-ish sort of way." He later opined: "While the football was spotty—three players tackled each other well after an incomplete pass fell to the ground—the crunching contact was oddly compelling. Both teams sported shoulder pads and hockey-style helmets and appeared to be putting their equipment to good use." Most of his article was a complaint about the players wearing too much, but even his faint praise for the level of play indicated that the athletes were taking the game somewhat seriously.[20]

The referees did take their flags out long enough to give Team Dream a first down on the 5-yard line after a pass interference penalty. Two plays later, actress Nicole Silva scored the game's only touchdown. Fortunately for those who had paid $29.99 for the right to watch the game, which was already in its second half, the only score came with 6:42 left in the event. Team Euphoria had one last play to score as time ran out, but Moore dropped what would have been a touchdown pass, and the game ended.[21]

It was unclear how many fans paid the price to watch the game. Mortaza and his production company predicted that around 1.5 million fans would pay to view the event, but Paul Bond of the *Today Show* wrote that the number was "closer to 100,000 buys." He claimed that number came from "published estimates," though none of those were readily accessible. According to Bond, Mortaza stated, "actual numbers for the show, which was made available via pay-per-view for about six weeks beyond the live event, are being audited and will be released next month."[22] If the statistics were ever released, research has not located them. A 2010 press release announcing the Lingerie Football League being televised on the MTV2 network contained the assertion that "the LFL is an extension of the most popular Super Bowl halftime counter-programming special in history called the *Lingerie Bowl*. Since its premier in 2004 the bowl is seen annually by millions of die-hard football fans worldwide."[23]

Whichever number range one accepted, the event proved successful enough that Mortaza repeated the game for the next two Super Bowls using much the same formula. For Lingerie Bowl II, ex-NFL players included coaches Jim McMahon and William (The Refrigerator) Perry. Based on the badly edited YouTube video, the banter between Goldberg and his two unnamed female co-announcers lowered the tone even further from the normally staid fare that the NFL prefers and that had been featured in the previous bowl. Before the game started, one mentioned, "The only thing protecting them is their helmet and shoulder pads," to which the other added, "And their implants." On the first play from scrimmage, the New York Euphoria's Sheena Mariano, who appears to have been one of the few athletes without movie or television credits, ran off the right side for a sizable gain. One of the female announcers yelled, "Get that little bitch!" and added, "Oh, I want New York to die." After chanting "Get her, get her!" repeatedly when the Euphoria had the ball, later in the game the same voice commented, "Am I supposed to do color commentary and not root for one side?" Goldberg responded, "It's way too late for that." At another point in the game, as the camera panned in on the women crouched to hear the call in the huddle, the woman said, "Oh, talk about tight ends." Goldberg commented, "This game is not played with one tight end. This game is played with fourteen tight ends, much to the delight of all of you around the world here with us."[24]

Although the play on the field appeared to be improved over the first year, the announcers' comments sexualized the players and the event even further than their uniforms already had. The crowd attending the event in person seemed to have grown from the first game, and the skill level of the athletes had also gone up. Mariano, who played in all three of the Lingerie Bowls, was apparently already a gifted athlete who improved her football skills as the seasons passed. A majority of the athletes still seemed to be minor celebrities, but even they had seemingly picked up their games.

The alternative halftime series ended with Lingerie Bowl III in 2006. There were attempts to stage more games, but various issues arose, reportedly including, according to a master's thesis by Amirah M. Heath, "a variety of decency concerns." Heath mentioned Dodge pulling their sponsorship and added that the 2009 version of the game was canceled due to concerns over the venue. The game was set to be played at Caliente Resorts, "a luxury clothing optional resort," but concerns over Federal Communications Commission decency rules led Mortaza to ask the resort to mandate clothing for the event. When the resort refused, Horizon Productions pulled the plug on the match. The gods of irony must have been roaring when media director Stephen McMillen released a statement announcing, "The league will not place our fans, players, staff nor partners in a less-than-comfortable environment that would ultimately jeopardize the mainstream perception and reputation of the brand that so many have worked diligently over these past five years to build."[25]

While it lasted, the players in the Lingerie Bowls also foreshadowed what Jeff King offered as a possibility during the buildup to the Women's Football Alliance's 2009 debut: that women's football in the United States could become a magnet for women around the world to come here to play. Hruby's ESPN article mentioned that, according to the game's website, there were "three Aussies and a single solitary Swede" among the players. He also mentioned that one hailed from Canada and another from the United Kingdom.[26] By using the Internet Movie Database (IMDb), it was possible to identify that host Didiayer Snyder and player Michelle Van Der Water were from Australia. Players Gwendolyn Osborne-Smith and Nicole Silva were from the United Kingdom, and sideline reporter Kylie Bax was born in New Zealand.[27] For the second bowl, Anca Marcus, from Romania, scored the first touchdown.[28] When Mortaza transitioned the halftime shows into the Lingerie Football League in 2009, international players from Australia, Canada, France, Nigeria, and Mexico would play there at various times.[29]

After the cancellation of Lingerie Bowl VI in 2009, Mortaza announced that instead of attempting to produce a single halftime show, he would instead debut the Lingerie Football League. In an interview Darren Rovell of CNBC asked Mortaza why he had decided to begin the league at that point, after having discussed the possibility for several years. Mortaza replied, "I think obviously more now than ever before [in the midst of a recession] we all need an escape from what's going on around us. And just the success we've had with the Lingerie Bowl, we thought if we can grab that kind of audience as a one-off halftime special, what if we built a year-round brand in all these pockets of fan bases around the country to watch their teams year round? That's why [I] came to the realization we need to launch a league here." So, in addition to making money, the league founder argued that he was performing something of a public service. He laid out the organization of the league for CNBC. There would be local owners, but he would keep "51 percent ownership of the teams." The teams would play in venues used by other professional leagues, including professional basketball, hockey, and soccer leagues. He maintained that while his players would be attractive, "Obviously beauty is skin deep. . . . So athletics are going to be a key component of it [which athletes were chosen]." When asked about pay, he replied, "That's the best part of it. There is no salary. The players get a percentage of the gate based on them winning and losing. There's a big discrepancy between those percentages. The players are going to be incented to play fierce football and win games." He differentiated his league proposal from other football startups that had failed by arguing that his league was not interested in directly competing with the NFL. "This is a fun Friday night out with you and your buddies or you and your girlfriends to watch lingerie football and be part of this Disneyland for football fans type setting that we're putting together in all the host stadiums and arenas."[30]

The league started with ten teams in major U.S. cities, with each playing a four-game schedule. Aside from some localized team names such as the Seattle Mist and Tampa Breeze, most of the teams were named to support the league's motto: True Fantasy Football. Of the original teams, those with suggestive names that still played in the league included the Chicago Bliss, the Denver Dream, and the Los

Angeles Temptation.[31] Players were chosen from the women who attended mini-camps in the cities chosen to host a team. Mortaza issued a November 2008 press release stating that "hundreds of women came out to minicamp in San Diego."[32] Judging from a YouTube video that included clips from the San Diego event, there were a fair number of women trying out to make the twelve-woman roster, perhaps more than one hundred. LA Temptation player Riley Madex echoed Mortaza's contention that the players should be beautiful and athletic when she said, "There's a lot athletes out here. Good looking girls, and a lot of girls showing a lot of aggression, so I think that's really good."[33]

The women in the video appeared thin, attractive, and athletic, with perhaps the emphasis on the first two. In 2010 prospective players were informed via the official LFL website that they should "bring your resume and fullbody [sic] picture in two-piece bikini to leave behind," which indicated that beauty would be a deciding factor.[34]

In 2013 Mikaila Perrett wanted to try out for one of the LFL teams forming in Australia. After she sent her photo, she received a reply that informed her she was not selected for a tryout and that "she needs to lean out from what I can tell in this photo." After the story broke in the Australian press, league spokeswoman Kelly Campbell told the Australian Associated Press, "Unfortunately, Ms Mikaila Perrett did not take being physically prepared seriously, and as a result was not cleared to compete last week." Campbell did offer Perrett the chance to try again, "if she demonstrated a commitment to get into 'great physical condition.'"[35] Marirose Roach, who played for the Philadelphia Passion, had to wait a year to begin playing because Mortaza reportedly told her coach that "she doesn't have the look" and was "too big."[36]

Many of the hopefuls seemed to be similar to Rachel Carrocio, who made the San Diego Seduction's first roster. Carrocio told ESPN reporter Mary Buckheit, "I came out here to pursue semipro athletics at all costs. I don't care if it's in lingerie. That's how much I would love to be able to make a living playing sports."[37] In a 2015 *Grantland* article by Jordan Ritter Conn, Chicago Bliss quarterback Heather Furr echoed Carrocio, telling the reporter that even though she was hesitant to even try out for the LFL, when she went to the first practice the workout was so strenuous that she "nearly threw up." Furr told the reporter, "It was like I was back in college," where she competed in basketball and track for Valparaiso University and Elmhurst College. After graduation, Furr tried to find the same athletic experience in recreational leagues but was looking for something "that would push me beyond my limits." Conn's article asserted that "dozens of female athletes, many of whom had considered themselves retired, were finding the exact same thing. They were thrilled by the game's pace and intensity." Amber Mane of the Green Bay Chill, who had been a member of the wrestling team in high school, enthused to the reporter, "I'd never been around that many girls who were just as hardcore as I am." Most of the players quoted in the article were embarrassed to one degree or another by the uniform they had to wear, but as with Carrocio, they agreed to be embarrassed, as long as they had the chance to play football.[38]

Initially, the athletes were paid a percentage of gate, "20% of ticket sales if they win and 10% if they lose." LFL media director Stephon McMillen told Elizabeth Suman of the *Baltimore Brew*, "We do not pay salaries because LFL player[s] are not employees." Rather, he and the league classified the athletes as "independent contractors."[39] That changed after Jennifer Delarosa, Coryn Salazar, and Nicole Bate, three LA Temptation players, sued the league in a California court in 2010, claiming that state law required that they be paid an $8 per hour minimum wage, receive overtime pay, and have deductions itemized on their paychecks.[40]

After that season, players were no longer paid. The LFL justified that by stating that it "would have ceased to exist in 2011 'due to financial losses.'" Instead, the LFL classified itself as an amateur league and required players to pay a $45 fee to play. As an amateur league, the LFL was not subject to various state and federal laws regarding minimum wages, overtime, and the like.[41]

Attempting to get a better deal, Las Vegas Sin quarterback Nikki Johnson attempted to form players into something like a union and then became the lead plaintiff in a 2014 federal lawsuit, along with

Melissa Margulies, who was the lead plaintiff in another California state suit.[42]

Male football players have not traditionally been strong union supporters, as the National Football League Players Association found during their 1982 strike when several players decided to cross the picket line and play.[43] The same held true for the LFL. When Heather Furr received Johnson's letter asking the players to present a united front against Mortaza, she remembered that "she contacted me and I was like, 'Eeeeeeeek!' What are you doing? . . . I'm not going to put my name on anything. I don't know how this is going to go."

How it went is that Johnson was kicked out of the league, and Mortaza said of Johnson, "She was a cancer. This is the last fifteen minutes of fame. She'll never be heard from again."[44] Furr's Bliss teammate Alli Alberts also distanced herself from any legal action, echoing the LFL line that the league was not very profitable. "If I thought they were making just millions and millions of dollars and they weren't trying to share it at all, I'd be like, 'Oh, come on,' but we're not making that much right now."[45]

What eventually became of the various lawsuits against Mortaza and the LFL is unclear. Mortaza reportedly never bothered to show up to defend himself in the lawsuit, and so the last word on the legal actions was that Margulies (and presumably Johnson) was "in the process of filing for a default judgment."[46] Websites with that information now have broken links that lead instead to a law firm's website. Had the plaintiffs won, it was likely that news of that would have appeared in the press. Perhaps the plaintiffs accepted some sort of settlement, or maybe Mortaza's version of the league as an amateur sport league prevailed.

Mortaza justified not paying players by stating, "If we paid a dime to a player, we wouldn't sustain a season of play," but he also argued that the unpaid athletes received increased opportunities for publicity due to their participation in the league. The women who appeared in *Pretty. Strong.* did receive pay for their participation, as, presumably, did Miami Caliente athlete "Ashley Helmstetter and nine other players from across the league" who appeared in the February 2011 issue of *Playboy* magazine.[47] Danielle Moinet, who played cornerback for the Bliss, used her experience to become Summer Rae of the World Wrestling Entertainment, so some women have parlayed their unpaid labor into a career, although for most that remained merely a dream.[48]

With the launch of a regular league, and after players quit receiving even a percentage of the gate, the press attention the LFL received changed. Shifting from the slightly bemused or mocking but still positive coverage it had received when it was a halftime novelty, many in the press began to express outrage at the league's business model.

Brad Rock of the *Deseret News* in Salt Lake City might not have been the first to critique the league idea, but his condemnation was indicative of the narrative that would define the LFL. Rock savagely ridiculed the idea of women playing football in lingerie, arguing the league was a joke, and that the women were not real athletes. "If it's supposed to be taken seriously, how many of the players played college football? . . . How many got an athletic scholarship in ANY [Rock's capitalization] sport?" He critiqued the Lingerie Bowls, which he called "ill conceived," by arguing there was little passing, and he added, "And just for the record, they tackle like girls," and then denigrated the women even further by adding, "Stats. Yeah, they have stats—36D being the most prevalent."[49]

Although some of the comments on the article echoed the author's attitude, "It's these kind of women that degrade our gender," according to Melissa, for instance, a surprising number took him to task for his opinion. Several comments were left by women who claimed to be LFL players. Toni_K claimed to play for the Dallas Desire and commented that she had "played 4yrs full scholarship womens [*sic*] basketball in college . . . For the first time sports have found a way to make things sexy." Lauren, purportedly a Philadelphia Passion player, told Rock that she "was a 4yr Division 1 2x All American full scholarship athlete." Another Philly Passion player challenged the author by writing, "I can assure you we do not tackle like girls. If you would like me to demonstrate, I would be more than happy to oblige."[50]

The similarity in the style of some of these posts, and that women from Philadelphia were commenting on an article in a Utah newspaper, perhaps indicated that the comments were part of an LFL-directed counternarrative program, or, as Neal Rozendaal suggested in his *Women's Football Encyclopedia*, perhaps Mortaza used various internet aliases to push back against criticisms of the league.[51] However, several of the other postings that did not appear canned indicated that Mortaza's idea had struck a chord in the popular imagination.[52]

If one subscribes to the theory that any publicity is good publicity, then the Lingerie Football League received an enormous amount of publicity for a women's sporting league. As the LFL proved to be successful, later articles would continue to lambast Mortaza and the league but, as with Conn's *Grantland* article quoted above, would describe the athletes involved more positively.

Despite the often caustic criticism of the league, in 2010, in their second year of existence, the Lingerie Football League and Mortaza had secured a broadcaster to televise their games.[53] MTV2 began running LFL *Presents: Friday Night Football on* MTV2, which featured highlights from that week's featured game. In announcing the deal with the new league, MTV2 senior vice president of programming and production Eric Conte announced the network's rationale for buying rights to what was already a controversial entity, asserting, "We are excited to partner with the Lingerie Football League to bring all the feminine ferocity of 'Friday Night Football' to MTV2 every week. We are eager to build upon all the excitement that the LFL and its hardcore fanbase [*sic*] have generated to date to deliver fast-paced head turning programming that fits perfectly within MTV2 fall programming slate."[54]

Having at least their highlights televised was an enormous step for the league and guaranteed that when the women's football blinders fell off of many people's eyes, their discovery of the sport would include provocatively dressed women. The IWFL had been in existence for ten years at that point, and the WFA had begun in the same year as the LFL, yet their games would not be available to whatever audience MTV2 was able to draw.

That the first woman's football league to receive television exposure was one that catered to the prurient interest angered many women who played in full uniform. In 2011, after Mortaza sent a letter to Michael

Jackson's daughter Paris, who was thirteen at the time, to become the spokesperson for a proposed LFL youth program,[55] Liz and Katie Sowers made a YouTube video to express their disgust.

At the time, they were reacting to Mortaza's contention in his letter to Jackson, who had received publicity for being the only female on the flag football team at her school,[56] that there was "a lack of options for competitive female football." The video showed the sisters holding up cards that introduced themselves and then read: "We play tackle football . . . Yes real tackle football . . . No, not in our bra and underwear . . . Real Football." Interspersed with their cards were photos from WFA games, and Liz held up her KC Tribe jersey to prove that they were a real team. They admitted that it was likely that viewers probably did not know that their team or league existed since, as another card read, "It seems that women need to undress in order to be seen." Addressing Mortaza's offer to Jackson directly, their cards read, "It makes me sad to think that young girls, such as Paris Jackson . . . Will grow up thinking that the only way to Play [Sowers' capitalization] the game they love . . . Will involve a uniform you would NEVER See [Sowers' capitalization] in the men's game." They made a distinction between their peers who played for the love of the game, and the LFL players who made money (by this time, LFL players also paid to play). "We play b/c we love the game, and believe that football is not just a sport for the guys and half naked girls . . . So to LFL Commissioner Mitchell S. Mortaza, when you said there is a 'lack of options for competitive female football' . . . Maybe you just haven't noticed us with our clothes on." The video finished with a photo of the sisters in their Tribe uniforms.[57]

The Sowers sisters were at that time players for the Kansas City Tribe of the WFA. Katie Sowers has since gone on to become one of the first female full-time assistant coaches, with the San Francisco 49ers in her case, and Liz, at that time, was the quarterback for the Kansas City Titans of the WFA.[58] Both also played for Team USA at the International Federation of American Football Women's World Championship (see chapter 6). Liz has also played for the USA Women's National Flag team and was hired to coach flag football at Ottawa University.

Criticism that LFL football was not real football was, and still is, a common theme from critics of the league. However, as mentioned above, most of those critical articles contain somewhat favorable descriptions of the athletes and their reasons for playing. Neal Rozendaal's *Women's Football Encyclopedia*, however, did not exempt LFL players from criticism. He devoted one of the final sections in his work to "The Case against Lingerie Football." He led off by discussing how the LFL deliberately chose women with a certain body type to fill the teams, concluding, "When a 'sport' rejects female athletes based not on their talent but based—first and foremost—on whether or not a man subjectively thinks she looks sexy in lingerie, it's not a legitimate sport. Period."[59]

Rozendaal proceeded to argue that critiquing the sport while supporting the players was a "fallacy": "Too many mainstream stories on the LFL gloss over all this [choosing players for 'marketability'/sexiness instead of talent] for some reason and still treat lingerie football like it's a legitimate sport; most media sources that glorify LFL players try to ignore the reality that it was only by being chosen in a glorified wet T-shirt contest that they made it into the league in the first place."[60]

He rebutted the common argument of LFL players that their uniforms were not that much different than what women in beach volleyball and track and field wore by returning to his first point. "Track and beach volleyball players may universally fit a certain body type, but that's because success at those sports demands that body type; the athletes weren't vetted to ensure they all fit that profile."[61] Although, in that section, he only briefly mentioned that "track and beach volleyball aren't contact sports like football," this was perhaps the best counter to those who point out uniform similarities.

Even though he argued that "you can have respect for the athletic ability and work ethic of lingerie football players and still acknowledge that lingerie football is in no way a real sport," he later quoted "one anonymous online commenter," who "summarized Mortaza's relationship with the players perfectly." The source reportedly compared the players' support for the league as being "similar to the Stockholm syndrome [where hostages come to identify with their captors] in certain ways."[62]

Much of Rozendaal's critique of the league, outside of the body shape requirements, dealt with Mortaza's failings, accusing him of neglecting player safety, criticizing his micromanagement of the league, suggesting that the league commissioner might have fixed game results, and highlighting the LFL's failures. This section of his *Women's Football Encyclopedia* was unique in that it is extensively footnoted. His thirteen pages of narrative on the LFL are backed up by 114 citations.[63]

Despite this documentary evidence supporting most of Rozendaal's assertions, his, and others', primary contention that the LFL is not "real" football is problematical. Whether they were suffering from the Stockholm syndrome, the current and former players who have been quoted over the years obviously believe they are playing football. The action on the field is indeed a variation of football, as is arena football or, for that matter, flag football. All of these variations, including the seven-on-seven LFL version, owe their origin to American football, which is, as are the variations growing out of the parent sport, real football. Arguing that this is not real football was therefore a philosophical position based on aesthetics, economics, and value judgments. The athletes were most certainly exploited for their sexual appeal. Their labor was not compensated, so they were also economically exploited. Participation in the league was also made more dangerous due to the lack of protective equipment. And, finally, the women of every body type who play full-kitted tackle football understandably are irritated that when the average person is aware of women's football, it is the provocatively clad version that has caused the blinders to fall. All of those factors do not, however, mean that the athletes engaged in the LFL are not playing football. The games are real, as are the runs, passes, and the hits; hence the league's inclusion in this work.

Dr. Jennifer Welter, who played with the Dallas Diamonds for several years, along with Team USA in 2010 and 2013, who then went on to become the first woman to play in a men's professional football game, and who became the first woman to coach in the NFL, had the "not real football" attitude about the LFL before she went to a tryout. She wrote about her encounters with the "models" of the LFL in *Play Big: Lessons in Being Limitless from the First Woman to Coach in the NFL.*

> After playing pro football for many seasons, I popped by an open tryout for the Dallas Desire, a team starting in the lingerie league. I went to their tryout with some serious attitude, assuming I'd show these pretty girls a thing or two about playing football. Let me be clear: talk about underestimated performers. Sure, these girls were beautiful, many of them models, but a good number of them were also exceptional athletes. They won me over, and in a sense, laid the groundwork for me to open my mind about how a person can be more than one thing.[64]

The LFL's failures that Rozendaal chronicled were accurate, but there were also successes. The MTV2 broadcast package turned out to be a win for both. In a 24 August 2011 press release, the network announced the expansion of the network's coverage to include broadcast of "20 regular season games that will air LIVE [press release capitalization] every Friday night on MTV2 over the course of the season."[65]

The network's decision to expand their coverage reflected the success of the previous season's highlight show. According to the press release, "In its first season on MTV2, 'LFL Presents: Friday Night Football' improved its time period (Fri/11pm–11:30) with all key MTV2 demographics, including a +13% increase among M[ales]12–34. At the time LFL was MTV2's most watched original series launch ever with M12–34 and highest rated since 2006 with P[ersons]12–34 and M12–34." The press release also claimed, according to *MyNetwork TV*, that the LFL was "2nd in Primetime TV ratings," and that the league had performed better than Ultimate Fighting Championship and World Wrestling Entertainment in "growth, national television viewership, attendance and business prosperity." The new contract moved the league's games from its original 11:00 p.m. time slot to

10:00 p.m., which presumably would allow for an increased share of younger viewers.[66]

A 2012 story by Megan Stewart of the *Vancouver Courier* confirmed the success asserted in the press release and added additional information about the league's television ratings. "In its 2010–11 season, games drew an average of 165,000 viewers, according to Nielsen television ratings. In 2011–12, viewership rose to an average 219,000 viewers per game and 493 tuned in Feb. 5, flipping the channel away from the Super Bowl half time show to watch the LFL championship."[67]

More than two hundred thousand viewers was a decent share of the 12–34 audience, particularly on Friday nights, when young males might be expected to have other things to do. However, the league and network ended their partnership with the 2011-12 season, though no rationale for parting ways has been found. Possibilities exist that the network bowed to outside pressure, although that likely would have been noted in the press. Perhaps the more likely explanation was that Mortaza might have wanted more money than MTV2 was interested in offering, but that is merely supposition based on the largely less than favorable press that the league's owner/commissioner has received over the years.

The MTV2 press release also announced that MGM Resorts International had established "weekly betting lines across all MGM properties."[68] Having a Las Vegas betting line could be considered a mark of success. The only other time that was the case was when the NWFA's 2002 and 2003 SupHer Bowls had betting lines established for those two games (see chapter 2).

Nor were media depictions completely negative. The American Broadcasting Company's *Nightline* ran a feature on the league in 2013 that included much of the negative views of the league—sexual exploitation and danger primarily—but nevertheless had an overall positive tone. Much of that came from interviewing several Chicago Bliss players, including defensive tackle Yashi Rice, wide receiver Alli Alberts, and tight end Jamie Barwick, who was interviewed with her young son. The final editing included their positive comments about the game they all professed to love.[69]

Reporter Juju Chang spent time with the Bliss, and claimed that "I've become their mascot" as one of the players yelled "Juju in the house!" when coach Keith Hac stormed into the locker room and began an expletive-laced diatribe about his team's performance against the Green Bay Chill. Chang excused his behavior, intoning, "After eighteen years of coaching men, Coach Hac feels the biggest compliment he can pay these ladies is to treat them just like the guys." Discussing the concussion risk posed by the hockey-style helmets, Chang allowed to pass without comment or context Mortaza's contention that one of the reasons for concussions in the NFL is that players use their protective gear incorrectly: "There's a reason why the NHL has far less sustained concussion, sustained concussions in the NHL versus the NFL, because once you put them in a football helmet, often times it's used as a weapon. They tend to spear one another. These women are smart. If they felt in any way that they weren't protected out there, . . . they wouldn't come back." Alberts, who was concussed while playing defensive back by LA Temptation quarterback Ashley Salerno in her first game, laughed off the danger. After admitting that this was what her family found most objectionable about her playing in the LFL, Alberts told Chang, "I can't not do it . . . I love it." At the end of the report, Chang posited, "With their skimpy outfits and trash-talking ways, these athletes may just be the unlikely vanguard of the new feminine mystique."[70]

News stories can be produced and edited in any number of ways. Chang included the critiques of the league but also left the audience with a positive feeling toward the league, Mortaza, and the spectacle of women playing tackle football in skimpy uniforms. She was no doubt attempting to present a balanced look at the league and its athletes, although critics such as Rozendaal would likely accuse her of glossing over the player selection process and glorifying the players at the expense of exposing the inherent inequality of the league, or perhaps accuse her of being an LFL apologist. That Chang and her editors chose this way to present their report on the league, instead of locating former players who had become critics of the sport, indicated that ambivalence about reporting on the lingerie football continued.

The league also succeeded, for a time, when it expanded internationally. As with the IWFL (see chapter 3), the LFL early on attempted to tap into the popularity of football in Canada. In 2011 Mortaza and the LFL played their All-Fantasy Game featuring the league's best players demonstrating their sport in Hamilton, Ontario. Later in the fall the Toronto Triumph became the first LFL team outside the United States. The team had a rocky start when sixteen of the team's twenty-two players left the team in protest after their head coach (or Mortaza?) fired four players and the defensive coach following their first game loss. Indicative of the possibilities for the league succeeding in Canada, the LFL quickly rounded up new players, perhaps including some from American teams, but the Triumph finished the season without winning a game.[71] Mortaza justified the league's action by stating that they were "concerned about producing high-quality football and getting rid of the ladies who just want to be celebrities."[72]

Locating athletes did not appear to be a problem, but other issues created roadblocks for the league. For instance, according to Katrina Krawec, in her master's thesis, "Shaping and Being Shaped: Examining Women's Tackle Football in Canada" (2014), when Mortaza expanded from one team in Toronto to LFL Canada, a four-team league, he had difficulties securing venues. His original plan was for six teams in Canada, but he had to change the number and the proposed locations of the teams. In a footnote, Krawec mentioned without much detail that "an arena in Victoria, BC declined to host the LFL."[73]

The Canadian league began its one and only season in 2012, as the U.S. LFL was transitioning away from playing in the fall to games in the spring, bringing it in line with, and in direct competition to, teams in the IWFL, WFA, and other full-kitted teams.[74] Teams were a mixture of local talent and imported Americans. Stevi Schnoor, a former member of the Canadian national rugby team, became a star for the BC Angels, and Americans such as Furr and Tamar Fennell teamed up on the Saskatoon Sirens.[75] Fennell is one of a handful of women who have played in the LFL and also for more traditional teams. Laure Gelis-Diaz (see chapter 6) played for the St. Louis Slam and the Chicago Bliss, and Fennell also has played for the Cincinnati Sizzle of the WFA.[76] For their eventually canceled 2013 season, the Sirens reached even further afield to sign Alexandra Markova, a native of Kostroma, Russia.[77]

Fennell talked with me about her career playing in very different leagues. While in high school, the athletic director there had tried to recruit her to kick for the boys' team, but her mother did not agree. When she began playing for the Sizzle, "I went and tried out and told her I'd be playing. She told me that she was never coming to see me play, but she did. I think she came to my first game after I scored the first one [touchdown]. I could hear her from the stands, and then she was at every game after that." With her mother on board, after her first season with the Sizzle, in which she was named to the WFA All American Team, she still wanted to improve her game. "I still didn't feel like I really understood football. I understood what Ickey [former NFL star Woods, then the owner of the Sizzle] told me to do, and I could execute that, but I didn't really understand football. So, I was searching for a football camp in women's football, and that's when I came across the LFL on MTV. I was teased a lot for being maybe a little bit more feminine than other players, so I found 'that looks fun.' I thought all these girls are super feminine, and it's super athletic—let me try out for this. So, I tried out and made the team in Cleveland to play there for a few years, and I had success with the LFL—I was an All-Star, and things of that nature, so that it's very obviously the differences between the two things I love about both so I've tried to maintain both seasons throughout the years."[78]

When I asked her the common question of what she thought about having to play in the skimpy uniform, she told me, "Yeah. So the uniforms have never affected me. Again, I've run track all my life, so yeah, I think I've been accustomed to having to perform in a two-piece uniform so it wasn't really a problem for me. I think maybe more of the criticism was because the uniform that kind of blinded people to the athletes and the athleticism that was in the league. Girls in the LFL, and in both leagues for that matter, but they put in a lot of training. They're legitimate athletes who take being out there seriously, for the most part. There's the social media aspect of it, but the ones who are at the top of their game, and their teams are doing that, really take it seriously. So if anything the uniform, you know—it's just frustrating that people would see that before they would see the product going out on the field."[79]

LFL Canada, the four-team league, ended after only one season of operation. The BC Angels, led by Schnoor, who had possibly suffered an MCL/ACL tear during the team's regular season meeting, won the 2012 championship game 25–12 over the Sirens.[80] The Canadian champion then played an "interleague" game against the Seattle Mist in an international match that the Mist won 38–18.[81] The Canadian teams seemed set for the 2013 season, and the league announced that the Calgary Fillies would be a new franchise, while Toronto suspended operations. However, on 16 September 2013 the Canadian season was postponed by the league. Although plans were announced to resume operations in 2014, that never happened. Some Canadian players such as Schnoor would catch on with American teams, and, as of 2019, she was still playing for Seattle.[82]

The cancellation of the 2013 season reportedly began with "a mass exodus of players from the Calgary Fillies, a new expansion squad, amid complaints of league disorganization and safety concerns." Following that, when the league cut the number of games for Canadian teams from four to two, the Sirens "voted not to suit up in 2013." With two of their four teams in turmoil, Mortaza evidently canceled the entire season. Kate Marshall of the defending champion Angels told the *Abbotsford (BC) News*, "Our team was definitely ready to go. It's a pretty big disappointment for us, because of the time commitment and everything we'd put into this season and launching the season in Canada." Countering the perceived tight control that Mortaza maintained over every aspect of the game, BC coach Kevin Snell told the paper, "To be a coach in this league, you have to be a self-starter. They kind of give it to you and let you run with it, which is awesome—nobody likes to be micromanaged."[83]

The league's stated reason for the cancellation of the season was "concern over the caliber of football that would be played by teams that lacked the proper preparation window due to new coaching staffs and instability within the coaching ranks. . . . Our greatest value as a global sport and brand is the importance we place on the caliber of football and the reputation we have built as a sport that prides itself on preparation and commitment. We are now broadcast to over 120 territories around the world and our fans/viewers have certain level of expectation. We do not want to jeopardize what we have worked all of these years to build."[84]

A similar pattern of initial success but long-term failure occurred when the LFL expanded to Australia. A week before Mortaza pulled the plug on the Canadian league, he announced that his expansion to Australia would be televised. The LFL announced on their website that "Australia's top broadcast network, Seven Network," had signed on to broadcast their games.[85]

As with Canada, Mortaza prepared Australia for the sport by bringing the LFL All-Fantasy Game Tour to Brisbane and Sydney in 2012. Chloe Butler, a native of Queensland and a wide receiver for the LA Temptation, acted as captain of the Western Conference team and as an ambassador to introduce the league to Australians. LFL Australia also featured four teams, although their names were less provocative than the American originals. The New South Wales Surge, Queensland Brigade, Victoria Maidens, and Western Australia Angels made up the roster of teams for the first, and only, season. Following the established pattern, some U.S. LFL stars such as Monique Gaxiola and Fennell traveled there to provide some veteran experience for the new football players. Gaxiola's NSW Surge won the championship, defeating the Angels 36–12.[86]

The creation of LFL Australia came with the typical negative reaction in the press, including a savage critique of the idea by Senator Kate Lundy, the Australian minister of sport, who charged, "Lingerie Football isn't just a distraction; it's an assault on sport," along with her denunciation of the exploitation of women that she argued was inherent in the league.[87] The condemnation in the media was coupled with success with the fans. The first game between the Maidens and Angels, which Victoria won 32–26, was a ratings hit on television. It peaked at 280,000 viewers and averaged 75,000. In contrast, the highest rated A-League (men's soccer) game only averaged 49,000 viewers.[88]

Despite the ratings success, Mortaza was reportedly "unable to secure television coverage for the 2014–15 season." The announcement by email to the teams came with only weeks to go before the start of the new season.[89] Mortaza asserted that even though the league "had a successful first year, . . . as we don't fill stadiums, we rely on television coverage" to explain the reason for his decision. As was the case in Canada, the outlook for the second LFL Australia season had appeared to be bright. The offseason news included plans to expand to Adelaide, and "another expansion market to be announced shortly."[90] Mortaza might be many things, but he is always optimistic, at least in his public communications, and so the league once again promised to be back the next year, with a new television deal and even more expansion, this time into New Zealand.[91]

What happened to the deal with Seven Network was as transparent as was the reasoning for MTV2 dropping their partnership—in other words, not at all. Before games had even begun, the network had received a petition circulated by Collective Shout, an organization described as "a grassroots campaign movement against the sexualisation of women." Caitlin Roper of Collective Shout argued that broadcasting the league "undermines the achievement of female athletes in other sports, who struggle for sponsorship and media coverage." Bridget Fair, the Seven group's chief of corporate and regulatory affairs, maintained that the network "did not believe the LFL breached Commercial Television Industry Code of Practice," as some had reportedly charged. When it came to sign a new contract, perhaps the network, after defending its decision, bowed to pressure and halted the telecasts. Once again, it might have also been the case that Mortaza asked for more money than the network wanted to pay or that he alienated them in some other way.[92]

The LFL has had other successes in finding broadcast partners, at least for a short period. After MTV2 canceled its broadcast partnership with the LFL (by then rebranded as the Legends Football League), Mortaza found other broadcasters to carry his games. In 2015 Fuse, a network that began as a music channel, transitioned to a variety of programming aimed at young adults, which that year included "18 regular season games, two conference Playoff games as well as the Legends Cup Championship game." Bill Hilary, the president of Fuse Media, told media reporter R. Thomas Umstead of *Multichannel News*, "This is a key acquisition for Fuse as we continue to roll out programming that extends beyond music and resonates with our core audience of New Young Americans as well as the established LFL fan base. LFL is primed to become the next major sports and entertainment franchise on television and we are excited to build on this momentum and bring these athletes, games and compelling stories to the network."[93]

That same year, the Oxygen network broadcast *Pretty. Strong.* The program was a reality series that followed the on- and off-the-field lives of several Bliss players, including Furr, Alberts, Rice, and Barwick.[94] The series was fairly typical of reality television fare. Most of the content followed the women during their daily lives, with a few minutes each episode devoted to football. That both *Nightline* and *Pretty. Strong.* featured the same athletes indicated that they must have been the best league ambassadors on the team, or those least likely to criticize Mortaza and the LFL.

Writing for ESPNW, Sarah Spain praised the athletes as being "former Division I athletes who can seriously ball. They're the kind of women you'd want your daughter to look up to: strong, athletic, passionate, empowered and confident." After that laudatory start, Spain identified her only problem with the league: "Those damn uniforms." She then proceeded to provide a more brief critique of the league than Rozendaal, but similar in spirit. The point here is not Spain's critique, which has been covered previously, but to illustrate why so many women who play full-kit football have issues with the LFL. Spain is a fairly prominent member of the media who often writes about women's sports. She is a radio personality for ESPN and tweets daily about sports. But her article about the LFL is balanced by only one article about the traditional women's football, a relatively brief write-up of the 2016 Women's World Games.[95] When even writers who might be expected to notice women's football, which she glossed over in the LFL article, do not, then women in more traditional leagues arguably have a reason to be upset.

The Oxygen program did negatively influence the league in one way. On one of the later episodes, Alberts revealed that she was dating Ashley Salerno, the quarterback of the Los Angeles Temptation. Salerno was ironically the player who leveled Alberts and gave her a concussion during the Chicago player's first game. YouTube has the video of Salerno's hit and Alberts's revelation linked to highlight what may be one of the more interesting first meetings of a couple.[96]

The episode ran in August, and by November the LFL and Mortaza took action to punish the players for violating the league's discipline policy. Both Alberts and Salerno were suspended for the 2016 season. According to TMZ reporting, the commissioner asserted that the policy, which forbade employees from dating, whether male or female, "was put in place to protect the integrity of the game—'It's all about fairness. The rules are in place to ensure we put the best product on the field.'" On the surface, that made sense. To have the quarterback from one team dating a defensive back from another would represent a potential conflict of interest, and the league likely also had an interest in preventing relationships that might lead to dramatic breakups or charges of sexual harassment, leading to even more bad publicity. The TMZ report, however, suggested that "some women in the league" were upset and claimed the rule was designed ensure that "players dating would take away from the sex appeal of the brand and push a more 'butch' image instead." Mortaza disagreed with those players, stating, "As for being open to the gay community, I don't think there's another league that's been more receptive. We'd never regulate what sex people could date."[97] Both players returned for the 2017 season, although Salerno was again suspended for violating the discipline policy in 2018.[98]

Other broadcast partnerships included deals with the Extreme Sports Channel in the United Kingdom, the Super Channel in Canada, and internationally on Eleven Sports.[99] LFL games, as of 2019, were not broadcast on any cable channels covered in a basic package in the United States, but while visiting my in-laws in France in 2016, I did find games being broadcast there. The color commenter on the broadcast was Sarah Riahi, who began the first French women's (full-kitted) football team, the Sparkles de Villeneuve-Saint-Georges in 2012. The LFL in the United States can be found on their YouTube channel, where games are broadcast on the week following the contest, which currently has 475,688 views.[100]

This was perhaps one of the largest successes that the LFL had. More so than any other women's football league, their games could be easily viewed. The game broadcast team featured Mortaza doing the play-by-play and Bobby Hewko, who played quarterback for the Florida Gators in the 1980s, adding color commentary. The broadcasts, one per week, were professionally produced and included sideline reporter Heidi Golznig's pregame and halftime interviews, instant replay, and professional graphics. In short, the LFL games, interspersed with commercials and located on the LFL Channel on YouTube, featured everything that the typical NFL broadcast did. They included much more as well. In particular, the coaches had microphones that recorded them screaming at officials and their players in profanity-laced tirades. Cameramen were positioned on the field to provide close-ups of the players and to record their trash talk, which was clearly audible. Halftime talks, or rants, were also available for viewers. Players also often interacted with the fans after scoring and provided something of a party atmosphere.

Although full-kitted leagues and their games are also available on YouTube, aside from championship games that are sometimes originally broadcast on ESPN3, the production qualities generally do not come close to those of the LFL. There is usually only one camera, and while the announcers are often enthusiastic, they are not generally as talented as the LFL crew.

Raphaëlle Duché, one of the French women in the LFL, playing for the Denver Dream in 2018, told me about her football career. From Montpellier, she played roller derby before she began playing football with the Argocanes, a combined team from Montpelier and Aix-en-Provence (see the introduction). She played on the losing side in two championship games of the Challenge Féminin. When she went to Scotland for university, she found that the women's team there played seven-a-side, so she played on the Predators, a men's team. "I didn't want to play seven-a-side. The level was not as good as I had in France, and I wanted to get better." It was not easy in the beginning, but by the end of the season, "they trusted me. At the last game I started defense, and I was captain of the team for one game."[101]

Her path to the LFL was a circuitous one. "It was not my plan at the beginning. I had a tough breakup last summer [2018]. My boyfriend was American, and I was planning the whole year to go in the USA with him. Well, it didn't work out that way, but I decided that I, I have my visa, I have everything. So fuck it, I'm going to go anyway, and I'm going to road trip." While in the home of American football, she decided that she wanted to try out for a team or teams, "just to see how is the level." She tried out for the Seattle Majestics of the WFA and made the team. It was just at the beginning of her road trip, and the season was still some time away, however, so she decided to keep traveling.

Her path led her to Denver. "I knew there was tryouts for the LFL in Denver early in December, something like that. Just out of curiosity, I wanted to do it, just to see how it is. I made the team, and it was winter, so I didn't want to road trip all around during winter. I found a place to stay, and I was like, I'm going to go to practice, because I love football, so I'm going to do some practice and see how it is. And then, weeks after weeks after weeks, I had my place on the team, I'm doing good, the team wants me ... it just kind of all happened, without me really thinking about it."[102]

She was well aware of the negative press that the LFL had. "Coming from Europe, I know that especially girls, they hate the LFL, and it has a really bad view from people. Because of the uniforms, and because ... I wanted to see from the inside how it is. How are the practices? Now I can tell all these girls in Europe who think the LFL is just girls showing off—I can tell them it is not. Absolutely not. We practice as hard as we practiced when I played football in Scotland or France. It's way faster. I don't think it has the reputation it should have, because it's actually very intense."[103]

Duché played defensive end for the Dream and played fairly well. In the games available on YouTube, "Frenchy" as Mortaza unimaginatively nicknamed her, demonstrated good athletic ability. She charged up field on the snap and showed good football speed in pursuit.[104]

When I asked her about the uniform, which at the time included full leggings instead of shorts, she told me, "It's one of the reasons people don't like—especially girls. I don't think men really care. I think girls are like, 'Oh, it's not respecting our bodies, not respecting our personhood.' I've never seen it that way. I'm not a feminist at all. At all. If I had to wear a panty, I would have done it, even though I really appreciate the fact that we wear leggings now. It's so much better." Her parents were a bit more skeptical about the uniforms, but the change to leggings helped.[105]

I did not have the chance to talk to Duché after the uniforms went back to shorts, and she was not sure she could afford to stay for the entire season, so maybe she left before the change. In a conversation on Messenger on 10–11 March 2020, Duché told me that she was not playing with the Dream, nor had she returned to Scotland to play there. Instead she was still in Denver but planned to play for the Denver Bandits of the WNFC, which she described as being "more professional and organize[d] than the LFL, and in my opinion, where the future of women's football is."[106] COVID did in the 2020 season, so Duché did not have the chance to report further on the differences between playing in the different leagues.

Bridget McDonnell, who played rugby for the Black Rose team at Ohio Northern University, and then for the Chicago Bliss, gave me a more detailed, or less pro forma, answer on the question of the uniform. "Did it bother me? Uh, no. I mean, I come from, I guess you could say conservative Christian background, but to me it was just a bathing suit. . . . The only thing that I think bothered me with the uniform was just the concern, if I don't look good in it then I can't play. Not so much [that I] had a problem with the uniform, [but] that I worried because I had to wear this uniform, [so] I need to make sure that I'm keeping up with my fitness and my healthy eating. The whole time I was with the league, I had my own personal trainer that I had hired that I had worked with. So, I followed a very strict eating regimen, because I never wanted to be in a spot where I felt, for myself, that I didn't look good in this thing that I now have to go play in, in front of people."[107] When comparing the athletic abilities of the LFL players to the other women against whom she previously played football, she said, "Overall, all the girls, even at tryouts and now in the team, are more athletic. There is not a single girl who is not athletic, who doesn't have an athletic background. . . . In France; it was more open to everybody." She argued that women in general in the United States were more athletic because of the opportunities that girls had in school.[108]

Duché was open to talking about her experiences in the LFL, but she asked me not to post the recording of our interview. She talked about the game day routine and told me that the players were issued the uniforms and had to turn them in when the game was over. "I think that Mitch [Mortaza], the owner, doesn't want us to have the uniforms with us. It's his product, and he's very protective of his product." Game days were very busy, with photo shoots, walking through plays ("He makes sure we know what we're doing so we don't look stupid on TV"), listening to Mortaza's pregame speech that lasts "about an hour." The day is heavily scripted. "It's very controlled from the inside. I've never seen any journalists," which was why Duché was hesitant to have her interview widely disseminated.[109]

In 2010 *BusinessWeek* magazine called the LFL "the fastest growing sports league in the United States."[110] That was reinforced by the international expansion of the league to Canada, Australia, and plans for a European league in 2013. However, those leagues eventually failed, and the European effort never materialized. Other events also began catching up with Mortaza that threatened the league.

After the commissioner canceled the 2014–15 Australian season, "a number of former support staff were organizing a class action lawsuit in the America[n] state of Nevada, where the company [Horizon Productions] is registered." According to Brendan Foster, a reporter for *WA Today*, various people claimed that "Mr Mortaza still owes players and coaches around $30,000 in payments after he cancelled the 2014/15 season two weeks before it was about to kick off." Foster also reported that "former WA Angels coach J. R. Rogers says Mr Mortaza still owes him $6500." Mortaza reportedly claimed Rogers "had not returned equipment and would not be paid until he did so." According to Mortaza, quoted in the article, "He knows that and is under contractual obligation to return [items of equipment]." Some of the dispute between Rogers and Mortaza seemed to stem from the plan that former LFL coaches and players had to create their own Ladies Gridiron League with a similar business model. Additional anger by former LFL players came when the LFL Facebook page contained some of their images. Nicole Harvey and Leah Warner also charged that "Mr Mortaza failed to respect them as athletes and reacted in an over-the-top manner to losses." They also claimed that he had "made a promise he would make the uniforms bigger, but he made them smaller," and revealed that they planned to stage protests when the LFL held tryouts for the new season.[111]

One metric of the LFL's success is that it has inspired imitators in other countries. In addition to the Ladies Gridiron League in Australia, which only lasted one year, three other leagues began in Mexico.[112] The sport there peaked with six separate leagues with nearly fifty teams in 2016, before contraction began, leaving the Women's Football League as the main bikini league there as of 2019.[113]

When asked about the uniforms, Carly Machuca, a defensive linewoman for the Mambas Negras (Black Mambas) de Puebla (Mexico), gave me a similar answer as most of the American women. "Yes, it is tough [to play wearing a bikini]. It [is] different than a regular uniform because when you get hurt, it hurts a lot more. We have less protection than other kinds of teams, but I don't think it's very different from other sports like volleyball or running. The uniform is kind of the same—we have even more clothes on. But it's kind of invigorating." She told me that her parents were "not that happy," not because of the uniform but because it was American football. Acting as a translator for Paulina Vidal, the Mambas Negras owner, she told me that the team averaged around 750 fans watching, which would be a good turnout for most women's teams.[114]

This is one area where full-kitted women's football has had much greater success, with traditional leagues spread over Europe and around the world. Mortaza still had his sights set on Europe, where women's football has spread to a majority of the countries. The league planned to create a league to debut in 2021 with "six national clubs in the United Kingdom, Ireland, Germany, Italy, Spain, and Belgium."[115]

Somewhat ironically, the creation of the Amsterdam Cats and the Queens Football League in the Netherlands resulted from the LFL. Kanessa Muluneh-Coerman, who built both leagues, which feature traditional uniforms, told me that her inspiration came when she happened to find a video of the LFL on the internet.[116]

In addition to changing the league motto to Women of the Gridiron, and the abortive attempt to change the uniform, Mortaza has also posited his league as the antidote for the NFL, which he has called the "No Fun League." When the San Francisco 49ers quarterback Colin Kaepernick began his 2016 protests during the national anthem, other athletes at various levels and in various sports followed his example. In 2017 Danielle Harvey and Sherri Awagah, two African American players from the LA Temptation, took a knee during a game with the Omaha Heart. Given the control that Mortaza reportedly exerted over the players, it is quite possible that he allowed, or even directed, the move to show that the league was relevant to current events. Fan reaction was somewhat negative; some fans could be heard yelling, "Get off your knees!"[117] After testing the waters, if that was staged, Mortaza and the league announced that official LFL policy required that "all of its players are going to stand when the national anthem is played," appealing to the sizable group of football fans who want their sporting experience politics-free.[118]

Other changes to the LFL have included increasing the diversity of the players. To use one team as an example, the Temptation team that played in Lingerie Bowl III was mostly white and blond, whereas the 2019 version of the team had seventeen players, only six of whom were Caucasian.[119]

The body type of the players has also changed, with the contemporary players being more solidly built than the runway models of the original Lingerie Bowls. On the Chicago Bliss roster for the 2011–12 season, for instance, the athletes averaged five feet seven inches tall and weighed an average of 136.5 pounds. For the 2018–19 season, the height had gone down to five feet six inches, but the weight had gone up to 152.4 pounds. That was not definitive, but it was indicative that perhaps Mortaza was easing off of the body standard that had been the norm in previous years.[120]

McDonnell had played during the 2014 season, which coincided with the first years of Mortaza's rebranding the league as the Legends Football League, and she noticed the change. "I will say that once I left the league that seemed to change. When I left the league, I started to see an evolution of beautifully strong athletic women who weren't the typical thin-bodied women from previous years, and it seemed to have kind of the evolution of yes, this is an athletic sport, you know, this is a physically demanding sport, and kind of the overall appearance of the league started to change and be strong, built women, which I thought was really cool. And then they eventually went to panty–sports bra–type thing to, I think, maybe appease more of the people who had a bigger problem with the uniform. But I think that the evolutions that were made and formed definitely went in a more positive direction."[121]

Mortaza has also elevated Danika Brace, formerly a linebacker for the Seattle Mist, to be the head coach and general manager of the Nashville Knights.[122] With the change to Legends Football League, the names for new teams have been less sexualized, with teams such as the Austin Acoustic and the Omaha Heart replacing the more provocatively named teams. After the uniform change that angered hard-core fans, the skimpy shorts have returned, and the game is largely the same sexualized version of football that has always marked the LFL brand.

Mortaza and the LFL, rebranded the Legends Football League in 2013, continued to operate in its tenth season in 2019. Although Mortaza has made changes around the periphery, the game remained much the same as it was in 2004. Teams have come and gone with some regularity, although the Bliss, Temptation, and Mist remain from the original league. The LFL, as of August 2019, had eight teams, each playing a four-game schedule. Aside from a spate of stories on the league's national anthem policy in 2017, the free (but largely negative) media that Mortaza received for the league in its first several years seems to have evaporated.

Mortaza again caused a stir in late 2019, when he posted that the LFL would "not be producing a 2020 season."[123] After four days, during which many people on social media welcomed this news, Mortaza pulled the rug out from under the celebrations of the league's demise and announced that he was merely rebranding once again.[124] The league would now be known as the X League, and he even disclosed plans for expansion. The now disappeared press release announcing the X League seemed to indicate that its athletes would be able to earn money from "branding and revenue opportunities." It went on to say, "Superstar athletes will generate revenues from merchandise that depicts their name, as well as sponsorship revenue share and opportunities to represent the X League with international press tours and games." In addition, "athletes who establish tenure and [have] proven their worth to the league and their individual teams will be presented ownership stake within their team, at the conclusion of their playing career." There were also team changes. The Nashville Knights reportedly did not comply with deadlines set by the league, so they would be replaced by the Kansas City Force. The Chicago Blitz would keep its name, but the Seattle, LA, Omaha, Austin, and Denver teams would all have new names.[125] Mortaza had apparently retired and sold the league to legendary Chicago Bears player and coach Mike Ditka.[126] Following the 2020 shutdown, the new X League season is scheduled to begin with the Chicago Blitz playing the Kansas City Force on 10 June 2022.[127]

Regardless of whether one considers the Lingerie Football League, the LFL, or the X League to be real football, it has survived all of the negative press. The league continued to offer women who want to play football in front of fairly large crowds, and gain notice by thousands of others online, the opportunity to do so. The league's YouTube channel often has more than two hundred thousand views for games, and as discussed above, it is the most accessible of any women's football league online.

The increased societal freedom that allowed the women of the WPFL to live out their football dreams also permitted entrepreneurs such as Mitchell Mortaza to make money from sexualizing the sport. Freedom, as we have learned, in many times and places, has not always been neat and tidy in the way that we might wish.

That freedom and the lack of an overriding monetary interest provided by one supreme league have meant that whenever disputes arose over league decisions, the aggrieved parties were at liberty to take their game to a different setting. When dissatisfaction grew among some WFA and IWFL teams, they had the ability to do something different and form their own league. That was how teams from Utah, Texas, Washington, and California created the Women's National Football Conference.

**1.** Sarah Viola of the Molosses, wearing a Boston Renegades helmet, versus Argocanes in the Challénge Féminin 2016. Photo by Jean-Marc Burtscher.

**2.** Sophie Aillaud (17) of the Argocanes taking a hand-off versus the Molosses in the Challénge Féminin 2016. Photo by Jean-Marc Burtscher.

**3.** Iris Smith, Toledo Troopers. Photo by the author.

**4.** Kasey Carter, Toledo Furies, and Eunice White (80), Toledo Troopers. Photo by the author.

**5.** Mitchi Collette (wearing scarf),
Toledo Troopers and Reign. Photo by the author.

**6.** Cynthia "Red" Bryant, Jodi "Moose" Rehlander, and Michele Braun, Minnesota Vixen. Photo courtesy of Jonathon Rehlander.

**7.** Melissa "Missy" Bedwell, Lake Michigan Minx. Photo by the author.

**8.** (*opposite top*) Louise Bean (Utah Falconz 13) against the Seattle Majestics. Photo by Sophie Crawford.

**9.** (*opposite bottom*) Columbus Comets versus Cleveland Fusion. Photo by the author.

**10.** (*above*) Thee Toledo Reign versus Pittsburgh Passion. Photo by the author.

11. (*opposite top*) Detroit Dark Angels versus Minnesota Vixen. Photo by the author.

12. (*opposite bottom*) Texas Elite Spartans versus Nebraska Nite Hawks. Photo by the author.

13. (*above*) Manitoba Girls Football Association players getting ready to play Indiana in the Battle of the Borders. Photo by the author.

**14.** Canyons Lethal Angels and the West Granite Quake of the Utah Girls Football League playing a demonstration during the halftime of the Utah Falconz versus Seattle Majestics game in 2018. Photo by Sophie Crawford.

**15.** Sam Gordon of the UGFL. Photo by the author.

**16.** (*above*) Team Finland versus Team USA at the 2017 IFAF Women's World Championship. Photo by the author.

**17.** (*opposite top*) Sami Grisafe (15) leads Team USA versus Team Canada at the 2017 IFAF Women's World Championship. Photo by the author.

**18.** (*opposite bottom*) Australian fans at the Women's World Championship, 2017. Photo by the author.

**19.** (*opposite top*) When Mexico played, the enthusiasm level in the stands increased. Photo by the author.

**20.** (*opposite bottom*) Mexican fans with noise-makers kept the energy up. Photo by the author.

**21.** (*above*) British fans sporting the Union Jack. Photo by the author.

**22.** Future Cleveland Browns coach Callie
Brownson (behind the 40-yard-line marker)
at the 2017 Women's World Championship.
Photo by the author.

**23.** Australia versus Mexico for third place
at the Women's World Championship, 2017.
Photo by the author.

**24.** Phoebe Schecter (56) of Great Britain playing against Mexico at the Women's World Championship, 2017. Photo by the author.

# The Women's National Football Conference

SUNRISE MOUNTAIN HIGH SCHOOL,
LAS VEGAS, NEVADA, 21 JULY 2018

The Texas Elite Spartans had not given up a single point in their inaugural 2018 Independent Women's Football League (IWFL) season. The Utah Falconz had not lost a game since 25 July 2015, when the Pittsburgh Passion defeated them 41–37 in the IWFL Championship game.[1] The 2018 IWFL season had been marred by blowouts and forfeits, and those problems resulted in two of the top women's football teams in the United States playing for the Best of the West Women's Football Championship (BWWFC) in Las Vegas.

The Elite Spartans' streak of not allowing a score came to an end when the Falconz' Louise Bean threw a 27-yard touchdown pass on fourth down to Veronica Siqueiros. Their scoring drive had only taken eight plays to move 55 yards. The Falconz added the 2-point conversion via a pass from Bean to Sara Galica to lead 8–0. The Elite Spartans came back when Odessa Jenkins scored on a 2-yard run to cap a 68-yard drive that included two unsportsmanlike conduct penalties on the Falconz and a sideline warning for the Elite Spartans. Shelby Valdepena kicked the extra point to make it 8–7. The teams took that score into halftime, but Utah scored on their first drive in the third quarter. The first Texas drive of the quarter ended when Falconz defensive back Tasha Aiono intercepted Texas quarterback Brittany Bushman's pass on the Texas 42-yard line. The Falconz converted on another fourth down deep in

Dallas territory when Keeshya Cox ran for the first down and then had her helmet ripped off when she went out of bounds. After the half-the-distance-to-the-goal penalty moved the ball to the 4-yard line, the Falconz took two plays to score on an option pitch from Bean to Aiono, who was in at wide receiver. Maira Alcala added the extra point to put Utah in the lead, 15–7. Jenkins then scored on a 6-yard run, and Jessica Gerhart, who split time with Bushman at quarterback, added the 2-point conversion to tie the game.

Jenkins, who was one of the Dallas owners as well as a running back, then scored on a 29-yard run off the right tackle, and when Valdepena added the extra point, the Elite Spartans were ahead 22–15. The Falconz, with around three minutes left, had their chances but failed to pick up a fourth down when Olivia Griswold sacked Bean with 2:08 left. Utah held the Elite Spartans on fourth down and got the ball back for one last shot with 23 seconds left, and Bean completed a long fourth-down pass to Cox at the Texas 47-yard line with 1.4 seconds left, but defensive back Liz Landry batted down Bean's last-ditch pass attempt to preserve the Elite Spartan victory.[2]

The path to the BWWFC in Las Vegas also began, in part, in the same place, seven months before the game. In early December 2018, Mike Rivera organized an all-star game for women football players that included fifty-two athletes primarily drawn from the western IWFL teams. Bean, who played in the game, posted on Facebook her summary of the experience: "52 Allstar players representing 10 teams from the West. 13 fabulous coaches representing 3 western Women's teams and 2 from the Hall of Fame organizations. Destination? Vegas! 10 hours of practice in two days. Then an EAST vs WEST game which we won 30 to 0. All in the hopes of promoting this awesome sport and to show how working together as one unit . . . empowers the whole!"[3]

The Vegas all-star game provided a base of relationships between the players from the west, and issues with the IWFL brought things to a head. According to Bean, Surge owner Christina Suggett sparked the conversations that led to the event when her team lost to the Falconz and saw that her team would have to expend a great deal of money to travel for the playoffs. To avoid spending the money that Suggett asserted they could not afford, she "suggested a tourney-style type playoff."[4]

On Oscar Lopez's *Gridiron Beauties* podcast, Suggett told the host, "To get to these games has been a challenge. I can't remember the last time we went regular-season airfare, but take a look at some of the scenarios that would have played out. I mean we're looking at— you know, of course, every team wants to get to that last game . . . that championship game—that would have put us at three air flights. Three! That's catastrophic. Look at Seattle's situation. Scott [Seattle coach McCarron], you were looking at four . . . I mean, who can afford that kind of travel? But, through no fault of Dallas, we were looking at some of the teams on this side [West Coast] really incurring some catastrophic airfare to get to Dallas. I'm not sure any of us could have made It, and so at some point I took a look at finances and reached out to a few teams, and said—how are we going to do this? I can't do it, so what where does that leave us? Between the four of us we came up with a great idea."[5]

Travel was one challenge that brought the teams together, but chaotic conditions within the IWFL was another. In 2018 the league seemed poised to showcase a higher level of play than it had for several years. The teams that took part in the BWWFC had all been members of the IWFL at the start of 2018. Utah had dominated the IWFL since the Pittsburgh Passion had left in 2016, and the addition of the Elite Spartans, along with the shift of the San Diego Surge and Seattle Majestics from the WFA, offered the chance for the longer-established league to regain some of the luster it had lost to its major competitor.

That did not happen however, and Jenkins told Lopez, "I think the main reason for this was that there was some insurmountable expenses, particularly for the folks on the West Coast . . . but I think we all came together because we were not achieving what we were told would be achieved, with the IWFL when it comes to competitive football. I mean, to be realistic, there's a higher level of football, where there's the blue bloods, and there's about potentially ten teams that could play each other and not blow each other out. So you talk about the competitive level of football that's really been playing, in any league, there is a clear differentiation now, and our goal is just to put on the best opportunity for girls, and not to see people get blown out."[6]

Falconz coach Rick Rasmussen echoed Jenkins and told Lopez: "The way the schedule worked out, the way the season played out, we were looking at two home games, and a trip to Austin hopefully. The travel impact would affect Seattle the worst and then San Diego second, but what we really wanted was the opportunity to play in a tournament setting where we knew we wouldn't have a forfeit, because we were frankly worried about a first-round forfeit. So when it was presented to us a couple of days after the seed began to sprout—yeah, we sacrificed possibly two home games, and possibly two forfeits, one due to a team with low numbers and one due to a team that was running out of money. So rather than saying, look we're going to bye, bye, and then try to go to Austin, it made more sense to play with top-level teams in a setting where everybody could easily get to, at a relatively inexpensive amount. We don't incur airfare during the season. . . . We take a bus everywhere. We had a trip to LA, and those take their toll on you. It just made sense when it was presented to us. Sure, we sacrificed the home field advantage, and clearly, the elevation is relatively stable here. So, the opportunity to play against Seattle, San Diego, and Dallas was just too tempting for us not to consider. Once we really started to think about it, it made sense. So, that was our motivation."[7]

When asked what the tournament meant for the IWFL, and what the ultimate goal of the BWWFC was, McCarron reported that his team had "sent a contract termination letter to the IWFL this morning, before the tournament announcement," and that the league had already removed the Majestics from their website. On the future of the league, he did not want to speculate. "Obviously, the four of our teams are no longer affiliated with the IWFL. They've removed our team logos from the website. I don't know that we can speak to the future of the league. That will obviously be up to them what they decide to do moving forward, but I would imagine that, in some capacity, there will still be an IWFL championship, although that will not involve any of our four teams."[8]

After Lopez ran down all of the changes that had taken place in 2017 and 2018, which included the Majestics and Surge moving to the IWFL and then this latest shift, he asked McCarron about what this event signaled for the future. McCarron told Lopez: "In fairness, Oscar, we want to see a particular vision of women's football to take place. Unfortunately, until we get to that point, our organization is not going to be satisfied. I think that is the great thing about having our four teams come together on this. While we may have different ideas about how we get there, we all have the same common goal in mind, which is great. Now it's a matter of how we put all those pieces together." The Seattle coach proved that he believed in the adage that one should always focus on the next game, and so he was not ready to speculate on what this meant for the future. "I think a lot of that is to be determined. The four of our groups are really focused on getting through this first. Then we'll see what comes of it, but collectively, I think our four organizations are excited about the opportunity to work together."[9]

Jenkins was more forthcoming about the future: "I think it's important to note that we talked a lot about this and what the future looks like, and that there needs to be a differentiation in order to have what we have always talked about achieving, which is competitive football every single weekend, with every matchup. And so, although we are coming together to do this tournament, we all have very similar goals, so I definitely look at this as a launch for something that sets us up for the future. What that is, we'll probably be back on your show to talk about it at some point."[10]

The tournament announcement, posted on the Falconz' Facebook site, stated in part:

There is a revolution happening in women's football. Some of the greatest franchises in the sports' history have folded. Others are finding it impossible to make it through a season due to enormous blowout victories, forfeits and/or insurmountable travel responsibilities.

Each of the so-called "major leagues" will see a new champion in 2018. Not because of league parity, but because the opposite is true. As a result, when attending a women's football game in any existing reputable league, you have over a 50% chance of witnessing a blowout. Even worse, 50% of all women's football games played by the most successful teams in the sport have ended in forfeit or with one team scoring ZERO points!

So where does the sport turn?

A group of powerhouse teams out west have decided that enough is enough! The "blue bloods" of West Coast women's football have banded together to bring fans the *Best of the West Women's Football Championship*. The tournament format creates head-to-head match ups with some of the best teams in the country. This group of owners has come together to show what can be achieved when a group has a willingness to combine resources for a shared vision.

The Utah Falconz, Texas Elite Spartans, San Diego Surge and Seattle Majestics have made a commitment to providing the best product that women's football has to offer. As a first step, they have worked together to bring about one of the most exciting events in recent history.

The "BIG 4" is among the most reputable and most distinguished women's sports organizations in the world. Combined, these teams have won over six national titles, boast over 40 All Star players, and have 10+ Team USA Gold Medalists, who have won all three World Championships since the introduction of women's football to the world stage in 2010.

The event will be held July 19th—July 21st in Las Vegas, NV. The 3-day round-robin style tournament will include an owner's forum, a player's clinic, as well as an evening social event. This event will be the launchpad for professional level women's football, and will change the sport forever.[11]

The tournament was largely successful, particularly in the down-to-the-wire finish in the final game. There were challenges, however. The Las Vegas heat, which hovered around 105 degrees Fahrenheit each day, was difficult enough for the fans and even worse for the players. This caused considerable criticism on social media, but the teams shortened the quarters from fifteen minutes to twelve in order to lessen the exposure to the heat. When no serious issues arose during the first day, the final games went back to the usual fifteen-minute quarters. Bean reported that the Falconz did not experience any problems and told me, "We had done a lot of heat training." The Majestics, according to the Utah quarterback, "said they struggled some. But it's not as hot up there."[12]

The live feed for the games was erratic, which led to several complaints that were sampled on the "Recommendations and Reviews" section of the BWWFC Facebook page.[13] The weather also wreaked havoc with one game.

The tournament began on 19 July 2018 with a rematch of the 14 April 2018 Utah-Seattle game that opened chapter 3. The Majestics made a closer game of it but lost again to the Falconz, this time 14–29.[14] The Surge played the Elite Spartans in the second game. Unfortunately, the live-feed problems were eclipsed by a massive storm that blew sand and rain, accompanied by lightning, which delayed the game after only three minutes into the first quarter. After a two-hour delay, the teams finished the game, and the Texans cruised to a 47–0 victory.[15]

After a rest day, the Surge and the Majestics played on 21 July 2018 in the early game to determine third place. In a tightly fought defensive battle that featured only one offensive score, San Diego defeated Seattle 16–6.[16] That was followed by the Utah-Texas nail biter. The only game of the tournament that was a blowout was the weather-delayed game on the first night. The four teams were demonstrably in good playing shape, since there were few serious injuries during the three days of intense play. With the exception of the storm game, the other games can be viewed on the BWWFC YouTube channel, and the games were professionally produced with play-by-play provided by Tony Cradasco and Melissa Farris.[17]

Between game days, the organizers held an owners' forum. The representatives included Samantha Smith-Meek of the Falconz, Cindy Butz-Houghton of the Majestics, Brian Sewell of the Surge, and Jenkins of the Elite Spartans. Kandace Mitchell, a former player with several teams and then the assistant director of athletics with the Atlanta Public

Schools, moderated the panel. One of the first issues that Jenkins led off with was the perennial goals of what purpose women's football teams should follow, amateur/recreational versus professional/competitive, that is a perennial discussion point in women's football. Jenkins outlined what the teams sought by telling the audience, "It is all about raging against the machine that is mediocrity in women's football," placing her and the others firmly in the professional/competitive camp.[18]

There was some talk about possible next moves, and it appeared clear that something new would come out of the tournament, but there were no details on what that might be. McCarron continued to be cagey about what would come next, but he did tell me that what he was thinking of how to move women's football to a new model. "Some of the stuff we have talked about collectively as a group over the last two days has all been conversations we have had as an organization. How do we get the organization financially viable on its own? Consistently, year after year after year, so that we can eliminate players fees all together? Once I get to that point, then I can start looking at, 'Okay, how do I start paying players?' but I can't do it until I don't have to worry about the team needing to bring in money to pay for fields, for practice, for equipment, for travel, for whatever. We can't get to that point yet, so we've started doing some things on our organization's side that can get us there. It just takes time. These guys have similar processes in place—they have the same idea about how they get that done from a league perspective, same as we did for a team. So it's really a natural fit for us, which is good. Hopefully it works out. If it doesn't, it doesn't, but hopefully it does."[19]

McCarron argued that the tournament, despite the technical issues and the storm, had already been a success. "I think the success of this was getting four teams together that had similar ideas on how things should be done, understanding that we were all going to have to give and take to pull this off. You don't find this a lot in women's football because everybody is out for themselves. They all want to look at, 'Well, how does this benefit my individual team? How does this affect my individual team without having an umbrella view?' We want to pull this umbrella view off, and I'm going to have to sacrifice something that will benefit Texas and San Diego and Utah. They're going to have to make sacrifices that will benefit us."[20]

McCarron also provided additional background on how the tournament originated from the Majestics' perspective: "When we left [the WFA] to come over to the IWFL, there were people that were put in place that were promised to be able to run the league like it needed to be run. . . . At the end of the day, they weren't, and all the support from within the league was just pushed aside. So we were left hanging. We had eight games to start, then we had seven, then we were down to six, and now we got another team that was folding right before the season, and now we're down to four. Where is the league stepping in and helping us get this stuff? We all had the same thing."[21]

On the possible future of the IWFL, McCarron, who had been a successful coach, proved to be a poor prognosticator. "I don't think the IWFL is ever going to be dead, just because they can look like an opportunity for a new team that wants to exist and say, 'I want to be a team,' and the IWFL will take me, and the IWFL will take their money."[22] The league did hold a championship in 2018, but their loss in the Minnesota court discussed in chapter 3 likely caused them to cease operations.

As had been the case in women's semiprofessional football in the United States since play resumed in 2000, as one league died, another was born. On 30 August 2018, a little more than one month after the BWWFC, the Majestics and the other BWWFC teams posted a press release on Facebook that announced the creation of the Women's National Football Conference (WNFC). The league had fourteen teams, along with a developmental team for the inaugural 2019 season.[23]

The WNFC named Kandace Mitchell, the moderator of the BWWFC Owners Forum, as the commissioner of the new league.[24] This addressed one of the issues that critics had complained about with previous leagues—that the leaders of the leagues were also team owners, which created implicit conflicts of interest.

The comments from the Surge, Majestics, and Falconz that accompanied the initial press release were aspirational, as had been the case for every new league in American women's football history. Mike Suggett of the Surge stated, "The WNFC provides a stable platform to grow the sport of Women's Football. The Surge is excited to be part of this new family." Smith-Meek added, "The Utah Falconz are thrilled to be joining the WNFC, which includes teams with proven track records on and off the field. It takes great innovation and courage for this sport to grow and we believe the WNFC embodies just that. We are honored to lead the charge in their ranks." McCarron added a bit more detail and ramped up the hopes for the future: "After seeing the business model, 3–5 year plan, and tremendous amount of successful, business-minded professionals involved with the WNFC, this was an easy decision for us to make. . . . This brings about a paradigm shift in the sport of women's football that not only gives us a platform to attract the highest caliber athletes, but will provide the type of professional league branding that will attract high level corporate sponsors."[25] For whatever reason, the Elite Spartans were not a part of the press release but were certainly connected to the league.

The league got off to a fast start in the sponsorship arena. In December the league announced that they had secured a sponsorship with athletic manufacturer Adidas. The support was part of Adidas's *She Breaks Barriers* initiative, which sought to "provide access, remove stereotypes, and to address the inequality for female athletes at all levels and ages." In addition to supporting the WNFC, the company also provided funds to cohost Jennifer Welter's nationwide flag football camps for girls.[26] Adidas joined Riddell, the helmet maker, to sponsor the first Title IX Bowl, the league's championship game.[27] According to the WNFC Facebook page, Riddell's sponsorship included awarding "equipment grants totaling $7,500" to the two teams who played in the game.[28] They also connected with USCREEN to broadcast their games on a variety of platforms.[29]

The sponsorships allowed the WNFC to pay some of their players. The league announced in March that each team would nominate one "Breaking Barriers" Player of the Week. One player from each conference (Pacific and Atlantic) would be selected and "be awarded a $250 cash prize, and $100 in [A]didas gear." In addition, there would be a player of the month, who would win "a brand new Riddell Speed

Flex helmet." The press release asserted that the WNFC was the "only league without player registration fees, or team registration fees in the history of women's football." It further specified, "The WNFC has assumed approximately $90,000 YTD ($60,000 directly to teams) in order to alleviate burdens from teams in the league."[30]

Since the WNFC was a new league in 2018, the information available for it was more readily available than it was for earlier leagues. The league clearly got off to a quick start financially, perhaps more so than other women's football leagues. However, the difficulty in finding sources for those other leagues might obscure any initial successes that they might have had. Still, the WNFC seemed to be off to a good start.

In addition to the BWWFC teams, the league picked up other experienced teams such as the Los Angeles Bobcats and the Atlanta Phoenix. They also accepted new teams such as the Nebraska Nite Hawks, which had a core group of players that had competed with the Nebraska Stampede of the WFA and the IWFL.[31]

The WNFC also benefited from the sisterhood of traveling shoulder pads and welcomed several international players. The Majestics led the way with three expat players. Defensive back Sylvie Aibeche attended the 2016 Women's World Football Games (WWFG) III in New Orleans, where she made connections, particularly with Majestics quarterback Rachel Wood, which "played a big role in my arrival to Seattle."[32] Aibeche had played with the Paris Dragons before she decided to take her game to Seattle.[33] Danielle "Dani" de Groot, who played quarterback for several Australian teams, including the Canberra Mustangs of the LGL, also saw playing time in Seattle.[34] So did Gabrielle "Gaby" Knops, who played on both sides of the ball for the Majestics, and who came to Washington by way of the Leeds Carnegie Chargers and the GB Lions.[35]

The Falcons and Spartans likewise served as destinations for women who wanted to play the American game in its homeland. As discussed in chapter 3, Utah has had several international players on their team. The Elite Spartans had Bruce Jurado, who was born in Mexico City. It was unclear from a 2019 *Diario AS* article whether Jurado still lived in Mexico, but the Spanish online sports site seemed to claim that, and the

Elite Spartan's site listed her birth place as Mexico City.[36] Their roster also included two players from Canada, one from Windsor, Ontario, and another from Montreal, Quebec.[37] The Elite Spartans also had players leaving teams in other leagues to join them. Jelani Kelly had played linebacker for the St. Louis Slam of the WFA. When she joined the team, the St. Louis team was on hiatus, but Kelly remained with the Texas team even after the Slam restarted.[38] Kelly was not alone in traveling to Texas to pursue her football goals, and the Elite Spartans roster listed players from thirteen states outside of Texas.[39]

Although *Gridiron Beauties* provided no information on where she would play, it reported that Andrea Romero, lately of the Mexico City Vikingas, would play in the WNFC in 2020.[40] When I asked the Falconz' Bean where Romero would play, she told me that probably she would go to the Elite Spartans, which would make sense geographically.[41] Nausicaa Dell'Orto, who parlayed her days playing football in Italy to a job with NFL Films, told me that she would be playing for the Philly Phantomz in 2020, and since they joined the WNFC, that would be one more international player.[42] Whether those last two players' plans to play for WNFC teams would survive the COVID-canceled season was unknown.

The Phoenix also brought in players from Mexico, and according to the team's Facebook page, the first touchdown scored in league history was a reception by wide receiver Lizbeth Mondragon, who had played for the Querétaro Titanes in Mexico.[43] In a comment on a post about Romero, AC Hris Tler, presumably of the Phoenix, wrote that "the Atlanta Phoenix has welcomed not one, TWO [her capitalization] of the best receivers from the National Team Mexico this season."[44] The name of the receiver was not provided, and the second Mexican woman would play with Atlanta in 2020. On Facebook Messenger, Mondragon told me that Ana Maria Barbosa, who was a teammate of Romero on the Vikingas, would be joining the Phoenix for the 2020 season. Mondragon, Barbosa, and Romero all played for the Mexican National Team at the IFAF WWC in 2017.[45]

There might have been more international players, but not every team had an available roster with player origins. However, teams such as the Majestics, Falconz, Elite Spartans, and Phoenix, along with the teams in other American leagues and in Europe, served as a microcosm of the sisterhood of traveling shoulder pads. They demonstrated the existence of a global talent pool whose members were willing and had the freedom to travel outside of their home country to play the game they love.

As had the WFA, the WNFC has also launched what they call their Global Football Development Program (GFDP). The league selected Gaby Knops to lead the effort as the director of global development, and she will be joined by regional directors including, among others, Phoebe Schecter and Laura Dye of the United Kingdom and Hedvig Palocci of Sweden. Their inclusion was interesting to me since I had the opportunity to interview those three women when they were only players. This initiative is set to launch in 2023.[46]

The fourteen regular teams in the WNFC played a six-game schedule before the league's playoffs. The four original teams, along with the Phoenix, Nite Hawks, Bobcats, and the first-year Alabama Fire made the playoffs. The Elite Spartans dominated the regular season. They won every game and only gave up points against the Falconz (18) and the Phoenix (7). Their rematch with the Falconz during the regular season did not live up to expectations. They played the game in Salt Lake City, but the altitude that troubled many teams had no effect on the Texans, and they won easily 55–8. The drubbings by the Elite Spartans were the only losses for Utah and Atlanta. The Majestics and the Surge both had 4-1-1 records, with the tie coming in their second meeting of the season—Seattle had won the first. Bringing up the rear, the Bobcats and Nite Hawks had 4 and 3 wins, respectively.

Aside from games that included Texas, Utah, and Atlanta, the other teams fulfilled the league's goal of having competitive games. For the WNFC playoff teams, the average margin of victory in their regular season games was 17.5 points per game (PPG), and none of the top teams reported having been the beneficiary of a forfeit.[47] For all fifteen teams, including the developmental Phoenix Prowlers, offenses scored an average of 20.5 PPG and gave up exactly the same 20.5 PPG, which indicated a certain amount of parity. On a team-by-team basis, the Elite Spartans led the way with a 34.5 PPG victory margin. The New Orleans Hippies had the worst of it, with a -34.5 PPG margin.[48]

For comparison, the six WFA teams from their Division I had a 24.3 margin of victory, and the Arlington Impact had a team (the Arkansas Wildcats) forfeit the game to them.[49] The WFA's Division II and III had more parity. DII offenses (eighteen teams) averaged 23.5 PPG and gave up 19.9 PPG, for an average point differential of 3.6 PPG. DIII teams (thirty-eight teams) averaged scoring 16.4 PPG and surrendered 22.9 PPG, which resulted in an average point differential of -6.4 PPG. As a league, WFA teams scored 26.9 PPG and ceded 19.7 for a league-wide point differential of 7.2 points. The DI champion Boston Renegades had the best victory margin of 48.2 PPG, and the DII Jacksonville Dixie Blues had the worst with an average point differential of -45.2 PPG. Over the course of the 2019 season, more than thirty WFA teams forfeited at least one game.[50]

The relative size of the two leagues—sixty-two teams for the WFA and fifteen for the WNFC—skewed the numbers. Also, when considering those numbers, one should keep in mind that they were calculated by a historian, so they should be viewed with some caution, if not skepticism. What they seemed to indicate, though, was that the WNFC largely met their goal of providing a competitive league. Aided by a six-game schedule, as opposed to the WFA's eight games, none of the WNFC teams forfeited. By limiting the number of teams, the league controlled, to a certain extent, the quality of those programs, and it also allowed teams to better manage travel expenses. As Jenkins mentioned in the owners' meeting, the new league sought to raise the level of play for women's football, not provide an organization for recreationally based teams.

On 11 May 2019, I had the chance to watch the Elite Spartans play the Nite Hawks in Omaha, Nebraska. Unfortunately for the Nite Hawks, the visiting Texans were too tough for the game to even be close, and the home team lost 0–30. I was disappointed that my home-state team lost, but the trip was worth it, since before the game, I had the chance to interview players, coaches, and owners from both teams.

The score reflected that the Nite Hawks were a first-year team. They had some veterans who had played for the Nebraska Stampede, but they were no match, talent-wise, for the Elite Spartans. Elizabeth Jenkins, Rachel May, Jewelle Grimsley, and Angelica Grayson, four of the Texans with whom I talked, had been members of Team USA at the 2017 WWC. I also wanted to interview Hannah DeGraffinreed, another member of the national team, but she was delayed, and we ran out of time. Tight end Umeki Webb had also won a gold medal, but hers was from the 1999 Pan American Games in basketball, and she was another women's football athlete who had played in the WNBA. Wide receiver Rasan Gore, the final Elite Spartan I interviewed, was named the MVP for the WNFC in 2019. So the Texans were stacked with talent.[51]

"OJ" Jenkins, who hung up her cleats and picked up a clipboard as the head coach of the Elite Spartans, had played in multiple WWCs. Jenkins was the catalyst for putting together the Texas team, and both Grimsley and Amber Kimbough joined the team specifically to play with the former all-star running back.[52]

Offensive tackle Ashley Box of the Nite Hawks had played eight-man high school football in Pawnee City, Nebraska, and then had played six years for the Stampede before they folded. Defensive end Jerrina "Snoop" Vaughn had also played for the Stampede for eight years and was a WFA All-American twice. The 30-point differential that night was at least under the Elite Spartans average margin of victory, and so the enthusiasm that Box and Vaughn displayed was likely undiminished. The Stampede had already overcome considerable difficulty, in the form of massive flooding earlier in the year, so even making it to the field at Bellevue West High School was something of a victory.[53]

The smaller number of teams also allowed the WNFC to have a more straightforward playoff format. On 13 and 15 June 2019 the top four teams in the Atlantic and Pacific conferences played in a tournament format to decide the competitors for the championship game. The Atlantic teams played their tournament in Grapevine, Texas, and the Pacific tournament took place in San Bernardino, California.[54]

The WFA continued to use the Massey rating system, which once again left the 7-1 Portland Fighting Shockwave out of the playoffs, while the KC Titans (2-7) and the Maine Mayhem (3-6) qualified for the postseason.[55] This was a common occurrence with the league, particularly for West Coast teams, and, as we have seen, was one of the reasons for the Majestics leaving the league.

The tournament format also lessened travel costs for the teams involved, which was one of the reasons for the original BWWFC tournament. The Title IX championship game, held at Marv Kay Stadium at the Colorado School of Mines in Golden, Colorado, was another rematch of the BWWFC final, but the game was closer than during the regular season meeting between Utah and Texas.

The Falconz once again scored first when Elizabeth Lane completed a 15-yard pass to Cox for the touchdown, and Alcala added the extra point. The Elite Spartans answered with a 17-yard touchdown run by Hannah DeGraffinreed, but Valdepena missed the extra point. Lane scored on a 4-yard run with 1:00 left in the first half, and Alcala added the point after to give the Falconz a 14-6 halftime lead. The Texans scored quickly in the second half when running back Rasan Gore ran 4 yards for the touchdown. Gore was unable to reach the goal line for the 2-point conversion, however, and the Falconz maintained a 2-point lead. The lead held into the early fourth quarter, but Gore scored her second rushing touchdown of the day, this time from 3 yards out. Valdepena made the extra point to make the score 20-14 in favor of the Elite Spartans. As the game wound down, Craig Chatman and Adam Collins, the announcers, agreed that this championship had been as good as advertised. "Both teams had done the WNFC proud tonight. The game lived up to its billing." With 2:22 left, the Falconz held on fourth down and took over at their own 22. On their ensuing drive, however, a personal foul sent Utah back to the 12, and they failed to convert a fourth down. Instead of taking a knee, the Elite Spartans ran the ball down to the 1-yard line but let time run out.[56]

A somewhat balanced regular season, efforts to lessen the costs to teams, cash and equipment awards to players and teams, high-profile sponsorships, and a closely fought final game. All of those were goals that the WNFC set out to accomplish, and then did so. The initial season was a success for the league, but whether that success would continue was an open question. Various leagues have had good starts but then faltered.

The WNFC went into their second season seemingly in better shape. The Surge ultimately folded, but they were replaced for 2020 by the Washington Prodigy, which had won three consecutive United States Women's Football League championships.[57] The Hippies left for the WFA, but La Muerte De Las Cruces from New Mexico and the Philly Phantomz also joined after they both posted 3-5 records during the 2019 WFA season. Las Cruces was chosen as the site for Title IX Bowl II. The North Florida Pumas left for the potentially greener pastures of the Women's Tackle Football League (WTFL), a startup league reportedly with twenty-two teams that was set to begin play in 2020.[58] The WNFC made up that loss and added the Kansas City Glory, the Oregon Ravens, and the Florida Avengers as expansion teams. The Phoenix Prowlers also became an official team, and that brought the number of WNFC teams up to twenty.[59] The league also secured a new sponsor, Rock Tape, which would provide injury treatment materials for the WNFC.[60]

The league continued to schedule a six-game season that would begin on 4 April 2020. The tournament format also remained the same, with playoff tournaments scheduled for 18–20 June 2020. Once again, their games would be streamed on Facebook and at wnfctv.com. They also planned to add a WNFC Tackle Football TV show to be aired on 12 April 2020 on the Youtoo America channel. As mentioned, the Title IX championship game was scheduled to be held in Las Cruces, New Mexico, on 11 July 2020.[61] Of course, no plan ever survives its first contact with the enemy, which in this case was COVID, and so that game, and the entire season, never happened.

The WNFC was in the growth arc in the life of their league in 2020. Elizabeth Jenkins told me: "One day we want to be able to say women can get paid to play football too, and that's just not the reality right now, but looking at how we started, being year one as the WNFC, we came out and got a six-figure apparel sponsorship from Adidas, which was huge for us. Everything we print out, we can put an Adidas logo on it with our logo, and that's powerful. We have a partnership with Riddell also, so again, another huge brand. USA Football, they are kind of aligning with us to help us again market and partner together to bring women's football to the next level. So much exciting stuff happening, and again, we're not even through year one yet. Plans for year two, phase two, we're going to expand. We hope to become more Midwest to East and bring some powerhouse teams over. We're going to round out the league at around thirty teams. It's not going to be one of those leagues that gets watered down with sixty to seventy teams. We are trying to produce a product that we can market and continue to get sponsors and investors' attention and have them continue to buy in, because that's the only way this is going to succeed."[62]

Elizabeth Jenkins had been playing for quite some time and had seen teams and leagues come and go. She started playing with the Cleveland Crush and remembered how that team's fortunes rose and fell when ownership changed. The Elite Spartans charged their players a relatively small annual fee. "We ask the players for $250, and even that really doesn't put a dent in the expenses that it takes to run a team. If you're running it the right way, you're probably spending at minimum $60,000 a year, but we try to do our best to not pass those expenses on to our players."[63]

The team furnished helmets, which also cut down on expenses that athletes had to pay. The league also made it less expensive for their teams by extending a grant of $4,000 to each team, along with a complete game set of uniforms provided by Adidas.

The WNFC also helped avoid the forfeits that plagued the game by helping teams in need. "Now one thing that the league is doing, and we have had to dip into this season, we had an emergency fund so if there were challenges, financial challenges, with teams being able to make road trips to avoid forfeiture, we would extend some financial help to those teams to get them to where they need to be to go play the game. That's one thing the league does to help prevent that. Obviously, we're giving the teams all the necessary tools to hopefully be able to stand on their own two feet. It is their individual business to run. What we're doing is we're trying to make that easier for them to do. Again, sticking logos like Adidas and Riddell next to the WNFC logo, next to their team logo, that adds more clout to it, gives it more power. Another thing is teams are going to be fined if they forfeit, and there's almost a nontolerance, so if there is a forfeiture, it would be highly scrutinized, and we might not invite you back into the league next season."[64]

As Jenkins said, "It's exciting times for women's football!" It will be interesting to see how far they will continue to expand, and if the thirty-team limit holds. Perhaps they will seek to challenge the WFA for team numbers. They seem to have decided to keep a relatively small league composed mainly of stable teams. Based on their public statements, that will most likely be the case, but as mentioned before, historians make poor prophets.

There were two new leagues that planned to compete for female athletes: the Women's Tackle Football League (WTFL), previously mentioned, and the Women's Football League Association (WFLA), which reportedly had thirty-two teams ready to go in 2020.[65] The WFLA, with the help of investors such as R&B artist Ja Rule, who has signed on as the owner of the New York Stars, had even promised to pay players.[66] This has caused a great deal of interest among the women's football community. Many were skeptical that the league will be able to make good on its promises, but others such as Elisa de Santis, Laura Roussel, Marine Urie, and Melissa Zandu of the French Molosses have signed on to play for the Phoenix Red Tails.[67] Christelle Harnais, also of the Molosses, signed to play with the Las Vegas Devils.[68] The league made something of a splash when it announced that Santia Deck, a "social media fitness and sport influencer," had become a "multi-million dollar player" for the league's Los Angeles Fames.[69] I wondered if COVID might derail those plans, but other issues arose.

By the time I was going over final edits on this manuscript, the skeptics had been proven correct. Lupe L. Rose, Sonja F. Shelby, and Katherine E Dirden, the league's founders, were accused by the Securities and Exchanges Commission of defrauding investors in SHE Beverages of several million dollars. With that, the WFLA, which had signed social media star and former LFL player Santia Deck as the purported "multimillion-dollar contract" to play for the Los Angeles Flames but had never actually played a game, disappeared in a cloud of recriminations and declarations of I told you so.[70]

It did seem that women's football has made significant strides in the past few years, or perhaps once the blinders fell away, it became easier to see the game and the athletes more frequently. The game and the athletes have begun to gain an increased measure of visibility. During Super Bowl LIII, female football players had considerable exposure, with commercials that featured Sam Gordon, Antoinette "Toni" Harris, and a team of young girls who ran a play against the New York Giants in a public service announcement for Girls Inc. Phoebe Schecter had an insert in the official Super Bowl program.[71] During broadcast of the NFL playoff game between San Francisco and Minnesota, on 11 January 2020, a commercial for Microsoft Surface featured 49ers assistant Katie Sowers using the product. When the game resumed, sideline reporter Michele Tafoya mentioned that Sowers had "played eight seasons in the Women's Football Alliance before pursuing her dream to coach." Tafoya then mentioned that there was "another trailblazer on the field—down judge referee Sarah Thomas, who last season became the first woman to be part of an NFL postseason officiating crew. I saw her before the game and she said, 'I'm glad my daughter is old enough to see this, and understand how significant it is.'"[72]

Despite leagues gaining corporate sponsorships, there are likely no teams anywhere near the break-even point financially. As of 2020, even the WNBA, which has the backing of the NBA, still hemorrhaged cash and struggled to find an audience. Although there was a niche market for mega-events such as the U.S. National Team at the Women's World Cup, once that was over, women's professional soccer shared the problem of the WNBA—that sports fans felt no urge to see more. Women's sports, with the possible exception of professional tennis, have never appealed to a mass audience. Women's American football faces all of the challenges with which other women's sports must contend, and without television coverage, a large fan base, or billionaire owners, the game is in worse shape than the others mentioned above. Social media has had a significant impact on the sport, but while Facebook,

Twitter, VK, and the like have done wonders for the game in creating connections among the players and teams, it has not led to widespread interest among fans. That does not mean that thousands of women worldwide will not continue to enjoy what is at best a niche sport. They will. However, the probability is that they will play only for the love of the game and in front of mostly empty seats. The WFLA exists only as a website, at least to this point.

The athletes, for the most part, will still have the times of their lives. They will learn to love the controlled violence or the legalized assault of the collision sport. They will learn the difference between being hurt and being injured, as many generations of players have. They will overcome concussions and torn ACLs, along with a host of more minor injuries, because that is the price that football demands, and they will gladly pay it. They will gain self-confidence and perhaps go from being in a bad place in life to a good place in football, to use WWFG coach Jim Farrell's oft-repeated phrase.[73] They will find a global sisterhood of football, which will be a place where they will find a sense of belonging.

The generations of girls and women who came before them fought for the freedom to play a man's sport, and now that such freedom is available, they will take advantage of it to experience life-changing moments. Perhaps one day enough women will have the freedom and desire to play that the game will be accepted by the International Olympic Committee, and women's football will gain even greater visibility, at least until the games are done. But during those games, should they ever be held, the women will be able to walk with the swagger of athletes who know they are the best players in their countries, and perhaps in the entire world of women's football.

Women have made their mark on the football world, but in 2012 in Canada, girls also began to take their place on the field. From Manitoba, leagues spread to New Brunswick, Utah, and Indiana.

# Girls Take the Field

**7**

On Saturday 18 November 2017, the North Winnipeg Nomads of the Manitoba Girls Football Association (MGFA) defeated junior and senior teams made up of players from the Indiana Girls Tackle Football League (IGTFL) in the first international games pitting teams composed of schoolgirls from grades 4 through 12.

The first game, played at Mooresville High School in Mooresville, Indiana, was a closely fought match between the junior teams made up of girls in grades 4 through 8. The Nomads, leavened by players from other teams in the MGFA, defeated the IGTFL side 33–31. The second game, played by the senior sides, made up of players from grades 9–12, was not so close. A fierce thunderstorm with driving rain caused officials to suspend play for a time, but that did nothing to improve the chances for the home team. The Nomads continued rolling after the delay to win 40–6, demonstrating that the greater experience of the Canadians had paid dividends.[1]

Lisa Zueff-Cummings and Tannis Wilson created the MGFA in 2011 to give girls a chance to play tackle football. The two had helped create and played together for the Manitoba Fearless, the first women's football team in the province, but they hadn't started playing until they were already in their thirties. Zueff-Cummings loved the game and wanted to give her daughter, along with other young girls, the chance to play when they were young. Zueff-Cummings related that she thought it was "crazy" that her daughter would have to wait that long until she was able to give football a try. The MGFA was the first organized girls' tackle football league in the world, and after seven years of hitting each other, their coaches and athletes were ready to test themselves against American teams. The league started with about 40 girls playing six-a-side, and in 2017 they had over 180 athletes playing on eight senior and four junior teams.[2] For 2018, Zueff-Cummings expected more than 200 players in an area with less than 1.5 million in population, so the league was continuing to expand, but in 2017 they were looking for more.

The MGFA began looking for an opponent. They contacted "a couple of organizations." When those efforts hadn't been successful, Dennis Radlinsky, the head coach of the junior team, "decided on his own to contact Indiana, and they were more than willing to play a game." After rejecting a plan to meet somewhere in between Winnipeg and Mooresville, a suburb of Indianapolis, the Canadians decided they would make the trip south. Their goal in playing the game was "bringing the girls' programs to the forefront and show that we can actually play internationally, and just kind of see where we're at. It would be nice to kind of gauge. We see how things go with the world, and the U.S. is always on top, and we'd kind of like to see how our future is going to go with these young girls starting from a young age, and ours have been playing for a while, most of them, so we'd kind of like to see how we're going to fare, and if we can keep this going year-after-year, it would be phenomenal."[3]

The junior and senior games were therefore something of a departure from the norm of the United States defeating all comers at our national game (see chapter 8). For the players, though, there did not seem to be a great deal of thought given to international power relations. They were simply enjoying the chance to play the game they loved with like-minded girls from across the border. They were, however, also conscious of the historical import of the game. The Canadian team's quarterback, Kaity Cummings, Zueff-Cummings's daughter, focused on the history that the players were making on the field. She mentioned that the MGFA was the first all-girls tackle football league and called the game "a really big part, moving forward, for girls altogether."[4] MGFA running back Aiyana Hart focused on the chance the game provided for "meeting new girls—another sister bonding."[5] Faith Skaggs, the quarterback of the IGTFL team, was also aware that she was taking part in a historic event. She knew that even though the Utah Girls Football League (UGFL) had been around longer, it was her league that had the opportunity to play in this first international friendly game. Skaggs said she had been "looking forward to the game and now that it is here, it is awesome!"[6] Her teammate Ale'sha Christy, who played running back and receiver, had more prosaic notions about the game: "I wasn't really nervous until I actually met them, and they got forty-two players, and we have to work together, and I'm confident that we can beat them, as long as we work together. We never give up, just be strong together."[7]

The IGTFL had not been in action as long as their Canadian opponents, having begun play in the summer of 2016. Chad Oldham started the league after he and his wife refused to permit their daughter Emily to play football in the Mooresville boy's league. When he informally questioned girls watching their brothers play, he found that many of them would have liked to play, but their parents would not likely have even considered giving permission. He searched the internet and discovered the UGFL that had started in 2015. He then decided to do the same in Mooresville. According to Kyle Neddenriep of the Associated Press, Oldham hoped for fifty girls the first season.[8] Christy hesitantly estimated that the IGTFL had around thirty suited up for the November game.[9]

The teams had met for the first time the night before the game, when the Indiana athletes, coaches, and parents hosted the visitors at a banquet, complete with sheet cakes in the form of a football field, with "Indiana" in one end zone and "Winnipeg" in the other. Despite the more-than-twenty-hour bus trip, the Nomads and the many parents who came along were buzzing with excitement after the meal. The Indiana girls had gone home already, but the Canadians were still waiting to gather everyone and get back on their bus to go to a hotel about ten miles away. The parents were showing some fatigue, but there was a general excited vibe that the long anticipated game would finally be played.

Despite high winds and driving rain the next day, the athletes from both countries played with reckless abandon. The field, with aluminum grandstands on the home side, had been decorated with American and Canadian flags, and recordings of both national anthems were played before play started. The home side was doing whatever they could to welcome their northern opponents, but they had no control over the weather. The junior game, as mentioned above, was the closest contest. The girls in that game had roughly similar amounts of experience, and so the 2-point win by the Canadians kept the crowd of around two to three hundred cheering until the end.

When the rain started during the second game, and the temperature rapidly dropped by at least fifteen degrees, the crowd thinned out, as some of the junior girls and their parents sought shelter. The on-field enthusiasm was undiminished, however, and the hitting was spirited. The Nomads took a while to get rolling, and neither team scored until the end of the first quarter when Cummings scored on a quarterback-keeper play, and Juliana Raposo added the point after.

The IGTFL did not feature a kicking game, but the MGFA did, so there had to be some compromise on the rules, which resulted in the Canadians kicking unopposed extra points. Another point for compromise during the game was the number of players. Indiana played eight-a-side, while the Canadians played six-on-six.[10] The hybrid rules caused a few instances of confusion among the officiating crew, composed of volunteers from both teams, including Zueff-Cummings's son Kieran, but the zebras largely remained in the background. The weather intruded on the game, and shortly after Cummings's touchdown caused a long delay. This seemed to help the more experienced visitors, some of whom had been playing for five or more years, and gave them the advantage for the rest of the game. After play resumed, they outscored the Indianans 33–6, with Canadian touchdowns by Ashanti Tshiovo, Sherisa Gretsinger, Hart, and Hannah Stewart. The sole Indiana score came when Alexis Ervin scored on a long run from her own territory to make the score, briefly, 21–6.[11]

Although the senior game was not close, the players, coaches, and parents were happy with the game. There was talk of a return match in Canada in 2018, but that never materialized. The IGTFL posted their thanks to everyone involved in the Battle of the Borders for their "support as well as the professionalism during the entire process."[12] Radlinsky stated: "The North Winnipeg Nomads and the Manitoba Girls Football Association are grateful to be able to give these young ladies an international football experience of a lifetime. Being ambassadors from Manitoba, it was a priority to reach out and create long term bonds with the Indiana girls tackle football community."[13] Emily Radlinsky, his daughter, focused on the chance to meet her peers, telling Ligia Braidotti of the *Winnipeg Free Press*, "Meeting up with all the girls was so much fun, and the game in itself was amazing. I believe that everyone on our team and their team played a great game." She also told the reporter that even though the two programs were set to compete, "they had become friends so fast . . . that it was difficult to be competitive against them."[14]

The lopsided victory in the senior game was likely due to the Canadian players having much more experience than their southern opponents. The Canadians had practiced and played for several years before these games. Many of the Nomads had also already had experience playing internationally. In 2014 twenty-four players from the MGFA staged an inter-league showcase game during the finals of the Independent Women's Football League (IWFL) championships in Rock Hill, South Carolina. Zueff-Cummings remembered that the game received little attention, even from the fans at the game. "I think we had maybe twenty people in the stands, and most of them had been members of the Toledo Troopers."[15]

The Troopers veterans were there to be inducted into the Women's Football Foundation's (WFF) Hall of Fame, as its first class, and the theme for the weekend was the "past, present, and future" of women's football. The girls who played in the game traveled to South Carolina with the support of the MGFA, which held fundraisers to help defray the $1,700 (CAD) that each girl's parents had to pay.[16] Confirming Zueff-Cummings's lament that few noticed the game, the article from the

*Winnipeg Free Press* quoted above seemed to be the only press report that took note of the groundbreaking experience. Given that it was reportedly the first ever game that featured all females playing, coaching, and officiating, it is interesting that the game did not garner more attention, but as Zueff-Cummings and many others noted, a primary challenge that women's football faces is "getting coverage and press, and for people to really know what we are doing."[17]

The girls who played remembered having a great experience, though. Brooke Pirrie of the Nomads was excited to have played in the "first all-girls playing, reffing, and coaching game ever." She also remembered meeting several of the Toledo Troopers who "talked to us about how they started," and felt it was "really cool!"[18] Her sister Montana called the game a "really fun learning experience," and more than the historical nature of the game, she focused on having the ability to play with a hybrid team made up of girls from several of the MGFA teams.[19] Sherisa Gretsinger came home with a "signature ball" signed by the players from the championship game, and while Gianna Donnelly didn't remember much about the game, she did remember the heat, which was "110 degrees Fahrenheit," and that one of her friends had to be treated for "heat stroke."[20]

Again confirming Zueff-Cummings's contention that women's football receives little coverage, none of the players interviewed had ever heard of the Troopers, who were seven-time champions of the National Women's Football League (NWFL) in the 1970s.[21] When asked whether she had heard of the Troopers, Kaity Cummings replied: "Honestly? No. I actually had no idea. And then when we finally met them, I was kind of surprised. I had never heard of them until that point."[22]

The athletes, young and old, did have more of an audience at the banquet where the Troopers were inducted into the WFF Hall of Fame. In a YouTube video on the induction ceremony, Tamara Jarrett, then the executive director of the WFF, introduced the Troopers as the "greatest women's football team in history." The scene then cut to Guy Stout, the son of Bill Stout, the head coach of the Troopers. Stout followed the theme and pointed to the crowd of women that included many of the Trooper veterans, the MGFA girls, and current IWFL players, saying, "Back here, we have three generations of professional football players. We have the past, the present, and the future." The remainder of the video had more speeches, a clip showing the Manitoba girls running onto the field and receiving high-fives from the Troopers, and shots of Trooper and Manitoba players saying, "I am a football player, and I love football!"[23]

---

### GIRLS PLAYING TACKLE FOOTBALL: PRE-TITLE IX

Since football began in the latter part of the nineteenth century, it has been seen as a manly sport, played by manly men. That has not been completely true. Even before the turn of the century, there was a recorded instance of football being played by college women in New York. Where games did take place, they were often played for the amusement of the male spectators, as was the case in that first recorded game.[24] Since that first mockery of a game, reports of girls playing the rough game appeared here and there in the early twentieth century. Sometimes, the girls played boys, and defeated them, as was the case in 1905, when the team from "Mrs. M. E. Mead's seminary . . . defeated the second eleven of the Overlook-Selleck Military academy of Norwalk, CT . . . by a score of 12 to 0."[25] Sometimes the girls played other girls, as was the case in Twin Falls, Idaho, where girls played a full-contact game in a gymnasium and liked it so well that they wanted a regular team.[26]

Not only did the females play the game, but some also coached. Walter Camp's wife Alice often helped the "father of football" with his practices and was honored as the "co-coach" of the 1888 Yale team in a1913 event. Stella Stagg, wife of Amos Alonzo Stagg, likewise helped her husband in a variety of football roles, including scouting the University of Chicago's opponents. There were also women such as Lillian Merrell, Estelle Sherwin, and Annie Bragdon who were head coaches of boys' teams on their own—without being married to the male head coach.[27]

Athletic opportunities for girls and women expanded during the 1920s, and that included the freedom for some to play football. In research for her dissertation at DeMontfort University in Leicester, England, Katie Taylor has amassed a startling number of girls and women who played the game. Hopefully, she will publish her findings once she finishes her PhD program.

The 1920s saw the birth of the "Powderpuff" game, a form of football that gave many high school girls a chance to play. The first game allegedly took place in Huron, South Dakota, in 1926.[28]

After the growing opportunities for women in the 1920s, physical education professionals, which included a number of influential women, began arguing that females put their physical and mental health at risk by playing any competitive sport. In combination with medical specialists, the physical educators promoted what we now realize was questionable science that posited females put their reproductive health at risk, and that tampering with menstruation "could bring women to 'the very borderline of the pathological.'" Not only did these advisers assert that sports posed a danger to women's physical and mental health, but they also added that "the public and commercial elements of sport left female athletes vulnerable to sexual and economic abuses."[29]

With science seemingly arrayed behind them, the physical educators kept a stranglehold on female sports for much of the period between the 1930s and the 1970s. Some girls and women still managed to play football during that period, but the obstacles they had to face to get onto the gridiron were substantial. That did not end with the passage of Title IX in 1972.

---

POST-TITLE IX

In the third chapter of her *Female Gladiators: Gender, Law, and Contact Sports in America,* Sarah K. Fields wrote about the struggles that girls had to face to play football, even after the passage of Title IX. She delved deeply into the facts of the cases and also the legal rationales that helped judges decide the cases. The first case of a female suing to be allowed to play football took place in Ohio, the scene of so many football firsts. Brenda Clinton, who was twelve years old in 1974, wanted to play for a local junior team in Cleveland. Despite her mother signing a waiver that absolved Cleveland Muny Football from any liability, the director of the league still denied her request. In *Clinton v. Nagy* the defendant's lawyers argued that the game was not safe for girls; therefore Clinton should not be allowed to play. Judge Thomas D. Lambros disagreed, because the league had not argued that football was more dangerous for girls than for boys. He ruled that denying Clinton's request to play a game that he acknowledged was a "rough and sometimes brutal contest" was "irrational" and insisted that the focus needed to be on the capability of the individual and not the class. He did stipulate, however, that his order did not require Clinton's coach to play the girl, if she was not a better player than her teammates.[30] Judge Lambros essentially ordered that young girls must have the freedom to risk their safety that we already allowed boys.

Fields's consideration of the legal challenges brought by girls and women who wanted to play football concluded with the case of Heather Sue Mercer. In 1999 Mercer wanted to participate in practices with Duke University and had done so during the previous season. The Duke coach, however, told her that she could not. She sued and won a $2 million punitive damage award. The U.S. Fourth Circuit Court of Appeals also found that universities were not required to allow women to try out for football, but where they chose to do so, as in Mercer's case, they could not discriminate on the basis of gender.[31]

Even though the courts backed girls' freedom to play football, it was still fairly uncommon. When they did make it to the field, it was most commonly as a kicker. A very few, such as Tami Maida of Philomath High School in Corvallis, Oregon, did play other positions. Maida played quarterback and started for the school's junior varsity team in 1981. Her experience formed the basis for the television movie *Quarterback Princess* (1983). Despite the occasional girl who kicked, or the rarer position player, the number of girls who played tackle football remained low, not topping 1,000 until the first years of the twenty-first century, when participation surged from 658 during the 2000–2001 season, to 2,604 for 2018–19.[32] Before 1980, if a high school girl wanted to play, she was most likely to get the chance in a powder-puff exhibition game.

Long before 2017's Battle of the Borders, my first experience with female tackle football was a powder-puff game held at Ainsworth High School in 1978. I should have paid better attention at the time, but I had no idea that I would one day be writing about such things. My friend Bob Beatty reminded me of the game and suggested I should talk to some of the players, so I did.

My clearest memory of the game was of Wanda Moore, who played quarterback, and who threw a better ball than many males. I also remembered Jackie Hamilton, who wore my borrowed uniform. She was large and strong—she once defeated our school's male arm-wrestling champion. I remember her plowing through opposing players until she tripped over their supine forms. She might have been able to hold her own on the varsity team, if she had had the desire to play, and the opportunity. In 1978 Title IX was still relatively new, and the possibility of some of my female classmates playing football did not even seem to be a possibility. Jackie was also not very popular in school, so to my recollection, nobody ever talked to her about what she thought about her exploits on the field. She was, in short, the sort of person who might have found herself and thrived on the gridiron—see the interview with Sydney Sessions below in the section about the Utah Girls Football League (UGFL). Unfortunately, I was unable to speak with either Moore or Hamilton.

I did communicate by Facebook Messenger with Julie (Weiss) Ferguson and JoAnn (Kirkpatrick) Walthour. Ferguson told me that she didn't remember much, just that "it was fun, but no details."[33] Walthour remembered a little more. She messaged me: "I don't remember too much about it. Except that it was held on an open week when the boys did not have a game, so we borrowed gear from the boys. Maybe the football players helped coach. I remember that I think Mike Howard [a teacher and coach] was one of the refs. I don't remember that we had practices—I don't think we had practices." She did mention, "I will say this, though. I think playing that powder-puff game has helped me understand the game of football better."[34] Gina Reyman, our school's

Athlete of the Year for 1979–80 (I finished second), also remembered playing, but we were never able to find a time to talk about the game.

My classmate Gaylin (Talbot) Tutnick remembered more: "I feel like it was maybe a fundraiser either for student council or for the football team—maybe student council. I remember that the girls had to arrange to borrow pads and uniforms from one of the boys on the team. I don't know how it was decided which of the boys coached which team, or how the teams were divided up. I have no idea or remembrance of how that happened. I just remember that my sister was on the opposite team, and she came gunning for me on every single play. She knocked me down so many times. She was aggressive. She was a feisty, scrawny little thing. So yeah, I remember waking up the next day so sore. My brother Greg was like, 'Well now you know how I feel every Saturday morning,' and I'm like, 'Why? Why do you do this to yourself—this is punishing.' I just remember thinking: yeah, this is not for me, because I'm really too much of a wimp to do this, but I think my sister Dea really dug it." Of the battle between her and Dea, she said: "I remember my sister being just right across from me, so I think maybe I was defensive tackle and she was an offensive tackle. We were like nose-to-nose. When we would do the downs and she would like look at me, and I could tell she was like, 'I'm going to take you down!'" She felt that playing in the game gave her a greater appreciation for the "toughness of football players, because, like I said, that was like the sorest I've ever been in my entire life." Tutnick teaches music and chorus in Scottsdale, Arizona, and she compared the amount of training and pain that went into being a football player with what musicians must often do to excel at their art. "I would imagine that, you know, when you're doing the [football] training, and they do that day in and day out, that their bodies get used to it. They suffer for their art just like, you know, ballet dancers do. People that are really committed to mastering their instrument—I mean pianists practice like six or seven hours a day until their fingers bleed. That certainly gave me a real respect for football players and made me realize that I need to just be a spectator of the games, and not a participant." When asked what her parents thought, she remembered that her mother was at the game supporting her and her sister. Her father, who taught chemistry at the high school, had been an athlete, and Tutnick remembered that he encouraged his children to play whatever sport they wanted to.[35]

Although in many areas girls are playing tackle football with the boys, or, as with girls from Manitoba and Indiana mentioned above, in their own leagues, powder-puff games are still the only contact some girls have with the gridiron game. Many of those games are now flag football, but in Jupiter, Florida, Dan Frank, the principal at Jupiter High School in 2016, attempted to cancel the annual full-contact game after fifty years. The game's cancellation outraged current students and alumni alike. Senior Amanda Montigney told a local news reporter, "It's very sexist, I believe, because I mean we are women, we can play any other sport in our high school. But we can't play football? I mean it's like crazy." Frank was unmoved, however, and went ahead with plans for cancellation of the game that had regularly packed the high school's stadium, and which raised $7,000 in 2015. Frank stated that the reason for the move was student safety. "A girl broke her leg a few years ago, each year players get bruises and sprains, and there is always a chance of more serious injuries. The narrow window of time for student preparation and practice and the limited availability of properly fitting safety equipment would put our students at risk."[36]

However, supporters of the game gathered about three thousand signatures on a petition to keep the game, and it lasted one more year.[37] According to a Facebook post by Amie Sardhina, the 2017 game was canceled due to lack of players.[38] Absent the motivation of administrative opposition to drive them, apparently not enough players or parents were outraged enough to keep the game going.

In citing student safety as the reason for the cancellation, Jupiter High's principal Frank was only echoing the rationale that many had used before him, and others would continue to use, to keep girls, and women, from playing the dangerous game. The concern for the safety of girls and women who wanted to play or were playing is still a contemporary concern, although it has been expanded to argue that football is unsafe for anyone.

There are still places where powder-puff games continue, but unlike in Jupiter, they play the flag variant of the game. Wallingford, Connecticut, is one such place where the game has been played the day before Thanksgiving since 1972. Judy Samaha, who was then the athletic director at Sheehan High School, which could likely be another interesting story, "wanted to create more athletic opportunities for girls in Wallingford," and the tradition has continued. The annual game pits Sheehan against Lyman Hall High School. Reportedly, the game draws four to five thousand spectators, and each team has more than 100 players on their rosters.[39] In 2017 Lyman Hall won the game, dubbed the Samaha Bowl, 28–20, and Lyman coach Ed Neidlander reported that their 21–0 halftime lead allowed him to make sure all 130 girls on his team got to play.[40]

The past couple of years have seemingly been something of a golden age for girls playing on boys' teams, and several girls made national headlines, not just for their presence, but for their performance on those teams. The following is a sampling of some of the athletes who broke into the limelight during recent football seasons (2016–17).

In 2016 Savanah Melton of North Little Rock High School made seven of nine field goals, with her longest being from 42 yards. She also converted on fifty-six of fifty-eight extra points.[41] At the end of the season, Arkansas Varsity named her second team kicker on their all-state team.[42]

In 2016 Eriana Pula, a starting guard and defensive tackle from Centennial High School in Compton, California, was the first girl selected to play in the California Classic All Star Game. The scout who recommended her for the game stated, "I did not know when I scouted her that she was a girl. She was a good player."[43]

During the 2016 season Becca Longo made thirty-five of thirty-eight extra points and one 30-yard field goal as a senior at Basha High School in Chandler, Arizona. As a result, in 2017 Longo became the first woman to earn an NCAA football scholarship when she signed to play with Division II Adams State, in Alamosa, Colorado.[44]

On 31 August 2017, Holly Neher, a quarterback for Hollywood Hills High School, became the first girl in Florida to throw a touchdown pass in a high school game. The 45-yard touchdown pass came on her first-ever passing attempt.[45]

K-Lani Nava of Strawn High School in Texas became the first girl to score points during the Texas playoff. She did this during the final of the University Interscholastic League played in the Dallas Cowboys' AT&T Stadium on 20 December 2017. She converted nine extra points in her team's 78–42 victory.[46]

Olivia Perez did not score points in the Texas high school championship game, but she is credited with saving football in Harrold High School in the state where calling football a religion might be giving religion too much credit. The school's team was down to only five players when Perez stepped in to save the day.[47]

These are only a few examples of young women making their mark on the gridiron. Brooke Liebsch, for instance, played quarterback not only for her high school but also for the KC Titans of the Women's Football Alliance.[48] There seems to be, if nothing else, an increase in the frequency of stories of girls playing football with the boys. I have no data to back up that claim, and it may simply be a matter of my seeing more of these stories since the blinders fell off, but there does seem to be an acceleration of young women playing well on male teams. In addition to Longo earning a scholarship as a kicker, defensive back Antoinette Harris became the first position player to be offered a full scholarship to an NAIA school when Bethany College of Lindsborg, Kansas, signed her up to play for them.[49] After Harris finished her playing days in Kansas, she has kept going. The WFA's Facebook reported on 21 February 2022 that Harris had signed on to play with the Cali War.[50]

Despite the courts typically siding with girls who want to play with the boys, and the numbers of girls who want to play in one manner or another, there are still locales that attempt to keep girls from playing.

Michaela Jenkins, from a town near Columbus, Ohio, had played youth football with her male counterparts in the Liberty Union–Thurston school district, and wanted to continue in middle school. The school district denied her request, arguing that Title IX contains a contact sports exemption that would allow them to keep her from playing. They held firm, at least until the Civil Liberties Union threatened to sue, and even an unnamed member of the Ohio State High School Athletic Association wondered why the district had "its knickers in a twist." Despite Title IX's contact sports exemption, the school district folded, and Jenkins was allowed to play.[51]

Since schools are controlled by local school boards, the situation for girls who wanted to play on boys' teams was not consistent. Jenna Mitchell, one of my advisees at Ohio Northern University, did not have a great deal of difficulty playing middle school football at Baker Middle School in Marion, Ohio. Mitchell, who was teaching high school social studies in Phoenix, Arizona, when I talked to her, remembered that she even had four sacks in her last game. As is often the case, despite working in a city with several current or former women's football teams, Mitchell had never heard of any of them.[52]

The persistence of school officials who continue to hold that football is too dangerous for girls to play with the boys, along with similar parental concerns, has led some such as Zueff-Cummings and Oldham to start leagues specifically for girls. These leagues have proved to be amazingly popular with girls from grades 4–12 and with their parents.

## ALL-GIRLS TACKLE FOOTBALL LEAGUES

After the 2011 debut of the MGFA, other leagues devoted to girls playing tackle football, including the IGTFL, began play, both in Canada and the United States. Kevin Hirschfield, writing on the Football Canada website, credited the Manitoba league with setting the pattern for other leagues.[53] Zueff-Cummings likewise argued that the 2014 game in South Carolina "helped spearhead some of the groups that have been coming out now with the younger girls' programs."[54]

Hirschfield and Zueff-Cummings gave credit to the MGFA for being the first all-girls football league in Canada, and the world. However, according to Lisa Harlow, girls in New Brunswick, on Canada's East Coast, began play at around the same time. Harlow told me that "close to forty" girls in that province had started practicing on all-girls teams in 2008. "The Junior girls actually started in 2008 as their first year. We would've taken one of the local minor football associations here in New Brunswick and Saint John, and we would've started within the association. We made small teams, everybody practiced together, and we would scrimmage on Sundays in a controlled scrimmage. So that was kind of year one, and then year two expanded into Fredericton Capital Minor Football doing the same sort of concept, and then we did scrimmages against one another. And then in year three is when it really formed into being a league, and so today [2018] we would have five teams across three minor football associations. Three teams in St. John, one in the Capital Fredericton Area, and then one as a part of the Greater Moncton Association. They play against each other, six-a-side, and then we crown a New Brunswick Champion every year."[55]

The New Brunswick Junior Girls Football League (NBJGFL) began when Harlow and her father, Larry, who had been involved in women's football in the province since 2004, decided they "needed to start a feeder program, so it was natural to go to that high school level and build a program there." The senior Harlow was the head coach of Team Canada at the 2010 Women's World Championship sponsored by the International Federation of American Football (see chapter 8), and his daughter Lisa played on the team that year. Harlow not only played, but she ended a German drive deep in Canadian territory with a sack that sent Canada into the finals against Team USA.[56]

The NBJGFL started practicing in 2008, but the first website for the league that featured three teams was for the 2012 season. Therefore, the MGFA's claim to being the first girls' league seems to be correct.[57] In the interview with Harlow, she inferred that the first seasons were developmental, not competitive. As of 2018, the NBJGFL had nearly ninety athletes playing on the various teams.[58] According to the Football New Brunswick site, the Varsity Girls Football League has five teams for girls from age fourteen to seventeen.[59] The site only had a schedule for 2018, and the last post on the NB Varsity Girls Football League Facebook page was from 12 January 2019. However, the league was still active in 2020, and a representative told me that they were "still active and have about 75 players depending on the year."[60]

As of 2020, there were three tackle leagues for girls in Canada, and opportunities were increasing. In addition to the MGFA and the NBJGFL, a new girls-only league began in Ottawa sponsored by the Cumberland Panthers Football Club (CPFA). According to a 28 November 2019 article by Martin Cleary in the *Ottawa Sun*, CPFA president Mark Oullette was leaving that position to create a six-a-side girls' tackle football program in Ottawa. Cleary wrote that girls had been cheerleaders and played flag football, and also "about 40 were on rosters" of co-ed youth teams in 2019. Oullette had been coaching and operating the girls' touch football league, and he sent a questionnaire to ask those athletes if they would be interested in playing tackle football. "The 102 players from the seven touch teams . . . blitzed Oullette with a 75% acceptance of the idea."[61]

As evident in the discussion of the Utah and Indiana girls' football leagues below, when girls have freedom and are presented with the opportunity, they will jump at the chance to play tackle football. During a time when enthusiasm for the boys game was reportedly waning, everywhere that adults have overcome their fear of allowing their daughters to play the rough sport, girls have rushed onto the gridiron.

In his article, Cleary also wrote, "During the past decade, Football Canada has made female tackle football a priority," and that support has apparently helped spread the girls' sport to other parts of the Canadian capital.[62] St. Mark's High School in Ottawa created a girls' team and played an intrasquad game on 29 April 2019. Eighty girls signed up for the team, and the Canadian Football League's Ottawa Redblacks, together with the Ottawa Sports and Entertainment Group, sponsored a training and game day at the Redblacks' TD Place stadium.[63]

The Canadian girls playing in Manitoba, New Brunswick, and Ontario reportedly were to be joined in 2020 by a new girls' tackle league in Nova Scotia.[64] They planned to play six-on-six, and their post called for girls under eighteen to sign up. No other details were provided, but it seemed that Football Canada's support was having positive results.

Along with the Canadian leagues and the girls' leagues in Utah and Indiana, there was also a new league seeking to start in Georgia during the summer of 2018.[65] Louise Ibsen, who played for the Copenhagen Tomahawks in Denmark, has likewise expressed interest in starting a girls' team there, so perhaps the sport may expand globally as well.[66]

Girls-only tackle football leagues in the United States suffered from the same disadvantages that semiprofessional leagues have. They were sometimes short-lived. As of 2020, Canada seemed to be leading the way in the creation of new teams and leagues. Football Canada's support no doubt was a key reason for that. The United States has no such organization that has promoted girls' football leagues. USA Football has focused on providing opportunities for women to gain technical skill, but aside from promoting flag football, they have not promoted girls playing tackle football. The Georgia league mentioned in the previous paragraph seemed to have settled on flag football.[67] Although Facebook posts continue to tantalizingly mention new leagues—a proposed Xikon-Arizona Girls Tackle Football league reportedly led by Raven Delaney, a former player who coached with the UGFL, for instance—only two leagues have actually formed teams and held competitions.[68] Rather than tackle leagues, the momentum, fueled no doubt by fears of concussions, has been toward expanding flag leagues.

In the United States, Utah led the way in the creation of girls' football programs. Crys Sacco, who had played center on the Utah Jynx and Utah Falconz teams, helped start the third all-girls league in North America in 2015. Sacco remembered that he and a friend discussed starting a girls' football league, so he began posting online about the idea. They decided that they should gain some experience first, so the two of them went out and coached a season of boys' junior high football. While they were doing that, he said that girls came up to him and told him that "if you start a league for girls, our parents will let us play."[69]

A girl playing football in Utah had already caused an internet sensation when Brent Gordon posted a video of his daughter, Sam, playing against boys in youth football. The video posted on YouTube in 2012 quickly went viral. It was a highlight of her first season playing, during which she scored thirty-five touchdowns and rushed for nearly 2,000 yards.[70] In the video Gordon can be seen running through defenses with seeming impunity, scoring again and again. The fame that came to her as a result of the video made her something of a "brand" for the league to build upon. Her notoriety attracted the press, and articles such as the one quoted above appeared in the *Washington Post*, a video report was posted on the *Guardian* (UK) site, she appeared on ESPN's *SportsCenter* and ABC's *Good Morning America*, and she became the first girl football player to appear on a Wheaties cereal box.[71]

At the same time that Sacco was doing preparation work to create a league, the young star spoke to a middle school audience and asked how many girls would like to play football. Her father, Brent, told Euna Park, a reporter for *UpWorthy*, "I'm not kidding, every single girl's hand shot up."[72] He emailed Sacco, and they began collaborating on the project. Sacco was unsure whether they should immediately start the league, as time was short to accomplish the task. Gordon was adamant though. Once they had decided on the course of action, he told Sacco, "If I'm going to sign my daughter up, it's going to be a football league, and we're going to do it now." With only four weeks to work, they moved quickly, contacting others and getting a registration website set up. Three days before their first orientation, the site went live, and they had "fifty girls—four teams of fifth and sixth graders." Since the 2015 season, Sacco reported that their player and team numbers had doubled each year. In 2017, they had "six teams of grade school, six teams of high school, and four teams of junior high." For the 2018 season, they expanded from the Salt Lake City area to nearby Utah County. Sacco predicted that they would have around 400 girls playing, up from 210 in 2017.[73]

The UGFL received a great deal of press, which is unusual for females playing football. The novelty of the idea that girls were signing up to play a sport with many critics, both in the media and in medicine, was likely a source of much of the interest. There was, however, considerable attention and possibly hope invested that the new league represented a step forward in furthering gender equality. *Good Housekeeping* hailed the league with a subheading declaring "They're not afraid of big hits—or busting stereotypes." The article mentioned that "the start of this new program does coincide with increased worry over sports-induced concussions. . . . But for these girls, the opportunity to be on the field far outweighs anything else."[74] A *Washington Post* article contained a passage from a *Huffington Post* story quoting the elder Gordon stating, "That's what this league is all about: fulfilling the dreams of girls who want to play football."[75] *Time* magazine ran a photo from Gordon's grandfather of Kami Gold, an eleven-year-old player with the headline "Girls Can Tackle Football, Too."[76] A story on Yahoo! Sports mentioned that the UGFL "had the blessings of USA Football and the NFL." It quoted Sam Rapaport, then the director of development at USA Football, stating, "The ultimate goal is for women to get paid to play football." Rapaport added, "We'd love to see women's tackle football played at the pro level."[77] For her, the UGFL was apparently a step in that direction. *Teen Vogue* mentioned that the Utah example had already inspired another league in Indiana, and asserted, correctly, it seems, "The exponential growth of the Utah League shows that if you create a space for girls to play tackle football, they will show up."[78] Combined with the glowing media coverage that Sam Gordon had received, the UGFL was riding high on a wave of positive press. That has continued, in some outlets such as the *Teen Vogue* article quoted above, but there has also been a pushback against the idea of girls playing the sport. More on that later.

I had the chance to see that "exponential growth" for myself on 14 April 2018, when I went to watch UGFL games in Midvale, a suburb of Salt Lake City. Sacco had described the phenomenal growth of the league, but hearing about it is one thing, and seeing it on the ground is quite another. The games were being held at Midvale City Park that day, and when I arrived, I observed the entire area of one side of the park covered with girls playing, practicing, or waiting in their football uniforms. The sidelines and other areas were packed with parents, siblings, and other spectators in lawn chairs watching the spectacle.

When I finally located Sacco, he told me that there were six teams of grade school, junior high, and high school athletes playing that year.[79]

Sacco introduced me to Jason Dixon, the head coach of the West Jordan High School team. He in turn organized some of his players to talk to me. I interviewed six players, after they had finished doing team photos, and all were positive about their experience playing football. His daughter, middle linebacker Lauren Dixon, setting the tone for most of the interviews, said she enjoyed the physicality of the game, since "the first person that crosses my face I'm allowed to hit."[80] Running back Olivia Green enjoyed being able to "take her anger out on people." She had played with the boys, but after she got hurt, her mother stopped that, so the girls' league gave her a chance to resume playing.[81] Quarterback Lacie Jacobson was told by her mother that she couldn't play with the boys because they were "too rough," but once she found out about the girls' league, she took advantage of the opportunity it presented. During her first year, she tore her LCL, which made her mother "hesitant," but not her—she said her goal was to "come back and play even better."[82] Tight end Aria Wagaman liked being able "to get down and get dirty, and like, hit other people without getting in trouble."[83] Cornerback Railey Tucker played against boys in a flag league that a local recreation center sponsored. She felt that playing in the girls' league allowed her to "get the full football experience," instead of just watching the game. She would like to continue playing at the college level and has contacted some teams about her hopes. She has not, however, received any encouragement from the local schools and realized that it would be a long shot.[84] Wide receiver Mary Coester had played basketball on her high school team but felt that playing that sport "made me feel bad about myself, like I had zero confidence." Football, to her, was "a dream come true . . . I really love hitting people." While applying to universities, Coester wrote an essay about "something she had overcome," and she wrote about "how football brought confidence back into her life." Her essay apparently impressed admissions officials at Brigham Young University–Hawaii, and she was admitted to their program.[85]

Those interviews completed, I found Sacco again, and he introduced me to Sam Gordon, the young celebrity-athlete who helped create the league. Gordon has been interviewed by so many journalists that it is likely something of a routine for her. Since the initial wave of media attention, she has continued to make news. Along with other UGFL athletes, Gordon filed a Title IX lawsuit against three school districts in the Salt Lake City area and against the Utah High School Activities Association to force them to create girls' high school football teams sponsored by the schools, rather than the UGFL.[86] During the celebrations around Super Bowl LII, to recognize her accomplishments, she was awarded the first-ever Game Changer Award presented by the NFL. The award "was established to recognize individuals who are committed to moving the game forward while making a positive contribution to their community."[87] In receiving the award, Gordon became the first female to be honored by the NFL during their end-of-the-year awards ceremony that also awards the Most Valuable Player and the Coach of the Year.[88] So, an interview with an obscure historian was likely just a distraction from preparing for her soon-to-start game.

Still, she was a good sport about it and said that "it is fun to be interviewed. I like talking about football." She retold the story of how she was speaking to middle school girls and asked how many wanted to play football. Gordon, now a ninth grader who was thinking about going to Stanford to play soccer and for their academic reputation, also reflected on the historical impact of her actions, including perhaps her legal action, although that was not part of the question. "Me and my dad have had conversations about how this is going to change the future. I mean, if you get this into college and stuff like that, [it] gives many more opportunities for girls to get scholarships and go to college. Like, it could change the lives of so many people, and it's insane that just doing simple things like giving girls the opportunity to play football can change so many people's lives, and I can see this being a monumental thing in women's sports." The media exposure Gordon has had at an early age has seemingly not created a monster but rather has given her a maturity that belies her age. She answered many of the questions like a seasoned athlete, giving credit to her teammates and using "we" more than "I."[89]

Sacco then turned the tables and interviewed me using Facebook Live. He press-ganged Stephanie Bracken, a spectator there to watch her daughter play, into holding the camera. Afterward, Bracken mentioned that her daughter loves the game so much that she has played through two concussions, so I asked her to do an interview.[90] She accepted, and as we were about to begin, her daughter Maddie and her teammate Sydney Sessions arrived, so they joined in. The younger Bracken lived up to what her mother had said, telling me that in addition to wanting to play with a concussion, she also once concealed from her coaches that she had broken her rib, so they wouldn't sit her out of the game. She also mentioned that in the games when she was concussed, her mother had been crying, not because her daughter was injured, but because she was sad that Maddie would have to come out of the game.[91]

The casual, matter-of-fact approach toward injuries and their possibility stands in stark contrast to the concern over the injury potential of playing football that is evident in the national media. As more and more girls begin playing football, despite some positive national press coverage from the *Wall Street Journal* on the start of the second all-girls football league in Indiana, or perhaps because of that positive coverage, newspapers such as the *New York Times* spearheaded a backlash against these efforts.

In Indiana, Chad Oldham noticed the UGFL through the press they had received, and reached out to Sacco for help in setting up a league that would allow his daughter to play. Sacco recalled that Oldham was concerned he wasn't having any luck in recruiting—all of the girls who wanted to play were "mainly older girls—like junior high." Sacco's advice to Oldham was "Take them! It doesn't matter. Just get your first fifty girls!" Oldham followed that advice and formed the second league in the United States, and the fourth in North America, for girls to play tackle football.[92]

During the 2017 season, the league's second year in existence, they too made a splash in the national press when Rachel Bachman of the

*Wall Street Journal* wrote a feature article about the IGTFL. The article set the scene by relating, "It's nearly game time on an early Saturday afternoon, so 17-year-old Alexis Ervin drops her earrings in the cupped hand of a burly, bearded coach and pulls on her helmet." Despite that slightly condescending start, the tone of the article, along with a video that accompanied the online version, was largely positive. Bachman paid some attention to the specter of concussions, particularly for girls, but still the article hewed closely to the "girl power" narrative of the early UGFL coverage. The video accompanying the online version featured players such as quarterback Alexis Ervin, who admitted that the first days of training were a "hot mess," as players struggled to learn the rules and techniques of playing the game. "But we've progressed so much!" she added, and argued that "football has really helped, like, all of us. We're not as mad, like, towards other things. When we get on the field, we definitely take everything out."[93]

Since the IGTFL was the second league for girls, it may have caught the attention of the *Wall Street Journal*, but it has received less press in other national media sites on its own. The IGTFL does appear in articles in conjunction with the UGFL, but the coverage it has garnered has not been as widespread as that of the older league. It is arguable that once a barrier is broken—creating an all-girls football league, for instance, the press tends to move on to the next cause célèbre. Responding to a tweet by Minnesota Lynx (WNBA) head coach Cheryl Reeve on the lack of media coverage in women's sport, Natalie Weiner, a staff writer for *Bleacher Report*, tweeted on 26 February 2018 that "the mainstream coverage of women's sports is almost exclusively centered on firsts and boundary breaking, which reinforces the idea that women's success in sports is the exception, not the rule."[94] That may or may not be true, but it seems to be the case with press coverage of the IGTFL. There may be another explanation, however.

Even while some media sources were hailing the new girls' leagues as a step forward, others were furthering the counternarrative surrounding the game—that it is dangerous for adults, and more so for children, especially girls. Maxwell Strachan wrote an article for the *Huffington Post* in February 2015, before the UGFL was a reality, that suggested youth football might be more dangerous for athletes than high school, college, or professional players. The article focused on research done by Boston University on forty-two former NFL players that found "there is an association between participation in tackle football prior to age 12 and greater later-life cognitive impairment measured using objective neuropsychological tests."[95] However, according to Strachan, the authors of the study also warned that since their research dealt with adults, it should not be used to draw conclusions about "the population at large." Strachan quoted author Julie Stamm, then a PhD candidate, who argued, "It does make sense that children whose brains are rapidly developing should not be banging their head again and again." Strachan added some balance to the article, also quoting Pop Warner's Dr. Julian Bailes, who pushed back against the Boston University study, arguing it was "'flawed' because of its small sample size."[96]

Sacco also remembered that during their first year, when ESPN's *Outside the Lines* program did a feature on the league, "they had this doctor on there talking about concussions, and he was like, 'I think this is a horrible idea,' and he tried to make it sound bad that we started girls' football." The league founder also mentioned that whenever one of their stories went viral, the comments underneath often had remarks such as "girls belong in the kitchen," "football is a man's sport," and the like. To the first critique from the doctor, Sacco argued, "We are super big on safety. We make sure that all of our coaches are USA [Football] certified." Sacco himself is a "therapist for people with spinal cord injuries, so I'm a little more cautious than a lot of people." He stated that the league is "very cautious about concussions," and cited safety concerns as being a reason the league started as eight-a-side, rather than the traditional eleven. To the second source of critique, Sacco and the league recommend that players "stay off social media" so they will not see those caustic comments.[97]

For the Indiana girls who might have read the comments below Rachel Bachman's *WSJ* article about their league, the negative comments were there. In a 6 September comment on the article, David Phillips was positive but still mentioned health concerns when he commented, "Life has risks—more power to them." However, Carrie Gorringe, the next commenter, retorted, "Because late-onset encephalopathy is so much fun . . ." Flinky Sminkleman, presumably an alias, commented, "So we're going to damage our girls' brains too?" In a less snarky comment, Richard Gaylord wrote that "it is utterly irresponsible for parents, now that the brain damage has been firmly established as a primary result of participating in sports that employ 'head banging' as a fundamental 'tool of the trade,' to allow their children, girls or boys, to play football." He also labeled allowing children, of any sex presumably, to play football, or even soccer, as "parental abuse."

The UGFL and Gordon's lawsuit received some of the online vitriol as well. Michael Schimp commented, "'A handful of those players and their parents are suing three Salt Lake City–area school districts and the Utah High School Activities Association. They want them to comply with a federal gender-equity law by creating high school football teams for girls.' After they win and bankrupt the school districts, or more likely, the school districts will drop the male sports, can we all give 'feminism' three cheers?"[98]

Michele Braun, a twenty-year veteran of the Minnesota Vixen and now a coach for the team, did not share Schimp's scorn about Gordon's efforts. In an 18 February 2018 interview, she praised the young star and told me, "We still have a majority of people coming into a sport who have never played the sport before, so you have to train them and teach them what to expect. That is a very difficult aspect at times to work with women on that, because we just haven't been used to playing the sport. I hope there are people like Sam Gordon who are making strides in our sport to have girls play football at a high school level because I think it is very, very important for girls to have that opportunity, so when they do come to our level that they have a better understanding. It's going to make teams better, and it's going to help the sport. I think that's really, really neat that they are doing that. I think it needs to happen, you know, at that level. I'm seeing more girls trying out for fifth- and sixth-grade football. I think that is great. I think there should be more girls getting the opportunity. There are still a lot of Stone Age people out there that don't think that girls should be able to do that. I think it is sad, because if there is no other alternative, if there is no other opportunity for a girl to play football, I think she should at least have that chance."[99]

Girls playing tackle football do not, however, have to delve into the comment sections to articles or on social media to find out they are endangering their health. They can read all about the risk of concussions in youth sport from a variety of sources including the "newspaper of record" to learn the same thing. Just to take away from the fun, February and the Super Bowl brought a slew of articles about the risk of concussions in youth sport. On 2 February 2018, a *New York Times* article headline asked: "More Girls at Playing Football. Is That Progress?"[100] Author Frankie de la Cretaz began by mentioning high school players such as Holly Neher, who became the first girl to throw a touchdown pass in a Florida high school game, and kicker K-Lani Nava, "who became the first girl in Texas to score points in a high school state championship game." Then he got down to the topic. "But as a growing body of research suggests that youth tackle football is harmful to children's brains, not everyone is cheering." De la Cretaz then quoted some of the same research authored by Robert Stern from Boston University noted above that found "kids who played tackle football before age 12 may be at higher risk for emotional and behavioral problems later in life." He added additional studies, with links to the online version, that found "a change in the brain's white matter (which connects different regions of the brain—the gray matter)" after just one season of play.[101] The article quoted other studies that mentioned chronic traumatic encephalopathy (CTE), and that stated female concussion rates, when compared to boys in the same sport, were higher. Dr. Donna Duffy, the codirector of the Female Brain Project at the University of North Carolina Greensboro, agreed that while more research was needed, "prepubescent kids should avoid playing tackle football."[102]

The article did quote Sacco, who stated, once again, that he "doesn't hear many concerns from parents about their daughters playing tackle football." Sacco went on to repeat what he had told other interviewers, including me: "I think they [the parents] feel safe because they're playing against other girls." Sacco, or de la Cretaz (it is unclear from the article), quoted Dr. Robert Stern, the lead researcher for the Boston University study, as having stated "that it is not possible to say whether the research—which looked only at boys—can be generalized to include girls because in an all girls league, the force of the hits could be different." Dr. Jen Welter, who was the first woman to play professional football with men, who later became the first woman to coach in the NFL, and who now organizes Grrridiron Girls camps to teach flag football to girls, was also quoted as saying, "if a girl is interested in playing football, rather than shutting down the conversation entirely, parents could discuss what drives her desire to play and consider ways to play safely."[103]

An article by Jason Chung, Peter Cummings, and Uzma Samadani quoted from the Boston University study and quoted the Concussion Legacy Foundation as announcing "a national campaign called F14G Football to convert all under-14 football into flag football, thereby eliminating tackle football." The authors pointed out that the message being sent by the CLF was that "eliminating tackle football is the key to safeguarding the brains and futures of America's youth."[104]

However, despite the provocative headline, the bulk of the article was devoted to debunking the narrative that youth football is unsafe at any level. The authors made the point that a study by Ling et al. in *Acta Neuropathologica*, a British journal, demonstrates that CTE can be found in "approximately 12 percent of normal healthy aged people who died at an average of 81 years." They also mention that Dr. Goldstein, one of the authors of the BU study, "was more measured" in an article that he wrote. "His article speaks in terms of likelihoods and qualifiers in noting that 'the causal mechanisms, temporal relationships, and contextual circumstances that link specific brain pathology to a particular antemortem insult are impossible to ascertain with certainty based solely on post-mortem neuropathology.'"[105] In other words, the science is far from settled and cannot be used to condemn all football all of the time.

That is not, however, the narrative that is posited by media sources, and the frequency of these articles has continued as more and more girls have begun playing. A sampling of headlines that have warned parents of the dangers of their children playing football includes "Not Safe for Children? Football's Leaders Make Drastic Changes to the Youth Game" in the *New York Times*; "Football's Concussion Crisis Is Killing Former High School Players, Too" on the *Huffington Post* website; and "Flag Football is MORE Dangerous to Children than Tackle, Study Reveals as Fears over Long-Term Injuries Caused by Concussions Continue to Rise" in the United Kingdom's *Daily Mail*.[106] This has been going on for some time, but particularly so in the wake of the 2011 lawsuit by former players against the NFL.[107] The narrative critical of football has been furthered by public figures who have weighed in on the subject. President Barack Obama, for instance, stated, "I would not let my son play pro football" and compared playing football to smoking.[108] A number of former NFL players, including Troy Aikman, Adrian Peterson, and Terry Bradshaw, have also stated on various media platforms that they would not let their sons play.[109]

These media headlines and stories amount to what Daniel J. Flynn has called a war on football. In his *The War on Football: Saving America's Game* (2013), Flynn argued: "Conventional wisdom, as readers of this book will soon discover, clashes with reality. . . . But the oft-repeated falsehoods buttress the interests of lawyers seeking billion-dollar settlements from the National Football League and doctors rolling in hundreds of millions of dollars in concussion grants. The fibs make dollars, so they make sense. They also propel a tired media narrative that accentuates the negative and ignores the positive. The *news* about football may be uniformly negative, but the *facts* are overwhelmingly positive, if well hidden [original italics]. Football plays safer than ever."[110] Even as he makes the point that football safety has improved considerably over the years, after profiling Briannah Gallo, a player for the Boston Militia of the Women's Football Alliance, Flynn quoted studies indicating that "women's football, unfortunately, conjures up a perfect storm for head injuries."[111] He noted that research has shown that although football accounts for half of the concussions reported in high school athletics, "girl's soccer placed second."[112]

Sacco believed parents felt safer letting their daughters play in the UGFL because they were competing against other girls, but Flynn argued, "Briannah and her fellow competitors in the Women's Football Alliance may actually play a more dangerous game than those in the National Football League. The physics say no. The physiology says yes."[113]

Flynn was not in any way advocating that women not play football. He was merely arguing that women's physiology meant they faced greater dangers of head injuries than their male counterparts. Both Gallo and Jessica Cabrera, another Militia player whom Flynn profiled, had suffered serious concussions, but rather than calling for banning women's football, he argued that the sport has a value that outweighs the risk. "Hang around the Boston Militia, and the profound benefits of athletics become personified. . . . Women's professional football exudes an infectious exuberance the likes of which could only emanate from amateurs. Observers can't help but experience a vicarious thrill. . . . Somehow, banning women's football because of female concussion rates seems reactionary; banning men's football because of the sports concussion rates seems progressive."[114]

There is some evidence, which may suffer from some of the same problems as studies on former football players, that indicates female athletes do have a higher risk of injury. In a compilation of the results of several published studies, researchers found that "females appear to sustain concussions at higher rates than men, with women playing basketball, lacrosse, and soccer at highest risk. They often have more severe signs and symptoms, and recover less quickly than men."[115]

As noted above, these studies may suffer from issues such as small sample size, selection bias, and other problems that have been noted in CTE research from Boston University and in other studies. However, the headlines and stories amount to a mountain of evidence arguing that football is unsafe for anyone to play, and even supporters of women's football such as Flynn acknowledge that the game may be more dangerous for girls and women. That begs the question: what are the athletes thinking when they decide to play, and what are parents thinking when they allow their children put themselves at risk?

The athletes with whom I spoke seemed to be having too much fun to worry about the possibility of injury. Even when they were concussed or had one of the many other injuries that football players are liable to encounter, they returned to the gridiron as soon as they could. Neither Maddie Bracken nor Lacie Jacobson were unique in the sangfroid with which they considered the possibility of injury. To them, and the other athletes that I interviewed, the positives of playing football far outweighed the negative.

Several focused on the camaraderie that being part of a team provided, and they often used the word "family" when speaking about that. Kaity Cummings of the North Winnipeg Nomads of the MGFA said she liked "the family aspect of the team. Football is one of the only sports, I think, that you have such a close contact family in, but especially in our league."[116] Sydney Sessions of Bingham in the UGFL stated, "It's a family—it's more about making friends and having another family than it is for playing the game really. I know that I have a thirty-plus girls behind my back if something happens to me."[117] Stephanie Bracken, whose daughter Maddie is on Sessions's team, added: "I just love how they hang out on and off the field. If they hear, you know, a friend being bullied a little bit, and they're like, you don't want to mess with these girls. They're football players, and they are family."[118]

Other players focused on more of the personal advantages playing brought them. Montana Pirrie of the Nomads told me, "It's definitely made me . . . I used to be really shy but now it made me more of a talkative person and like I used to never talk to news reporters about it and like now it's like really easy for me to talk to them."[119] Railey Tucker of the West Jordan High School team of the UGFL said, "Before this I didn't really have anything to, like, dedicate everything that I had and all my power and effort to, and now that I am playing football I'm able to dedicate all that power and effort in my life to football and kind of help motivate me for everything especially in school to keep my grades up."[120] West Jordan's Macy Coester, when asked what she liked about football, replied, "Everything, like I just love, I love hitting people. I really love hitting people." As mentioned above, she credited football with bringing confidence back into her life, and she added, "Like it's been . . . I'm so much more confident. I'm so much happier when I have football practice and I just . . . yeah, life's good."[121]

Many players focused on football as a means of coping with the stress, and anger, that had troubled them before joining their teams. The Nomads' Gianna Donnelly told me: "My dad kind of wanted me to try it out because I was just in general a violent person, I guess, but I liked hitting people and stuff. I always used to play football with the boys in middle school and stuff like that, so I was like, I might as well try girls' football, so that kind of clicked with me. . . . Basically it caps my anger a little bit too." She said that her mother was "actually really supportive, and she thought it was, like, a good idea to play, and she also thought it was a good idea so I could just get out all of my anger and frustrations on other people, and I wouldn't get in trouble for it. So it was good."[122] Natalie Hanson of the IGTFL felt, "I like if you have something going on you, like, you can take it out in football. Like, your anger, you hit someone, you just get the . . . it's just the adrenaline in you."[123] Olivia Green of West Jordan, whose nickname on her jersey was "Try Me," because when she gets angry, she will tell that to whoever makes her angry, reported that football helped with that. "I mean I got to take my anger out on people. It helps a little bit, and that it's just a lot of fun. I have a lot more, like, friends and people actually, like, talk to me and think I'm pretty cool now." She added with a chuckle— "They're kind of afraid of me, to be honest."[124]

One of the enduring fascinations that both players and spectators have with football is the violence of the sport. It is also one of the main concerns of critics of football, but the commonly used phrase that "violence is as American as apple pie" has some validity. Hampton Stevens, writing "An Intellectual's Defense of Football" in the *Atlantic*, argued, "Football tells us that violence can be beautiful when performed for the sake of a greater good," and that "violence, for good or ill, is the beauty of it [football]."[125] One needn't search very strenuously to find hundreds of articles, essays, and other writings affirming that the violence of football is a positive trait of the game. That many of the girls interviewed felt the same way flies in the face of traditional roles assigned to males and females but demonstrates that the fascination with aggression, once thought to be a male domain, actually cuts across gender lines.

The desire to strike a blow for gender equality also motivated many of the athletes interviewed for this project. Noah Harris of the IGTFL responded, "My chain of thought changed on how I would not only look at sports but look out on life, like it doesn't have to be split down the middle—girls and boys do this all. You can do what you want."[126] Her teammate for the Battle of the Borders Ale'sha Christy agreed, reporting that most people, including her teachers, were largely positive about her playing, "except for the boys' football team. They don't like it, and say, 'We can't wait to see you get creamed.' I can't wait to prove them wrong."[127] Lauren Dixon of West Jordan made it even clearer. She gave her reason for wanting to play as "I just thought it would be fun to show boys what, like, girls can do, and I just thought it would be a lot of fun. You know you talk to boys, and they're, like, 'Girls can't play football, you know—they're too sissy to hit somebody.' And I'm just like, 'No, I'll kill you.'" When asked if she had indeed shown the boys what girls can do, she responded affirmatively, saying, "Yeah. They're kind of scared."[128]

As with Green, she gave a little laugh that presumably demonstrated she thought this was a good thing, as well she should. These girls were doing something that most of their mothers never had the chance to do. They were playing a game that many people in the United States and around the world see as a manly game for manly men. They are reveling in the knowledge that they can be just as rough as their male counterparts, when playing against other females.

Sam Gordon, in her acceptance speech at the NFL award ceremony, had thought out what she wanted to say, and so she delivered her remarks more grammatically, if not more enthusiastically, than her peers in Winnipeg, Mooresville, and Midvale. She told the audience: "I want to let you all in on a little secret: girls love football. Millions of girls will be watching the Super Bowl. But watching the sport we love the most is not enough. We want to play football too, on separate girls' teams. I know girls want to play because I asked them. Before Title IX, some people thought the girls were not interested in playing sports, but they were wrong. They were just as wrong as people who argued that women did not want to vote, to hold public office, or be lawyers or doctors. People who think girls don't want to play football are wrong too. Throughout history women have had to fight for the right to follow their dreams. My dream is that high schools and colleges will offer girls' football teams, and I'm going to fight to see my dream come true. Utah will be the birthplace of girls' high school football. By growing up playing football, women will have the same experience and knowledge of the game that men have; men that end up coaches, scouts, executives, and broadcasters. If we are allowed to play, the doors to those opportunities will be thrown wide open. Equality is our Super Bowl."[129] Those are lofty goals, and while colleges offering girls' tackle football teams might be a stretch, Gordon and her co-plaintiffs are fighting for their dreams by continuing with their lawsuit against the school districts and the state association.

The athletes in the various leagues, along with those who play, or have played, on boys' teams around the nation embody the qualities of toughness, aggressiveness, and bravery that proponents of football have claimed the game instills. Maddie Bracken, whose mother cried because concussions kept her daughter out of the game, embodies the toughness and bravery that once was widely celebrated in our culture. She told me that her father wanted her to play football because "I got bullied a lot as a kid, and my dad was, like, super pissed off that I, like, couldn't stand up for myself 'cuz it was, like, when I was about second grade, so he wanted me to learn some self-defense, so he signed me up for football." When I asked her about her mother's reports that she had been injured several times but kept playing, she responded: "Yeah. I had, like, a broken rib about two weeks ago, and I didn't tell my coaches. I don't want to be out, and last year when I played with the boys, I broke my ankle and tore a ligament in my knee. I still played the playoff game, all of the championship practices, and the championship game. No excuses. I'm always going to play no matter what." When I commented that she must have a high pain threshold, she disagreed but asserted: "I won't show it. I'm a baby, but I won't show it. I cry in the car."

One must acknowledge that freedom to play includes the freedom to risk one's health, and that has traditionally been a hurdle that girls have faced when trying to take their place on the gridiron. However, when those obstacles, typically imposed by adults trying to protect girls, disappear, and girls have the freedom, they and their parents have been willing to pay that price.

When Kerri Strug stuck the landing in her vault with two torn ligaments in her ankle to win the team gold medal for the U.S. Olympic Team, she became a national hero. When Willis Reed played with a torn muscle in his right leg in the seventh game of the 1971 NBA championship series, we label that a "Top NBA Moment."[130] When Jack Youngblood of the Los Angeles Rams played in the playoffs, the Super Bowl, and the Pro Bowl with a broken leg, we remember that as one of the "Manliest Moments in NFL History."[131] When coaches such as Vince Lombardi sent players back into the fray after concussions, it was celebrated as part of his myth.[132]

While many still hold that athletes should exhibit toughness in the face of injury, many others might feel that Maddie's mother should be prosecuted for child abuse. Online commenter Richard Gaylord is not alone in arguing that allowing children to play football is parental abuse. Bennet Omalu, the doctor who is "credited with discovering" CTE, reportedly "likens children playing football to abuse and says there is nothing we can do to make the game safer." He added: "Someday there will be district attorney who will prosecute for child abuse [on the football field] (brackets in article) and it will succeed. . . . It is the definition of child abuse."[133] In 2018 the legislatures in the states of Illinois, California, New Jersey, and Maryland considered legislation that would have banned tackle football for children under twelve. Though none have as yet become law, the media concentration of concussions and CTE is having an impact.[134]

The voices of commenters such as Gaylord have been magnified through social media. Their commentary has in turn extended the impact of medical professionals such as Omalu, Stern, and Duffy, and they have caused a split in our culture between those who value football, despite its dangers, and those who think the game is unsafe at any age. This split also reflected the political chasms that exist in our society, with conservatives such as Flynn, who writes for *Breitbart*, and Rush Limbaugh arguing that critics of football are attacking the game from the left, because "they don't like displays of patriotism, strength, [and] rugged individualism."[135] Dave Zirin, the sports editor for the leftwing magazine *The Nation*, after summarizing how "science is not football's friend," asked and answered the question, "So does this mean it's not 'moral' to watch a ceaselessly brutal sport that is 70 percent black but has no black ownership?"[136] When they publish stories about youth and high school football, articles or posts by left-of-center media sources such as the *New York Times* and the *Huffington Post* tend to focus on the dangers, not the benefits.

During the height of the concussion debate, critics of football, and the parents who heed their warnings, have caused participation rates for boy's high school football to drop. According to the National Federation of State High School Associations (NFSHSA), the number of high school boy athletes playing football has dropped from 1,135,052 in 2009 to 1,086,690 in 2016, which is a decline of a little more than 4 percent.[137] The Sports & Fitness Industry Association (SFIA) reported a 30 percent drop in pre–high school participation between 2008 and 2013.[138] However, USA Football, quoting more recent data from SFIA, indicated that this trend has reversed, and participation in tackle football, for children aged six to fourteen, grew by 2.5 percent from 2014 to 2015, from 2.128 million to 2.169 million. Contra to NFSHSA's numbers, USA Football, again quoting SFIA numbers, reported that participation rates for high school age athletes rose 2.5 percent to 1.248 million. The numbers of athletes playing flag football are growing at an even greater rate.[139]

Regardless of the drop in high school participation, if one exists, tackle football remains the nation's most popular sport, which indicates that millions of parents are ignoring the news that the game is unsafe for their children. Moreover, more and more girls are playing football. The number of girls in youth football has been estimated, reportedly by USA Football, at being around 25,000 girls.[140] High school participation for girls has increased from 85 players in 1980, the first year that NFSHSA reported female players, to 2,120 in their report for the 2015–16 high school season. They also report a growth in girls playing flag football, from 3,855 in 2002, the first year with numbers reported, to 11,254 in 2017.[141]

So football seems to be alive and well, despite numerous reports of its decline. That is good news for the girls of the tackle leagues in Manitoba, Utah, Indiana, and New Brunswick. The same is true for the flag leagues in Florida and elsewhere, because the benefits that girls gain from playing football far outweigh the dangers. It may be somewhat hyperbolic, but in addition to the other benefits discussed previously, some girls reported even greater benefits. When asked what football had done for her, Sherisa Gretsinger of the Nomads told me simply, "It saved my life." She did not explain how it had done so, but the conviction in her voice was absolute.[142] Bingham's Sydney Sessions was more loquacious, but no less convincing. She said: "Well, I've always been kind of that tomboy. I mean, I never really had a sport I stuck to. I switched around from every sport really, and none of them really stuck with me. I saw this advertisement for this league, and I started. It's the best thing I've ever done. . . . Before football I never really had friends. I was just kind of that kid at school that walked around minding her own business. I mean, I was nothing special. I had no stories. I was just there to be there. I started playing football, and I became someone. I found my personality. I found who I really was, and it was just such a great experience, because, like, I presented myself. I wasn't there before, and now I'm this person who goes up to teammates, and I talk to people. I have friends. I have a special thing about me, saying to people, 'Yeah, I play football,' and everyone finds that really cool now. At first everyone kind of—it was something bad. It was, 'Oh you're going to get a concussion, you can't play—you're a girl.' But now, everyone, they support me, and I have more friends, and I'm better than ever in life."[143]

Sydney's father, who walked up while we were talking, confirmed the changes that he had seen in his daughter, and Stephanie Bracken, who is called "Momma B" by the team, added, "You lead this team. She's a leader."[144] "It saved my life" and "I became someone" are powerful testimonies to what football has done for those individuals and what it might do for many more girls and women like them. Those seem like good reasons to take a calculated risk.

Something that was not mentioned may provide another. Several of the adult players I interviewed made statements along the lines that they didn't have bodies that were thought to be traditional for girl athletes when they were in school. Body image issues have widely been reported as being a problem for teen girls.[145] None of the young athletes to whom I talked, even those who were larger, mentioned that their body image had improved by playing football. Perhaps they started playing at an early enough age, and being big is not a bad thing in football, so they did not suffer from that particular problem, or it was not as severe as in other girls their age. However, in a study of fifteen Canadian players, "'It Doesn't Matter How Big or Small You Are . . . There's a Position for You': Body Image among Female Tackle Football Players," the authors reported, "For these women, football provided a body-image friendly opportunity that motivated players to engage in more physical activity."[146] This was a small sample, to be sure, but other studies have linked sports participation with increased positive body image, and so the contention may well be valid.

In recent years the UGFL has garnered a great deal of positive publicity. After her NFL award, Sam Gordon appeared in an NFL commercial that had her showing off her football moves along with several current and former NFL stars.[147] Two all-star teams from the UGFL also recently played a scrimmage during the halftime of the 2020 NFL Pro Bowl.[148] Those are positive moments, but it remains to be seen if a national organization will get behind girls' football the way that Football Canada has.

More than two thousand girls are playing tackle football with boys in schools around the United States. Thousands more are playing flag football. Added to them are the hundreds that play in all-girls tackle leagues that began in Canada, and that are now found on both sides of the northern border. The road for this participation has had to be paved by girls and their parents who challenged existing notions that football was too dangerous for girls, and now, too dangerous for anyone. They have been aided by adults, both male and female, who have put aside old notions of what sports are proper for girls.

They are learning the joys of visiting violence on their peers and are on the receiving end of that violence, which they accept stoically. They are absorbing the lessons that football can teach when it is done well—courage, perseverance, team work, and working toward a concrete goal. That football truly provides these values has come under question from a number of sources, but not from the young athletes themselves. They have embraced the sport with the fervor of the new convert to the secular religion of the gridiron.

They are also joined in their love for the sport by thousands of women in North America and around the world. Interest outside the United States has been sufficient to encourage the creation of international championships in the women's game. Three times since 2010 the International Federation of American Football (IFAF) has sponsored championship contests that have provided women from Canada, Mexico, Australia, and various European nations the chance to test their mettle against their American counterparts. As we shall see, it has not gone well for the international teams.

# American Women Tackle the World

Football is a violent sport, and it attracts athletes who are comfortable with or who love that violence. According to some women who have played in the International Federation of American Football's (IFAF) Women's World Championship (WWC), the violence is part of what they love. Some were more overt than others about what they were doing.

Danilynn Welniak, of the Dallas Diamonds and the 2010 Team USA, said: "I'm going to have to say my favorite part of it is the fact that it's pretty much legalized assault. I know I'm little, but I'm kinda powerful sometimes. So you get out there and you get that pancake block, and you have your running back go behind you, it's a pretty awesome feeling."[1]

Others did not go that far, but in interviews during the 2017 WWC, they gave much the same message. Alicia Wilson, of the Calgary Rage and the 2017 Team Canada, told me: "You get to hit people sometimes. That's a lot of fun. There's nothing more satisfying than a good hit."[2]

Laura Dye, of the Leeds Carnegie Chargers and the 2017 Great Britain Lions National Team, mentioned: "I'm an angry person. That is one of my . . . attributes, so I like being able to hit people without getting in trouble for it, and releasing that anger, without doing it the wrong way. I love playing with the girls because we're just a big family . . . I really, really love the hitting people though!"[3]

Likewise, Anna Greta Medina, of the Legionarias UNINTER and the 2017 Team Mexico, commented: "It has a lot of intensity, and that's what I was liking about it. So I say okay—it was my first day about hitting, and I say okay, I can do this!"[4]

The quotes above are just a few from women who have reveled in their ability to play the rough sport. I considered adding a subtitle to this chapter along the lines of "The Success of Anglo-North American Aggression," but I have also been told by girls and women from countries outside of the United Kingdom or North America that this is a feature of playing tackle football that appeals to them. Suvi Mantyniemi of the Tampere Saints Ladies and the 2017 Finnish National Team, for instance, told me, "I like being able to legally punch somebody on the field!"[5] Nausicaa Dell'Orto of the Bologna Underdogs, who also played for the Italian National Team, though not in any of the IFAF Women's World Championships, echoed that when I talked to her at USA Football's Women's World Games in New Orleans. After watching her launch herself into the tackling dummy in a one-on-one drill, I mentioned that she seemed to have a grudge against the dummy. She smiled and replied, "I have some anger issues."[6]

The athletes typically smile or give a nervous laugh when they tell me about their enjoyment of the rough side of the game they love. They likely are acknowledging that a proclivity toward violence is not viewed positively in today's world. They might also be demonstrating awareness that if violence is not socially acceptable for males, it is even less so for females. But they like it. Just as several of the youth players from Manitoba, Utah, and Indiana enjoyed having an outlet for their aggressive tendencies.

No—the adrenaline rush that women football players feel when they pancake block or flatten an opponent to the ground is not restricted to Anglo-North America. But they have managed to play the violent game on the international stage better than their sisters from other countries. Of the three IFAF WWCs, the Americans have finished first and the Canadians second in each. In the 2017 WWC, Mexico and Great Britain sent national teams for the first time, and they finished third and fourth, respectively.

The athletes obviously revel in the violence of the collision sport, and all of those with whom I have talked also told me that it was a special experience to play for their country. Defensive linewoman Monica Lewinska told me: "Literally when we are standing out there doing the anthems, you can feel the emotions rising, and I'm always thinking control it because then you've lost it. I get that every time we come out for the anthems, and I feel it in my chest rising, and there's no feeling like it."[7] Lewinska's teammate and Great Britain National Team cocaptain, quarterback Jo Kilby, echoed her. "It's a great honor to be apart of, and we wear our jerseys with great pride, and to be one of the captains is, you know, is very special."[8]

Team Mexico offensive linewoman Sandra San Juan Chavez said, "Well, playing at this level, representing my country, well, it's a big responsibility for me, but also I feel very happy, and it's an honor. Definitely it's a big honor, and I feel very blessed."[9] Her teammate defensive end Medina, who was barely out of high school when she played for Mexico, told me that she felt "goosebumps" each time she took the field for her nation.[10]

All of the women I interviewed had something similar to say. Leah Hinkle, the first athlete I interviewed, added, "Being on Team USA was obviously an incredible experience. I've been able to travel the United States because of football. I've been able to travel the world because of football. I have friends all over the world because of football."[11]

That was another common theme that came up in many of the interviews. In the age of social media, the women often reported that their friend list on Facebook had exploded. Linebacker Kellie Hopkins of the Perth (Australia) Broncos mentioned, "I had about a hundred friends before I started this. Now I've got like six hundred Facebook friends."[12]

The IFAF WWC has given women such as Sami Grisafe and Knengi Martin who play tackle football the opportunity to accomplish something that NFL players such as Tom Brady and Nick Foles have never been able to do—they have won a true world championship. The Philadelphia Eagles claimed the title of "World Champions in 2018," but that was not proven in actual international competition.[13] Admittedly, had the Eagles played the champion of the Canadian Football League (CFL), or the champions of any other league around the world, they would crush their opposition. They did not, however, and so their claim to be world champions, no matter how likely to be true, is a fictive title. Not so for Team USA, which has defeated all opponents in international competitions for as long as they have been held.

To be fair, there are male players who do represent their country in international competition. USA Football sponsors male junior and senior national teams, but their selection criteria specify that these players must be currently in college or within the first year after graduation. They cannot be under contract with an NFL or CFL team. In practice, this means that the players are those who are not likely to become professionals, and if there are any players who went on to a career in a top professional league, their names were well concealed.[14]

I had the chance to attend the 2017 WWC held in Langley, British Columbia, not far from Vancouver. While there, I was able to interview five players from Team Mexico, seven from Team Canada, three from Team Finland, and four from Team UK. *American Football International*, a blog devoted to the spread of the American game, helped me receive a press pass, and I wrote posts on the championships for them.[15] Once I finally got into the swing of things, I also asked questions of American, British, Finnish, Mexican, Canadian, and Australian players during the postgame press conferences. Since then, I have managed to interview several other players who were at the championships from the United States, Australia, and the United Kingdom.

I did not interview any athletes from Australia, outside of the postgame media availabilities. On the off day that followed the first day's games, I was watching the Aussies practice, when Team Outback's head coach, Jen Welter, in fine NFL fashion, sent an assistant to tell me that the session was closed to the public and press. After that, I was too intimidated to try to talk to the players. That did, however, make me feel more like a reporter than just a mere historian who had managed to finagle a press pass.

I had only seen a few Women's Football Alliance games before arriving at the WWC, so I was somewhat unprepared for the level of football that I saw there. The athletes were in good shape, and there were few of the injuries that had marred some of the WFA games that I had seen. These were the best football players from the six nations who had been chosen to represent their countries in international competition. Observing their demeanor around the stadium, it was clear that these women were well aware of their elite status. They walked with a certain swagger that is typical of top athletes, and when they went onto the field, they demonstrated that they belonged in that category.

The games started on 24 June with something of a grudge match. The Finns had defeated the British in the 2015 Women's European Championships sponsored by IFAF Europe. That championship had been the GB Lions' first foray into an international tournament. The Finns were ranked third in the championships and the Brits were ranked fourth, so it was set to be a competitive game, even though the Lions had lost 50–12 in their previous match. It proved to be so. The Finns outgained the Brits, but a long touchdown run by Lions' running back Ruth Matta, an interception return by Lucy Kirk, and two touchdown passes from Jo Kilby to Jessica Anderson gave the Lions a 27–21 victory. The Finns played well throughout behind Jonna Hakkarainen, who passed for two touchdowns, one to Emmi Järn, and another to Kristi Nirhamo. Those three Helsinki Wolverines were joined by their cross-town rival Jenni Linden of the Helsinki Roosters, who gained 153 yards on twenty-four carries in the losing effort.[16] Late in the fourth quarter, the Finns were on the British 5-yard line but wasted seventeen precious seconds and failed to score as time ran out.[17]

The Lions had aimed to revenge their loss to Finland. UK linebacker Phoebe Schecter told me: "So coming into this, it's basically been in our minds since we found out we're going to the Worlds, and since we found out we had our game against Finland: this is the rematch. And I knew from then—the whole team knew from then—that we did not want to lose to Finland. So we based everything around that."[18] Defensive tackle Monica Lewinska echoed: "Our mantra was basically, 'Beat Finland!' That's because every year, we are trying to build and get better. That's the next level we needed to get to."[19]

The UK-Finland rematch turned out to be the closest game of the championship. The second game of the opening day pitted Team USA versus Team Mexico. The Mexicans would eventually defeat the Australians and the British to take third place, but they struggled against the defending champions and lost 29–0. The last game of the day saw the Canadians rolling over the Australians 31–6.

That pattern continued on the second day. The surprise of the day, and the championships, was how well Team Mexico played. The Mexican Miracle began on 27 June, when they led off the second day with a 31–10 victory over the Australians. Along with their opponents that day, Mexico was appearing in its first international competition. Women had only been playing full-contact football in the Liga Extrema de Football Arena (LEXFA) since 2014, and their thirteen teams had only expanded to eleven-a-side in 2016 to prepare for the world championships.[20] Whether that plan actually took place was unclear. Team Mexico head coach Giovanni Carrillo told reporters in the postgame conference after their victory against Australia that this championship had been their first experience at playing with elevens. Despite the newness of their program, LEXFA made their ultimate goals clear on their website in 2015: "The most important mission for us is to unite football . . . with the purpose of . . . mak[ing] it very clear that the women of Mexico play the best American football in the world." The website article continued, stating that they were "not wanting to compete to compete," but rather they were forming "14 arena teams converted into a single objective . . . BE THE CHAMPIONS OF THE WORLD !!!"[21] Their loss to Team USA demonstrated they had some work to do before that objective was realized, but with their defeat of their fellow newcomer to the international stage, Australia, they were making a start.

Andrea Romero Vasquez, a running back from the Vikingas of Mexico City, was happy with the result of their first game against the Americans. She told me: "It was a hard game, a very physical game. We have to move faster than we thought, but it was a great match for us. Because the United States, they always scored more than 60 points, so we only received only 29, I think that it's a good result. So I am proud of my team with that result."[22] Vasquez, though a slight woman, transformed into a punishing runner on the field and was one of the reasons Mexico did so well. She gained 35 yards in seven carries against the United States, and 102 yards on fourteen carries against Australia.

Vasquez's teammate Maria Fernanda Mandujano Abrego, a wide receiver, told me that playing against Australia, "We felt more relaxed. We know what we have to do. So the first game was just to see how Mexico plays. Then with Australia, it was like okay, we know how to play football. We are good, let's do this." On representing her country in international competition, she summed up what most of the players I interviewed said: "It's a dream. A lot of girls in Mexico have this dream. It's very exciting. When you hear the Mexican anthem, it's like a dream."[23]

With a little over two years' experience, the Mexican team may not have even been invited to the tournament if IFAF had not experienced a schism in 2015. Under the leadership of Tommy Wiking, IFAF had planned to hold the 2015 Men's World Championships in Stockholm, Sweden, but financial irregularities threatened to postpone or cancel the games. USA Football stepped in, and IFAF accepted their bid to hold the games at the field next to the Pro Football Hall of Fame in Canton, Ohio.[24] The games went on as scheduled, but at the IFAF meeting that accompanied the games, Wiking, who had previously submitted his resignation as president, reneged on his action. He and his supporters, which included many European federations, walked out of the meeting when the others moved ahead to elect a new president. This led the federation to a split into two contending IFAFs, one based in Paris, with Wiking as the president, and another based in New York, with Roope Noronen as their president.[25] Wiking flexed his presidential muscles by suspending several federations, including Federación Mexicana de Fútbol Americano, for purportedly violating the federation's anti-doping rules.[26] Germany and Sweden, who had participated in the championships in 2010 and 2013, followed IFAF Paris and so absented themselves from the pool of nations available for the 2017 games. Teams such as Mexico, Great Britain, and Australia were the beneficiaries of those decisions.

In the day's other games, USA and Canada continued to roll. Team USA defeated Finland 48–0. USA head coach Jim Farrell had to deal with some questions after his team failed to score quickly in the opening quarter of their first two games. Farrell's main difficulty, seemingly, was making sure that all of his players got quality time on the field. He used a platoon system with his three quarterbacks (Sami Grisafe, Lisa Horton, and Allyson Hamlin) and the other position players splitting time. In his postgame comments, Farrell downplayed his team's ability to score quickly and instead emphasized that his players were still getting to know each other and mesh as a team.[27]

There was no doubt that the USA had the most experienced players. Both Grisafe and linebacker Knengi Martin were playing in their third wwc. Running back Odessa Jenkins, defensive back Callie Brownson, wide receiver Jeanette Gray, linebacker Vicky Eddy, offensive linewoman Dawn Pederson, and wide receiver Liz Sowers were playing in their second wwc. Sowers's two sisters, Rusty and Katie, had also each played in one wwc, the first and the third, respectively. So the championships were something of a family affair for her.

In the final game of day two, the Canadians defeated the British 35–0. Team UK had come to the games with the goal of defeating the Finns, and having accomplished that, they struggled for the rest of the championship. The players made it clear that they were focused on defeating Finland, and that seemed to represent "mission accomplished" for them.

On 30 June the women from the various teams, likely a bit tired from having to play three football games in a week, gathered for the medal round. In the fifth-place game, Finland defeated Australia 35–0.[28] Australia had made a significant splash by hiring Welter, the first woman to play in a men's professional football game, as well as the first woman to earn a coaching internship in the NFL. During the championships, the Australians' inexperience was evident. Their teams at home played seven-a-side, so even though they had talented athletes, Team Outback struggled at playing eleven-a-side. They also seemed to have been overly focused on playing a finesse game, using unusual formations to try to confuse their opponents. Their offense seemed to work better when they settled down to straight-ahead football. The much longer experience that the Finns brought to the game was too much for the newcomers.

Team Mexico continued their march to football success by defeating the United Kingdom 19-8. The surprise team of the championships, Mexico featured a great deal of team speed, which they used to great effect. Romero continued to impress. She scored two touchdowns against Australia and was chosen player of the game in the medal match against Great Britain. The UK Lions came back from the let-down they seemed to suffer in the wake of defeating Finland. Running back Ruth Matta scored the Lions' only touchdown and continued her strong performance in the WWC (192 yards on twenty-seven carries in the first two games). For her efforts, Matta was named the British player of the game.[29]

The championship matched Team Canada against Team USA. The same two teams had contended for the championship in each of the previous two WWCs, and Canada was the only team with players who could match the experience of the Americans. In the first two WWCs, the United States had defeated their neighbors by scores of 66-0 in 2010 and 64-0 in 2013. In 2017, the Canadian players had a goal of toppling the USA from its top place in women's football.

Alicia Wilson, a slotback who played for the Calgary Rage, told me: "It'll be a good game. I think . . . uh, how do I say this nicely, their attitude towards football is, hold on, I have to put this nicer . . . sorry, um . . . because it is called American football, it is theirs. Okay? We have Canadian football, but we are learning American. I think they underestimate us. And I cannot wait to prove them wrong."[30]

Beth Thomson, a linebacker who played for the Saskatoon Valkyries, said: "Tomorrow? Well, that's the nerves asking. They look good, right? They always look good. So they are tough, they are strong, they are big, but we are too. We have speed. We have toughness. We have good coaches that coach us the proper schemes. We've been watching their film, and I think we're gonna . . . I believe that we have a chance to win this gold, and we're gonna take it when we are out there tomorrow. So."[31]

They were not able to do that, but they were able to make it something of a close game.

Prior to this championship, Team USA had only given up one touchdown in the eight previous games—in a 107-7 demolition of Germany in 2013. This time, however, Canada scored the first points of the game when Carly Dyck kicked a 38-yard field goal to put Team Canada up 3-0. Team USA scored three touchdowns, on a pass from Grisafe to Gray, another catch by Gray on a double-pass trick play from wide receiver Angela Baker, and a 3-yard run by Odessa Jenkins. Canada was not finished though, and after a fake field goal had failed, Team Canada's Aimee Kowalski hit Alex Kowalski on a 39-yard scoring pass to make the score USA 21 to 9 for Canada. After USA quarterback Lisa Horton ran the ball in from the 11-yard line with only 1:11 gone in the third quarter, the Canadians answered when defensive back Rebeckah Heninger recovered a fumble on her own 24 and ran it back for Canada's final score of the game. After that, Team USA scored twice more on runs by Alexis Snyder and Hannah DeGraffinreed to make the score 41-16. They might have scored again, but their last drive stalled when a naked man wearing a red cowboy hat streaked across the field. After the commotion, the Team USA quarterback took a knee and ran out the clock.[32]

In the final press conference sponsored by Football Canada, Team USA head coach Jim Farrell summed up the experience: "These women are warriors. They were the best athletes on the soccer field, the lacrosse field, at field hockey, a basketball star, whatever it was, they were the best athletes. And now they find what football gives. It's a very, kind of like, visceral experience. It's a collision sport, not a contact sport, and they would tell you that there's nothing better than the feeling of this ultimate team game, and what it can give to you, and what it pushes you to do and know about yourself. I'm very proud to be around them and to know what kind of women they are. They affect change, all of them. They are the change makers. We have players on our team that are in their early forties, versus players on our team that are twenty-one. It's a whole different experience between what our forty-year-old players had to do to play tackle football to now what some of our younger players are able to do, and the ease of which they're finding opportunities." Farrell issued a call to high school coaches in the nations that had gathered to play the WWC to find a team to help coach. "They're unbelievable athletes. I've coached more Division I players coaching women's football than I did in eighteen years of coaching high school."[33]

He also predicted that some of his more experienced players would be the next generation of coaches, which turned out to be true. The San Francisco 49ers hired Team USA wide receiver Liz Sowers as a full-time coach in 2017, and Team UK running back Phoebe Schecter served an internship with the Buffalo Bills for the 2018 season. Team USA running back Odessa "OJ" Jenkins finally hung up her cleats and became coach Jenkins of the Texas Elite Spartans. There may be even more, but those were the players that I knew for sure.

Canada had been chosen to host the 2013 WWC, but after some contractual issues with IFAF, the games went to Vantaa, Finland.[34] After IFAF's schism, the Canadians finally got their chance, and they made the most of it. Football Canada (FC) and IFAF New York put on a good show, and in the awards ceremony, the hosting organization even brought in two Royal Canadian Mounted Police (Mounties) in full red dress uniforms and their traditional peaked hats to hand out the awards. McLeod Stadium in Langley, which is about thirty miles west of Vancouver, had plenty of seating, even for the final game, when the stands were mostly full.

For the other games, a few hundred fans backed their favorites. Aside from the Canada-USA game, the largest crowd was likely for the match pitting Australia against Mexico. Both of those national teams traveled well, and their fans were particularly evident. The Australians were a bit quieter but featured Rachael Cary, a woman dressed in a kangaroo "onesie."[35] Whenever Australia played, kangaroos were everywhere, including on the sidelines as the team stood for their national anthem.

The Mexican fans were more numerous, and more raucous. They draped banners, hung streamers, and livened up the atmosphere with a variety of noise makers. As mentioned above, after the first game against the United States, the Mexican fans had much more to cheer about than the Australians. That and their greater numbers were likely reasons for the Mexican fans' greater displays of enthusiasm.

Fans of the UK Lions were also evident and were dressed for the occasion. One super fan made more noise than most of the rest of the fans at the games. Wearing a blue Matthew Stafford jersey with Union Jack sweatpants, he kept up a continuous drumbeat on the metal trashcans around the stadium. Another fan wore a blue dress with red flowers and sported a British flag umbrella.

The U.S. fans seemed to be mostly players, likely from Washington and Oregon teams. Since Canada was the host of the games, they had the largest fan base, and they wore the usual team gear, along with Canadian maple leaf insignia. The Americans and Canadians were enthusiastic but didn't stick in the memory as the fans from nations farther away did.

The main takeaway from the games seemed to be that the global playing field was becoming more level. Team USA still won, but their margin of victory was less than in previous WWCs. The UK Lions upset the balance of European power by defeating Finland, a team that had finished in third place in the first two WWCs. As the surprise team of the week, Mexico demonstrated, at least for 2017, that North American teams were dominating women's tackle football. The British rounded out the top four teams, thus providing my thoughts on Anglo–North American violence.

The WWC also has created and expanded the network of women playing football around the world. Some of the Mexican players mentioned that Team USA players had made the point to congratulate them after they defeated Australia, and it took some time to clear the field after the championship game since the players were hesitant for the week to end. Though few noticed in the larger world, for one week the athletes experienced the life of a professional football player—practicing, playing, and likely eating and sleeping football, all in the pursuit of securing a world championship on the gridiron. Doing something that most male football players would never have the chance to do. For some of the players on the field, this would be the third time they had had that chance, and it all started in Sweden.

## WWC 2010, STOCKHOLM, SWEDEN

IFAF first held the WWC in Stockholm between 27 June and 3 July 2010. The organization had been holding world championships for men since 1999 and had also staged flag football championships for women and men since 2002.[36] The "ultimate goal" IFAF pursued through the games was International Olympic Committee (IOC) recognition of tackle football as an Olympic sport.[37] If the federation could demonstrate that the sport was played at a high level by both men and women, the chances of adoption would likely increase. The 2015 IFAF schism has no doubt set back efforts to have tackle football added to the Olympic Games, since one of the prerequisites for inclusion is that the sport must have an international federation, not dueling federations.[38]

To coach the inaugural national team, USA Football chose John Konecki, who was at the time the head coach of the Chicago Force of the Independent Women's Football League (IWFL).[39] The players also came from the IWFL, which was the only "full-kitted" semiprofessional league for women at the time. The Lingerie Football League began play in 2009, but players from that league were not eligible.[40] IFAF used data from a 2009 Benchmarking Study, which counted the number of female athletes playing American football in each country, to rank the national teams. The top six teams, in order, were the United States, Canada, Germany, Austria, Finland, and Sweden. These nations were ranked from one to six in the same order for seeding the championship. They were then invited to form national teams and attend the 2010 games.[41]

North America had the largest group of athletes from which to draw. The pool of talent for Team USA came from the fifty-one IWFL teams with some 1,800 athletes and was coached by Konecki. Larry Harlow, the head coach of the Saint John (New Brunswick) Storm of the Maritime Women's Football League (MWFL), coached Team Canada. The ninety Canadian players who tried out for the forty-five woman squad primarily came from the MWFL, which was, at that time, the only Canadian women's football league. In addition to the "13 players from Saint John and nine from Winnipeg," there were other MWFL and independent teams such as "Fredericton, Montreal, Calgary, Edmonton, Moncton, Saskatoon, and Halifax" that provided athletes.[42]

Women in Germany had been playing since 1990 and had 120 players try out for Team Germany. Nearly a third of their roster, 14 of the 45, was made up of players from the Berlin Cowboys and Berlin Kobras, who contributed 7 players each. Those two teams had contested the previous year's Ladies Bowl, the German women's national championship. Other teams contributing players included the Dresden Diamonds, the Mainz Lady Warriors, and the Muelheim Shamrocks.[43]

Austrian women joined their German gridiron neighbors in 1997 and had four teams, including the Budapest Wolves. Although the Finns had been playing flag football since the 1980s, their Suomen Amerikkalaisen Jalkapallon Liitto Ry (SAJL) had only adopted tackle football in 2008.[44] Sweden, the sixth-ranked team, had only three teams in 2010—the Stockholm Mean Machines, the Arlanda Jets, and the Limhamn Griffins. Some Swedish women had played on male teams, and some had played flag football. They had some international experience, having played and lost to Finland in 2008 and 2009.[45]

The United States and Austria played the first game of the historic championship on 27 June 2010 at Stockholm's Zinkensdamms IP Stadium. Austria was undoubtedly hoping for an upset, but God was on the side of the big battalions, so the outcome of the match between a nation with fifty-one teams versus one with four was close to a sure thing. Team USA won handily, outscoring the Austrians 63–0. Adrienne Smith, a wide receiver for the New York Sharks, scored the first touchdown for the Americans on a 59-yard pass from Chicago's Grisafe, and Boston Militia running back Mia Brickhouse added two rushing touchdowns. Team Austria was not prepared for the USA's aerial bombardment that saw Grisafe pass for three scores. Melissa Gallegos of the So Cal Scorpions and Jenny Schmidt of the KC Tribe added one touchdown pass each. It is unclear if Danilynn Welniak, the player whose quote opened the chapter, was able to pancake block an Austrian, but she caught a scoring pass. The sole bright spot for the Austrians was Marie-Theres Michelitsch of the Raiffeisen Lady

Vikings, who rushed for a respectable 71 yards on twenty-two carries. Michelitsch joined wide receiver Rusty Sowers of the KC Tribe, who caught eight passes for 83 yards and two touchdowns as game MVPs.[46]

Canada played Sweden in the second game of the day, and this was a closer match. Team Canada only scored one offensive touchdown on a run by running back Julie Paetsch of the Saskatoon Valkyries. Jenn De Guise, a Canadian linebacker, intercepted a pass from Swedish quarterback Martina Karlsson and returned it 19 yards for the score. For that, and her five other tackles, De Guise was named the game MVP for Canada. Both extra point attempts failed, and Canada also missed a field goal. So when Sweden's Erika Hinders returned the kickoff that followed De Guise's touchdown for the first Swedish score, she cut the Canadian lead to 12–6. Despite a late Swedish drive into Canadian territory, and the stellar play of Swedish game MVP linebacker Pillan Plass, the Canadians secured victory when they recovered a Swedish fumble with fifty-one seconds left. The home team drew around five hundred fans to watch one of the closest games of the championship.[47]

Two days later, Finland played Austria in the second game of Group A. Finland began its march toward the medal round by defeating the Austrians 50–16. Finnish MVP Merita Bruun led the way with 116 yards on nine carries and scored two touchdowns. Austria's Michelitsch continued her strong play and carried the ball thirty-four times for 252 yards and was once again named the Austrian game MVP. Most of the scoring took place in the first half, with Team Finland leading by 44–16, and the second half became a defensive struggle. The only score of the second half occurred when Jenna Suhonen of the Jyväskylä Jaguars ran the ball into the end zone from 18 yards. The Finnish victory set up a match against Team USA, and Team Finland head coach Teemu Kuusistoof thought his team had a chance, if their offense continued to produce. "I think the U.S. is still the top team, but we showed today that we should be ranked higher than fifth place."[48]

The second game on 29 June was between the German team and the Swedes in Group B. Once again, in a close contest, Team Sweden lost another nail-biter to Team Germany 14–0. In the first half, Germany's game MVP Susanne Erdmann of the Nürnberg Hurricanes returned a

Swedish punt to the 13-yard line and ran the ball for a touchdown on the next play. Erdmann finished with two touchdowns and 96 yards on twelve carries. The Swedish defense continued their good play, and Michaela Rowett received the game MVP for her team. Germany's victory set up the next match against Team Canada.[49]

The point differential against a common opponent favored the Germans for their match with Canada on 1 July 2018. The Canadians had an extra bit of motivation, however, since July 1 is Canada Day, a national holiday celebrated as Canada's birthday. Canada's Paetsch opened the scoring with the first of her two touchdowns. She had her best game of the wwc against Team Germany, rushing for 201 yards on twenty carries and was named her team's game MVP. Paetsch's first run covered 69 yards, and her second was a 36-yard run after she picked up a fumbled snap. The Germans struck back with time running out on the first half, when quarterback Gabi Duvinage of the Nürnberg Hurricanes scored on a quarterback sneak to make the score at halftime 14–6 in favor of Canada. The only scoring of the second half came when Kendra Jones of the Saint John Storm scored on second and goal from the 5-yard line. The Germans were driving deep in Canadian territory when Lisa Harlow of the Saint John Storm sacked Duvinage on the last play of the game.[50]

Team Finland coach Kuusistoof had the correct plan for playing Team USA, but his athletes could not execute it. Their game followed the Canadian victory over Germany. The Finnish offense struggled, but their American opponent's attack did not. They scored 72 points and shut out the Finns. Jessica Springer, a running back from the Dallas Diamonds who had rushed for 120 yards on twelve carries and a touchdown in the game against Austria, added another touchdown and rushed for 35 yards on five carries. Demonstrating that figuring out a somewhat equitable player rotation has always been one of the primary concerns of Team USA coaches, Julie Shockley from the Sacramento Sirens got the most touches in this game, and she rushed for 103 yards on nine carries. Likewise, KC's Schmidt started the game at quarterback and hit eight of ten passes for 88 yards and two scores. Grisafe added another two touchdown passes, and KC's Rusty Sowers once again won the game MVP award for catching eight passes for 83 yards and two touchdowns. The coaching staff did a good job of spreading playing time, and nine different players scored for Team USA in the game. Elina Seppala, a linebacker for Team Finland, was named their game MVP. Bruun, who surely wanted to reprise her 257-yard effort from the Austrian game, was held to only 11 yards on fifteen carries by the American defense that was led by linebacker Knengi Martin of the California Quake with eight tackles.[51]

The medal games took place on 3 July 2010 and began with the fifth-place game matching winless Sweden and Austria. Team Sweden won in another game that went down to the last play of the game. Austria took an early lead when Carissa Klupper of the Dacia Vienna Vikings scored the first touchdown of the game. Team Austria increased its lead to 12–0 when Pia Marrara, also of the Vikings, hit Caroline Friedl for the score. Sweden got on the scoreboard when Austria demonstrated that football was still a relatively new and sometimes disorienting sport. After intercepting a Swedish pass, the Austrian defensive back, whose name was not listed, perhaps out of pity, got turned around and ran the wrong way. The Swedes tackled her in the end zone for a safety to make it 12–2 Austria. Sweden scored more conventionally moments later when Erike Hinders ran 52 yards to make the score 12–8 at halftime. In the second half, Sweden blocked an Austrian punt, and quarterback Martina Karlsson connected with Anna Persson of the Arlanda Jets to take their first lead. Karlsson scored herself on a quarterback sneak to put the Swedes up by 20–12. Austria struggled a bit in the second half without the services of their star running back Michelitsch, who went out with a broken foot in the first quarter. Nevertheless, they scored with thirty-four seconds remaining when quarterback Saskia Stribrny of the Raiffeisen Lady Vikings found wide receiver Stephanie Kenecny for the score. The 2-point conversion attempt to send the game into overtime failed, however, as did the Austrian onside kick attempt, and Sweden held on for a 20–18 victory.[52]

Finland, although playing tackle football only since 2008, defeated the Germans, who had more than a decade of experience at the game, to win the bronze medal. Merita Bruun opened the scoring by catching a 90-yard touchdown pass from Jenni Wahlberg. Wahlberg then found Tiino Salo for the 2-point conversion. The Finnish quarterback then scrambled for a touchdown to make the score 14–0 Finland. The Finns increased their lead at half to 26–0 on two Bruun touchdown runs, one of 76 yards. The Finns did not score in the second half, and the Germans came roaring back with a touchdown by Manuela Scott of the Stuttgart Scorpions and two by Susanne Erdmann of the Nürnberg Hurricanes to pull them to 26–18. Team Germany was driving and made it to the Finnish 22-yard line, but they turned the ball over after Wahlberg's fourth-down pass attempt failed, and that sealed Team Finland's win.[53]

Outside of the games played by Team USA, the inaugural WWC featured a number of exciting games that went down to the final seconds before a victor emerged. Team Canada was no doubt hoping for a similar result in their game against the United States. They, and fans who wished to watch a back-and-forth struggle, were disappointed, however, as the Americans defeated their northern neighbors 66–0. Springer of the Diamonds rushed for 161 yards and scored four touchdowns to lead Team USA. Boston's Brickhouse contributed two touchdowns and was joined in the scoring column by the Siren's Shockley, Desiree Weimann of the So Cal Scorpions, and KC's Sowers, who caught a touchdown pass from Grisafe of the Force. The defense was led by Amy Satterfield of the LA Amazons, along with Jen Welter and Alberta Fitcheard of the Dallas Diamonds, who each had seven tackles. There was not a great deal to celebrate for Canada, but Paetsch once again played well, gaining 60 yards on nine carries. Michelle Young-Mather of the Saint John Storm led the Canadian defense with eight tackles.[54]

In something unusual, the game MVP was awarded to outside linebacker Jamie Menzyk of the Chicago Force. KC's Rusty Sowers was chosen as Offensive MVP for the championship and was joined by her teammate Sharon Vasquez of the Pittsburgh Passion, the Defensive MVP. The overwhelming victory meant that the United States held all three international championships in American football sponsored by IFAF—the men's junior and senior teams were also defending champions.[55]

The 2010 WWC had to be seen as a triumph for women's football, on the field. Most of the games had been closely contested, which should have thrilled any spectators who happened to attend. IFAF and Svenska Amerikansk Fotbollförbundet (SAFF), the Swedish football federation also led by Tommy Wiking, had done a good job of staging the event. Team USA demonstrated that the world had a way to go before they could effectively compete against athletes from football's birthplace, but virtually the same team lineup, with the exception of Austria being replaced by Spain, would be back in 2013 for another round, so enthusiasm for the event must have been strong. SAFF's Mikael Roos wrote the game stories and compiled the statistics that were referenced above, which provided one of the most complete records of any WWC.

Outside of Roos's efforts, there was very little in the press, at least in North America. Canadian newspapers, such as the *Daily Gleaner* published in Fredericton, New Brunswick, contained several articles, including profiles of the Capital Area Lady Gladiators' Julia Coleman. Two weeks before the WWC began, the linebacker on Team Canada told reporter Bruce Hallihan about the excitement that the Canadian players felt about representing their country in international competition: "Now that it's so much closer to being reality, we can hardly wait. We want to see how we stack up with the other teams and we want to do our best." She also told the reporter that she and her teammates stayed in touch through Facebook, which was starting to become pervasive by 2010, and which would carry so much news of women's football in the future. Hallihan mentioned that the budget for Team Canada was $150,000 CAD, and that each player would have to come up with $3,500 CAD of her own money to have the chance to play for Canada.[56]

The paper contained other, briefer articles as Team Canada moved toward its silver medal finish and was joined in carrying stories about the Canadian team by the CBC News and the *Calgary Herald*, who published one story each. The interest in Fredericton was no doubt due to the presence of the Moncton Vipers of the MWFL and perhaps the relative visibility of the other women's teams in the area.

The same was true for the American media's coverage of the 2010 WWC. Newspapers in Pittsburgh, Baltimore, and Munster, Indiana, carried stories. Those articles that did more than merely mention Team USA's victories focused on athletes from the local area that were members of the national team. Kaitlyn Carr of the *Baltimore Sun* wrote an article profiling Okiima Pickett and Tarsha Fain of the nearby D.C. Divas and Baltimore Nighthawks, respectively. In anticipation of the games, Pickett told the reporter: "Oh my gosh, it's amazing. As a child, I have always had this dream of walking through the airport with my team. And the other day, the coaches were talking about walking through the airport when we get to Sweden and I was like . . . it's a dream come true."[57]

The *Times* of Munster, Indiana, was the counterpart of the *Daily Gleaner* and carried several stories or box scores about Team USA. Munster is less than thirty miles from Chicago, so the paper's interest was piqued by national team athletes such as Grisafe, Angela Bandstra, Keesha Brooks, Dawn Pederson, Kimberley Marks, and Jamie Menzyk.[58] The local players mentioned in a longer profile on 27 June included Jeanette Gray, Dana Vermilye, Candace Griffin, Menzyck, and coach Konecki.[59] The same issue had longer profile pieces on Gray, Menzyck, and Konecki. A follow-up story on 4 July 2010 credited Menzyk and Konecki for leading Team USA to victory over the world.[60]

The various player profiles that preceded the games were unusual for the athletes, who generally labored in anonymity. Outside of the attention produced by the WWC, even the *Munster Times* had ignored women's football before the games and returned to their policy after the event. At the time, though, an opinion piece by Ken Karrson of the *Times* even indicated that his experience interviewing athletes for the paper had changed his mind about women playing football. He went into the interviews with the idea that "women watching [football] is fine. Women playing it is another story." After interviewing the players and writing profiles that featured Menzyck and Gray in particular, he admitted that the athletes had helped shatter his "definite preconceived notions about football-playing females."[61] There is little evidence, however, that Karrson continued to follow the game, at least in print.

Despite the historic nature of the WWC, the national press was silent on the event. If one only paid attention to national news sources such as the *New York Times*, the *Wall Street Journal*, *USA Today*, and *Sports Illustrated*, they would never know that the championship had been played.

One of the better personal accounts on the experience of playing for Team USA at that first championship can be found in *Play Big: Lessons in Being Limitless from the First Woman to Coach in the NFL* by Dr. Jen Welter. She wrote that she felt "honored and humbled to have been chosen to play among this exceptional roster of women, the best team in the world." She also felt the strain of having to find the money to pay the $3,000 that each player had to raise to take part in the championship. In a statement that she repeated as Australia's coach in 2017, she wrote: "Playing for Team USA was a new experience. It was the first time in my life I could actually focus 100 percent on football. When we reported to training camp in Round Rock, Texas, we left everything else outside the game."[62]

For the athletes, the 2010 WWC was a success. They had demonstrated that they could play high-level football on an international stage. USA games aside, the field for that first WWC was evenly matched, with an average margin of victory of only 12 points. Several of the games were decided on the final play. Only the Austrians had not won a game. IFAF had done a good job of staging the championship—the problems that would lead to their chaotic split would not become evident for another five years. So the various competitors left with a positive experience and began working toward their next chance to tackle the world.

---

## WWC 2013, VANTAA, FINLAND

On 11 June 2012, the Suomen Amerikkalaisen Jalkapallon Liitto Ry (SAJL), Finland's American football federation, announced that they had been awarded the right to hold the next WWC in 2013. Roope Noronen, who would later lead IFAF New York, announced that the games would be held at ISS Stadium in Vantaa, which is 22.5 kilometers (about 14 miles) north of Helsinki. Noronen stated: "We could not bypass the possibility of organizing such matches in Finland. We are proud that IFAF chose us." IFAF's Wiking stated, "We know that Finland is organizing fine matches," indicating his confidence in Noronen and SAJL.[63]

As mentioned above, Canada had originally been selected as the site for the WWC, but difficulties complying with IFAF demands caused Football Canada to drop their bid. Finland was the beneficiary of the change and would make the most of their opportunity.

The lineup for the games was much the same as in 2010, with one exception—Team Spain replaced Austria, who had struggled in Stockholm. Spanish women began playing in 2011 under the umbrella of the Federación Española de Futbol Americano (FEFA). Roberto Torrecillas of the Barberà Rookies has been credited with being one of the founders of the women's game there, and his team had won the first league championship.[64] Torrecillas and the Rookies began even earlier, in 2008, when "five or six girls" wanted to play the sport, and he started recruiting.[65] The players for Team Spain came largely from the Rookies, who hailed from the Barcelona region, the Las Rozas Black Demons from near Grenada, and the Terrassa Reds, also from near Barcelona. The two had contended for the 2013 championship of the women's section of the Liga Nacional de Fútbol Americano.[66]

Several players, including Grisafe, Menzyck, Welter, Brickhouse, and Vasquez, from the 2010 Team USA returned to action in Vantaa. Rusty Sowers did not make the team, but her sisters, twins Liz and Katie Sowers, kept the family name fresh. The same was true of the other national teams. Germany returned their backfield combination of Duvinage and Erdmann, among others. Canada also had the services of De Guise, Young-Mather, and Paetsch, who had performed well before, and had a total of nine athletes returning for Team Canada. Hakkarainen returned to quarterback Team Finland, but star running back Bruun did not play. Jenni Lindén, however, would easily pick up the slack at the position. Tea Törmänen of the D.C. Divas, who also played in 2010, was also back playing for Finland. Sweden had a large talent turnover and returned only Anna Persson and defensive linewoman Frida Ångström from the 2010 team.[67]

Despite most teams having three more years of experience, the 2013 games were not, in general, as tight as they had been three years earlier. The point differential, once again excluding USA games, increased from 12 points in 2010 to 32.5 in 2013, but contracted to 22 in 2017. Part of that was due to the drubbings that the Spaniards took at the hands of Finland (47–0), Canada (50–0), and Sweden (64–0). Germany was involved in two of the closest matches of WWC 2013, defeating the Swedes 25–14 and losing once again to the Finns in the third-place match, but this time by a single point, 20–19. The Germans' other game, against the United States, was a devastating blowout that saw Team USA defeat the German 107–7.

Host country Finland played Spain in the first match of WWC 2013 on 30 June 2013, and it became clear quickly that Team Spain was in for a long week. Spain gained only 2 yards on their first series before punting to Finland, who took only five plays to score their first touchdown. Quarterback Tiina Sliver of the Seinajoki Crocodiles scored from the 15 with 6:45 left in the first quarter, and Janina Virtanen of the Turku Trojans added the 2-point conversion. Team Finland scored again with 3:42 left when Sliver hit wide receiver Sari Kuosmanen of the Jyväskylä Jaguars for a 19-yard touchdown. Virtanen once again added the conversion to make the score 16–0 at the end of the opening quarter. From there, the home team added a touchdown by Elina Seppälä of the Helsinki GS Demons and another touchdown throw from Sliver to Kuosmanen, but both conversions failed, to make the score 28–0 at the half. In the second half Jenni Lindén of the Jonesuu Wolves got into the scoring column twice on touchdown receptions of 27 yards from Sliver and 13 yards from Laura Hautakangas of the Jaguars. She was joined in the scoring column by Janna-Jemima Seiles of the Helsinki Roosters who caught a Sliver pass for 21 yards, and Jutta Luhtala kicked an extra point along the way to make the final score Finland 47–0 over Spain.[68]

Team USA played in the evening game, and they picked up where they had left off in 2010 by defeating Sweden 84–0. The coaches again spread the load among their athletes. Scoring for the Americans were Cassey Brick of the San Diego Surge, who found the end zone three times, and Odessa Jenkins of the Dallas Diamonds, who caught two touchdown passes. Scoring single touchdowns were Grisafe, Brandi Hatcher of the Chicago Force, Adrienne Smith of the Boston Militia, Katie Sowers of the Titans, Gray of the Force, and Ashley Berggren of the Force. Donna Wilkinson of the D.C. Divas contributed four 2-point conversions, Mia Brickhouse added three, and Angela Larsen of the Central Cal War Angels added two successful extra-point kicks. Jennifer Plummer of the West Michigan Mayhem and Rachel May of the Diamonds led the defense in tackles. Leah Hinkle of the Portland Fighting Shockwave, playing in her second WWC, had an interception, and Katie Sowers recovered two fumbles.[69]

The games continued two days later with a rematch of Sweden and Germany. Both offenses played better this time, but the result remained the same. Germany won 25–24 on the strength of three touchdowns by Erdmann of the Hurricanes, who was selected as the game's MVP. Christina Schampel of the Berlin Kobra Ladies scored the other touchdown for Team Germany. One of Team Sweden's touchdowns was scored by Alison Mana, who, like Törmänen, played in the United States, in this case for the California Quake. The other was by Marianne Gimhag of the Stockholm Mean Machines. As a result of their victory, the Germans earned the right to play against Team USA in the Group A final.[70]

Canada and Spain played in the second game, and Canada rolled to a 50–0 victory. Julie David of the Saskatoon Valkyries ran for three touchdowns to lead the scoring. Sophie Roy of the Montreal Blitz and Julie Paetsch of the Valkyries each scored one touchdown. The Canadian athletes who scored the final two touchdowns and the extra points were not listed in the game article. Despite their second crushing loss, Spanish head coach Roberto Torrecillas Sanchez said that he was "proud of his team," and that they were happy to be playing in the WWC. Canadian head coach Jeff Yasuie also praised the Spaniards, saying, "Spain was having fun and playing with emotion."[71] Canada and Finland would meet next for the championship of Group B.

Team USA played Germany on 4 July 2013. Just as the Canadians had seemed to gain an extra quickness in their steps on Canada Day in 2010, the Americans seemed have a little extra motivation when they played Germany on Independence Day. Sami Grisafe, who, when she was not playing football, is a musician, played a ukulele and sang the "Star Spangled Banner" before the game. As with Sam Gordon's touchdown video, the video of Grisafe performing the national anthem went viral. According to the Women's Football Alliance post about her, "Buzzfeed called her performance 'The most inspiring combination of sports and music you will ever see.'"[72]

Fired up by the emotion of the moment, Team USA unloaded on the hapless Germans. Game MVP Katie Sowers had five interceptions and scored two touchdowns to demonstrate that her presence on the team was not just as a "legacy" pick.[73] Perhaps there were a few Hessians on the opposing team with a historical grudge, because Germany had come out seeking to ruin the American birthday. After Jeanette Gray caught a 31-yard touchdown pass from Grisafe, the Germans ripped off a 34-yard touchdown run on their first play to make the score 8–7 USA. That was the first touchdown ever scored on the Americans, and it seemingly pissed them off. They scored on the next eight possessions of the first half, and led 60–7 at halftime. Ten different players scored that day. Jenkins scored three touchdowns to lead the way. Sowers's two interception-return touchdowns were matched by Hatcher and Brick. Kimberley Klesse of the Columbus Comets, Boston's Smith, Alexis Snyder of the Phoenix Phantomz, Chicago's Gray, Nicole Vilarino of the Shockwave, and KC's Liz Sowers each scored one. West Michigan's Plummer, Boston's Vicky Eddy, and Andreana Campolo of the Seattle Majestics were the leading tacklers. The final score of 107–7 propelled Team USA into the gold medal game for the second straight time.[74]

The evening game that day featured first-time opponents Canada and Finland. Both had medaled in 2010, so it promised to be a closer game. The Demons' Seppälä scored the opening touchdown for Finland, but Marci Kiselyk of the Valkyries caught a touchdown pass from Saadia Ashraf of the Blitz to even the score. Finland scored again on a 2-yard run by Kristi Nirhamo of the Trojans, and Finland went into the half leading 12–6. Canada's halftime adjustments worked, and they scored four straight touchdowns to win. Lya Jolicoeur of the Dragons de Beauce-Appalaches scored two of them on runs of 5 and 6 yards. She was joined by Aimee Kowalski of the Regina Riot and Saskatoon's David. Lara Guscott, another member of the sisterhood of traveling shoulder pads, playing for the KC Tribe, scored on four point-after touchdown kicks to make the final score 34-12 Canada.[75]

Sweden played Spain for fifth place on 6 July 2013 and continued the Spaniards' woes by defeating the team making its international debut 64-0. Team Sweden scored four times in the first quarter and led 38-0 at halftime. They continued to roll in the second half, and Team Spain could not find the end zone. The winless Spaniards were not deterred, though. Quarterback Ada Quintana Mota of the Rookies said: "I hope that now after the tournament, women will wake up to the [game]. We now have only six teams in Spain and would like to have more. Now, we got the first touch on the highs and we saw the level of the other teams. Four years to see!" Team Sweden's head coach Johan Sedin was happy with his team's effort. He told the unnamed reporter from the SAJL who left the records quoted here: "We played a good game. Every player got into the field today to play; that's good. We expected a tough match, Spain is a tough country. We've been watching them through Facebook before the tournament."[76]

The bronze medal match pitted Germany and Finland in a rematch of the 2010 finals. This time Germany came closer, losing by only a single point, 20-19. With rain pouring down, Berlin's Erdmann scored the first touchdown. Finland answered with Seinajoki's Sliver finding the end zone to make the score 7-6. The Trojans' Nirhamo scored in the second quarter, but Germany came back to maintain their lead on a touchdown by Sarah Walther of the Mülheim Shamrocks. In the second half, Sliver scored again and then threw a touchdown pass to Nirhamo to give the running back her second score. Christina Schmidt of the Kobra Ladies finished the scoring in the fourth quarter when she caught a 62-yard touchdown pass. The German attempt to go for a 2-point conversion, rather than the tie, was unsuccessful, and Team Finland repeated as bronze medalists. The decision to go for 2 points and the win was shared by all of the German coaches, according to the defensive coordinator, Daniel Koch: "We decided together that it was the right solution to try to get two extra points." Team Finland head coach Jorma Hytönen said of the game: "Hard fight. Great game. We did today defense, attack, special teams, everything. We have talked about our story all the time and today we wrote the story of the ending."[77]

The gold medal game was another rematch, this time of North American teams. Canada was hoping for a better result than 2010, and they succeeded. But only marginally. The 64-0 USA victory was a 2-point improvement over the previous meeting. Brickhouse led the way this time, scoring four rushing touchdowns. Five other players, including Jenkins, Wilkinson, Gray, Smith, and Liz Sowers, also had touchdowns. The defense was again led by Eddy, Plummer, and Katie Sowers, among others. Menzyck repeated as final game MVP. Grisafe, who threw for three touchdown passes in the final, and nine for the WWC, was named the tournament MVP. Team USA head coach Konecki remarked: "These women are amongst the best players in the world at their respective positions. It has been a privilege for me to coach athletes of this caliber. I couldn't be more proud of my team than I am right now."[78]

After they returned home, Callie Brownson and Becky Worsham of the D.C. Divas told Alex Parker of *WJLA Sportstalk* about their experiences. At age twenty-four, Brownson was the youngest member Team USA. She told Parker: "It was an amazing experience. It was really cool to see American football played passionately by other countries. You know the scores don't reflect the attitude that they all had and the passion that they all had for the game. Talent wise, we had the upper hand, but those teams, like Sweden, they just love playing. They love it. So it was an amazing experience to see a sport like that we find so accustomed to our culture spread among all these countries." Worsham echoed Brownson in praising her opponents: "Actually, after the whole tournament was over, they came and they talked to us, and they were like, it's just an honor to even play with you guys, and you could see on the field, like they would never quit. They wouldn't give up, even though they were losing by a lot. They would just keep going. Keep trying to make a tackle, or try to learn from their mistakes."[79]

In spite of local interviews of players such as Brownson and Worsham, media coverage of the event was as sparse or even worse than in 2010. Karrson of Indiana's *Munster Times* might have left the paper, or returned to his previous views of women playing football, because he published no stories that could be found. The paper contained one story about the triumphal return of Konecki, Menzyck, Gray, and defensive coordinator Adam Lewandowski, but that was it.[80] The national press continued to ignore the event.

The Canadians, perhaps because of their loss in the final game, did not have any discernable stories about the games. There were a few profiles in the American local press of players such as Knengi Martin in the *San Diego Union Tribune*, Liz Okey in the *Manchester (MI) Mirror*, and Adrienne Smith on CBS *New York*, but not much more in traditional places.[81]

If traditional media avenues were closed to the athletes, the new media offered a chance for them to communicate with each other, and anyone else who might be willing to listen. In addition to the websites that store the game summaries and some statistics, other social media sites contained information on the games. Postgame player and coach interviews for the 2013 and 2017 WWC are available on YouTube, and some videos of the full games also existed there.[82]

The official websites of the various host countries still carry a good amount of material on the games. Most of the games can still be found, either on their sites or on YouTube. The final games from each WWC are readily available on the video-sharing site, so anyone interested can watch them at their leisure. Finding those who are interested seems to be the problem, though. The 2010 USA-Canada game had 1,087 views on the site.[83] The 2013 final had 3,301 views.[84] Unfortunately, the 2017 USA-Canada game was not available on YouTube when I wrote this, but it could be found, with some searching, on Ten Feet Sports and Entertainment, which did not have viewing statistics.[85] When the USA versus Canada game was finally posted to YouTube by someone named Zach Gratz a little over a year after the game, it had fewer than 1,000 views when I saw it in 2020.[86]

Facebook had become entwined in the fabric of millions of people's lives by 2013, and women football players found the social media site to be perfect for getting their news out to a wider world. The 2013 Team USA had fans who created the 2013 Women's Team USA Tackle Football Fan Club, which had a variety of posts on the championship and beyond.[87] There was also a page dedicated to the 2017 National Team and games.[88] Both pages have become aggregation sites for news on women's football. These pages are joined by those created by the myriad of teams, in the United States and abroad, where women play the game.

The 2013 WWC also attracted the attention of filmmaker Mansfield Daniel, who produced *Tackle the World—Tough Game/Tougher Women*. The documentary followed the players and teams from WWC 2013 as they played their way through the games. It captured some of the spectacle that SAJL put on for the games. The first game began with a flyover by the Finnish Air Force and concluded with fireworks set off from the field as Team USA celebrated. Consideration of Team Finland opened *Tackle the World*, and they were billed, correctly at that time, as the top women's football team in Europe. Interviews punctuated images of the games being played. Coaches were seen motivating players along with athletes joyfully hitting one another. Narrator Ronald James informed viewers that a third of Team Sweden's athletes were teenagers in the WWC. IFAF's Tommy Wiking spoke of the dream that football might one day be an Olympic sport. Sami Grisafe shook hands with young girls in the stands—one fan told an interviewer, "I want to be as cool as she is." A short clip of Team Spain doing the Macarena dance, which also went viral, demonstrated that the Spanish enthusiasm for the game was undiminished by their losses. Coach Konecki's pregame speech was excerpted. The documentary was not a hard-hitting exposé of the dangers of the game, nor did it mention that the women paid their own way. It was rather a celebration of everything good in women's tackle football.[89]

All of the images and interviews sent a clear message that these women loved the game of football. One of Spain's team captains, identified only as the wife of defensive coordinator Sebas Serrano, stated, "I can't imagine a better sport to play. It's pure adrenaline, and I'm happy to play." This linebacker added, "It's a sport that you can hit people, and it's the only one that you can hit as hard as you can to somebody else." Asked what she loved about the game of football, Finland's Sliver replied: "Everything. The tactics. The speed. The roughness—I like to give a hit, and I like to take a hit."[90]

The focus then turned to Team USA. An uncredited narrator, perhaps Grisafe, intoned: "It's July 4th, and I cannot think of a better celebration of our Independence Day than to represent the USA in the game that was once called the final frontier of women in sports. It has been hard work getting here, and work is not done. However, independence from outdated ideals was a great start. One of the beautiful things about football is the diversity required to make a team successful. Player talents, skill sets, and personalities vary significantly from player to player and from position to position. There is a synergy among football players that forms a team that has to rely on each player to complete her individual job for the play to be successful. It is beautiful really. If all the players on the team were built same way and had the same talents, we would not be successful. Ultimately, our diversity is our strength. As magical as Team USA is on the football field, as impressive as our play is, I wish you all could know the amazing women beneath the red, white, and blue helmets. If the world knew the amazing women who sacrificed so much for this game, the world would fall in love with Team USA, and women's football."[91]

Another theme was that girls and women should have the ability to play the sport if they wanted. Samantha Rapaport of USA Football said: "When I watch these girls play and I have the USA Football on my heart, what I'm thinking about personally, and I know what all these girls are thinking about, is the first time that we ever touched a football. We're sending a message to everyone back in the United States that football is gender blind and, you know, are that all these girls that are being told no in the United States, that they can't play football; we're sending a message to show them what they can do with football when they're older. More importantly show these school administrators and league administrators what girls can do with football." According to

Wiking, "There are lots of women and girls who want to play football, and why should we not let them play? It's just plain insane not to do it." Holly Pederson demonstrated that Grisafe was not the only artistically talented member of Team USA when she recited her poem titled "We Play for Her" before the final game against Canada.[92]

*Tackle the World* was a tour de force for the world of women's football, but seemingly only for those in that world. The extent of its reach is hard to determine, however. It did not come up in a search of databases such as WorldCat or LexisNexis Academic. The WGF's site has a link to it, and it is not hard to find on YouTube, but other sites such as IMDb contain no information. It seemed to have something of a renaissance in late 2018, with 824 views, when the WGF reposted it with this message: "The entire short film is here to see as the world gets ready for WWC 3 in 2017." By 2022 it had passed 2,000 views.[93] Without a doubt, most of the players who contended in the 2013 WWC have the link saved on their computers, along with other athletes who have been inspired by it, but how many is also impossible to ascertain.

Jen Welter, the Dallas Diamonds linebacker who played in two WWCs, gave what seemed to be an accurate analysis of the lack of media coverage in *Play Big*: "We again won a gold medal in America's game. And yet, again, it seemed no one even knew we existed. Not one major media outlet covered our story." To her, "the underlying message was clear: women's football was not newsworthy."[94]

Perhaps not newsworthy, but the IFAF's WWC did provide a venue for women athletes from North America, Europe, and now Australia, to gather together for a celebration of the world of women's tackle football. In 2017 the games were in their third iteration, and some old competitors had dropped out to make way for a new wave of teams.

The IFAF schism worked in the favor of Mexico and Australia, injecting exciting new teams into the mix. What effect that will have in their home countries will be interesting to observe. For the Mexican team, at least, this did provide a much greater level of exposure for the women's game. Team Mexico's games in the 2017 WWC were streamed live in Mexico, and the medal game against the United Kingdom was broadcast live on one of their television stations.[95]

Team Canada was steadily improving, cutting their margin of loss to the USA from 66 points in 2010 to 25 in 2017. Most might not have noticed that the USA dominated the 2010 and 2013 WWCs, but some who were there were concerned that the U.S. dominance might not be that good. In *Tackle the World* Rapaport asserted that the 2013 Team USA was the "best female sports team I have ever seen in my life— take football out of it." She was aware that the rest of the world was not at that level, however, and began to think about how to address that. "It is incumbent on the U.S., and on Canada as well, to help the world grow. I think our goal has to be to get the level of international play up. These women want it. I mean they love football."[96]

Rapaport and Elizabeth Faust, who was Rapaport's intern at those games, set about to "throw ideas around" on how to level the international playing field. According to Faust, "After the 2013 games, there wasn't a whole lot of competition for the U.S. So it was kind of like, how do we not only grow women's football in the U.S. but also help develop the world." The winning idea that Rapaport and her team came up with was the Women's World Games, which debuted in 2014.[97]

But that is a story for another day, and another project.

# Postscript   

The Boston Renegades, back-to-back champions of the Women's Football Alliance (WFA), finally received primetime attention from the Entertainment and Sports Network (ESPN), but events beyond the team's and league's control lessened the impact of their moment in the spotlight. What might have been a chance to drive curious football fans to the stadium to see the Renegades in action was rendered moot by the global reaction to the COVID-19 virus.

*Born to Play*, a documentary film by Viridiana Lieberman, debuted on the sport network from 9 to 11 p.m. on a Wednesday night.[1] The film followed the Renegades through their 2018 season, during which they overcame various obstacles, including injuries, a forfeit, and two losses, to win the WFA national championship. Lieberman did a masterful job of switching scenes from the field, where the Renegades demonstrated the drive and focus that made them exceptional athletes and champions, to their workaday lives that illustrated how much their routines differed from the other football champions in Massachusetts. Particularly effective was Lieberman's use of transitions that showed the Renegades on their rented field, in the midst of practicing when the stadium's lights switched off as their two-hour time expired.

As with many football documentaries, Lieberman showcased the team's quarterback, in this case Allison Cahill. Viewers heard from Cahill's mother about a party when, at an early age, she surprised her family by donning shoulder pads over her dress and telling them her dream was to be a football player. Although she was angry when everyone laughed at the sight, she made good on her dream. According to her biography on the team's website, as of 2019, Cahill "has amassed more than 20,000 passing yards with nearly 300 passing touchdowns. Over her career, she has tallied a win-loss record of 123-27 including a 26-8 postseason record. She has a career 60.7 percent completion percentage and a 115.96 quarterback rating."[2] Although not explicitly stated, Cahill's day job was apparently as a physical trainer, and one humorous scene took place at a family dinner, where the normally confident quarterback struggled to put a live lobster into boiling water.

Chanté Bonds and Whitney Zelee, a current and former offensive star, respectively, were also featured. After starting off as primarily a defensive back (she was named the WFA's defensive player of the year in 2017), Bonds became increasingly important in the offense as the season progressed. Bonds scored three touchdowns, two receiving, including a 73-yard run off of a screen pass, and also returned a punt for a score in the final. As a result of her play in the championship game against the Los Angeles Warriors that the Renegades won 42–18, the WFA named her as the MVP for the championship game. She was also later chosen as the overall league MVP.[3]

Injuries had forced an end to Zelee's on-field career, but during the 2018 season she helped coach the team. During the 2013 season, she had one of the greatest seasons of any running back, male or female. She rushed for 2,326 yards on 140 carries, for a 16.6 yards per carry average, and scored thirty-seven touchdowns. She added three more receiving scores to give her a total of forty touchdowns for the year and also scored eight 2-point conversions.[4] The WFA named Zelee their championship game MVP twice in her brief career. She won her first award as a rookie in 2011, when her 101 rushing yards and three touchdowns helped propel the Boston Militia to its second straight national title (one in the IWFL and one in the WFA).[5] Zelee won her second MVP, helping the Militia to their third league title in 2014. She had missed much of the season due to injuries and had only gained 162 yards. She nearly doubled her offensive production in the final against the San Diego Surge, when she rushed for 291 yards, added 16 yards in receptions, and scored six touchdowns.[6]

Most of Zelee's time in the documentary, save for a brief section that described her playing career, dealt with her relationship with her partner Cahill. How many yards she might have rushed for had she been healthy falls into the same category as speculation about Gayle Sayers or other high-level athletes whose careers ended early. According to Neal Rozendaal, the oft-cited author of the *Women's Football Encyclopedia*, Zelee had 2,832 yards in 2013, and amassed 6,240 for her career.[7] A search of the WFA season score database only turned up a total of 4,495 yards, but whatever the number, Zelee's 2013 season stood as one of the greatest of any running back.[8] She also had the unusual privilege of visiting the White House with her Militia teammates to celebrate their 2014 championship.

After winning their second WFA championship, the Militia became the first women's team in history to win a championship and then not play another game under that name.[9] The Cleveland Rams had done the same thing in 1946, moving to Los Angeles after they had won the NFL championship in 1945, but the Militia's move was the first for women. As was the case with the Rams, the core of the championship team continued to play in Boston, but under the Renegades name. This made sense in the case of the Rams' players, who were under contract, but the women playing for the Militia and then the Renegades were not being paid to play.

When *Born to Play* aired on ESPN, it was another indication that women's semiprofessional football was becoming more visible, and perhaps the documentary caused the blinders to fall away from the eyes of an increasing number of football fans. Since *The Oklahoma City Dolls* in 1981, there have been a few movies with women or girls playing football such as *Quarterback Princess* (1983), *Necessary Roughness* (1991), *The Longshots* (2008), and the French movie *Bande de Filles* (2015). There have been television programs such as *Bella and the Bulldogs* (2015–16), which followed a Texas middle school girl who played quarterback for her school.

*Born to Play*, however, seemed to have been the leading wave of a number of women's football documentaries. *Open Field* (2020) debuted shortly after the Renegades documentary. Documentarian

Kathy Kuras followed the careers of Sami Grisafe and Katie Sowers as they won IFAF championships and Sowers coached in the NFL.[10] The Toledo Troopers finally made it to the theaters in 2021, not as a feature film but as *We Are the Troopers*, a documentary. Actress Julie Bowen announced in August of 2021 that she and Andra Douglas had signed a deal to develop Douglas's book for television.[11] Crys Sacco of the Utah Girls Football League recently screened *First Down* at the Austin Film Festival. This is the story of the league's Kearns Cougars, which Sacco coached to a league title.[12]

There have also been a few novels. *The Legend of Jesse Smoke* was a 2016 novel by Robert Bausch that imagined the title character making the jump from the D.C. Divas to the Washington Redskins. *Black and Blue: Love, Sports, and the Art of Empowerment* (2019) by Andra Douglas, mentioned previously, was a fictionalized account of the author's football career as a player and owner of the New York Sharks.

Nonfiction works are also sparse. There is, of course, Neal Rozendaal's *The Women's Football Encyclopedia*, which I have leaned on for information on early teams and leagues. On 2 November 2021, Bold Type Books released *Hail Mary: The Rise and Fall of the National Women's Football League* by Frankie de la Cretaz and Lydsey D'Arcangelo. Katie Taylor, a British researcher, successfully defended her dissertation and is now working to turn it into a monograph on women playing football, largely prior to the 1970s. There are a few more books that were largely written for young girls, but the shelf is uncrowded.

Commercials have perhaps had the biggest impact, since a wide audience is exposed to them. As previously mentioned, the NFL featured Sam Gordon in a league commercial that aired during Super Bowl LIII in 2019, and another commercial that year featured Antoinette Harris, who was a scholarship defensive back at Bethany College in Kansas.[13] Secret Deodorant had a spot that showed a kicker making a game-winning kick and then taking her helmet off to reveal that she was a female.[14] The Los Angeles Bobcats of the WNFC appeared in an NFL commercial advertising their one hundredth season in 2019, and there have been other commercials for other products that have had girls and women in football gear.[15] Finally, ESPN featured *Born to Play* in 2020. The frequency that viewers can see images of girls and women playing football has certainly increased since the 1980s. Maybe this made more people aware, but maybe not.

My brother-in-law, Steve Dixon, and Steve Salzman, a high school friend, both texted me during the showing of *Born to Play*. They knew that I was writing about women's football, so they wanted me to know it was on and asked if I had interviewed any of the players. Unfortunately, after letting me know, they each surfed away from documentary, which illustrated the challenge that women's football teams and leagues faced. When ESPN rebroadcast the documentary on 26 July, I badgered them to watch so I could have some feedback.

Salzman could not convince his daughter, Liz, to watch with him, but he texted me some of his thoughts, most of which contained exclamation points. He told me, "They must love the game! They have to pay to play! Outrageous!" He added, "They play pretty well for only practicing a couple of days a week!" But he wondered about the business model: "I don't know if it [women's football] will survive money problems!"[16]

Dixon likewise texted me his impressions, which were not as positive, but just as filled with exclamation points. "Just seems wrong women playing tackle football! Some of them scare me to look at! [There were a] lot of men in coaching positions!" He extended his comments somewhat by telling me, "It's a shame the stands are so empty. Gotta respect them working their asses off for no pay. I'm old school though and believe football should be played by men. I enjoyed the two hours. I really hate [that] they work so hard and get so little recognition. They are more pure to the sport than the men who get paid millions of dollars to play. I noticed a decisively male dominance in the coaching area though, and they should also be women."[17]

*Born to Play* had decent advance publicity and even gained notice from the other prominent football team in the state. The New England Patriots tweeted the promotional video and added, "The story of passion, perseverance and proof that football is for everyone. Tune in as our fellow New England football team, @GoRenegades, is featured in @BornToPlayMovie tonight at 9 on @espn."[18] *Variety*'s headline announcing the airing read "How ESPN Documentary 'Born to Play' Shows Football in Its 'Purest Form.'"[19] The *Boston Herald* also previewed the video, with the headline "ESPN Doc Tackles Renegades— Boston's Champ Women's Tackle Football Team."[20] In what might be considered an unintended metaphor for women's football, another glowing preview appeared on the *Unseen Films* site.[21]

*Born to Play* also received at least one positive review in a prominent place. *Entertainment Weekly*'s Gerrad Hall wrote, "The film . . . hones in on the spirit, the tenacity, and the dedication of the Renegades, comprised of women ages 19–49 who pay to play, doing so outside their regular jobs."[22] Hall at least went to the bother of interviewing Lieberman and quoted her extensively in his article. Outside of that review, though, most of the notice the film received was from less prominent sites, and few of them seemed to notice.

I wrote a review of *Born to Play*, and Roger Kelly posted it on the *American Football International* blog, which caters to football fans around the world.[23] Oscar Lopez posted several mentions of the documentary on his "Gridiron Beauties" Facebook page and included links to the various reviews, and Michael Burmy's "Hometown Women's Football" Facebook site had several posts uploaded by Wyn Dom of the Mile High Blaze of the WFA.[24] Several women's football team accounts also posted and reposted news of the broadcast around the time of the film's debut. Prominent women's football players such as Odessa Jenkins, the owner of the Texas Elite Spartans, and Jen Welter, the former Dallas Diamond, tweeted about it as well.

In short the usual Facebook and Twitter suspects in the world of women's football took notice of *Born to Play*, but few others did. Prominent women sports media personalities seemed to have missed the documentary completely, even those associated with ESPN. Prolific tweeter and ESPN radio personality Sarah Spain, who had written at least one article about women's football, was silent on the documentary, as were other network personalities.

The dedication of the women depicted in the documentary impressed viewers, including at least a couple who would not typically be aware of women's football, as demonstrated in the comments from Salzman and Dixon quoted above. However, how many of those otherwise oblivious viewers did the ESPN broadcast actually reach? I have been unable to locate audience numbers for the documentary. The reach of various tweets and Facebook posts also seem constrained compared to other events. The most-liked "Gridiron Beauties" post had only 35 likes. When I posted a photo of my wife, Sophie, with our new kitten, Dagobert, draped over her shoulder, the post garnered 39 likes. A tweet by the Women's Sport Foundation on 17 July 2020 received 50 likes and was retweeted 25 times.[25] The Patriots' tweet only received 27 likes and 9 retweets. To draw a contrast on Twitter, when hot-dog-eating-contest winner Miki Sudo ate 48.5 hotdogs and buns in ten minutes, an ESPN tweet from 4 July 2020 had 4,600 likes and 1,800 retweets.[26]

This analysis may be merely anecdotal, but after following social media for the past several years, it is my impression that even those who are involved in women's football do not support each other much. At least arguably, a primary reason for this lack of exposure was due to the lack of one central site that was acknowledged as the place to go for women's football news. Each team had its own social media presence, which was not likely followed by other teams. The aforementioned "Gridiron Beauties" and "Hometown Women's Football" have attempted to create a go-to site for the game. Both sites are still going strong, although HWF's Burmy has occasionally discussed reducing his active role.

This balkanization of the sport's social media reach has likewise always been an issue for the larger world of women's football. Women's freedom to play the game they love has not been constrained by any overriding financial interests. Therefore, a chaotic environment has reigned in the sport.

Successful leagues such as the National Football League are economic cartels, held together by the mutual interests of owners and players. Major League Baseball's reserve clause may have been an unfair constraint on labor, but it also helped create the professional sport we know today.

Since there is no such economic motivation holding women's players, teams, and leagues together, an entropic force has operated in women's football. So, teams come and go. Teams join and leave leagues, sometimes for somewhat trivial reasons. Owners who seemed to be making progress seemingly angered their peers and were forced out of leagues. Therefore the available players and funds are widely dispersed and, unlike the case of the Women's National Basketball Association, there was no central league that can command focused attention.

Women's football now faces additional uncertainty beyond their control. After reaction to COVID compelled the cancellation of the 2020 season for many in the United States and around the world, how many women will decide that they can do other things with their time? Some no doubt will find that life has happened to them, and will hang up their cleats. The various leagues did play their 2021 season, but COVID restrictions meant that several teams, including the Columbus Comets, the Toledo Reign, and the Pittsburgh Passion, were unable to play. The Passion did send a team of former and current players to a tournament in Provincetown, Massachusetts, that Diane Beruldsen's International Women's Flag Football Association sponsored in 2021, just to keep their hand in the game, and their Facebook page does announce a six-game schedule for spring 2022. Mitchi Collette of the Reign was hopeful that the team could come back in 2022, although the team does not appear on the WFA website as of March 2022. The Comets have apparently folded, but the Columbus Chaos appears to be their successor. The Cleveland Fusion is holding tryouts, so it looks like they will be back. Perhaps the Midwest will return to the game soon.

The WFA even made a splash by holding their 2021 championship at Tom Benson Hall of Fame Stadium in Canton, Ohio—across the street from the Pro Football Hall of Fame. The Division I champion Boston Renegades even drew the attention of Robert Kraft, the owner of the New England Patriots, who loaned his team's plane to them for the trip to Ohio.[27] In addition, the number 7 jersey that Renegades quarterback Allison Cahill wore in the championship final was displayed in the Pro Football Hall of Fame, and the Hall announced that they would continue to display WFA Pro Division Championship MVP jerseys.[28]

The WFA also announced in 2022 that ESPN2 will be televising their 2022 championship. During the 2021 season Eleven Sports and Roku televised twelve games, and the final was streamed on ESPN3, so moving up to live broadcast television is a significant step.[29]

The current state of women's football seems to be improving, although the athletes still compete in relative anonymity. However, as long as football remains a popular sport, women will continue to remain "desperate for a fix" of the football drug.[30] They will also continue to enjoy the freedom to visit legal violence on their peers. So, if you care to remove your blinders, there is a good chance that you will see that they are still out there. Everywhere.

# Appendix
LIST OF INTERVIEWEES

**Ainsworth Bulldogs**
Julie (Weiss) Ferguson
Gina Reyman
Gaylin (Talbot) Tutnick
JoAnn (Kirkpatrick) Walthour
**Atlanta Phoenix**
Lizbeth Mondragon
**Austin Rage**
Dee Kennamer
**Boston Renegades**
Erin Diette
Ruth Matta
Sarah Viola
**Capital City Rage**
Robin Grove
**Carolina Queens**
Ebony Kimbrough
**Cincinnati Sizzle**
Tamar Fennell
Shannon Helseth
Angela Mason
Pam Schreiner
Kendra Spencer
Michelle Terrell
**Cleveland Fusion**
Martina Latessa
Sophia Pagan

**Colorado Freeze**
Elecia Kruise
Erin Pounds
**Columbus Comets**
Allie Fair
Lorrain Harris
Denise Jones
Carolyn O'Leary
Coach Hank Patterson
Lindsay Rice
Sierra Robison
Christi Sabatucci
**D.C. Divas**
Callie Brownson
Natalie Gaston
**Detroit Dark Angels**
Jacquie Bennington
"Miami" Henry
Tessa Marie Sharman
Alecia Sweeny
**Eugene Ladyhawks**
Erin Miller
**Everett Reign**
Gina Buckmiller
**Houston Heat**
Jennifer Kadlitz

**Indiana Girls Tackle
Football League**
Ale'sha Christy
Natalie Hanson
Noah Harris
Elise Scaggs
Faith Skaggs
Kelsie Tanner
**Indiana Women's Flag
Football League**
Julie Sadler
Kayla Steffee
**Indy Crash**
Christy Fox-Martini
Lea Kaszas
Christa Martini
April Priest
Olivia Taplin
**Legends Football League**
Raphaëlle Duché—Denver Dream
Tamar Fennel—Chicago Bliss
Bridget McDonnell—Chicago Bliss
**Los Angeles Bobcats**
Jane Brinkman
Olivia Morgan
**Maine Mayhem**
Alicia Jeffords
**Mile High Blaze**
Chantel Hernandez
**Miscellaneous**
Diane Beruldsen—International
Women's Flag Football Associ-
ation
Michael Burmy—Club Burmy
Jim Farrell—Team USA
Elizabeth Faust—USA Football
Dale Glossenger—American Foot-
ball Events, USA All Stars

Steph Jackson—NFL Flag Ambas-
sador
Coach Lisa Limper—Hillsboro &
Glencliff High Schools
Oscar Lopez—*Gridiron Beauties*
Jenna Mitchell—Baker Middle
School
Sydney Williams—USA
**Molosses d'Asnieres-sur-Seine**
Elisa De Santis
Christelle Harnais
Sarah Viola
**Music City Mizfits**
Jaimie Lock
Heidi McGuire
Jennika Watts
**Nebraska Nite Hawks**
Ashley Box
Jerrina "Snoop" Vaughn
**New Brunswick Junior Girls
FB League**
Lisa Harlow
**New York Sharks**
Andra Douglas
Collette Smith
Anna "Tonka" Tate
**North Winnipeg Nomads**
Kaity Cummings
Gianna Donnelly
Sherisa Gretsinger
Aiyana Hart
Brooke Pirrie
Lisa Pirrie
Montana Pirrie
Lisa Zueff-Cummings
**Pittsburgh Passion**
Kimberly Beaver
Jana Meister

Kaitlan Neidermeyer

Lisa Horton

**Portland Fighting Shockwave**

Jessica Gerdes

Leah Hinkle

Dani Riggelman

**San Diego Rebellion**

Leslie Hubbell

Knengi Martin

**Seattle Majestics**

Cyndi Butz-Houghton

Holly Custis

Scott McCarron

Julia McComas

McKenzie Tolliver

Kase Tukutau

**St. Louis Slam**

Kendall Park

**Tampa Bay Inferno**

Ty Baldwin

Melissa Bedwell

Chrissy Clingan

Corynn Franklin

Jennifer Marshall

Jennifer Moody

**Team Canada**

Kristen Chatterton

Trina Graves

Emilie Halle

Wendy Iwaasa

Rienna Rueve

Beth Thomson

Alicia Wilson

**Team Finland**

Petra Eloranta

Mirva Honkonen

Suvi Mantyniemi

**Team Great Britain**

Laura Dye

Jo Kilby

Monica Lewinska

Phoebe Schecter

**Team Mexico**

Maria Fernanda Mandujano
Abrego

Sandra San Juan Chavez

Sybil Odette Gonzalez

Anna Greta Medina

Andrea Romero Vazquez

**Texas Elite Spartans**

Rasan Gore

Angelica Grayson

Jewell Grimsley

Elizabeth Jenkins

Odessa "OJ" Jenkins

Amber Kimbrough

Rachel May

Umeki Webb

**Thee Toledo Reign**

Lynn Eubank

Octavia Griswold

Brianna Patman

Tonya Shinaul

Miika Vining

**Toledo Troopers**

Mitchi Colette

Iris Smith

Eunice White

Kasey Carter—Toledo Furies

**Tulsa Threat**

Chris Gee

Bri Lynch

**Utah Falconz**

Tasha Aiono

Maira Alcala

Louise Matthews Bean

BreAnn Hillhouse Cintron

Sara Galica

Coach Marc "Hutch" Hunter

Chanel Johnstun

Coach Rick Rasmussen

Samantha Smith-Meek

Jasmine Teters

Jody Thompson

**Utah Girls Football League**

Maddie Bracken—Bingham HS

Stephanie Bracken—Bingham HS
parent

Sam Gordon—West Harriman
Mustangs

Crys Sacco

Sydney Sessions—Bingham HS

**West Jordan High School—UGFL**

Macy Coester

Lauren Dixon

Olivia Green

Lacie Jacobson

Railey Tucker

Aria Wagaman

**West Michigan Mayhem**

Tiffany Grzybowski

**Winnipeg Wolfpack**

Laura Dacey

# Notes

INTRODUCTION

1. I use weasel words such as "around," "approximately," and "nearly" because at any one time definitive numbers are impossible as teams and leagues rise and fall with some regularity.

2. James Dator, "A Short History of the Banning of Women's Soccer," *SB Nation*, 6 July 2019, https://www.sbnation.com/soccer/2019/7/6 /18658729/banning-womens-soccer-world-cup-effects.

3. David J. Leonard, Kimberly B. George, and Wade Davis, eds., *Football, Culture, and Power* (New York: Routledge, 2017), xiv; see also Gretchen Reynolds, "Hits to the Head May Result in Immediate Brain Damage," *New York Times*, 31 January 2018, https://www.nytimes.com/2018/01/31 /well/move/hits-to-the-head-may-result-in-immediate-brain-damage .html; and Joe Drape, "'The American Dilemma': Why Do We Still Watch Football?" *New York Times*, 2 February 2018. These are only a few examples of how football is critiqued in the media and academia.

4. Russ Crawford, "The 'Sun of Austerlitz' Shone for the Molosses," *Sport in American History*, 21 July 2016, https://ussporthistory.com/2016/07 /21/the-sun-of-austerlitz-shone-for-the-molosses/.

5. Russ Crawford, *Le Football: The History of American Football in France* (Lincoln: University of Nebraska Press, 2016), 253.

6. Interview with Christelle Harnais conducted by author, Ada OH, via Messenger, 6 September 2017 (Genevieve and Christian Mercadier, translators).

7. "Molosses Football Féminin 2015 Bande De Filles," YouTube, accessed 18 March 2018, https://www.youtube.com/watch?v=5QXRaeEVejU.

8. Christine N. Ziemba, "*Girlhood*," *Paste Music*, 30 January 2015, https://www.pastemagazine.com/articles/2015/01/girlhood.html.

9. Harnais interview.

10. Crawford, "Sun of Austerlitz."

11. Crawford, "Sun of Austerlitz."

12. Interview with Elisa De Santis conducted by author, Ada OH, via Messenger, 9 August 2017 (Sophie Crawford, translator).

13. Interview with Sarah Viola conducted by author, Ada OH, via Messenger, 11 September 2017.

14. Interview with Louise Matthews Bean conducted by author, Ada OH, via Facebook Messenger, 19 March 2018.

15. Russ Crawford, Women Playing American Football, accessed 9 December 2020, https://womenplayingamericanfootball.weebly.com/.

16. "Press Release: The WFA & the Women's World Championships 2017," Women's Football Alliance, Canton OH, accessed 22 March 2018, https://wfaprofootball.com/press-release-wfa-womens-world-championships/.

## 1. WOMEN'S PROFESSIONAL FOOTBALL BEGINS

1. Jennifer A. Carter, "'Let's Bang': Constructing, Reinforcing, and Embodying Orthodox Masculinity in Women's Full Contact, Tackle Football" (PhD diss., University of Cincinnati, 2014), 34–35.

2. Joseph A. Kotarba, "Women's Professional Athlete's Injury Care: The Case of Women's Football," in *The Social Organization of Sports Medicine: Critical Socio-Cultural Perspectives*, ed. Dominic Malcolm and Parissa Safai (New York: Routledge, 2012), 111.

3. "The Flapper Magazine, Thanksgiving 1922 Issue," Pinterest, accessed 16 July 2018, https://www.pinterest.com/pin/114138171779960296/?lp=true.

4. Don Van Natta, *Wonder Girl: The Magnificent Sporting Life of Babe Didrickson Zaharias* (New York: Little, Brown, 2011), 12.

5. Seymour Rothman, "I've Heard," *Toledo Blade*, 5 September 1978, 41.

6. Rothman, "I've Heard," 41.

7. Dale C. Mayer, *Lou Henry Hoover: A Prototype for First Ladies* (New York: Nova History, 2004), 33.

8. Susan K. Kahn, *Coming on Strong: Gender and Sexuality in Women's Sports* (Urbana: University of Illinois Press, 1994), 56.

9. Kahn, *Coming on Strong*, 167.

10. *Uncle Sam's Feminine Football Fans*, British Pathé, 1 January 1932, accessed 16 July 2018, http://www.britishpathe.com/video/uncle-sams-feminine -football-fans/query/football.

11. British Pathé, "*Women Battle on the Gridiron aka Lady's Rugby March (1934)*," YouTube, 13 April 2014, https://www.youtube.com/watch?v= eOAsZIUvVyk.

12. Michael Oriard, *King Football: Sport and Spectacle in the Golden Age of Radio & Newsreels, Movies & Magazines, the Weekly & the Daily Press* (Chapel Hill: University of North Carolina Press, 2001), 352.

13. Erica Westly, "The Forgotten History of Women's Football," *Smithsonian*, 5 February 2016, https://www.smithsonianmag.com/history/forgotten -history-womens-football-180958042/.

14. Interview with Diane Beruldsen conducted by author, Ada OH, via Google Voice, 13 July 2018.

15. Interview with Andra Douglas conducted by author, Ada OH, via Google Voice, 29 October 2020.

16. Neal Rozendaal, *The Women's Football Encyclopedia* (Rockville MD: Roze-hawk, 2016), 3.

17. Interview with Mitchi Collette conducted by author, Temperance MI, 1 May 2018.

18. Rozendaal, *Women's Football Encyclopedia*, 2.

19. Teams identified as "professional" are not in the truest sense professional, in that most women who played never received any compensation. I continue to use the term, however, to differentiate adult athletes, teams, and leagues from youth league teams and athletes.

20. M. Ann Hall, *The Girl and the Game: A History of Women's Sport in Canada*, 2nd ed. (Toronto: University of Toronto Press, 2016).

21. "Scorecard: Padded Figures," *Sports Illustrated*, 31 August 1969, 9, https:// www.si.com/vault/issue/43013/11, accessed 25 July 2018.

22. Katrina Krawec, "Shaping and Being Shaped: Examining Women's Tackle Football in Canada" (master's thesis, University of Windsor, 2014), Electronic Theses and Dissertations, 5156, https://scholar.uwindsor.ca/etd /5156.

23. Frankie de la Cretaz and Lyndsey D'Arcangelo, *Hail Mary: The Rise and Fall of the National Women's Football League* (New York: Bold Type Books, 2021), 57.

24. Rozendaal, *Women's Football Encyclopedia*, 4.

25. Tom Henry, "Remembering Toledo's Troopers," *Toledo Blade*, 16 July 2013, http://www.toledoblade.com/Movies/2013/06/16/Remembering-toledo-s-Troopers.html.

26. De la Cretaz and D'Arcangelo, *Hail Mary*, 122.

27. Tom Lorenz, "Coming of Age on Colony Field," *Blade Sunday Magazine*, 10 November 1974, 4–14, accessed 25 July 2018 via Google News.

28. Mike Tressler, "Inside Today," *Blade Sunday Magazine*, 10 November 1974, 4–14, accessed 25 July 2018 via Google News.

29. Lorenz, "Coming of Age."

30. Gary Kiefer, "A Woman's Place Is in the Game," "Women in Football" clipping file, Pro Football Hall of Fame, Canton OH.

31. Lorenz, "Coming of Age."

32. "Weaker Sex?—My Foot: Women Take to the Gridiron in Their Own Version of the National Football League," *Ebony*, November 1973, 182–90.

33. Lena Williams, "Award Brings Only Publicity for Halfback," *New York Times*, 8 June 1975, 21.

34. "Weaker Sex?"

35. Rozendaal, *Women's Football Encyclopedia*, 7.

36. Henry, "Remembering Toledo's Troopers."

37. "Linda Jefferson Athlete of the Year," "Women in Football" clipping file, Pro Football Hall of Fame.

38. Chris Schmidbauer, "Former Football Star Jefferson Still Running Strong," *Toledo Free Press*, 17 February 2011, https://issuu.com/toledofreepress/docs/tfp_022011.

39. "Linda Jefferson Athlete of the Year."

40. Tom Melody, "Jefferson Cannot Run Down a Decent Date," *Akron Beacon Journal*, 14 November 1978, "Women in Football" clipping file, Pro Football Hall of Fame.

41. Schmidbauer, "Former Football Star Jefferson."

42. Beth Sheboy, "After 7-Year Stint, Gal Piles Up Yards," "Women in Football" clipping file, Pro Football Hall of Fame.

43. Art Schrock, "Elusive: HOF Speaker's Directions Guide Her to Minerva," *Canton Repository*, 14 November 1978, "Women in Football" clipping file, Pro Football Hall of Fame.

44. Beth Sheboy, "Jefferson Is the New HOF Sweetheart," *Canton Repository*, 28 November 1978, "Women in Football" clipping file, Pro Football Hall of Fame.

45. Jeff McGinnis, "A Perfect Interview: What It Meant to Meet Linda Jefferson," *Toledo Free Press*, 27 May 2014, https://archive.li/Rde9B.

46. "Perfect Season: The Untold Story of the Toledo Troopers," Toledo Troopers Hall of Fame Induction, YouTube, 16 January 2017, https://www.youtube.com/watch?v=09UA7gXlfsY.

47. "Bio—Linda Jefferson," Toledo Troopers, "Women in Football" clipping file, Pro Football Hall of Fame.

48. "1975 Women's Final," United States Superstars Competitions, Rotunda West FL, 27–29 January 1975, http://www.thesuperstars.org/comp/75women.html, accessed 2 September 2018.

49. Melody, "Jefferson Cannot Run Down."

50. Rozendaal, *Women's Football Encyclopedia*, 7.

51. Tom Henry, "Troopers Saluted for Inspiring Girls to Play," *Toledo Blade*, 24 March 2016, https://www.toledoblade.com/local/2016/03/24/Toledo-Troopers-saluted-for-inspiring-girls-to-play/stories/20160323262?abnpageversion=evoke.

52. Interview with Iris Smith conducted by author, Toledo OH, 21 April 2018.

53. Smith interview.

54. Interview with Eunice White conducted by author, Toledo OH, 19 May 2018.

55. Bill C., "Don't Ask Nebraska Fans about Penn State's National Title. Just Don't Do It," *SB Nation* Football Study Hall, 26 May 2016, https://www.footballstudyhall.com/2016/5/26/11764420/1982-college-football-season-penn-state-nebraska.

56. Interview with Mitchi Collette conducted by author, Temperance MI, 1 May 2018.

57. Collette interview.

58. Collette interview.

59. Scott Munn, "Gridiron Girls Oklahoma City Dolls Blitzed Tradition, Had Fun in '70s Show of Nonconformity," *The Oklahoman*, 23 July 1991, https://newsok.com/article/2363605/gridiron-girls-oklahoma-city-dolls-blitzed-tradition-had-fun-in-70s-show-of-nonconformity, accessed 2 September 2018.

60. Scott Munn, "Catching Up: After Years of Playing Football and Living Abroad, Jan Hines Has Settled Down in Virginia," *The Oklahoman*, 14 July 2010, https://newsok.com/article/3476282/catching-up-after-years-of-playing-football-and-living-abroad-jan-hines-has-settled-down-in-virginia; Karen Klinka, "Football Was Dolls' Game," *The Oklahoman*,

14 February 2000, https://newsok.com/article/2686223/football-was
-dolls-game.

61. Lacey Lett, "'We Had to Learn Everything': Women Fighting on and
off the Field for Equal Rights with the Oklahoma City Dolls," KFOR, 8
December 2016, https://kfor.com/2016/12/08/a-league-of-their-own
-how-womens-football-won-in-the-70s/.

62. Munn, "Gridiron Girls Oklahoma City Dolls."

63. Munn, "Gridiron Girls Oklahoma City Dolls."

64. Elana Levine, *Wallowing in Sex: The New Sexual Culture of 1970s American
Television* (Durham NC: Duke University Press, 2007), 37–38.

65. Lett, "'We Had to Learn Everything.'"

66. Munn, "Gridiron Girls Oklahoma City Dolls."

67. Oklahoma Historical Society Film and Video Archives, "All Female Oklahoma City Dolls Football Game, c. 1976–1977," YouTube, 29 May 2012,
https://www.youtube.com/watch?v=pVU2gPCU6qU.

68. Munn, "Gridiron Girls Oklahoma City Dolls."

69. *The Oklahoma City Dolls*, directed by E. W. Swackhamer, performed by
Susan Blakely, David Huddelston, and Eddie Albert, ABC Television,
1981, https://www.youtube.com/watch?v=hh9uzdORvAc&t=2s, accessed
7 October 2018.

70. John J. O'Connor, "TV Weekend; Football 'Dolls' and California Dreams,"
*New York Times*, 23 January 1981, https://www.nytimes.com/1981/01/23
/movies/tv-weekend-football-dolls-and-california-dreams.html, accessed
8 October 2018.

71. Peter J. Boyer, "'City Dolls' Do a Jiggle Tonight," *Annapolis Capital*, 23
January 1981, 9.

72. Paul Mavis, "The Oklahoma City Dolls (Sony Choice Collection)," DVD
*Talk*, 21 June 2013, https://www.dvdtalk.com/reviews/61230/oklahoma
-city-dolls-sony-choice-collection-the/.

73. Louis Fowler, "The Oklahoma City Dolls," *Colorado Springs Independent*,
17 April 2013, https://www.csindy.com/blogs/IndyBlog/?page=218.

74. Louis Fowler, "MIO Movie Reviews: The Oklahoma City Dolls," *Lost
Ogle*, 9 July 2014, https://www.thelostogle.com/2014/07/09/mio-movie
-reviews-the-oklahoma-city-dolls/.

75. Andrew D. Linden, "Revolution on the American Gridiron: Gender, Contested Space, and Women's Football in the 1970s," *International Journal
of the History of Sport* 32, no. 18 (5 March 2015): 2171–89, https://www
.tandfonline.com/eprint/TneRSAGKbTICag6vTAdJ/full.

76. "Shades of O.J.: Petite Toledoan Best in Gals' Loop," Associated Press, 27 April 1976, "Women in Football" clipping file, Pro Football Hall of Fame.

77. Clementine Bloomingdale, "First Down for Women's Football," *Playgirl*, 1975, "Women in Football" clipping file, Pro Football Hall of Fame.

78. Linden, "Revolution on the American Gridiron."

79. De la Cretaz and D'Arcangelo, *Hail Mary*, 237.

80. Jean Williams, *A Contemporary History of Women's Sport, Part One: Sporting Women, 1850–1960* (New York: Routledge, 2014), 2.

81. Christa Binswanger and Kathy Davis, "Sexy Stories and Postfeminst Empowerment," in *The Women's Liberation Movement: Impacts and Outcomes*, ed. Kristina Schulz (New York: Berghahn Books, 2017), 130.

82. Saucy, "Move Over Boys, Women's Football Coming Through," *Pretty Tough*, 29 January 2008, http://www.prettytough.com/move-over-boys-womens-football/.

83. Rozendaal, *Women's Football Encyclopedia*, 7.

84. Interview with Kasey Carter conducted by author, Toledo OH, 19 May 2018.

85. Carter interview.

86. "Coaching," "Women in Football" clipping file, Pro Football Hall of Fame.

87. Lett, "'We Had to Learn Everything.'"

88. De la Cretaz and D'Arcangelo, *Hail Mary*, 50.

89. Rozendaal, *Women's Football Encyclopedia*, 7.

### 2. WOMEN'S FOOTBALL ROARS BACK

1. George Dohrmann and Jim Caple, "Another Doomed Dream?" *St. Paul Pioneer Press*, 7 November 1999, 1A, https://savesb6.newsbank.com:8443/MNGsave/classic/doc?docid=1326454&q=(%20headline(another%20doomed%20dream)%20)&stem=false&spaceop=AND&ttype=xsl&tval=headline_mng&pos=0&hn=1&pubAbbrev=mng&dtokey=qtgwjuvlorik#anchor1326454, accessed 18 November 2018.

2. Kelley King, "Saturday Night Lights a Self-Proclaimed Smash-Mouth Women's League Had a Not-So-Smashing Debut," *Sports Illustrated*, 18 October 1999, https://vault.si.com/vault/1999/10/18/saturday-night-lights-a-self-proclaimed-smash-mouth-womens-league-had-a-not-so-smashing-debut, accessed 18 November 2018.

3. "History," Minnesota Vixen, accessed 18 November 2018, http://www.mnvixen.com/history/.

4. "The History of Women's Professional Football League," "Women in Football" clipping file, Pro Football Hall of Fame.

5. Laura Billings, "Women's Football Doesn't Quite Reach the End Zone," *St. Paul Pioneer Press*, 12 October 1999, 1B, https://savesb6.newsbank .com:8443/MNGsave/classic/doc?docid=1322597&q=(%20(minnesota %20vixen)%20)%20AND%20date(01/01/1998%20TO%2011/18 /2000)&stem=false&spaceop=AND&ttype=xsl&tval=headline_mng&pos =3&hn=4&pubAbbrev=mng&dtokey=kuzdhgwhnhafys#anchor1322597, accessed 18 November 2018.

6. Dohrmann and Caple, "Another Doomed Dream?"

7. Billings, "Women's Football Doesn't Quite Reach."

8. Jessica Barnett, "True Hearted Vixens," *AlterNet*, 15 July 2001, https:// www.alternet.org/2001/07/true-hearted_vixens/.

9. "*True-Hearted Vixens*," Berkeley Media, accessed 18 November 2018, https://www.berkeleymedia.com/product/truehearted_vixens/; Robert Koehler, "True-Hearted Vixens," *Variety*, 27 July 2001, https://variety .com/2001/film/reviews/true-hearted-vixens-1200468992/.

10. "History," Minnesota Vixen.

11. Interview with Michele Braun conducted by author, Ada OH, via Google Voice, 18 February 2018.

12. Interview with Melissa Bedwell conducted by author, Metairie LA, 22 February 2018.

13. Braun interview.

14. Bedwell interview.

15. Bedwell interview.

16. Braun interview.

17. Bedwell interview.

18. Braun interview.

19. Bedwell interview.

20. Michele Braun, "Feeling nostalgic," Facebook, 12 September 2018, https:// www.facebook.com/profile/1159354114/search/?q=feeling%20nostalgic.

21. Women's Football Hall of Fame, Facebook, 15 October 2018, https://www .facebook.com/1938174076243575/posts/2040938762633772/.

22. Bedwell interview.

23. William Dean Hinton, "Stumbling, Bumbling, Tumbling," *Orlando Weekly*, 27 September 2001, https://www.orlandoweekly.com/orlando/stumbling -bumbling-tumbling/Content?oid=2261803.

24. Hinton, "Stumbling, Bumbling, Tumbling."

25. Andra Douglas, *Black and Blue: Love, Sports, and the Art of Empowerment* (New York: BookBaby, 2019), 81.

26. Neal Rozendaal, *The Women's Football Encyclopedia* (Washington DC: Rozehawk Publishing, 2016), 22.

27. King Kauffman, "Women's Football: Ready for Prime Time?" *Salon*, 19 December 2001, https://www.salon.com/2001/12/19/wafl/.

28. Hinton, "Stumbling, Bumbling, Tumbling."

29. Rozendaal, *Women's Football Encyclopedia*, 22.

30. "Women's Professional Football League," Wikipedia, accessed 23 November 2018, https://en.wikipedia.org/wiki/Women%27s_Professional _Football_League.

31. Chris Shott, "Korpacz Is Pioneer of Women's Football," *Cranston Herald* (Warwick RI), 27 August 2002, http://cranstononline.com/stories/korpacz -is-pioneer-of-womens-football,9024?content_source=&category_id=& search_filter=&event_mode=&event_ts_from=&list_type=&order_by=& order_sort=&content_class=&sub_type=stories&town_id=.

32. Shott, "Korpacz Is Pioneer," 28, 34, 42, 48, 53, 64.

33. Rozendaal, *Women's Football Encyclopedia*, 42, 48, 53, 58, 64.

34. "Korpacz v. Women's Professional Football League," Casetext, 27 January 2006, https://casetext.com/case/korpacz-v-womens-professional -football-league.

35. Wendy Grossman, "Winning Ways in a Losing League," *Houston Press*, 27 December 2001, https://www.houstonpress.com/news/celebrating-a -houston-texans-thanksgiving-weekend-11057864.

36. Rozendaal, *Women's Football Encyclopedia*, 34.

37. Joshua Truksa, "H. Energy Captures IWFL Crown," *Alvin (TX) Sun*, 31 July 2018, http://www.alvinsun.net/sports/article_8d64fe0a-9436-11e8 -9bab-4b244a78e42e.html.

38. Truksa, "H. Energy Captures IWFL Crown."

39. Women's Football Alliance, "Houston Energy Surges into the WFA," Facebook post, 12 September 2018, https://www.facebook.com/wfafootball /posts/houston-energy-surges-into-wfathe-womens-football-alliance -is-pleased-to-announc/10157147548585931/.

40. Albert Burford, "Filmmaker Sean Pamphilon Defends His Actions on the New Orleans Saints Bounty Audio Tapes," *New Orleans Times-Picayune*, 5 June 2012, https://www.nola.com/saints/index.ssf/2012/06/filmmaker _sean_pamphilon_defen.html; Sean Pamphilon and Royce Toni, dirs.,

*Playing with Rage* (Rtistic Camp, 2006), https://www.imdb.com/title/tt1413564/fullcredits/?ref_=tt_ov_st_sm.

41. Pamphilon and Toni, *Playing with Rage*.

42. Sandy F. Glossenger, "American Football Events Women's Team USA All Stars," Facebook post, 25 July 2019, https://www.facebook.com/groups/1682333595209974/permalink/2119771034799559?sfns=mo.

43. "Playing with RAGE," Facebook, accessed 18 December 2018, https://www.facebook.com/groups/AustinRAGE/.

44. Royce Toni, "Playing with RAGE—Tiffany," YouTube, 28 April 2008, https://www.youtube.com/watch?v=q7vCFaip7Q4&feature=youtu.be&fbclid=IwAR08OLRRg16gdRCen4H1vyzjqjsbaL_1X72Vuv60kNOo1TCJpHfuh_vmCTY.

45. Interview with Dee Kennamer conducted by author, Ada OH, via Google Voice, 25 November 2018.

46. Eli Kabillio and Lorna Thomas, dirs., *First Down* (Mad Dog Films, 11 January 2018), https://vimeo.com/ondemand/firstdown.

47. Kabillio and Thomas, *First Down*.

48. Rozendaal, *Women's Football Encyclopedia*, 24–28.

49. Kennamer interview.

50. Kennamer interview.

51. Kennamer interview.

52. Rozendaal, *Women's Football Encyclopedia*, 28.

53. "The Austin Rage," Visit Wimberley, 2002, http://www.visitwimberley.com/rage/.

54. Kennamer interview.

55. Kennamer interview.

56. Douglas, *Black and Blue*, 99–100.

57. Douglas, *Black and Blue*, 178.

58. Interview with Andra Douglas conducted by author, Ada OH, via Google Messenger, 29 October 2020.

59. Michael Weinreb, "Playing for Fun, and Little Else, on Football's Edge," *New York Times*, 18 July 2006, https://www.nytimes.com/2006/07/18/sports/football/18football.html.

60. Kauffman, "Women's Football."

61. Lisa Davis, "Unsportsmanlike Conduct," *SF Weekly*, 23 January 2002, http://www.sfweekly.com/news/unsportsmanlike-conduct/.

62. Hinton, "Stumbling, Bumbling, Tumbling."

63. Davis, "Unsportsmanlike Conduct."

64. Rozendaal, *Women's Football Encyclopedia*, 35.

65. Associated Press, "Women's Football; Name Change Avoids Conflict," *New York Times*, 26 November 2002, https://www.nytimes.com/2002/11/26/sports/women-s-football-name-change-avoids-conflict.html.

66. "National Women's Football Association," Women's Football Association, accessed 19 November 2018, http://www.womensfootballassociation.com/.

67. Rozendaal, *Women's Football Encyclopedia*, 68.

68. Weinreb, "Playing for Fun."

69. "National Women's Football Association."

70. Donna Wilkinson, "Gender Bowl—Battle of the Sexes 2005," Donna Wilkinson website, accessed 21 November 2018, https://www.donnawilkinson.net/gender-bowl.

71. Jacqueline McDowell and Spencer Shaffner, "Football, It's a Man's Game: Insult and Gendered Discourse in the Gender Bowl," *Discourse and Society*, 19 August 2011, https://journals.sagepub.com/doi/pdf/10.1177/0957926511405574.

72. "Women's Pro Football Scores with AFA Hall of Fame," PR Web, 21 May 2006, https://www.prweb.com/releases/2006/05/prweb388147.htm.

73. "Women's Football Goes Hollywood," Sports Critics, accessed 21 November 2018, http://www.thesportscritics.com/womens-football-goes-hollywood/.

74. "Award-winning actress, Julie Bowen, announced the project on the jumbotron before the WFA D1 Championship game this past weekend," Facebook, 25 July 2021, https://www.facebook.com/watch/?v=863503350931816.

75. Rozendaal, *Women's Football Encyclopedia*, 13.

76. Weinreb, "Playing for Fun."

77. Kim Grodus, "Football History," Kim Grodus website, accessed 19 December 2018, http://kimgrodus.com/football-history.html.

78. Neal Rozendaal, "The Greatest Players in Women's Football History: Part 2," Neal Rozendaal website, accessed 19 December 2018, http://nealrozendaal.com/womensfootball/greatest-players-history-2017-part-2/.

79. Ted Williams, Emily Haynam, and Aaron Stoller, "Detroit Holds the Power as It Demolishes Pensacola in NFWA [sic]," *The Lantern*, 4 August 2003, https://www.thelantern.com/2003/08/detroit-holds-the-power-as-it-demolishes-pensacola-in-nfwa/.

80. Grodus, "Football History."

81. "Detroit Demolition Women's Football Team Joins Independent Women's Football League; Four-Time National Champion Full-Contact Team to Begin Fifth Season April 29," *Business Wire*, 19 April 2006, https://www.businesswire.com/news/home/20060419005689/en/Detroit-Demolition-Womens-Football-Team-Joins-Independent.

82. Rozendaal, *Women's Football Encyclopedia*, 12, 29–37.

83. Royce Toni, "Playing with RAGE Movie Trailer," YouTube, 2 December 2006, https://www.youtube.com/watch?v=dKAP3HDwm_4.

84. Kendra Nordin, "Women's Pro Football . . . Oof!" *Christian Science Monitor*, 24 November 2000, "Women in Football" clipping file, Pro Football Hall of Fame.

85. Kennamer interview.

86. Jim Axelrod, "Throwing Like a Girl," CBS News, 26 January 2001, https://www.cbsnews.com/news/throwing-like-a-girl/.

87. Alexandra Powe Allred, *Atta Girl: A Celebration of Women in Sport* (Terre Haute: Wish, 2003), 38.

88. Cassandra Negley, "She Can—and Will—Play Football (Whether You Watch or Not)," *Sporting News*, 14 May 2014, http://www.sportingnews.com/us/nfl/news/womens-football-leagues-iwfl-legends-football-league-wnba-girls-usa-football-world-championships-jennifer-welter-low-viewership/5h9m2ldmd1gl1fr7iv6xjtdio.

89. "2017 Girls of Fall," Maine Mayhem Facebook page, accessed 20 December 2018, https://www.facebook.com/pg/mayhemfootball2016/photos/?tab=album&album_id=1835454016784991.

90. Adrienne Smith, "More Girls Than Ever Are Playing High School Football," Gridiron Queendom, 23 October 2018, https://gridironqueendom.com/more-girls-than-ever-are-playing-high-school-football/.

91. Bedwell interview.

92. Kennamer interview.

93. Kendra Nordin, "Women Pros Search for Niche," *Christian Science Monitor*, 10 November 2003, "Women in Football" clipping file, Pro Football Hall of Fame.

94. Douglas interview.

95. Shott, "Korpacz Is a Pioneer."

96. Shott, "Korpacz Is a Pioneer."

97. Rozendaal, *Women's Football Encyclopedia*, 13–14.

### 3. THE INDEPENDENT WOMEN'S FOOTBALL LEAGUE

1. Interview with Marc Hunter conducted by author, Ada OH, via Google Voice, 14 March 2018.

2. Interview with Rick Rasmussen conducted by author, Ada OH, via Google Voice, 8 March 2018.

3. Louise Matthews Bean, Facebook post, 14 June 2018, https://www.facebook.com/1271750163/posts/10216062137447515/.

4. Interview with Samantha Smith-Meek conducted by author, Ada OH, via Google Voice, 4 May 2018.

5. Cassandra Negley, "She Can—and Will—Play Football (Whether You Watch or Not)," *Sporting News*, 14 May 2014, http://www.sportingnews.com/us/nfl/news/womens-football-leagues-iwfl-legends-football-league-wnba-girls-usa-football-world-championships-jennifer-welter-low-viewership/5h9m2ldmd1gl1fr7iv6xjtdio.

6. Neal Rozendaal, *The Women's Football Encyclopedia* (Washington DC: Rozehawk Publishing, 2016), 12.

7. Negley, "She Can—and Will—Play Football."

8. Rozendaal, *Women's Football Encyclopedia*, 75–76.

9. Negley, "She Can—and Will—Play Football."

10. "History," Independent Women's Football League, accessed 22 December 2018, http://www.iwflsports.com/theiwfl/history/.

11. Negley, "She Can—and Will—Play Football."

12. Sports Destination Management Team, "An Interview with Laurie Frederick, President & CEO, Independent Women's Football League," Sports Destination Management, 31 August 2010, https://www.sportsdestinations.com/sports/football/an-interview-with-laurie-frederick-president-ceo-i-4631.

13. Mandi Woodruff-Santos, "Inside the World of Women's Tackle Football—Where Women Pay to Play," Yahoo! Finance, 30 March 2016, https://finance.yahoo.com/news/women-s-tackle-football-iwfl-wfa-183132959.html.

14. Interview with Alecia Sweeny conducted by author, Detroit MI, 28 April 2014.

15. Marvin Goodwin, "Demolition Owner and GM Put on Suspension List," *Oakland Press*, 12 July 2009, https://www.theoaklandpress.com/news/demolition-owner-and-gm-put-on-suspension-list/article_090746fd-4a4e-55a0-bbb5-f3f5d732260b.html#disqus_thread.

16. Cosmo, "KC Forfeits; Detroit Rejects Replacement," *Crack-Back* (blog), 3 July 2007, http://crack-back.blogspot.com/2007/07/rather-than-show -up-to-get-bitch.html.

17. Rozendaal, *Women's Football Encyclopedia*, 61.

18. Cosmo, "KC Forfeits."

19. Rozendaal, *Women's Football Encyclopedia*, 54, 60.

20. Goodwin, "Detroit Owner and GM."

21. Merle Exit, "Taking Credit When You've Actually Screwed It Up," *Merle's Whirls*, 20 July 2016, http://merleswhirls.blogspot.com/2016/07/.

22. Interview with Andra Douglas conducted by author, Ada OH, via Google Voice, 29 October 2020.

23. Neal Rozendaal, "Soap Operas and Sorting Out the 2016 IWFL Play-off Mess," Neal Rozendaal website, accessed 23 December 2018, http:// nealrozendaal.com/womensfootball/soap-operas-sorting-2016-iwfl -playoff-mess/.

24. Rozendaal, *Women's Football Encyclopedia*, 75–76.

25. "History of the Divas," D.C. Divas Football, accessed 23 December 2018, http://dcdivas.com/wp-content/uploads/2015/02/D.C.-Divas-2014 -Yearbook.pdf.

26. Peter Rugg, "Women's Football Champions the Kansas City Tribe Suing to Leave Their League," *The Pitch*, 25 August 2010, https://www.thepitchkc .com/news/article/20586962/womens-football-champions-the-kansas -city-tribe-suing-to-leave-their-league.

27. Ross Forman, "Chicago Force Leaves One League, Starts Another," *Windy City Times*, 27 October 2010, http://www.windycitymediagroup.com/lgbt /Chicago-Force-leaves-one-league-starts-another/29268.html.

28. Rozendaal, *Women's Football Encyclopedia*, 82, 85.

29. "*The Tackle Girls* Preserves Landmark Moment in Women's Football for Generations to Enjoy," *Fourth and Feminine*, 13 January 2014, https:// fourthandfeminine.wordpress.com/2014/01/13/the-tackle-girls -preserves-landmark-moment-in-womens-football-for-generations-to -enjoy/.

30. Women's Football Alliance, "Pittsburgh Passion and Toledo Reign Rejoin WFA for 2016 Season," Pittsburgh Passion Women's Football, accessed 29 December 2018, http://pittsburghpassion.com/news/2015 -press-releases-2/.

31. Matt Gephardt, "Semi-Pro Football Players Question the Disappearance of League Fees," *Get Gephardt*, KUTV, 4 March 2014, https://kutv.com/news

/get-gephardt/semi-pro-football-players-question-the-disappearance-of
-league-fees-05-29-2015.

32. Matt Gephardt, "Women's Football League Leaves Supporters Hungry,
for Cookies," *Get Gephardt*, KUTV, 1 July 2014, https://kutv.com/news
/get-gephardt/womens-football-league-leaves-supporters-hungry-for
-cookies.

33. Interview with Louise Bean conducted by author, Ada OH, via Google
Voice, 7 March 2018.

34. Amy Donaldson, "Women's Football Team Helps Mormon Family Tackle
Conflicts over Son's Sexuality," *Deseret News*, 18 September 2015, https://
www.deseretnews.com/article/865637135/Womens-football-team-helps
-Mormon-family-tackle-conflicts-over-sons-sexuality.html.

35. Salt Lake Chamber, "This Is Me: Hiroko Jolley, Women's Excellence 4
Life," YouTube, 1 December 2016, https://www.youtube.com/watch?v
=jAdJA5vlxBU.

36. Salt Lake Chamber, "This Is Me."

37. Interview with Marc "Hutch" Hunter conducted by author, Ada OH, via
Google Voice, 14 March 2018.

38. Hunter interview.

39. Smith-Meek interview; "54 Kelly Colobella," Utah Falconz, 29 April 2016,
https://www.utahfalconz.com/player/kelly-colobella/.

40. Interview with Jody Thompson conducted by author, Ada OH, via Google
Voice, 4 April 2018.

41. Smith-Meek interview.

42. BreAnn Hillhouse, "Utah Falconz Announce New Board President, Same
Game Plan," *Deseret News*, 8 February 2018, https://www.deseretnews
.com/article/865695754/Utah-Falconz-announce-new-board-president
-same-game-plan.html.

43. "Chicago Force Finale—Team Ends Operation," Chicago Force Football,
18 February 2018, http://chicagoforcefootball.com/news.asp?ID=220.

44. "2018—The Final Shark Season: Team Sold to New Owners," NY Sharks
Football, accessed 31 December 2018, http://nysharksfootball.com/.

45. Interview with Andra Douglas conducted by author, Ada OH, via Google
Messenger, 29 October 2020.

46. Bean interview, 7 March 2018.

47. Rasmussen interview, 8 March 2018.

48. Rasmussen interview, 8 March 2018.

49. Rasmussen interview, 8 March 2018.

50. Rasmussen interview, 8 March 2018.

51. Bean interview, 7 March 2018.

52. Brett Kennedy, "Great Falls Resident Louise Bean Balances Motherhood and Quarterbacking in Football," *Montana Sports*, 9 January 2019, https://montanasports.com/more-sports/2019/01 /09/great-falls-resident-louise-bean-balances-motherhood-and -quarterbacking-in-football/?fbclid=IwAR36Aht7L5iIMnDcpfPAmO _eJiAiDdgToFUEOy1kIgvEohE65E2NRlrQRuM.

53. "About the San Diego Surge," San Diego Surge Women's Football, accessed 11 January 2019, https://www.sandiegosurge.com/about.

54. UtahVOD, "Utah Falconz vs. San Diego Surge @ Utah," YouTube, 20 May 2018, https://www.youtube.com/watch?v=ewOBXQ231PU.

55. UtahVOD, "Utah Falconz vs. San Diego Surge."

56. Interview with Rick Rasmussen conducted by author, Ada OH, via Google Voice, 21 May 2018.

57. Bean interview, 7 March 2018.

58. "IWFL Championship Weekend," Utah Falconz, accessed 4 January 2019, https://www.facebook.com/womensfootballchampionship.

59. Interview with Louise Bean conducted by Oscar Lopez, *Gridiron Beauties Blitz Radio*, Episode 217, 11 April 2018, http://www.blogtalkradio .com/gridironbeauties/2018/04/11/gridiron-beauties-blitz-radio# .WsyI9vYtmn8.facebook.

60. Smith-Meek interview.

61. Interview with Sara Galica conducted by author, Ada OH, via Google Voice, 14 March 2018.

62. Utah Falconz, Facebook, 24 February 2018, https://www.facebook.com /utahfalconz/posts/1572310386199170.

63. Galica interview.

64. Interview with BreAnn Hillhouse Cintron conducted by author, Ada OH, via Google Voice, 15 March 2018.

65. Cintron interview.

66. Interview with Maira Alcala conducted by author, Ada OH, via Google Voice, 16 March 2018.

67. Interview with Tasha Aiono conducted by author, Ada OH, via Google Voice, 14 April 2018.

68. Interview with Louise Bean conducted by author, Ada OH, via Facebook Messenger, 19 March 2018.

69. Jo Light, "Hard-Hitting," *Oklahoma Gazette*, 28 September 2018, https://m.okgazette.com/oklahoma/hard-hitting/Content?oid=4499421.

70. Interview with Chanel Johnstun conducted by author, Midvale UT, 14 April 2018.

71. Alcala Interview.

72. Interview with Jasmine Teeters conducted by author, Ada OH, via Google Voice, 16 March 2018.

73. "About Us," Seattle Majestics, accessed 7 January 2019, https://theseattlemajestics.com/about/.

74. Molly Yanity, "Play for Free? They'll Pay to Play," *Seattle Post-Intelligencer*, 12 June 2008, https://www.seattlepi.com/sports/article/Play-for-free-They-ll-pay-to-play-1276436.php.

75. "Game Info," Women's Football Alliance, Hosted Sports, accessed 7 January 2019, https://www.hostedsports.com/league_data.asp?league=wfa.

76. Interview with McKenzie Tolliver conducted by author, Ada OH, via Google Voice, 16 March 2018.

77. Holly Custis, "A New Mountain: Knee Surgery," *Relentless21: A Gridiron Mindset*, 11 March 2016, https://relentless21.wordpress.com/2016/03/11/a-new-mountain-knee-surgery/.

78. Interview with Holly Custis conducted by author, Ada OH, via Google Voice, 30 March 2018.

79. Custis interview.

80. Custis interview.

81. Interview with Kase Tukutau conducted by author, Ada OH, via Google Voice, 10 March 2018.

82. Tukutau interview.

83. Interview with Julia McComas conducted by author, Midvale UT, 14 April 2018.

84. Interview with Cyndi Butz-Houghton conducted by author, Ada OH, via Google Voice, 1 April 2018.

85. Rozendaal, *Women's Football Encyclopedia*, 24.

86. Butz-Houghton interview.

87. Butz-Houghton interview.

88. Butz-Houghton interview.

89. Interview with Erin Miller conducted by author, Ada OH, via Google Voice, 9 March 2018.

90. Miller interview.

91. "2018 Eugene LadyHawks Team Summary for Weeks 1 through 12," Independent Women's Football League, Hosted Sports, 2018, http://www.hostedsports.com/football/team_stats.asp?league=IWFL&season=2018&selected_team=Ladyhawks&tier=.

92. Austin Meek, "'This Isn't the Lingerie Bowl': Eugene LadyHawks Show Football Is More than a Man's Game," *Eugene Register-Guard*, 22 May 2018, https://www.registerguard.com/news/20180522/this-isnt-lingerie-bowl-eugene-ladyhawks-show-football-is-more-than-mans-game.

93. "2018 Los Angeles Bobcats Team Summary for Weeks 1 through 12," Independent Women's Football League, Hosted Sports, 2018, http://www.hostedsports.com/football/team_stats.asp?league=IWFL&season=2018&selected_team=Bobcats&tier=.

94. Amanda Scurlock, "L.A. Bobcats Promote Equality and Health," *Los Angeles Sentinel*, 15 March 2018, https://lasentinel.net/l-a-bobcats-promote-equality-and-health.html.

95. Interview with Jane Brinkman conducted by author, Ada OH, via Google Voice, 22 March 2018.

96. Los Angeles Bobcats Facebook page, accessed 9 January 2019, https://www.facebook.com/bobcatsofla/.

97. *NFL 100 Kickoff*, WNFC Facebook share, 15 August 2019, https://www.facebook.com/NFL/videos/887775208247004/.

98. Interview with Sybil Gonzalez conducted by author, Langley BC, 29 June 2017.

99. Interview with Olivia Morgan conducted by author, Ada OH, via Google Voice, 19 March 2018.

100. Morgan interview.

101. Morgan interview.

102. Amanda Prestigiacomo, "Transgender Woman Wins Discrimination Suit, $20,000 for Being Cut from Women's Football Team," *Dailywire*, 28 December 2018, https://www.dailywire.com/news/39735/transgender-woman-wins-discrimination-suit-after-amanda-prestigiacomo.

103. Laura Yuen, "Snubbed by One Team, Transgender Football Player Feels at Home at Last," *MPR News*, 10 March 2017, https://www.mprnews.org/story/2017/03/10/snubbed-by-one-team-transgender-football-player-feels-at-home-at-last.

104. Anthony Gockowski, "Transgender Woman Wins Legal Battle against All-Female Minnesota Football Team," *Tennessee Star*, 24 December 2018,

http://tennesseestar.com/2018/12/24/transgender-woman-wins-legal-battle-against-all-female-minnesota-football-team/#comments.

105. "For Immediate Release," Minnesota Vixen Women's Football, Facebook, 28 December 2018, https://www.facebook.com/profile/100063740701274/search/?q=for%20immediate%20release.

106. Donaldson, "Women's Football Team Helps Mormon Family."

107. Rebecca Meiser, "Leather & Laces: When Football Alone Doesn't Fill the Stands, the Fusion Turns on the Charm," *Scene Magazine*, 19 May 2004, https://www.clevescene.com/cleveland/leather-and-laces/Content?oid=1486475.

108. My Gay Life, "The Best Kept Secret—A Women's Football Podcast," SoundCloud, https://soundcloud.com/mygaylife/best-kept-secret-episode-0.

109. Interview with Jane Brinkman conducted by author, Ada OH, via Google Voice, 22 March 2018.

110. Sarah K. Fields, *Female Gladiators: Gender, Law, and Contact Sport in America* (Urbana: University of Illinois Press, 2010), 45.

111. Brinkman interview.

112. Brinkman interview.

113. Brinkman interview.

114. Michael Burmy, Facebook post, 10 October 2018, https://www.facebook.com/100007530852265/posts/2173828719544802/.

115. Oscar Lopez and Louise Bean, "Bobby Hosea Jr. on Helmet Rule, Proper Tackling Techniques and IWFL 2018 Bobcats Season," *Gridiron Beauties Blitz Radio*, Episode 216, April 2018, http://www.blogtalkradio.com/gridironbeauties/2018/04/04/gridiron-beauties-blitz-radio.

116. "2018 Austin Yellow Jackets Team Summary for Weeks 1 through 12," Independent Women's Football League, Hosted Sports, accessed 10 January 2019, http://www.hostedsports.com/football/team_stats.asp?league=IWFL&season=2018&selected_team=Yellow%20Jackets&tier=.

117. "Standings," Independent Women's Football League, accessed 10 January 2019, http://www.iwflsports.com/schedule/standings/.

118. Ashley Edmiston, "2019 Four Point Stance: Episode 6," *Four Point Stance*, accessed 8 March 2019, https://www.mixcloud.com/AshlyEdmiston1340am/.

119. "Best of the West Teams Rejoin Forces in WNFC," Facebook, 30 August 2018, https://www.facebook.com/theseattlemajestics/photos/a.103704433028454/1965826363482909/?type=3&theater.

## 4. THE WOMEN'S FOOTBALL ALLIANCE

1. "Columbus Comets vs. Toledo Reign," Columbus Comets, 21 April 2018, http://www.columbuscomets.org/teams/default.asp?u=COLUMBUSCOMETS&s=football&p=boxscore&sportsHQ=COLUMBUSCOMETS&gameID=671677&archTog=1.

2. "2018 Toledo Reign Team Summary for Weeks 1 through 10," Women's Football Alliance, Hosted Sports, accessed 12 January 2019, https://www.hostedsports.com/hsi_stats.asp?league=wfa&season=2018.

3. "Overall Team Record," Columbus Comets, accessed 12 January 2019, http://www.columbuscomets.org/teams/default.asp?u=COLUMBUSCOMETS&s=football&p=NewsStory&newsID=39257.

4. Neal Rozendaal, *The Women's Football Encyclopedia* (Washington DC: Rozehawk, 2016), 79.

5. Rozendaal, *Women's Football Encyclopedia*, 68.

6. "Women's Football 2018 Program," Thee Toledo Reign.

7. Interview with Mitchi Collette conducted by author, Temperance MI, 1 May 2018.

8. "2018 WFA National Championship," Women's Football Alliance, Hosted Sports, 27 July 2018, https://www.hostedsports.com/hsi_schedule.asp?from=league_data&league=wfa&season=2018.

9. Rozendaal, *Women's Football Encyclopedia*, 8.

10. "Columbus Comets Football," Home Teams Online, accessed 12 January 2019, http://www.hometeamsonline.com/teams/?u=COLUMBUSCOMETSFOOTBALL&s=football.

11. Hanna Brooks Olsen, "For Female Football Players, It's Pay to Play (and Pray Someone Sees)," *The Nation*, 23 November 2015, https://www.thenation.com/article/for-female-football-players-its-pay-to-play-and-pray-someone-sees/.

12. "Another League?" *Women's Football Talk*, 3 August 2008, http://www.blogtalkradio.com/wfbtalk/2008/08/03/Another-League.

13. Mandi Woodruff-Santos, "Inside the World of Women's Tackle Football—Where Women Pay to Play," Yahoo! Finance, 30 March 2016, https://finance.yahoo.com/news/women-s-tackle-football-iwfl-wfa-183132959.html.

14. "Another League?," *Women's Football Talk*.

15. "Another League?," *Women's Football Talk*.

16. "Another League?," *Women's Football Talk*.

17. Luis F. P. Carranco, "Las mujeres también saben tacklear," *Horacero*, 21 August 2012, https://www.horacero.com.mx/reportaje/las-mujeres -tambien-saben-tacklear/.

18. Lea Kaszas, "An American in Finland: Playing for the Trojan Women of Turku," Gridiron Queendom, 1 November 2016, http://www .gridironqueendom.com/an-american-in-finland-playing-for-the-trojan -women-of-turku/4529?utm_source=www.gridironqueendom.com.

19. Interview with Lea Kaszas conducted by author, Ada OH, via Google Voice, 6 May 2017.

20. "Tooley chemins mènent au Flash . . . ," Flash de La Courneuve, 6 June 2018, http://www.flashfootball.org/coaching-section-feminines/.

21. "Livestream: Pro-Cloud Transatlantic Trophy—Women's Challenge— New York Sharks @Brimingham Lions, 2:30p (3:30p CET, 9:30a ET)," *American Football International*, 2 September 2018, https://www .americanfootballinternational.com/livestream-pro-cloud-transatlantic -trophy-womens-challenge-new-york-sharks-birmingham-lions-230p -330p-cet-930a-et/.

22. Jeff King, email to author, 16 February 2021.

23. "WFA International," Women's Football Alliance, accessed 9 March 2022, https://wfaprofootball.com/wfa-international/.

24. Women's Football Alliance, "WFA International Announces 2022 Game in Mexico City," Facebook, 25 February 2022, https://www.facebook.com /wfafootball.

25. Rozendaal, *Women's Football Encyclopedia*, 73–109.

26. Neal Rozendaal, "2017 Season Review," Neal Rozendaal website, accessed 27 January 2019, http://nealrozendaal.com/wp-content/uploads/2017 /08/2017-WFE-U.S.-Addendum.pdf.

27. "WFA Teams by State," Women's Football Alliance, accessed 27 January 2019, http://www.wfaprofootball.com/teams-by-state/.

28. Neal Rozendaal, "2016 U.S. Women's Football Leagues Addendum," Neal Rozendaal website, accessed 27 January 2019, http://nealrozendaal.com /wp-content/uploads/2016/09/2016-WFE-U.S.-Addendum.pdf.

29. "Women's Football Alliance," Hosted Sports, accessed 27 January 2019, https://www.hostedsports.com/league_data.asp?league=wfa.

30. Mark Staffieri, "Boston Militia Makes History as First Team to Capture Two WFA National Titles," *Fourth and Feminine*, 10 September 2014, https://fourthandfeminine.wordpress.com/2014/09/10/boston-militia -makes-history-as-first-team-to-capture-two-wfa-national-titles/.

31. "About the Team," Boston Renegades, accessed 4 March 2019, https://bostonrenegadesfootball.com/about-the-team/.

32 . Sam Goresh, "From Militia to Renegades: Women's Football Returns to Somerville," Wicked Local Somerville, *Somerville Journal*, 30 April 2015, https://www.bostonrenegadesfootball.org/wp-content/uploads/2015/05/From-Militia-to-Renegades_-Womens-football-returns-to-Somerville-Gate-House.pdf.

33. Goresh, "From Militia to Renegades."

34. Goresh, "From Militia to Renegades."

35. "Female Football Players Demand Respect from the NFL and a Professional League of Their Own," Change.org, accessed 4 March 2019, https://www.change.org/p/whenwnfl?recruiter=836313666&utm_source=share_petition&utm_medium=facebook&utm_campaign=psf_combo_share_initial.pacific_post_sap_share_gmail_abi.gmail_abi&utm_term=tap_basic_share&recruited_by_id=422ed410-ce20-11e7-8b80-05b1e5dc5d88&utm_content=fht-14243095-en-us%3Av5.

36. Russ Crawford, "Women's Football Arrives at Super Bowl LIII," *American Football International*, 6 February 2019, https://www.americanfootballinternational.com/women-athletes-gained-major-recognition-during-super-bowl-liii/.

37. Interview with Elizabeth Jenkins conducted by author, Bellevue NE, 11 May 2019.

38. Ken Belson and Victor Mather, "Patriots Owner Robert Kraft's Arraignment Is Scheduled for March 28," *New York Times*, 7 March 2019, https://www.nytimes.com/2019/03/07/sports/patriots-robert-kraft-charges.html.

39. Alex Wong, " A Season with the Sharks, New York's Pro Women's Football Team," *BuzzFeed*, 5 February 2017, https://www.buzzfeednews.com/article/stevenlebron/a-season-with-the-sharks-new-yorks-pro-womens-football-team.

40. "Israel Football League," *American Football International*, accessed 8 March 2019, https://www.americanfootballinternational.com/members/israel-football-league/.

41. Women's Football Alliance, "2018 WFA Championship on ESPN," YouTube, 29 September 2018, https://www.youtube.com/watch?v=kDn5SC2db_4.

42. Gridiron Queendom, "Boston Militia White House Visit Nov 2014," You-Tube, 26 January 2015, https://www.youtube.com/watch?v=n4s_bltrn_4 &t=34s.

43. "A New Milestone in Women's Sports and Football History," Boston Renegades, 16 May 2016, https://www.bostonrenegadesfootball.org/cahill -notches-100th-career-victory/.

44. Gridiron Queendom, "Boston Militia White House Visit."

45. Neal Rozendaal, "The Greatest Players in Women's Football History: Part 3," Neal Rozendaal website, accessed 5 March 2019, http://nealrozendaal .com/womensfootball/greatest-players-history-2017-part-3/.

46. Gridiron Queendom, "Boston Militia White House Visit."

47. Gridiron Queendom, "Boston Militia White House Visit."

48. Mark Staffieri, "Boston Militia Superstar Adrienne Smith Sets the Gold Standard with Team USA Documentary," *Fourth and Feminine*, 4 February 2014, https://fourthandfeminine.wordpress.com/2014/02/04/boston -militia-superstar-adrienne-smith-sets-the-gold-standard-with-team-usa -documentary/.

49. "Female Tackle Football Champion Inducted into Hall of Fame," MENAFN-PR URgent, 20 November 2018, https://menafn.com /1097722404/Female-Tackle-Football-Champion-Inducted-into-Hall -of-Fame.

50. "Boston Renegades Notch Victory in First Franchise Game," Boston Renegades Football, 18 April 2015, https://www.bostonrenegadesfootball .org/boston-renegades-notch-victory-in-first-franchise-game/.

51. Interview of Sarah Viola conducted by author, Ada OH, via Facebook Messenger, 11 September 2017.

52. Kaz Nagatsuka, "Kokura Finds Inspiration, Strength on Football Field," *Japan Times*, 28 March 2011, https://www.japantimes.co.jp/sports/2011/03 /28/more-sports/football/kokura-finds-inspiration-strength-on-football -field/#.XH2agehKiUl.

53. "Noriko Kokura, #81," Boston Renegades Football, accessed 4 March 2019, https://bostonrenegadesfootball.com/player/kokura-noriko/.

54. Interview with Elisa De Santis conducted by author, Ada OH, via Facebook Messenger, 13 August 2017 and 18 March 2018.

55. Mark Simon, "Mission Compl3te," Boston Renegades, 24 July 2021, https:// www.bostonrenegadesfootball.org/mission-compl3te/.

56. Neal Rozendaal, "Three-Point Playoff Loss Dashes Divas' Three-Peat Hopes, 27–24," D.C. Divas Football, Facebook post, 19 June 2017, https://m.facebook.com/dcdivasfootball/posts/10155292951870772.

57. "Franchise History," D.C. Divas, accessed 5 March 2019, http://dcdivas .com/history/.

58. "Tea Törmänen," D.C. Divas, accessed 5 March 2019, http://dcdivas.com /team/players/tea-tormanen/.

59. Mark Staffieri, "Allyson Hamlin Becomes First Quarterback in Washington Football History to Reach 200 TD Passes," *Fourth and Feminine*, 16 June 2015, https://fourthandfeminine.wordpress.com/2015/06/16/allyson -hamlin-becomes-first-quarterback-in-washington-football-history-to -reach-200-td-passes/; Ally Hamlin, Facebook post, shared by *Gridiron Beauties*, 5 January 2017, https://www.facebook.com/GridironBeauties /posts/1328576100519404.

60. Jenny Vrentas, "The Women Who Are Changing the Face of the NFL," *Sports Illustrated*, 18 August 2017, https://www.si.com/nfl/2017/08/16 /themmqb-women-nfl-coaches-training-camp-bills-falcons-jets-49ers -vikings.

61. D.C. Divas Football, Facebook post, 31 July 2017, https://www.facebook .com/dcdivasfootball/photos/a.380493205771/10155432253280772/ ?type=3&theater.

62. "Rachel Hahn," D.C. Divas, accessed 6 March 2019, http://dcdivas.com /team/players/rachel-huhn/; "Callie Brownson," D.C. Divas, accessed 6 March 2019, http://dcdivas.com/team/players/callie-brownson/.

63. Rich Cimini, "'Girl Scout' Details Groundbreaking Career, Life with the Jets," ESPN, 16 August 2017, http://www.espn.com/blog/new-york-jets /post/_/id/70353/girl-scout-details-groundbreaking-career-life-with -the-jets.

64. "Callie Brownson," Dartmouth Football, accessed 6 March 2019, https:// dartmouthsports.com/coaches.aspx?rc=2131&path=football.

65. "Callie Brownson," Cleveland Browns, accessed 13 December 2020, https://www.clevelandbrowns.com/team/coaches-roster/callie -brownson.

66. Paul P. Murphy, "Callie Brownson of the Cleveland Browns Is the First Female Position Coach in an NFL Game," CNN, 30 November 2020, https://www.cnn.com/2020/11/30/sport/first-woman-coach-nfl-game -trnd/index.html.

67. "Callie Brownson Makes History," Pro Football Hall of Fame, 12 December 2020, https://www.profootballhof.com/callie-brownson-makes -history/?fbclid=IwAR02avdHPJ9J9njM1F0_YdGEpJ-NTBDNr4wCmVJ mjpJHDd71qmAyaQi67lg.

68. Anthony Polsal, "Browns Announce Additions, Changes to 2022 Coaching Staff," Cleveland Browns, 25 February 2022, https://www.clevelandbrowns .com/news/browns-announce-additions-changes-to-2022-coaching-staff.

69. "Victorious Trailer," Vimeo, 2018, https://vimeo.com/148916313.

70. "Victorious: Women of the Gridiron. The Fourth Quarter Is Here!" *Indiegogo*, accessed 6 March 2019, https://www.indiegogo.com/projects /victorious#/.

71. "WFA 2019 Postseason," Women's Football Alliance, Hosted Sports, 2019, https://www.hostedsports.com/hsi_schedule.asp?from=league_data& league=wfa&season=2019.

72. San Diego Surge Women's Football shared Women's Football Hall of Fame Facebook post on Gallegos, 27 November 2018, https://www.facebook .com/148672595165845/posts/2251311498235267/.

73. Oscar Lopez, *Gridiron Beauties Blitz Radio*, 28 March 2018, https://www .blogtalkradio.com/gridironbeauties/2018/03/28/gridiron-beauties-blitz -radio.

74. "2019 Dallas Elite Team Summary for Weeks 1 through 11," Women's Football Alliance, Hosted Sports, 2019, https://www.hostedsports.com /hsi_schedule.asp?from=league_data&league=wfa&season=2019.

75. "2018 Standings," Women's Football Alliance, Hosted Sports, 2018, http:// www.hostedsports.com/football/league_standings3.asp?league=wfa& season=2018&division=WFA%20I.

76. Don Harrold, Facebook post in "Club Burmy: For Women's American Football Fans," 16 April 2018, https://www.facebook.com/libertocity /videos/2113715682182770/.

77. Mandi Woodruff-Santos, "Inside the World of Women's Tackle Football— Where Women Pay to Play," Yahoo! Finance, 30 March 2016, https:// finance.yahoo.com/news/women-s-tackle-football-iwfl-wfa-183132959 .html.

78. Interview with Michele Braun conducted by author, Ada OH, via Google Voice, 18 February 2018.

79. Interview with Laura Brown conducted by author, New Orleans LA, via Google Voice, 21 February 2018.

80. "About the Sharks," New York Sharks, accessed 7 March 2019, http://nysharksfootball.com/about-the-sharks/.

81. Interview with Laura Brown conducted by author, Ada OH, via Facebook Messenger, 7 March 2019.

82. "Allison Cahill, #7," Boston Renegades, accessed 7 March 2019, https://www.bostonrenegadesfootball.org/player/cahill-allison/.

83. "History," Minnesota Vixen, 7 March 2019, http://www.mnvixen.com/history/.

84. Interview with Laura Brown conducted by author, Ada OH, via Google Voice, 21 February 2018.

85. "Historical Standings and Stats," Minnesota Vixen, 2018, http://www.mnvixen.com/historical-standings-and-stats/.

86. Interview with Hank Patterson conducted by author, Columbus OH, 10 March 2018.

87. Patterson interview.

88. "Player Profile: Carrie Hall," Columbus Comets, 2018, http://www.columbuscomets.org/teams/default.asp?u=COLUMBUSCOMETS&s=football&p=profile&sportsHQ=COLUMBUSCOMETS&playerID=448673.

89. Rozendaal, *The Women's Football Encyclopedia*, 286.

90. Jody DiPerna, "Passion Play," *Pittsburgh City Paper*, 17 April 2008, https://www.pghcitypaper.com/pittsburgh/passion-play/Content?oid=1340093.

91. Rozendaal, *Women's Football Encyclopedia*, 287.

92. "2018 Pittsburgh Passion Team Summary for Weeks 1 through 10," WFA, Div. I, Hosted Sports, 2018, https://www.hostedsports.com/hsi_stats.asp?league=wfa&season=2018.

93. DiPerna, "Passion Play."

94. "History," Pittsburgh Passion Women's Football, accessed 8 March 2019, http://pittsburghpassion.com/history/.

95. Jennifer Yee, dir., *Pittsburgh Passion: Inside Women's Professional Football in the United States* (Back Light Productions, 2008).

96. Interview with Caitlin Kegley conducted by author, Ada OH, 2017.

97. Interview with Lisa Horton conducted by author, Columbus OH, 12 April 2018.

98. Interview with Shannon Helseth conducted by author, Cincinnati OH, 7 April 2018.

99. Interview with Pam Schreiner conducted by author, Cincinnati OH, 7 April 2018.

100. Rozendaal, *Women's Football Encyclopedia*, 162; Cincinnati Sizzle, WFA, Div. III, Hosted Sports, 2005–19, https://www.hostedsports.com/league _data.asp?league=wfa.

101. "2018 Cincinnati Sizzle Team Summary for Weeks 1 through 10," WFA, Div. III, Hosted Sports, 2018, https://www.hostedsports.com/hsi_stats .asp?league=wfa&season=2018.

102. Interview with Tamar Fennell conducted by author, Ada OH, via Google Voice, 17 April 2018.

103. Patterson interview.

104. "2018 Cleveland Fusion Team Summary for Weeks 1 through 10," WFA, Div. II, Hosted Sports, 2018, https://www.hostedsports.com/hsi_stats .asp?league=wfa&season=2018.

105. Interview with Jennifer Moody conducted by author, Tampa FL, 7 June 2017.

106. Monivette Cordiero, "Remembering Chris Bodman and Jahqui Sevilla, the First Two Pulse Survivors to Pass Away," *Orlando Weekly*, 7 June 2017, https://www.orlandoweekly.com/Blogs/archives/2017/06/07 /remembering-chris-brodman-and-jahqui-sevilla-the-first-two-pulse -survivors-to-pass-away.

107. Chris Connelly, "An Ambulance Shadow, a Timely Tourniquet and the Power of Teammates in Orlando Tragedy," ESPNW, 12 January 2017, http://www.espn.com/espnw/culture/article/17154818/orlando-anarchy -teammates-bond-tragedy-erupts-pulse.

108. Interview with Ty Baldwin conducted by author, Tampa Bay FL, 7 June 2017.

109. "2017 Orlando Anarchy Team Summary for Weeks 1 through 10," WFA, Div. III, Hosted Sports, 2017, https://www.hostedsports.com/hsi_stats .asp?league=wfa&season=2017.

110. Kyle Wescott, "DIV III Champs: Arkansas, Playing 'Old School' Football," Women's Football Alliance, 22 July 2017, https://wfaprofootball.com/2017 -div-3-championship-recap/.

111. "2018 Orlando Anarchy Team Summary for Weeks 1 through 10," WFA, Div. III, Hosted Sports, 2018, https://www.hostedsports.com/hsi_stats .asp?league=wfa&season=2018.

112. "2018 Tampa Bay Inferno Team Summary for Weeks 1 through 10," WFA, Div. II, Hosted Sports, 2018, https://www.hostedsports.com/hsi_stats.asp ?league=wfa&season=2018.

113. Interview with Jennifer Moody conducted by author, Tampa FL, 7 June 2017.

114. Erik Lacitis, "DUI Record Can Keep You Barred from Canada," *Seattle Times*, 30 September 2009, https://www.seattletimes.com/seattle-news /dui-record-can-keep-you-barred-from-canada/.

115. Joey Lafranca, "Women's Football Alliance Game Coming to Platts-burgh," *Press-Republican*, 3 July 2017, https://www.pressrepublican.com /sports/adult_youth_sports/women-s-football-alliance-game-coming -to-plattsburgh/article_a15d3c3f-273e-5b28-85f5-30f5e32323a2.html ?utm_content=bufferf5c1f&utm_medium=social&utm_source=twitter .com&utm_campaign=buffer.

116. Ameeta Vohra, "Saadia Ashraf, Pioneering Transition from National Team Player to Coach," Football Canada, 30 May 2017, https://footballcanada .com/news/saadia-ashraf-pioneering-transition-from-national-team -player-to-coach/.

117. Backseat Coach shared press release from the Montreal Blitz on Face-book, 18 October 2017, https://www.facebook.com/backseatcoach/posts /1414948938554285.

118. "2016 Tampa Bay Inferno Team Summary for Weeks 1 through 10," WFA, Hosted Sports, 2016, https://www.hostedsports.com/hsi_stats.asp ?league=wfa&season=2016; "2017 Tampa Bay Inferno Team Summary for Weeks 1 through 10," WFA, Div. II, Hosted Sports, 2017, https://www .hostedsports.com/hsi_stats.asp?league=wfa&season=2017.

119. "2018 Tampa Bay Inferno Team Summary for Weeks 1 through 10," WFA, Div. II, Hosted Sports, 2018, https://www.hostedsports.com/hsi_stats.asp ?league=wfa&season=2018.

120. Rozendaal, *The Women's Football Encyclopedia*, 314; for more on the St. Louis Slam, see seasons 2016 and 2017 at the WFA page at Hosted Sports, https://www.hostedsports.com/league_data.asp?league=wfa.

121. Sowanty89, "Laure Gelis-Diaz Women Professional Player High-lights," YouTube, 13 January 2009, https://www.youtube.com/watch?v =-kmRtmPeDkk.

122. "Coach Frenchy," Jennings Jr. Warrior Football, accessed 10 March 2019, http://www.kozlen.com/warriornation/frenchy.htm.

123. "Changes to the 2016 Season," Miami Fury Football, 16 January 2016, http://www.miamifuryfootball.com/2016/01/.

124. Mark Simon, "The Backseat Forecast for Week 9—6/2/2018," Women's Football Alliance, 2 June 2018, http://www.wfaprofootball.com/womens

-tackle-football-predictions-and-previews/the-backseat-forecast-picks
-for-week-8-6022018/?fbclid=IwAR0ja4LHiXju71CmJvEjIShjZ6eL
-t8wMQmAVs2pRSNtJM4veC0xtiR1H2w; "2018 Miami Fury Team
Summary for Weeks 1 through 10," WFA, Div. II, Hosted Sports, 2018,
https://www.hostedsports.com/hsi_stats.asp?league=wfa&season=2018.

125. "2017 Seattle Majestics Team Summary for Weeks 1 through 10," WFA,
Div. I, Hosted Sports, 2017, https://www.hostedsports.com/hsi_stats.asp
?league=wfa&season=2017.

126. "2017 Miami Fury Team Summary for Weeks 1 through 10," WFA, Div. II,
Hosted Sports, 2017, https://www.hostedsports.com/hsi_stats.asp?league
=wfa&season=2017.

127. Sean Fraser, "The BCS System Needs to Go," *Digital Journal*, 10 January
2012, http://www.digitaljournal.com/article/317685.

128. "Front Office Staff," D.C. Divas, accessed 10 March 2019, http://dcdivas
.com/team/front-office/current-front-office-staff/.

129. Neal Rozendaal, "The Massey Ratings and Women's Football," Neal
Rozendaal website, accessed 10 March 2019, http://nealrozendaal.com
/womensfootball/massey-ratings-and-womens-football/.

130. Coach Ashley Edmiston, *Four Point Stance*, Episode 17.2, accessed 19 April
2019, https://www.mixcloud.com/widget/iframe/?feed=%2F%2Fwww
.mixcloud.com%2FAshlyEdmiston1340am%2Ffour-point-stance-episode
-172%2F&hide_cover=1&hide_tracklist=1.

131. Gary Wolf, "The Data Driven Life," *New York Times*, 28 April 2019, https://
www.nytimes.com/2010/05/02/magazine/02self-measurement-t.html.

132. Jeff Kanew, dir., *Revenge of the Nerds* (20th Century Fox, 1984).

133. John Smith, "Kellen Moore and Boise State Broncos Expose BCS Fraud,"
*Bleacher Report*, 23 December 2011, https://bleacherreport.com/articles
/995339-boise-state-and-kellen-moore-expose-the-fraud-the-bcs-is.

134. Statistics for the Majestics and War Angels are available at "2017 WFA
I Statistics through Week 11," WFA, Div. I, Hosted Sports, accessed 19
April 2019, https://www.hostedsports.com/hsi_stats.asp?league=wfa&
season=2017.

135. "Road to the Championship," Women's Football Alliance, 2017, http://
www.wfaprofootball.com/wfa/wp-content/uploads/2017/07/PLAYOFF
-FINALS-2017.png.

136. Based on a comparison between "2018 National Rankings," Women's
Football Alliance, 2018, http://www.hostedsports.com/hsi_standings.asp
?from=league_data&league=wfa&season=2018, and "Teams by Divi-

NOTES TO PAGES 153–158

sion," Women's Football Alliance, accessed 20 April 2019, http://www
.wfaprofootball.com/teams-division/.

137. Michael Burmy, Facebook post, 9 April 2019, https://www.facebook.com
/100007530852265/posts/2284301955164144?sfns=mo.

138. "Meet the WFA's National Team Players," Women's Football Alliance,
accessed 19 April 2019, http://www.wfaprofootball.com/usa-football
-womens-national-team/.

139. "Teams by Division," Women's Football Alliance, accessed 9 March 2019,
http://www.wfaprofootball.com/teams-division/.

140. "Announcements," Iowa Crush, accessed 9 March 2019, http://www
.theiowacrush.com/.

141. "Houston Energy Surges into WFA," Women's Football Alliance, Facebook,
12 September 2018, https://www.facebook.com/wfafootball/photos/a
.409548020930/10157147548300931/?type=3&theater.

142. "New Teams Joining the WFA for 2018," Women' Football Alliance, 11
October 2017, https://wfaprofootball.com/new-teams-joining-wfa-2018/.

143. United States Women's Football League, accessed 19 April 2019, https://
www.uswfl.net/; "Teams," Women's National Football Conference,
accessed 19 April 2019, https://www.wnfcfootball.com/teams/.

144. "Roster," Los Angeles Warriors, accessed 19 April 2019, http://www
.lawarriorsfootball.com/teams/812367-Los-Angeles-Warriors-Womens
-Football-football-team-website/seasonal_roster; "2019 Cali Soldiers,"
Cali War, accessed 19 April 2019, https://caliwar.com/roster.

145. Women's Football Alliance, Facebook post, 10 October 2018, https://
www.facebook.com/wfafootball/posts/the-womens-football-alliance
-is-pleased-to-announce-that-the-cali-war-has-signed/10157214822
860931/.

146. Cali War Women's Football, accessed 20 April 2019, https://caliwar.com/.

147. Winston Churchill, BBC broadcast, October 1939.

### 5. THE X LEAGUE

1. Douglas Charles, "Well Shit, the Lingerie, I Mean Legends Football League
Just Went and Changed Their Uniforms for 2017," *BroBible*, 11 January
2017, https://brobible.com/sports/article/legends-football-league-new
-uniforms/.

2. Esteban, "LFL Tweaks Uniforms, Players to Wear Yoga Pants for the First
Time (Pics)," *Total Pro Sports*, 12 January 2017, https://www.totalprosports
.com/2017/01/12/lfl-new-uniforms-pants-pictures/.

330

3. Legends Football League, Facebook post, 30 January 2018, https://www
.facebook.com/mylfl/posts/lfl-unveiling-2018-uniforms-pictured-chicago
-bliss-away-unikickoff2018/10156048919782103/.

4. @MyLFL, "BREAKING: Shorts Uniforms set to make debut TONIGHT
in Seattle Mist vs Austin Acoustic game," Twitter, 21 July 2018, https://
twitter.com/MyLFL/status/1020729007992647680.

5. @MyLFL, "Fan Poll: Do you like the new Shorts Uniform?" Twitter, 24
July 2018, https://twitter.com/MyLFL/status/1021830504981483520.

6. Mark J. Burns, "With Series of Bold Moves, Legends Football League
Aims to Become a Global Sports Property," *Forbes*, 6 September 2014,
https://www.forbes.com/sites/markjburns/2014/09/06/with-series-of
-bold-moves-legends-football-league-aims-to-become-global-sports
-property/#739406b273a1.

7. Burns, "With Series of Bold Moves."

8. Anthony Sharwood, "Lingerie Football Players Demand to Be Paid for
Their Work," News.com.au, 28 July 2015, https://www.news.com.au/sport
/sports-life/lingerie-football-players-demand-to-be-paid-for-their-work
/news-story/9e39cd48e6976365a99736f91ad4e10d.

9. Spike Rogan, "Is the Lingerie Football League (LFL) Worth Seeing? A Can-
did Review," *Bleacher Report*, 13 December 2009, https://bleacherreport
.com/articles/307748-is-the-lingerie-football-league-lfl-worth-seeing-a
-candid-review.

10. Legends Football League, "LFL Week 11/2018 Season/Nashville Knights
vs Omaha Heart/Full Game," YouTube, 14 July 2018, https://www.youtube
.com/watch?v=-TcWk85X_n8.

11. Adena Andrews, "Women's Football Players' Passion Is Priceless," ESPNW,
30 July 2011, http://www.espn.com/espnw/features/article/6809422
/women-football-players-passion-priceless.

12. Amirah M. Heath, "Gridiron Goddesses: The Sport and Spectacle of Lingerie Football" (master's thesis, Pennsylvania State University, 2013), 31,
https://etda.libraries.psu.edu/files/final_submissions/7815.

13. mustangbarry, "lingerie-bowl-2003-highlight-reel," YouTube, 29 January
2007, https://www.youtube.com/watch?v=PlXM9hFqKtw.

14. mustangbarry, "lingerie-bowl-2003-highlight-reel."

15. Mary Connelly, "Dodge to Sponsor TV Lingerie Bowl," *Automotive News*,
1 December 2003, https://www.autonews.com/article/20031201/SUB
/312010743/dodge-to-sponsor-tv-lingerie-bowl.

16. "Lingerie Bowl Has New Sponsor," CNN Money, 13 January 2004, https://money.cnn.com/2004/01/12/news/companies/lingerie_bowl/.

17. Natalie Deibel, "Lingerie Bowl," in *American Sports: A History of Icons, Idols, and Ideas*, vol. 1, ed. Murray R. Nelson (Santa Barbara: Greenwood, 2013), 711–12.

18. Aman2k, "Lingerie Bowl 1—Sheena Mariano (2/1/2004)," YouTube, 9 December 2011, https://www.youtube.com/watch?v=90TD1bMaC_Y.

19. Rogan, "Is the Lingerie Football League (LFL) Worth Seeing?"

20. Patrick Hruby, "A Bust of a Lingerie Bowl," *Page 2*, ESPN, accessed 27 July 2019, http://www.espn.com/page2/s/hruby/040202.html.

21. Hruby, "Bust of a Lingerie Bowl."

22. Paul Bond, "Skins vs. Skins in Lingerie Football League," *Today Show*, 15 April 2004, https://www.today.com/popculture/skins-vs-skins-lingerie-football-league-1C9485550.

23. "MTV2 and the Lingerie Football League Score with 'LFL Presents: Friday Night Football on MTV2' Premiering September 3 at 11p," Cision PR Newswire, 17 August 2010, https://www.prnewswire.com/news-releases/mtv2-and-the-lingerie-football-league-scores-with-lfl-presents-friday-night-football-on-mtv2-premiering-friday-september-3rd-8pm-pt--11pm-est-100878699.html.

24. aman2k, "LINGERIE BOWL II Sheena Mariano (2/5/2006)," YouTube, 9 December 2011, https://www.youtube.com/watch?v=EVRTPcnI8Hw.

25. Heath, "Gridiron Goddesses."

26. Hruby, "A Bust of a Lingerie Bowl."

27. "Lingerie Bowl Full Cast and Crew," IMDb, 2004, https://www.imdb.com/title/tt0791320/fullcredits?ref_=tt_cl_sm#cast.

28. Anca Marcus, AncaMarcusFit, accessed 29 July 2019, https://www.ancamarcusfit.com/bio.

29. Alex Blair, "AFLW Star Jacinda Barclay Delves into Her Time Playing in the USA's Legends Football League," News.com.au, 19 March 2018, https://www.news.com.au/sport/sports-life/aflw-star-jacinda-barclay-delves-into-her-time-playing-in-the-usas-legends-football-league/news-story/18d51a4f1515d9bc43caa7beffc907b7; Mark Staffieri, "BC's Stevi Schnoor Soars towards All-Fantasy Status," *Canada Football Chat*, 20 October 2016, https://canadafootballchat.com/bcs-stevi-schnoor-soars-towards-all-fantasy-status/; interview with Raphaëlle Duché conducted by author, Ada OH, via Google Voice, 2 May 2018; Louis Brewster, "Lingerie Football Becoming the Stuff of Legends," *San Bernardino Sun*, 4 May 2013, https://

www.sbsun.com/2013/05/04/louis-brewster-lingerie-football-becoming -the-stuff-of-legends/; Moisés Castañeda, "ANA GARZA/Primera Mexicana en jugar en la LEGENDS FOOTBALL LEAGUE," YouTube, 25 October 2017, https://www.youtube.com/watch?v=s89KGhdZOTk.

30. Darren Rovell, "NFL Owners Interested in Lingerie Football?" CNBC, 18 May 2009, https://www.cnbc.com/id/30811629.

31. Bobbi A Knapp, "Garters on the Gridiron: A Critical Reading of the Lingerie Football League," *International Review for the Sociology of Sport*, 18 February 2103, https://journals.sagepub.com/doi/full/10.1177 /1012690212475244.

32. Mary Buckheit, "Can We Take Lingerie Football Seriously?" ESPN, 12 June 2009, http://www.espn.com/espn/page2/story/_/page/buckheit %2F090612.

33. Five Stone, "LFL Lingerie Football League—Music by Five Stone—San Diego Seduction Tryouts," YouTube, 1 December 2008, https://www.youtube.com/watch?v=2_OJXBnS7fY&list= FL9lAdds8Td60EjWl9G4XJ3w.

34. George Diaz, "LFL Brings Fantasy to Football," *Orlando Sentinel*, 21 January 2010, https://www.orlandosentinel.com/news/os-xpm-2010-01-21 -1001210166-story.html.

35. Rashida Yosufzai, "Not 'Lean' Enough for Lingerie Football," *Stuff*, 16 December 2013, http://www.stuff.co.nz/life-style/9522786/Not-lean -enough-for-lingerie-football.

36. Jordan Ritter Conn, "The Lingerie Football Trap," *Grantland*, 23 July 2015, http://grantland.com/features/legends-football-league-womens -lingerie-football-league-mitchell-mortaza/.

37. Buckheit, "Can We Take Lingerie Football Seriously?"

38. Conn, "Lingerie Football Trap."

39. Elizabeth Suman, "Baltimore Charm Plays Football in Lingerie—Is Their Pay Skimpy Too?" *Baltimore Brew*, 4 October 2010, https://www .baltimorebrew.com/2010/10/04/lingerie-football-league-players-paid -less-than-8-an-hour/.

40. June Williams, "Lingerie Football Champs Demand Wages," *Courthouse News Service*, 9 September 2010, https://www.courthousenews.com /Lingerie-Football-Champs-Demand-Wages/.

41. Lauren Chval, "The Chicago Bliss Sells Tickets and Wins Championships, but Its Players Are Unpaid," *Chicago Tribune*, 19 October 2015, https://

www.chicagotribune.com/redeye/redeye-chicago-bliss-sells-tickets-and
-wins-championships-its-players-unpaid-20151019-story.html.

42. Conn, "Lingerie Football Trap."

43. Len Pasquarelli, "Lengthy Strike Has Mostly Been Forgotten," ESPN, 21
September 2007, https://www.espn.com/nfl/columns/story?columnist
=pasquarelli_len&id=3030311.

44. Conn, "Lingerie Football Trap."

45. Chval, "Chicago Bliss Sells Tickets."

46. Ty Schalter, "'The Truth Is Not Always Sexy': Inside the Legends Football
League," *Vice News*, 29 September 2015, https://www.vice.com/en_us
/article/3d93a8/the-truth-is-not-always-sexy-inside-the-legends-football
-league.

47. Kyle Munzenreider, "Miami Lingerie Football Player Ashley Helmstetter Strips for Playboy," *Miami New Times*, 19 January 2011, https://www
.miaminewtimes.com/news/miami-lingerie-football-player-ashley
-helmstetter-strips-for-playboy-6546795.

48. Ryan Dilbert, "Summer Rae's Lingerie Football League Stint Prepared
Her for WWE Spotlight," *Bleacher Report*, 20 October 2015, https://
bleacherreport.com/articles/2580001-summer-raes-lingerie-football
-league-stint-prepared-her-for-wwe-spotlight.

49. Brad Rock, "New Lingerie Football Is a Joke and Not a Real Sport," *Deseret
News*, 22 July 2009, https://www.deseret.com/2009/7/22/20330296/new
-lingerie-football-is-a-joke-and-not-a-real-sport.

50. Rock, "New Lingerie Football."

51. Neal Rozendaal, *The Women's Football Encyclopedia* (Rockville MD: Roze-
hawk, 2016), 363.

52. Rozendaal, *Women's Football Encyclopedia*, 363.

53. I continue to spell out the league's name since in 2013 the Lingerie Football League rebranded as the Legends Football League, which allowed
Mortaza to keep the LFL designation.

54. R. Thomas Umstead, "MTV2 to Air Lingerie Football League Content,"
*Multichannel News*, 17 August 2010, https://www.multichannel.com/news
/mtv2-air-lingerie-football-league-content-362980.

55. Adam Wells, "Paris Jackson: Lingerie Football League Crosses the
Line Recruiting 13-Year Old," *Bleacher Report*, 19 October 2011, https://
bleacherreport.com/articles/901505-paris-jackson-lingerie-football
-league-crosses-line-recruiting-13-year-old.

56. Sarah Fitzmaurice and Mike Larkin, "Showing the Boys How It's Done!" *Daily Mail*, 26 October 2011, https://www.dailymail.co.uk/tvshowbiz /article-2053557/Paris-Jackson-shows-football-skills-girl-team.html.

57. Liz Sowers, "Lingerie Football," YouTube, 11 December 2011, https:// www.youtube.com/watch?v=3x6jMqUScho.

58. Audie Cornish, "How Katie Sowers Became the 2nd Woman to Coach Full-Time in the NFL," National Public Radio, 29 March 2019, https:// www.npr.org/2019/03/29/708170974/how-katie-sowers-became-the -second-woman-to-coach-full-time-in-the-nfl; "Kansas City Titans Team Summary for Weeks 1 through 11," WFA, Div. I, Hosted Sports, 2019, http://www.hostedsports.com/football/team_stats.asp?league=wfa& season=2019&selected_team=Titans&tier=.

59. Rozendaal, *Women's Football Encyclopedia*, 357.

60. Rozendaal, *Women's Football Encyclopedia*, 360.

61. Rozendaal, *Women's Football Encyclopedia*, 358.

62. Rozendaal, *Women's Football Encyclopedia*, 363.

63. Rozendaal, *Women's Football Encyclopedia*, 366–71.

64. Dr. Jen Welter, *Play Big: Lessons in Being Limitless from the First Woman to Coach in the NFL* (New York: Seal Press, 2017), 99–100.

65. "Lingerie Football League and MTV Return to the Gridiron with a New Season of 'LFL Presents: Friday Night Football on MTV2' to Premiere Friday, August 26th Live at 10pm ET," Cision PR Newswire, 24 August 2011, https://www.prnewswire.com/news-releases/lingerie-football-league -and-mtv2-return-to-the-gridiron-with-a-new-season-of-lfl-presents -friday-night-football-on-mtv2-to-premiere-friday-august-26th-live-at -10pm-et-128306933.html.

66. "Lingerie Football League and MTV."

67. Megan Stewart, "Pigskin and Lace," *Vancouver Courier*, 8 June 2012, https://www.vancourier.com/news/pigskin-and-lace-1.375717.

68. "Lingerie Football League and MTV."

69. Juju Chang and Allison Markowitz, "Lingerie Football: So Sexy or Just Sexist? Female Players Say They Love the Game," *ABC News Nightline*, 20 September 2013, https://abcnews.go.com/Entertainment/lingerie -football-sexy-sexist-female-players-love-game/story?id=20318487.

70. Chang and Markowitz, "Lingerie Football."

71. Katrina Krawec, "Shaping and Being Shaped: Examining Women's Tackle Football in Canada" (master's thesis, University of Windsor, 2014), https:// scholar.uwindsor.ca/etd/5156.

72. Larry Brown, "Lingerie Football League's Toronto Triumph Team Members Quit in Protest," *Larry Brown Sports*, 20 October 2011, https://larrybrownsports.com/everything-else/lingerie-football-leagues-toronto-triumph-team-members-quit-in-protest/93751.

73. Krawec, "Shaping and Being Shaped."

74. Andrew Bucholtz, "Lingerie Football? Only in Canada," Yahoo! Sports, 14 April 2012, https://ca.sports.yahoo.com/blogs/cfl-55-yard-line/lingerie-football-only-canada-023255568.html.

75. Mark Staffieri, "Stevi Schnoor a Key Building Block for the BC Angels Defense," *Fourth and Feminine*, 2 January 2013, https://bleacherreport.com/articles/1466355-stevi-schnoor-a-key-building-block-for-the-bc-angels-defense; Mark Staffieri, "Superstar Running Back Tamar Fennell Lands in Las Vegas," *Fourth and Feminine*, 23 May 2015, https://fourthandfeminine.wordpress.com/2015/05/23/superstar-running-back-tamar-fennell-lands-in-las-vegas/.

76. Interview with Tamar Fennell conducted by author, Ada OH, via Google Voice, 17 April 2018.

77. Mark Staffieri, "Saskatoon Sirens Ready for Another Chance to Play for the Title," *LFL 360*, accessed 3 August 2019, https://www.lfl360.com/lfl-north-america/usa/saskatoon-sirens-ready-chance-play-title/.

78. Fennell interview.

79. Fennell interview.

80. Mark Staffieri, "Lingerie Bowl Canada I Game Recap," *LFL 360*, accessed 3 August 2019, https://www.lfl360.com/lfl-north-america/usa/lingerie-bowl-canada-game-recap-lfl360-com-mark-staffieri/.

81. "USA's Seattle Mist Dominate Canada's BC Angels in Pacific Cup Debut, 38–18," *LFL 360*, accessed 3 August 2019, https://www.lfl360.com/lfl-north-america/usa/seattle-mist/usas-seattle-mist-dominate-canadas-bc-angels-pacific-cup-debut-38-18/.

82. "Mist Still Perfect after Handling Dream 62–22," *LFL 360*, accessed 3 August 2019, https://www.lfl360.com/lfl-north-america/usa/mist-still-perfect-after-handling-dream-62-22/.

83. "B.C. Angels Players 'Devastated' at Cancellation of LFL Canada Season," *Abbotsford (BC) News*, 18 September 2013, https://www.abbynews.com/news/b-c-angels-players-devastated-at-cancellation-of-lfl-canada-season/.

84. "LFL Canada 2013 Season Postponed to 2014," *LFL 360*, 16 September 2013, https://archive.is/20130916201304/http://www.lfl360.com/canada /bc-angels/lfl-canada-2013-season-postponed-2014/.

85. "LFL Announces Major Australian Broadcaster and Premiers LFL on 7Mate Commercial," *LFL 360*, 11 September 2013, https://www.lfl360 .com/australia/lfl-announces-major-australian-broadcaster-premieres -lfl-7mate-commercial/.

86. "NSW Surge—the Journey to the Legends Cup," *LFL 360*, 5 February 2014, https://www.lfl360.com/australia/new-south-wales-surge/nsw-surge -journey-legends-cup/.

87. Kate Lundy, "Sports Minister Slams Lingerie Football League," *Mamamia*, 22 May 2012, https://www.mamamia.com.au/why-cant-they-do-this-with -their-clothes-on/.

88. Steven Raeburn, "Ladies 'Lingerie Football' Scores More Viewers than the A-League," *The Drum*, 16 December 2013, https://www.thedrum.com /news/2013/12/16/ladies-lingerie-football-scores-more-viewers-league.

89. Lisa Herbertson, "Legends Football League Cancelled, Lingerie-Clad Players Left Searching for New Competition," *Daily Telegraph*, 2 October 2014, https://www.dailytelegraph.com.au/newslocal/parramatta/legends -football-league-cancelled-lingerieclad-players-left-searching-for-new -competition/news-story/18c34f9048b05210a28dcfb669da4bd5.

90. "LFL Announces Expansion into Adelaide and Coopers Stadium," *LFL 360*, 23 March 2014, https://www.lfl360.com/australia/legends-football -league-announces-expansion-adelaide-coopers-stadium/.

91. Herbertson, "Legends Football League Cancelled."

92. "Calls for Seven to Cut Lingerie Football," *Sydney Morning Herald*, 3 December 2013, https://www.smh.com.au/entertainment/tv-and-radio /calls-for-seven-to-cut-lingerie-football-20131203-2ynyf.html.

93. R. Thomas Umstead, "Fuse Tackle's Women's Football League," *Multichannel News*, 8 April 2015, https://www.multichannel.com/news/fuse -tackles-women-s-football-league-389545.

94. Sarah Spain, "Legends Football League Is Still the Wrong Packaging for Women's Game," ESPNW, 14 October 2015, http://www.espn.com/espnw /news-commentary/article/13882332/legends-football-league-wrong -packaging-women-game.

95. Sarah Spain, "Women's World Football Games Join Coaching with Competition," ESPNW, 20 March 2016, http://www.espn.com/espnw/voices

/article/14944177/women-world-football-games-were-time-coaching
-competition.

96. LFL Playmaker, "Ashley Salerno Hits Allie Alberts," YouTube, 23 September 2013, https://www.youtube.com/watch?v=YfektQIvaSE; Very Real Reality, "Pretty Strong: Alli Reveals She's Dating the Enemy | Oxygen," YouTube, 16 November 2015, https://www.youtube.com/watch?v=pvSN80XXleg.

97. "Star WR Upset She Can't Date Opposing Player," TMZ, 21 November 2015, https://www.tmz.com/2015/11/21/legends-football-league-players-dating/.

98. "Historic Rivals Set to Begin New Chapter in 2018 Season Opener," LFL Talk, 4 December 2018, http://www.lfltalk.com/lfl-articles.

99. "Lingerie Football: You Have to See It to Believe It," Extreme.com, 14 October 2014, http://extreme.com/blog/outdoor/961/lingerie-football-you-have-to-see-it-to-believe-it; "Super Channel Kicks Off New Sports Programming Sub-Brand with the Acquisition of Popular US Sports Franchise, Legends Football League," Cision, 22 February 2017, https://www.newswire.ca/news-releases/super-channel-kicks-off-new-sports-programming-sub-brand-with-the-acquisition-of-popular-us-sports-franchise-legends-football-league-614476173.html; "LFL Announces US Sports Broadcaster Partner, Eleven Sports," LFL 360, 12 April 2017, https://www.lfl360.com/featured/lfl-announces-us-sports-broadcast-partner-eleven-sports/.

100. "Legends Football League," YouTube, accessed 3 August 2019, https://www.youtube.com/user/LingerieFootball.

101. Interview with Raphaëlle Duché conducted by author, Ada OH, via Google Voice, 2 May 2018.

102. Duché interview, 2 May 2018.

103. Duché interview, 2 May 2018.

104. X League, "LFL | Week 3 | 2018 Season | Omaha Heart vs Denver Dream," YouTube, 11 February 2022, https://www.youtube.com/watch?v=efEIsO0Clu4.

105. Duché interview, 2 May 2018.

106. Interview with Raphaëlle Duché conducted by author, Ada OH, via Facebook Messenger, 10–11 March 2020.

107. Interview with Bridget McDonnell conducted by author, Ada OH, via Google Voice, 5 March 2021.

108. Duché interview, 2 May 2018.

109. Duché interview, 2 May 2018.

110. Rick Paulus, "Lingerie League Goes Legit," SB Nation, 20 November 2012, https://www.sbnation.com/longform/2012/11/20/3649738/lingerie-football-league.

111. Brendan Foster, "Legal Action Aplenty as WA Lingerie Football Spat Turns Ugly," WA Today, 17 February 2015, https://www.watoday.com.au/national/western-australia/legal-action-aplenty-as-wa-lingerie-football-spat-turns-ugly-20150217-13h9ph.html.

112. Kearyn Cox, "Women's Gridiron Players Ditch Skimpy Uniforms to Tackle Full-Contact League," ABC News, 20 August 2017, https://www.abc.net.au/news/2017-08-20/gridiron-west-womens-league-launched-in-perth/8814510; Krawec, "Shaping and Being Shaped," 5.

113. Patrick Seitz, "Mexico Loves Bikini Football," Tech-media-tainment, 7 February 2016, https://techmediatainment.blogspot.com/2016/02/mexico-loves-bikini-football.html; Women's Football League, accessed 4 August 2019, https://www.wfl.com.mx/.

114. Interview with Carly Machuca and Paulina Vidal conducted by author, Ada OH, via Facebook Messenger, 2 February 2018.

115. "LFL Nations League of Europe Announces Strategy and Inaugural Season," LFL 360, 8 January 2019, https://www.lfl360.com/europa/lfl-nations-league-of-europe-announces-strategy-and-inaugural-season/.

116. Interview with Kanessa Muluneh-Coerman conducted by author, Ada OH, via Facebook Messenger, 16 January 2018.

117. Steve DelVecchio, "LFL Players Protesting the National Anthem," Larry Brown Sports, 24 May 2017, https://larrybrownsports.com/everything-else/lfl-players-protesting-national-anthem/371505.

118. Brett Bodner, "Legends Football League, Formerly Lingerie League, Says All Players Will Stand for National Anthem," New York Daily News, 28 September 2017, https://www.nydailynews.com/sports/more-sports/lfl-players-stand-national-anthem-article-1.3528185.

119. "Lingerie Bowl III National Media Day," Bodog.com, accessed 5 August 2019, https://www.gettyimages.com/detail/news-photo/los-angeles-temptations-during-bodog-com-lingerie-bowl-iii-news-photo/115402322; "Team," LFL, accessed 5 August 2019, https://lflus.com/latemptation/player?id=19.

120. Bliss rosters, accessed 8 August 2019, https://www.lfl360.com/lfl-north-america/usa/game-23-bliss-roster/; https://lflus.com/chicagobliss/player?id=20. Temptation rosters, accessed 8 August 2019, https://

lflus.com/latemptation; https://www.lfl360.com/lfl-north-america/usa
/temptation-release-active-roster/.

121. Bridgett McDonnell interview.

122. Liz Lohuis and Stuart Ervin, "Lingerie Football League Comes to Nashville under New Name," WSMV NEWS4 National, 8 November 2017, https://www.wsmv.com/news/lingerie-football-league-comes-to-nashville-under-new-name/article_45e42d81-9172-5a7f-be3e-8b7143c4c27d.html.

123. Mitchell Mortaza announcement, posted by Michael Burmy, "The LFL Is Dead. My Thoughts in the Comments," Facebook, 13 December 2019, https://www.facebook.com/photo.php?fbid=2479267689000902&set=gm.3101185773243777&type=3&theater&ifg=1.

124. X League, "Extreme Football League (X League). The Beginning," YouTube, 17 December 2019, https://www.youtube.com/watch?v=bn1QH-E5KuM&feature=youtu.be&fbclid=IwAR0kntv2L9pCPkW34YPG0FdLfVEm2k9eWP1CW2aniFIqX9mU2PY6s172874.

125. X League press release, 15 January 2020, https://extfl.com/xwire/.

126. Barry Werner, "Chicago Bears Legend Mike Ditka Becomes Owner of Women's Football X League," *TouchdownWire*, 14 July 2020, https://touchdownwire.usatoday.com/2020/07/14/chicago-bears-mike-ditka-x-league-womens-football-lingerie-football-league/.

127. "2022 Season Schedule," X League, accessed 9 March 2022, https://xleague.live/schedule/.

### 6. THE WOMEN'S NATIONAL FOOTBALL CONFERENCE

1. Neal Rozendaal, *The Women's Football Encyclopedia* (Rockville MD: Rozehawk, 2016), 333.

2. Best of the West Championship, "Utah Falconz vs. Texas Elite Spartans Championship Game 2018," YouTube, 24 July 2018, https://www.youtube.com/watch?v=rESnboEXiqQ.

3. Louise Matthews Bean, Facebook post, 3 December 2018, https://www.facebook.com/photo.php?fbid=1677583322294648&set=a.860408027345519&type=3&theater.

4. Interview with Louise Matthews Bean conducted by author, Ada OH, via Facebook Messenger, 29 December 2019.

5. Oscar Lopez, "Gridiron Beauties Blitz Radio—Episode 225," *Blog Talk Radio*, 6 June 2018, https://www.blogtalkradio.com/gridironbeauties/2018/06/06/gridiron-beauties-blitz-radio.

6. Lopez, "Gridiron Beauties Blitz Radio."

7. Lopez, "Gridiron Beauties Blitz Radio."

8. Lopez, "Gridiron Beauties Blitz Radio."

9. Lopez, "Gridiron Beauties Blitz Radio."

10. Lopez, "Gridiron Beauties Blitz Radio."

11. Utah Falconz, "Best of the West Women's Football Championship Coming to Las Vegas," Facebook, 5 June 2018, https://www.facebook .com/notes/best-of-the-west-womens-football-championship /best-of-the-west-womens-football-championship-coming-to-las-vegas /891118421094766/.

12. Interview with Louise Matthews Bean conducted by author, Ada OH, via Facebook Messenger, 31 December 2019.

13. "Recommendations and Reviews," Best of the West Women's Football Championship Facebook page, accessed 31 December 2019, https://www .facebook.com/bestofthewestfootball/.

14. Michael Burmy, "Round 1 Recap," Seattle Majestics vs. Utah Falconz, Facebook, 20 July 2018, https://www.facebook.com/photo.php?fbid= 2110777052516636&set=gm.2187629024599461&type=3&theater.

15. Michael Burmy, "Round 1 Recap," San Diego Surge vs. Texas Elite Spartans, Facebook, 20 July 2018, https://www.facebook.com/photo.php?fbid =2111197905807884&set=gm.2188331234529240&type=3&theater.

16. Best of the West Championship, "San Diego Surge vs Seattle Majestics," YouTube, 25 July 2018, https://www.youtube.com/watch?v =JQnDVe-hzEE&fbclid=IwAR35Gamo9yZdoZUVrMjeu1B7Y7jgxgv5fsDv R3DaSqcGlzppTTH0pnJPYIo.

17. Best of the West Championship YouTube Channel, accessed 31 December 2019, https://www.youtube.com/channel/UCwKoC1fH_9c8E-g_xGHYnkg ?fbclid=IwAR1-DwBbdJmspMToks5aiNiw5g5TcqT8Vs4ktUkBKLLUD9 _Sv6_XMhy_qK4.

18. Best of the West Women's Football Championship, "Best of the West Owners Forum," Facebook, 20 July 2018, https://www.facebook.com /bestofthewestfootball/videos/931705237036084/.

19. Interview with Scott McCarron conducted by author, Las Vegas NV, 20 July 2018.

20. McCarron interview.

21. McCarron interview.

22. McCarron interview.

23. WNFC, "The Pre-Season Rankings Are In, and Guess Who's on Top?" Facebook, 8 March 2019, https://www.facebook.com/notes/wnfc/pre-season-rankings-are-in-and-guess-whos-on-top/397372811061881/.

24. Kaye Michelle, "2019 Athletic Director of the Year for the State of Georgia," Facebook, 25 March 2019, https://www.facebook.com/photo/?fbid=2052914974763132&set=a.147491631972152.

25. Seattle Majestics Women's Tackle Football, "Best of the West Teams Rejoin Forces in WNFC," press release, Facebook, 28 October 2018, https://www.facebook.com/theseattlemajestics/photos/a.103704433028454/1965826363482909/?type=3&theater.

26. "Adidas Kicks Off Initiative to Break Down Barriers Faced by Women and Girls in Sport," Adidas, 10 December 2018, https://news.adidas.com/American-Football/adidas-kicks-off-initiative-to-break-down-barriers-faced-by-women-and-girls-in-sport/s/87fa878d-dbe4-4619-826d-f4b71e1b33cc?fbclid=IwAR3aPemD1RXpgfo1Yyal7Ie9u9_wjOk7xZmiu9TITV3qWwMpi4851e2EfQ.

27. "Women's Tackle Football Is Taking Over Denver, Colorado," Cision PR Newswire, 11 June 2019, https://www.prnewswire.com/news-releases/womens-tackle-football-is-taking-over-denver-colorado-300865647.html.

28. WNFC, "Breaking News!" Facebook, 11 June 2019, https://www.facebook.com/thewnfc/posts/-breaking-news-adidas-and-riddell-have-stepped-up-to-be-the-title-sponsors-of-th/449077402558088/.

29. "WNFC and USCREEN Join Forces to Launch WNFC TV," *Newswire*, 2 March 2019, https://www.newswire.com/news/wnfc-and-uscreen-join-forces-to-launch-wnfc-tv-20818550.

30. WNFC, "WNFC Becomes First Women's Football League (Who Does Not Charge Teams or Players) to Offer Cash Performance Prizes," Facebook, 30 March 2019, https://www.facebook.com/notes/wnfc/wnfc-becomes-first-womens-football-league-who-does-not-charge-teams-or-players-t/407931753339320/.

31. "News Release: WNFC Professional Women's Tackle Football Will Call Bellevue Home in 2019," Greater Bellevue Area Chamber of Commerce, 2 August 2018, https://www.bellevuenebraska.com/news/details/news-release-wfa-professional-women-s-tackle-football-will-call-bellevue-home-in-2019-08-02-2018.

32. Sylvie Aibeche, "III. Season X—Just Do You," Facebook, 23 December 2019, https://www.facebook.com/ObiSeven7/posts/2409028352760530?_tn_=K-R.

33. Oscar Lopez, "Episode 266," *Gridiron Beauties Blitz Radio*, 26 March 2019, https://www.iheart.com/podcast/256-gridironbeauties-30953596/episode/gridiron-beauties-blitz-radio-31318077/.

34. Nick Armistead, "LGL Exclusive: 'De Great One' Dani de Groot," *Crunch Magazine*, 16 January 2016, http://www.thecrunchmagazine.com/degreatone/?fbclid=IwAR3LlHF9Mu5AjzUOJCZ_nZHWcM1n6z9-ooiM0Mh6C1Uq3QD4BFu5dB9EK_o.

35. Nick Wilson-Town, "DC Catches Up with Chargers Gaby Knops ahead of Move to Seattle Majestics," *Double Coverage*, 6 December 2018, http://dblcoverage.com/dc-catches-up-with-chargers-gaby-knops-ahead-of-move-to-seattle-majestics/.

36. Uriel Parrilla, "Bruce Jurado, la mexicana cameona de football en US," *Diario AS*, 1 July 2019, https://us.as.com/us/2019/07/01/nfl/1562005671_485703.html.

37. "Meet the Texas Elite Spartans," Texas Elite Spartans, accessed 10 January 2020, https://www.texaselitewomensfootball.com/meet-the-spartans.

38. "Texas Elite Spartans Sign Renowned All American Linebacker for 2018 Season!" Texas Elite Spartans, 18 March 2018, https://www.texaselitewomensfootball.com/single-post/2018/03/18/TX-Elite-Spartans-Sign-Renowned-All-American-Linebacker-for-2018-Season.

39. "Meet the Texas Elite Spartans."

40. Gridiron Beauties, "Breaking News," Facebook, 28 December 2019, https://www.facebook.com/156585881051771/posts/2799633340080332/?d=n.

41. Interview with Louise Matthews Bean conducted by author, Ada OH, 28 December 2019.

42. Interview with Nausicaa Dell'Orto conducted by author, Ada OH, via Google Voice, 17 August 2017.

43. Atlanta Phoenix, Facebook post, 7 April 2019, https://www.facebook.com/AtlantaPhoenixFootball/photos/a.225770857470067/2096508363729631/.

44. WNFC, "Breaking News," Facebook, 28 December 2019, https://www.facebook.com/page/283554952443668/search/?q=mondragon.

45. Interview with Lizbeth Mondragon conducted by author, Ada OH, via Facebook Messenger, 10 January 2020.

46. "The Women's National Football Conference (WNFC) Is Officially Going Global," WNFC, accessed 10 March 2022, https://www.wnfcfootball.com/single-post/the-women-s-national-football-conference-wnfc-is-officially-going-global.

47. Wayne's World of Women's Football, "Playoff Teams Season Results," Facebook, 8 June 2019, https://www.facebook.com/2259537717437598 /photos/a.2261455177245852/2326960944028608/?type=3&theater.

48. "2019 Women's National Conference Standings," WNFC, Hosted Sports, 2019, http://www.hostedsports.com/football/league_standings1.asp ?league=wnfc&season=2019.

49. "WFA 2019 Post Season Week 1—Weekend of June 15 (9 Games)," WFA, Hosted Sports, 2019, https://www.hostedsports.com/hsi_schedule.asp ?from=league_data&league=wfa&season=2019; "WFA 2019 Post Season Week 2—Weekend of June 29 (6 Games)," WFA, Hosted Sports, 2019, https://www.hostedsports.com/hsi_schedule.asp?from=league_data& league=wfa&season=2019.

50. "2019 WFA I Team Statistics through Week 11," WFA, Hosted Sports, 2019, https://www.hostedsports.com/hsi_stats.asp?league=wfa&season =2019.

51. Interviews with Elizabeth Jenkins, Rachel May, Angelica Grayson, Jewelle Grimsley, Umeki Webb, and Rasan Gore conducted by author, Omaha NE, 11 May 2019.

52. Interviews with Jewelle Grimsley and Amber Kimbrough conducted by author, Omaha NE, 11 May 2019.

53. Interviews with Ashley Box and Jerrina "Snoop" Vaughn conducted by author, Bellevue NE, 11 May 2020.

54. WNFC, Facebook, 16 June 2019, https://www.facebook.com/thewnfc /photos/a.29465768000073/452515128880982/?type=3&theater.

55. "WFA 2019 Postseason Week 1—Weekend of June 15 (9 Games)."

56. Score Sports Bat Idea, "WNFC Championship Utah vs Texas IX Cup," YouTube, 29 June 2019, https://www.youtube.com/watch?v=imGvDgvwcrQ &t=2686s.

57. "Prodigy Join WNFC," Washington Prodigy, 15 December 2019, https:// www.washingtonprodigy.com/new-blog/2019/12/15/prodigy-join-wnfc.

58. "Standings," Women's Tackle Football League, accessed 18 December 2020, https://thewtfl.com/standing.

59. "Follow Your Favorite WNFC Now!" Women's National Football Conference, accessed 9 January 2020, https://www.wnfcfootball.com/teams.

60. WNFC, "WNFC Announces Partnership with RockTape as Official Sponsor and Kinesiology Tape Supplier for 2020 Season," Facebook, 30 December 2019, https://www.facebook.com/notes/wnfc/wnfc-announces

-partnership-with-rocktape-as-official-sponsor-and-kinesiology-tap
/591221088343718/.

61. WNFC, "WNFC Announced It's 2020 Schedule!" Facebook, 16 December
2019, https://www.facebook.com/notes/wnfc/wnfc-announced-its-2020
-schedule/578766519589175/.

62. Interview with Elizabeth Jenkins conducted by author, Omaha NE, 11
May 2019.

63. Jenkins interview.

64. Jenkins interview.

65. "About Us," Women's Football League Association, accessed 18 December
2020, https://wflafootball.com/.

66. D. A. Romo, "Ja Rule Announces Ownership of First Ever Paid Women's
Football Team," *Grey Journal*, 2019, https://greyjournal.net/work/money
/ja-rule-announces-ownership-of-first-ever-paid-womens-football
-league/.

67. Nicolas Niel, "WFLA: Qautre Molosses à l'assaut des USA (Partie 1)" [Four
Molosses storming the USA], *Café Crème Sport*, 3 September 2020, https://
cafecremesport.com/2020/09/03/wfla-quatre-molosses-a-lassaut-des
-usa-partie-1/.

68. Christelle Harnais, "Road to Las Vegas Devils," *Leetchi*, 2020, https://
www.leetchi.com/c/equipe-deurope-2020.

69. Lupe Rose, "Santia Deck Becomes the Highest Paid Multi-Million Dollar Player for the WFLA," IssueWire, 10 December 2019, https://www
.issuewire.com/santia-deck-becomes-the-highest-paid-multi-million
-dollar-player-for-the-wfla-1652221414316762.

70. Matt Weiss, "WFLA League That Signed Guam Women Loses Prominent Player, SEC Sues Owner," *Guam Daily Post*, 8 October 2021, https://
www.postguam.com/sports/local/wfla-league-that-signed-guam-women
-loses-prominent-player-sec-sues-owner/article_e3ad8a58-26f4-11ec
-8141-dfcf266e3c91.htm.

71. Russ Crawford, "Women's Football Arrives at Super Bowl LIII,"
*American Football International*, 6 February 2019, https://www
.americanfootballinternational.com/women-athletes-gained-major
-recognition-during-super-bowl-liii/.

72. Juwan J. Holmes, "NFL Coach Katie Sowers Wins This Weekend, Both
on Screen and Sidelines," *LGBTQ Nation*, 12 January 2020, https://www
.lgbtqnation.com/2020/01/nfl-coach-katie-sowers-wins-screen-sidelines
-weekend/.

73. Interview with Jim Farrell conducted by author, Ada OH, via Google Voice, 3 May 2018.

### 7. GIRLS TAKE THE FIELD

1. Ligia Braidotti, "Nomads Girls Team Experience Big Time Football: North Winnipeg Club Plays Cross-Border Games in Indiana," *Winnipeg Free Press*, 27 November 2017, https://www.winnipegfreepress.com/our -communities/sports/Nomads-girls-teams-experience-big-time-football -460295783.html.

2. Interview with Lisa Zueff-Cummings conducted by author, Ada OH, via Facebook Messenger, 5 November 2017.

3. Zueff-Cummings interview.

4. Interview with Kaity Cummings conducted by author, Mooresville IN, 18 November 2017.

5. Interview with Aiyana Hart conducted by author, Mooresville IN, 18 November 2017.

6. Interview with Faith Skaggs conducted by author, Mooresville IN, 18 November 2017.

7. Interview with Ale'sha Christy conducted by author, Mooresville IN, 18 November 2017.

8. Kyle Neddenriep, "All-Girls Tackle Football League Coming to Moores-ville," *Washington Times*, 3 July 2016, https://www.washingtontimes.com /news/2016/jul/3/all-girls-tackle-football-league-coming-to-mooresv/.

9. Christy interview.

10. Rachel Bachman, "Girls Who Love Football Rush into Their Own Leagues," *Wall Street Journal*, 5 September 2017, https://www.wsj.com/articles/girls -who-love-football-rush-into-their-own-leagues-1504623692#comments _sector.

11. Russ Crawford, "Canada v. USA in Historic Girl's 'Battle of the Border' Club Team Challenge—Part 2," *American Football International*, 29 November 2017, http://www.americanfootballinternational.com/canada-vs-usa -historic-girls-battle-border-club-team-challenge-part-2/.

12. Indiana Girls Tackle Football League, "Thank you to everyone for your support of the inaugural 'Battle of the Borders,'" Facebook, 19 November 2017, https://www.facebook.com/Indiana-Girls-Tackle-Football-League -991718354257796/.

13. Crawford, "Canada v. USA."

14. Braidotti, "Nomads Girls Team."

15. Zueff-Cummings interview.

16. Cindy Chan, "Girls to Tackle New Football Experience: Twenty-Seven Female Footballers off to Rock Hill, S.C.," *Winnipeg Free Press*, 23 May 2014.

17. Zueff-Cummings interview.

18. Interview with Brooke Pirrie conducted by author, Mooresville IN, 18 November 2017.

19. Interview with Montana Pirrie conducted by author, Mooresville IN, 18 November 2017.

20. Interviews with Sherisa Gretsinger and Gianna Donnelly conducted by author, Mooresville IN, 18 November 2017.

21. "What Does a Football Player Look Like?" Toledo.com, 10 October 2014, https://www.toledo.com/news/2014/10/10/toledo-local-features/what -does-a-football-player-look-like/.

22. Kaity Cummings interview.

23. "I'm a Girl and I Play Football! Young Players Meet the Toledo Troopers," YouTube, accessed 5 April 2018, https://www.youtube.com/watch?v= 9hUh9FROsA4&feature=youtu.be.

24. "Football Game by Girls," *New York Sun*, 23 November 1896, 4.

25. "Mount Pleasant, a Notable Indian Athlete—Girls 'Defeat a Boys' Eleven," *Rock Island (IL) Argus*, 8 December 1905, 15.

26. "Girls' Football Team? Sure! In Idaho," *Rock Island (IL) Argus*, 25 March 1921, 22.

27. Katie Taylor, "From Camp to Sowers: A Needed History of Women Football Coaches," *Sport in American History*, 28 August 2017, https:// ussporthistory.com/2017/08/28/from-camp-to-sowers-a-needed-history -of-women-football-coaches/.

28. John Andrews, "Cavour's Lady Leatherheads," *South Dakota Magazine*, 15 February 2012, http://southdakotamagazine.com/cavour-lady -leatherheads.

29. Susan Cahn, *Coming on Strong: Gender and Sexuality in Twentieth-Century Women's Sport* (Cambridge MA: Harvard University Press, 1994), 63.

30. Sarah K. Fields, *Female Gladiators: Gender, Law, and Contact Sports in America* (Urbana: University of Illinois Press, 2005), 38–39.

31. Fields, *Female Gladiators*, 52.

32. "Participation Statistics (1969–2014)," National Federation of State High School Associations, accessed 7 May 2018, http://www.nfhs.org /ParticipationStatistics/ParticipationStatistics/.

33. Interview with Julie Ferguson conducted by author, Ada OH, via Facebook Messenger, 1 May 2018.

34. Interview with JoAnn Walthour conducted by author, Ada OH, via Facebook Messenger, 2 May 2018.

35. Interview with Gaylin Tutnick conducted by author, Ada OH, via telephone, 2 May 2018.

36. Associated Press, "Fla. High School Sacks Nation's Last Tackle Powder-puff Football Game," CBS News, 3 May 2016, https://www.cbsnews.com/news/florida-high-school-sacks-nations-last-tackle-powderpuff-football-game/.

37. "Tackle Powder-Puff Tradition Lives On in South Florida," *Orlando Sentinel*, 28 May 2016, http://www.orlandosentinel.com/sports/highschool/football/os-ap-jupiter-juniors-win-powder-puff-football-game-keep-tradition-alive-0528-20160528-story.html.

38. Amie Sardhina, "Jupiter Powderpuff 2017," Facebook, 21 February 2017, https://www.facebook.com/groups/418071681917617/user/100001611765746/.

39. Tony Terzi, "Nation's Longest-Running Powder Puff Game Draws Out Huge Crowds in Wallingford for 45th Year," Fox61, 23 November 2016, http://fox61.com/2016/11/23/nations-longest-running-powder-puff-game-draws-out-huge-crowds-in-wallingford-for-45th-year/.

40. Bailey Wright, "Lyman Hall Powder Puff Tops Sheehan, Wins Second Straight Samaha Bowl," *Wallingford (CT) Record-Journal*, 22 November 2017, http://www.myrecordjournal.com/News/Wallingford/Wallingford-News/Wallingford-powder-puff-teams-compete.

41. Jeremy Muck, "Getting Her Kicks: North Little Rock's Melton Zeroed in on Football Field," *Arkansas Democrat Gazette*, 18 November 2016, http://m.arkansasonline.com/news/2016/nov/18/getting-her-kicks-nlr-s-melton-zeroed-i/.

42. Luke Matheson, "2016 All-Arkansas Varsity Teams," ArkansasVarsity.com, 22 December 2016, https://arkansasvarsity.rivals.com/news/2016-all-arkansasvarsity-teams.

43. "California Lineman Eriana Pula Becomes First Girl to Earn Invite to All Star Game," *American Football International*, 18 December 2016, http://www.americanfootballinternational.com/california-lineman-eriana-pula-becomes-first-girl-earn-invite-star-game/?utm_campaign=coschedule&utm_source=facebook&utm_medium=John%20McKeon&utm_content

=California%20Lineman%20Eriana%20Pula%20Becomes%20First
%20Girl%20To%20Earn%20Invite%20to%20All%20Star%20Game.

44. Mirin Fader, "Drilling Kicks and Nailing Drills, Becca Longo Bids for
Starting Job on Adams State Football Team," ESPNW, 17 August 2017,
http://www.espn.com/espnw/sports/article/20357751/female-kicker
-becca-longo-bids-starting-spot-adams-state-football-team.

45. David Furones, "Hollywood Hills Female Quarterback Holly Neher
Throws Touchdown in Debut, and Makes History," *South Florida Sun Sentinel*, 1 September 2017, http://www.sun-sentinel.com/sports/highschool
/football/broward/fl-sp-hs-hills-neher-td-20170831-story.html.

46. Warner Todd Huston, "Teen Girl Makes History as First Female Football
Player to Score Points in Texas State Title Football Game," *Breitbart*, 21
December 2017, http://www.breitbart.com/sports/2017/12/21/teen-girl
-makes-history-first-female-football-player-score-points-texas-state-title
-football-game/.

47. Elizabeth Merrill, "Six-Man Forever," ESPN, 4 August 2017, http://www
.espn.com/espn/feature/story/_/id/20229005/high-school-girl-saves
-football-season-fading-texas-town.

48. Sabrina Villanueva, "Earn Your Stars," *Odyssey Online*, 31 October 2016,
https://www.theodysseyonline.com/earn-your-stars.

49. Karl Bullock, "Safety Antoinette 'Toni' Harris Joins Exclusive Company
with College Football Scholarship," *Sports Illustrated*, 19 January 2018,
https://www.si.com/college-football/2018/01/19/belthany-antoinette
-harris-woman-scholarship.

50. "Toni Harris Signs with Cali War for the 2022 Season!" Facebook, 21
February 2022, https://www.facebook.com/wfafootball/photos/a
.409548020930/10160282295080931/.

51. Bob Cook, "Ohio School Engaged in What Will Be Futile Fight to Keep
Girl off Football Team," *Forbes*, 16 August 2013, https://www.forbes.com
/sites/bobcook/2013/08/16/ohio-school-engaged-in-what-will-be-futile
-fight-to-keep-girl-off-football-team/#5adcb368301c.

52. Interview with Jenna Mitchell conducted by author, Ada OH, via Google
Voice, 11 May 2020.

53. Kevin Hirschfield, "Manitoba Pioneering Girls Tackle Football," Football
Canada, 24 June 2017, http://footballcanada.com/manitoba-pioneering
-girls-tackle-football/.

54. Zueff-Cummings interview.

55. Interview with Lisa Harlow conducted by author, Ada OH, via Google Voice, 23 May 2018.

56. Harlow interview.

57. "New Brunswick Junior Girls Football League," *Gridiron New Brunswick*, 28 October 2012, https://www.gridironnewbrunswick.org/girlstackle.html.

58. Harlow interview.

59. "About the Varsity Girls Football League," Football New Brunswick, accessed 4 March 2020, http://footballnb.ca/page.php?page_id=101633.

60. NB Varsity Girls Football via Facebook Messenger, 5 March 2020.

61. Martin Cleary, "Cumberland Panthers Will Start the First All-Girls Tackle Football Program," *Ottawa Sun*, 28 November 2019, https://ottawasun.com/sports/football/cumberland-panthers-will-start-the-first-all-girls-tackle-football-program.

62. Cleary, "Cumberland Panthers."

63. CFC Scout, "Ottawa's First Ever High School All-Girls Tackle Football Team Hits the Field," *Canada Football Chat*, 30 April 2019, https://canadafootballchat.com/ottawas-first-ever-high-school-all-girls-tackle-football-team-hits-the-field/.

64. Seahawks Minor Football Club, "Nova Scotia's First All-Girls Football Program!" Facebook, 1 March 2020, https://www.facebook.com/seahawksminorfootball/photos/a.490315027839853/1210196079185074/?type=3&theater.

65. "Tentative 2018 Schedule," Georgia Girls Tackle, accessed 6 April 2018, https://www.georgiagirlstackle.com/schedule.

66. Interview with Louise Ibsen conducted by author, Ada OH, via Facebook Messenger, 15 January 2018.

67. NFL, "Trail Blazers: Girls of Georgia," Facebook, 5 February 2020, https://www.facebook.com/NFL/videos/1065287720487897/UzpfSTIyMzgwOTc2MTA5MzkwNDoxNzcyMTk3NzY2MjU1MDg4/.

68. Jamie Warren, "Girls Playing Football: How Leaders Are Inspiring Young Women to Play the Game," ABC 15, 3 February 2020, https://www.abc15.com/sports/girls-playing-football-how-leaders-are-inspiring-young-women-to-play-the-game?fbclid=IwAR0otX9y88RwarJOv2sgfKbvCPgA6SyvCoF85Ihv70QJll3B-CtSZfLGl8Y.

69. Interview with Crys Sacco conducted by author, Ada OH, via telephone, 12 January 2018.

70. Cindy Boren, "Sam Gordon, 9-Year-Old Girl, Is Already a Football Star (Video)," *Washington Post*, 8 November 2012, https://www.washingtonpost

.com/news/early-lead/wp/2012/11/08/sam-gordon-9-year-old-girl-is
-already-a-football-star-video/?utm_term=.26e820815480.

71. Gabe Zaldivar, "Sensational Sam Gordon Becomes First Female Player on
Wheaties Box," *Bleacher Report*, 21 November 2012, http://bleacherreport
.com/articles/1417644-sensational-sam-gordon-becomes-first-female
-football-player-on-wheaties-box.

72. Euna Park, "How This Stigma-Defying Young Woman Started the First
All-Girls Tackle Football League," *UpWorthy*, 15 February 2018, http://
www.upworthy.com/how-this-stigma-defying-young-woman-started
-the-first-all-girls-tackle-football-league.

73. Sacco interview, 12 January 2018.

74. Caroline Picard, "The First All-Girls Tackle Football League Debuts in
Utah: They're Not Afraid of Big Hits—or Busting Stereotypes," *Good
Housekeeping*, 1 June 2015, https://www.goodhousekeeping.com/life
/parenting/a32758/first-girls-tackle-football-league-utah/.

75. Matt Bonesteel, "Utah Tween Girls Get a Tackle Football League of Their
Own," *Washington Post*, 22 May 2015, https://www.washingtonpost.com
/news/early-lead/wp/2015/05/22/utah-tween-girls-get-a-tackle-football
-league-of-their-own/?utm_term=.2cb9c355798b.

76. Sean Gregory, "Girls Can Tackle Football, Too," *Time*, 25 June, 2015, http://
time.com/3935253/girls-can-tackle-football-too/.

77. Eric Adelson, "Girls Tackle Football? Yeah, It's Happening," Yahoo! Sports,
26 May 2015, https://sports.yahoo.com/news/girls-tackle-football--yeah
--it-s-happening-150437166.html.

78. Jessica Luther, "The Rising Number of Girls Playing Football," *Teen Vogue*,
1 February 2017, https://www.teenvogue.com/story/girls-play-football
-females-teams.

79. Interview with Crys Sacco conducted by author, Midvale UT, 14 April
2018.

80. Interview with Lauren Dixon conducted by author, Midvale UT, 14 April
2018.

81. Interview with Olivia Green conducted by author, Midvale UT, 14 April
2018.

82. Interview with Lacie Jacobson conducted by author, Midvale UT, 14 April
2018.

83. Interview with Aria Wagaman conducted by author, Midvale UT, 14 April
2018.

84. Interview with Railey Tucker conducted by author, Midvale UT, 14 April 2018.

85. Interview with Macy Coester conducted by author, Midvale UT, 14 April 2018.

86. Adrienne Smith, "Famed Utah Teen Sues, Pursues High School Football," Gridiron Queendom, 19 September 2017, http://gridironqueendom.com /famed-utah-teen-sues-pursues-girls-high-school-football/4960?utm _source=gridironqueendom.com&utm_medium=article&utm_campaign =es_b1.

87. Brandon Judd, "Morning Links: Utah Youth Football Player Sam Gordon Delivers Strong Message during Super Bowl Festivities," *Deseret News*, 6 February 2018, https://www.deseretnews.com/article/865695684 /Morning-links-Sam-Gordon-receives-Game-Changer-award-Jamaal -Williams-talks-about-his-first-Lambeau.html.

88. Valkyrie Football, "NFL Honors Utah Girls Tackle Football with Game Changer Award," YouTube, 22 June 2018, https://www.youtube.com /watch?v=7W_qyjFUOr4&t=5s.

89. Interview with Sam Gordon conducted by author, Midvale UT, 14 April 2018.

90. Interview with Stephanie Bracken conducted by author, Midvale UT, 14 April 2018.

91. Interview with Maddie Bracken conducted by author, Midvale UT, 14 April 2018.

92. Sacco interview, 12 January 2018.

93. Bachman, "Girls Who Love Football."

94. Cheryl Reeve, Twitter, 26 February 2018, 9:36 a.m., https://twitter.com /natalieweiner/status/968193798403706880; Natalie Weiner, Twitter, 26 February 2018, 10:39 a.m., https://twitter.com/natalieweiner.

95. Julie M. Stamm et al., "Age of First Exposure to Football and Later-Life Cognitive Impairment in Former NFL Players," *Neurology*, 28 January 2015, http://n.neurology.org/content/84/11/1114.

96. Maxwell Strachan, "The Super Bowl Overshadowed a Disturbing New Study of Youth Football," *Huffington Post*, 3 February 2015, https:// www.huffingtonpost.com/2015/02/03/youth-football-concussions_n _6606554.html.

97. Sacco interview, 12 January 2018.

98. Comment section to Bachman, "Girls Who Love Football," 5 September 2017, https://www.wsj.com/articles/girls-who-love-football-rush-into -their-own-leagues-1504623692.

99. Interview with Michele Braun conducted by author, Ada OH, via Google Voice, 18 February 2018.

100. Frankie de la Cretaz, "More Girls Are Playing Football. Is That Progress?" *New York Times*, 2 February 2018, https://mobile.nytimes.com/2018/02 /02/well/family/football-girls-concussions.html?referer=http%3A%2F %2Fm.facebook.com%2F.

101. James Balm, "The Subway of the Brain—Why White Matter Matters," *On Biology* (blog), Biomed Central, 14 March 2014, http://blogs.biomedcentral .com/on-biology/2014/03/14/the-subway-of-the-brain-why-white-matter -matters/.

102. De la Cretaz, "More Girls Are Playing Football."

103. De la Cretaz, "More Girls Are Playing Football."

104. Jason Chung, Peter Cummings, and Uzma Samadani, "Does CTE Call for an End to Youth Tackle Football?" *Minneapolis Star Tribune*, 10 February 2018, http://m.startribune.com/does-cte-call-for-an-end-to-youth-tackle -football/473655913/#comments.

105. Chung, Cummings, and Samadani, "Does CTE Call for an End?"

106. Ken Belson, "Not Safe for Children? Football's Leaders Make Drastic Changes to the Youth Game," *New York Times*, 31 January 2017, https://www .nytimes.com/2017/01/31/sports/youth-football-wants-to-save-the-game -by-shrinking-it.html?smid=tw-nytsports&smtyp=cur; Andy Martino, "Football's Concussion Crisis Is Killing Former High School Players, Too," *Huffington Post*, 12 August 2018, https://www.huffingtonpost.com/entry/football -brain-injury-cte_us_598dc2dee4b0909642967529; Kelly McLaughlin, "Flag Football Is MORE Dangerous to Children than Tackle, Study Reveals as Fears over Long-Term Injuries Caused by Concussions Continue to Rise," *Daily Mail* (London), 14 February 2018, http://www.dailymail.co.uk/news /article-4224178/Flag-football-dangerous-children-tackle.html.

107. David Ariosto, "Former NFL Players Sue League over Head Injuries," CNN, 22 December 2011, https://www.cnn.com/2011/12/22/us/sport -nfl-concussion-lawsuits/index.html.

108. John Breech, "President Obama: I Wouldn't Let My Son Play Pro Football," CBS Sports, 19 January 2018, https://www.cbssports.com/nfl/news /president-obama-i-wouldnt-let-my-son-play-pro-football/.

109. Joe Delessio, "9 NFL Players Who Wouldn't Let Their Sons Play Football," *New York Magazine*, 14 November 2014, https://nymag.com/intelligencer /2014/11/9-nflers-who-wont-let-their-sons-play-football.html.

110. Daniel J. Flynn, *The War on Football: Saving America's Game* (Washington DC: Regnery, 2013), 1–2.

111. Flynn, *War on Football*, 20.

112. Flynn, *War on Football*, 21.

113. Flynn, *War on Football*, 21.

114. Flynn, *War on Football*, 23.

115. Jeannette Y. Wick, "Sports Injuries: Are Women More at Risk?" *Pharmacy Times* 80, no. 6 (16 June 2014), https://www.pharmacytimes.com/view /sports-injuries-are-women-more-at-risk.

116. Kaity Cummings interview.

117. Interview with Sydney Sessions conducted by author, Midvale UT, 14 April 2018.

118. Stephanie Bracken interview.

119. Montana Pirrie interview.

120. Tucker interview.

121. Coester interview.

122. Donnelly interview.

123. Interview with Natalie Hanson conducted by author, Mooresville IN, 18 November 2017.

124. Green interview.

125. Hampton Stevens, "An Intellectual's Defense of Football," *Atlantic*, 13 September 2010, https://www.theatlantic.com/entertainment/archive /2010/09/an-intellectuals-defense-of-football/62858/.

126. Interview with Noah Harris conducted by author, Mooresville IN, 18 November 2017.

127. Christy interview.

128. Dixon interview.

129. "Sam Gordon Wins Inaugural NFL Game Changer Award," *Sporting News*, accessed 26 April 2018, http://www.sportingnews.com /nfl/video/sam-gordon-wins-inaugural-nfl-game-changer-award /ewpmqlh1tfbv18rjmz7werz3p.

130. "Top NBA Finals Moments: Hobbled Willis Reed Inspires Knicks' Victory in Game 7," NBA.com, 17 May 2017, http://www.nba.com/top-nba-finals -moments-hobbled-willis-reed-inspires-game-7-1970-finals.

131. Alex Gelhar, "Pro Bowl Flashback Friday: Jack Youngblood's Broken Leg," NFL.com, 22 November 2013, http://www.nfl.com/news/story/0ap2000000285834/article/pro-bowl-flashback-friday-jack-youngbloods-broken-leg.

132. Barry Rothbard, "How NFL Teams Used to Treat Concussions: Ray Nitschke's Forearm," *Sportsgrid*, 21 October 2010, https://www.sportsgrid.com/real-sports/nfl/how-nfl-teams-used-to-treat-concussions-ray-nitschkes-forearm/.

133. Scooby Axson, "'Concussion' Doctor: Letting Kids Play Football Is 'Definition of Child Abuse,'" SI.com, 8 August 2017, https://www.si.com/nfl/2017/08/08/bennet-omalu-cte-football.

134. Jacob Feldman, "Four States Considering Youth Tackle Football Bans," SI.com, 4 April 2018, https://www.si.com/nfl/2018/04/04/four-states-consider-banning-youth-football-themmqb-newsletter.

135. Ellen [no last name provided], "Limbaugh: NFL Protests Are Part of Left's War on Football, Patriotism and Masculinity," NewsHounds, 29 September 2017, http://www.newshounds.us/limbaugh_nfl_protests_left_s_war_football_patriotism_masculinity_092917.

136. Dave Zirin, "Is It Okay to Watch Football?" *The Nation*, 5 March 2018, https://www.thenation.com/article/is-it-okay-to-watch-football/.

137. "High School Participation Survey Archive," National Federation of State High School Associations (NFHS), accessed 27 April 2018, https://www.nfhs.org/sports-resource-content/high-school-participation-survey-archive/.

138. Roger Pielke, "Has the United States Reached Peak (American) Football?" Play the Game, 25 September 2017, http://www.playthegame.org/news/comments/2017/048_has-the-united-states-reached-peak-american-football/.

139. David Lange, "Number of Participants in Tackle Football in the United States from 2006 to 2018," Statista, 22 February 2021, https://www.statista.com/statistics/191658/participants-in-tackle-football-in-the-us-since-2006/.

140. Melissa Isaacson, "Who Says Girls Can't Play Football? Certainly Not 13-Year-Old Auburn Robertson," ESPNW, 9 November 2016, http://www.espn.com/espnw/sports/article/18004876/who-says-girls-play-football-certainly-not-13-year-old-auburn-roberson.

141. "High School Participation Survey Archive."

142. Gretsinger interview.

143. Sessions interview.

144. Stephanie Bracken interview.

145. Pamela Trotman Reid, Shauna M. Cooper, and Kira Hudson, "Girls to Women: Developmental Theory, Research, and Issues," in *Psychology of Women: A Handbook of Issues and Theories*, ed. Florence L. Denmark and Michelle A. Paludi (Westport CT: Praeger, 2008), 249.

146. Toni Liechty, Katherine Sveinson, Fleesha Willfong, and Kate Evans, "'It Doesn't Matter How Big or Small You Are . . . There's a Position for You': Body Image among Female Tackle Football Players," *Leisure Sciences* 37, no. 2 (March/April 2015): 119.

147. Russ Crawford, "Women's Football Arrives at Super Bowl LIII," *American Football International*, 6 February 2019, https://www.americanfootballinternational.com/women-athletes-gained-major-recognition-during-super-bowl-liii/.

148. Amy Donaldson, "Big Time: Players from Utah Girls Tackle Football League Invited to Pro Bowl to Showcase Their Skills," *Deseret News*, 21 January 2020, https://www.deseret.com/sports/2020/1/21/21074470/utah-girls-tackle-football-invited-pro-bowl-sam-gordon-national-football-league?fbclid=IwAR3FfDkhrlADm5X4kT1gpFgBSPlSxv1s9zEl-EhEKitbVK5Xz8bqeMFArvU.

### 8. AMERICAN WOMEN TACKLE THE WORLD

1. "Women's Football Training Camp in Round Rock," YouTube, 1 July 2010, https://www.youtube.com/watch?v=IaSUxodryd0.

2. Interview with Alicia Wilson conducted by author, Langley BC, 29 June 2017.

3. Interview with Laura Dye conducted by author, Langley BC, 29 June 2017.

4. Interview with Greta Medina conducted by author, Langley BC, 29 June 2017.

5. Interview of Suvi Mantyniemi conducted by author, Langley BC, 26 June 2017.

6. Interview of Nausicaa Dell'Orto conducted by author, Metairie LA, 24 February 2018.

7. Interview with Monica Lewinska conducted by author, Langley BC, 29 June 2017.

8. Interview with Jo Kilby conducted by author, Langley BC, 29 June 2017.

9. Interview with Sandra San Juan Chavez conducted by author, Langley BC, 29 June 2017.

10. Interview with Ana Greta Medina conducted by author, Langley BC, 29 June 2017.

11. Interview with Leah Hinkle conducted by author, Ada OH, via Google Voice, 29 March 2017.

12. Interview with Kellie Hopkins conducted by author, Langley BC, 29 June 2017.

13. NFL, "The Philadelphia Eagles Are World Champions!" Facebook post, 7 February 2018, https://www.facebook.com/Nfl/videos/10156094335 806263/.

14. Garrett Shea, "Request from USA Football," 29 August 2014.

15 "Women's World Championships," *American Football International*, 23 June–5 July 2017, http://www.americanfootballinternational.com/?s= women%27s+world+championship.

16. "WWC 2017—Schedule and Results," Football Canada, accessed 10 May 2018, http://footballcanada.com/team-canada/2017-ifaf-womens-world -championship/wwc-2017-schedule-results/.

17. Russ Crawford, "Brits Upset Finns in 2017 IFAF Women's World Championships Opener," *American Football International*, 26 June 2017, http://www.americanfootballinternational.com/2017-womens-world -championships-start-upset/.

18 Interview with Phoebe Schecter conducted by author, Langley BC, 29 June 2017.

19. Interview with Monica Lewinska conducted by author, Langley BC, 29 June 2017.

20. "Femenil Equipada 2015," LEXFA, 17 February 2015, https://arenafootball .com.mx/femenil-equipada-2015/; "Premundial Femenil," LEXFA, 28 May 2015, https://arenafootball.com.mx/premundial-femenil/.

21. "Premundial Femenil."

22. Interview with Andrea Romero Vasquez conducted by author, Langley BC, 29 June 2017.

23. Interview with Maria Fernanda Mandujano Abrego conducted by author, Langley BC, 29 June 2019.

24. John McKeon, "How We Got Here: AFI on the 2015 Canton IFAF World Championship," *American Football International*, 9 July 2015, http://www .americanfootballinternational.com/afi-on-the-2015-canton-ifaf-world -championship-how-we-got-here/.

25. John McKeon, "IFAF Elects New President in Canton Congress—Or Did They?" *American Football International*, 18 July 2015, http://www

.americanfootballinternational.com/ifaf-elects-new-president-in-canton
-congress-or-did-they/.

26. John McKeon, "Wiking's IFAF Faction Suspends Six Nations Including
the United States, Canada, Mexico, and Japan," *American Football International*, 18 September 2016, http://www.americanfootballinternational
.com/wikings-ifaf-faction-suspends-six-nations-including-united-states
-canada-mexico-japan/.

27. "2017 IFAF Women's World Championship Press Conference: U.S. &
Mexico," Football Canada, 25 June 2017, https://www.youtube.com/watch
?v=N17qjiCT-mQ.

28. "WWC 2017—Schedule and Results."

29. "WWC 2017—Schedule and Results."

30. Wilson interview.

31. Interview with Beth Thomson conducted by author, Langley BC, 29 June
2017.

32. Russ Crawford, "United States Beats Team Canada, Captures Gold at
Women's World Championship," *American Football International*, 2 July
2017, http://www.americanfootballinternational.com/united-states
-captures-gold-womens-world-championship/.

33. Football Canada, "2017 IFAF Women's World Championships Gold
and Silver Medal Press Conference," YouTube, 1 July 2017, https://www
.youtube.com/watch?v=NhU-lBF6hXs.

34. Paul Clarke, "Port City Loses World Football Tournament; Football Canada," *New Brunswick Daily Gleaner*, 17 July 2012, accessed via Nexis Uni.

35. Stacey Speer, "Catching Up with the Fans at the WWC," Women's Gridiron
Leagues of Australia, Facebook post, 24 June 2017, https://www.facebook
.com/wglaus/videos/658105144385926/.

36. Jacob Feldman, "World Championships Give Local Football Players a
Shot to Play for USA: Some Are Looking for a Second Chance; Others
Want One Last Chance to Suit Up," *Washington Post Blogs*, 28 June 2015,
accessed via Nexis Uni; Katina Caraganis, "Leominster Athletes Join U.S.
Team at Flag Football World Championship," *Fitchburg (MA) Sentinel &
Enterprise*, 12 August 2010, accessed via Nexis Uni.

37. "IFAF Increases Reach of Benchmarking Study by Surveying American
Football Stakeholders Worldwide," SportsFeautres.com, accessed 14 May
2018, http://www.sportsfeatures.com/presspoint/pressrelease/52334
/ifaf-increases-reach-of-benchmarking-study-by-surveying-american
-football-stakeholders-worldwide.

38. Kurt Badenhausen, "How a Sport Becomes an Olympic Event," *Forbes*, 9 August 2016, https://www.forbes.com/sites/kurtbadenhausen/2016/08/09/how-a-sport-becomes-an-olympic-event/#4033fdc22ce9.

39. Matt Douthett, "Local Man Named Coach of USA Women's Football Team," *Northwest Indiana Times*, 12 March 2010, http://www.nwitimes.com/sports/local/local-man-named-coach-of-usa-women-s-football-team/article_3f4cb2f2-1f83-59a5-be7c-2dd659cadf28.html.

40. Walter Reiterer, "IFAF Women's World Championship of American Football," *Bleacher Report*, 23 February 2010, http://bleacherreport.com/articles/350880-ifaf-womens-world-championship-of-american-football.

41. Mikael Roos, "Seeding," Svenska Amerikansk Fotbollförbundet, updated 7 June 2016, https://iof1.idrottonline.se/IdrottOnlineForbund/AmerikanskFotboll/svenskaamerikanskfotbollforbundet/forbundet/2010ifafwomensworldchampionship/Schedule/Seeding/.

42. Lauren Hickey, "Sweden Welcomes First International Federation of American Football Women's World Championship," International Federation of American Football press release, 21 June 2010.

43. Hickey, "Sweden Welcomes."

44. "History," Helsinki Roosters, accessed 15 May 2018, https://www.helsinkiroosters.com/naiset/historia/.

45. Hickey, "Sweden Welcomes."

46. Mikael Roos, "USA Records 63-0 Victory over Austria to Open First-Ever IFAF Women's World Championship," Svenska Amerikansk Fotbollförbundet, 2010, https://iof1.idrottonline.se/IdrottOnlineForbund/AmerikanskFotboll/svenskaamerikanskfotbollforbundet/forbundet/2010ifafwomensworldchampionship/Schedule/Results/.

47. Mikael Roos, "Canada's Stifling Defense Leads to Thrilling 12-6 Victory over Sweden in IFAF Women's World Championship," Svenska Amerikansk Fotbollförbundet, 27 June 2010, https://iof1.idrottonline.se/IdrottOnlineForbund/AmerikanskFotboll/svenskaamerikanskfotbollforbundet/forbundet/2010ifafwomensworldchampionship/Schedule/Results/.

48. Mikael Roos, "Finland Defeats Austria 50-16 to Set Up Intriguing Clash with Team USA," Svenska Amerikansk Fotbollförbundet, 29 June 2010, https://iof1.idrottonline.se/IdrottOnlineForbund/AmerikanskFotboll/svenskaamerikanskfotbollforbundet/forbundet/2010ifafwomensworldchampionship/Schedule/Results/.

49. Mikael Roos, "Germany Wins Defensive Battle against Sweden during Groups Play at the IFAF Women's World Championship," Svenska Amerikansk Fotbollförbundet, 30 June 2010, https://iof1.idrottonline .se/IdrottOnlineForbund/AmerikanskFotboll/svenskaamerikanskfotboll forbundet/forbundet/2010ifafwomensworldchampionship/Schedule /Results/.

50. Mikael Roos, "Canada Triumphs 20-12 over Germany to Earn Place in 2010 IFAF Women's World Championship Gold Medal Game," Svenska Amerikansk Fotbollförbundet, 1 July 2010, https://iof1.idrottonline .se/IdrottOnlineForbund/AmerikanskFotboll/svenskaamerikansk fotbollforbundet/forbundet/2010ifafwomensworldchampionship /Schedule/Results/.

51. Mikael Roos, "USA Shuts Out Finland 72-0 for the Right to Face Canada in the 2010 IFAF Women's World Championship Gold Medal Game," Svenska Amerikansk Fotbollförbundet, 1 July 2010, https://iof1.idrottonline.se/IdrottOnlineForbund/Amerikansk Fotboll/svenskaamerikanskfotbollforbundet/forbundet/2010ifafwomens worldchampionship/Schedule/Results/.

52. Mikael Roos, "Host Sweden Claims Fifth Place with a 20-18 Win over Austria at the 2010 IFAF Women's World Championship," Svenska Amerikansk Fotbollförbundet, 3 July 2010, https:// iof1.idrottonline.se/IdrottOnlineForbund/AmerikanskFotboll /svenskaamerikanskfotbollforbundet/forbundet/2010ifafwomensworld championship/Schedule/Results/.

53. Mikael Roos, "Finland Defeats Germany to Win Bronze Medal at the 2010 IFAF Women's World Championship," Svenska Amerikansk Fotbollförbundet, 3 July 2010, https://iof1.idrottonline.se/IdrottOnlineForbund /AmerikanskFotboll/svenskaamerikanskfotbollforbundet/forbundet /2010ifafwomensworldchampionship/Schedule/Results/.

54. Michael Roos, "Stats," Svenska Amerikansk Fotbollförbundet, updated 7 June 2016, http://iof1.idrottonline.se/IdrottOnlineForbund /AmerikanskFotboll/svenskaamerikanskfotbollforbundet/forbundet /2010ifafwomensworldchampionship/Schedule/Stats/.

55. Mikael Roos, "USA Wins Gold Medal at First Ever IFAF Women's World Championship of American Football in Sweden," Svenska Amerikansk Fotbollförbundet, 3 July 2010.

56. Bruce Hallihan, "Coleman Ready to Take on the World," Daily Gleaner, B1, 18 June 2010, accessed via Nexis Uni.

57. Kaitlyn Carr, "Tackling the Status Quo," *Baltimore Sun*, D6, 3 July 2010, accessed via newspapers.com.

58. "Local Players Help U.S. Breeze to Title Game," *Munster (IN) Times*, 112, 2 July 2010, accessed via newspapers.com.

59. Ben Karrson, "Women's Work," *Munster (IN) Times*, 12, 27 June 2010, accessed via newspapers.com.

60. "Menzyck, Konecki Lead Team USA to Gold," *Munster (IN) Times*, 112, 4 July 2010, accessed via newspapers.com.

61. Ken Karrson, "(View)pointing in a New Direction," *Munster (IN) Times*, 15, 27 June 2010, accessed via newspapers.com.

62. Dr. Jen Welter, *Play Big: Lessons in Being Limitless from the First Woman to Coach in the NFL* (New York: Seal Press, 2017), 121–22.

63. "Naisten MM-kisat Suomessa 2013," SAJL—Jenkkifutsiliitto, 11 June 2012, https://jenkkifutis.fi/info/historia/maajoukkueet/naiset/mm-kisat/.

64. "La historia de un equipo hegemónico," *LaLiga4Sports*, 14 June 2016, https://www.laliga4sports.es/noticias/la-historia-de-un-equipo-hegemonico.

65. Sergi Quitian, "El major futbol americano femenino del país está en Barberà" [The best female football in the country is in Barberà], *La Vanguardia*, 29 December 2012, http://www.lavanguardia.com/local/20121229/54358425969/mejor-futbol-americano-femenino-pais-barbera.html.

66. FEFA, "Rookies y Demons se juegan el título femenino," NFL Hispano, 2 May 2013, http://www.nflhispano.com/2013/05/02/rookies-y-demons-se-juegan-el-titulo-femenino/.

67. For the 2013 rosters, see "The Teams," IFAF, 2013, https://web.archive.org/web/20131206041037/http://www.wwc2013.com/the-teams/; for the 2010 rosters, see "Nations," Svenska Amerikansk Fotbollförbundet, 2010, http://iof1.idrottonline.se/IdrottOnlineForbund/AmerikanskFotboll/svenskaamerikanskfotbollforbundet/forbundet/2010ifafwomensworldchampionship/Nations/. For Tea Törmänen, see Neal Rozendaal, "2013 Team USA Members: Three D.C. Divas Selected for USA Football 2013 Women's National Team," D.C. Divas, 2013, http://dcdivas.com/history/honors/wwc-participants/2013-team-usa-members/.

68. "Spain vs Finland (June 30, 2013)," SAJL—Jenkkifutsiliitto, 30 June 2013, https://jenkkifutis.fi/info/historia/maajoukkueet/naiset/mm-kisat/.

69. "USA Defeats Sweden 84–0," International Federation of American Football, 30 June 2013, https://web.archive.org/web/20130706031312/http://www.wwc2013.com/2013/06/usa-defeats-sweden-84-0/.

70. "Germany Beats Sweden 25–14," International Federation of American Football, 2 July 2013, https://archive.ph/20130703014711/http://www.wwc2013.com/2013/07/germany-beats-sweden-25-14/.

71. "Canada Defeated the Dancing Spaniards," International Federation of American Football, 2 July 2013, https://archive.ph/20130703014625/http://www.wwc2013.com/2013/07/canada-defeated-the-dancing-spaniards/.

72. "Team USA—Sami Grisafe, Chicago Force," Women's Football Alliance, 11 January 2017, https://wfaprofootball.com/sami-grisafe/.

73. "USA Flying to Saturday's Finals," SAJL—Jenkkifutsiliitto, 4 July 2013, http://www.sajl.fi/?x167512=1419747.

74. Joe Frollo, "U.S. Women's Team: Our Journey to a Second Straight Gold Medal," Dr. Jen Welter's Blog from the WWC, USA Football, 9 July 2013, https://blogs.usafootball.com/blog/2065/u-s-women-s-team-our-journey-to-a-second-straight-gold-medal.

75. "Finland Bent on Canada 34–12," SAJL—Jenkkifutsiliitto, 4 July 2013, https://jenkkifutis.fi/info/historia/maajoukkueet/naiset/mm-kisat/.

76. "Sweden Played to Victory in Spain," SAJL—Jenkkifutsiliitto, 6 July 2013, http://www.sajl.fi/?x167512=1425446.

77. "Finland Took the Bronze Medal," SAJL—Jenkkifutsiliitto, 6 July 2013, https://jenkkifutis.fi/info/historia/maajoukkueet/naiset/mm-kisat/.

78. Frollo, "U.S. Women's Team."

79. "July 8th Sportstalk with Team USA Women's Football," WJLA ABC 7, 10 July 2013, http://wjla.com/sports/sports-talk/july-8th-sportstalk-with-teamusa-women-s-football-91211.

80. Mike Nieto, "Four Locals Part of World Football Championships," Northwest Indiana Times, 18 July 2013, http://www.nwitimes.com/sports/high-school/football/four-locals-part-of-world-football-championships/article_328add62-b5b3-5503-8977-3988f6e51950.html.

81. Nina Garin, "Player, Coach on the Ball; U-T Profiles Notable Local People," San Diego Union-Tribune, 23 February 2013, accessed via Lexis Uni; Marsha Chartrand, "MHS Alum, Elizabeth Okey, Football World Cup Champion," Manchester (MI) Mirror, 11 November 2013, http://themanchestermirror.com/2013/11/11/mhs-alum-elizabeth-okey-football-world-cup-champion/?fb_action_ids=639078385040&fb_action_types=og.likes&fb_source=other_multiline&action_object_map=%5B535000616577672%5D&action_type_map=%5B%22og.likes%22%5D&action_ref_map=%5B%5D; "Female Football Player Won't Rule Out Possibility of Pro

Football League for Women," CBS New York, 8 October 2013, http://newyork.cbslocal.com/2013/10/08/female-football-player-wont-rule-out-possibility-of-pro-football-league-for-females/.

82. "2013 IFAF Women's World Championship—Vantaa, Finland," Football Canada, 8 July 2013, https://www.youtube.com/playlist?reload=9&list=PLraqQHaL8M_u_ZJTEIp-Vvr7YyLaC4F5c.

83. Lars Borg, "LGSPORTS WWC Canada vs USA," YouTube, 14 December 2010, https://www.youtube.com/watch?v=lch-mvEtmSM.

84. wwc2013fi, "USA-CAN WWC2013 Gold Medal Game 6.7.2013," YouTube, 6 July 2013, https://www.youtube.com/watch?v=mMLTlo-dnbg.

85. "Canada Football vs U.S.A.," Ten Feet Sports and Entertainment, 30 June 2017, https://portal.stretchinternet.com/tfsetv/portal.htm?eventId=370618&streamType=video&utm_content=buffer933a4&utm_medium=social&utm_source=facebook.com&utm_campaign=buffer.

86. Zach Gratz, "IFAF Women Championship 2017, USA vs Canada," YouTube, 16 July 2018, https://www.youtube.com/watch?v=x_xQB4wgDuU&t=1918s.

87. "2013 Women's Team USA Tackle Football Fan Club," Facebook, launched 1 January 2013, https://www.facebook.com/2013WomensTeamUsaTackleFootballFanClub/.

88. "USA National Women's Tackle Football Team," Facebook, 2017, https://www.facebook.com/USWomensNationalFootballTeam.

89. Mansfield Daniel, dir., *Tackle the World—Tough Game/Tougher Women* (ESI Entertainment, 2014), https://www.youtube.com/watch?v=FhdTSDZmjyk.

90. Daniel, *Tackle the World*.

91. Daniel, *Tackle the World*.

92. Daniel, *Tackle the World*.

93. Daniel, *Tackle the World*.

94. Welter, *Play Big*, 124.

95. Vasquez interview.

96. Daniel, *Tackle the World*.

97. Elizabeth Faust interview conducted by author, New Orleans Saints Practice Facility in Metairie LA, 23 February 2018.

### POSTSCRIPT

1. Viridiana Lieberman, dir., *Born to Play* (Center for Independent Documentary, 2020), https://www.imdb.com/title/tt12615654/.

2. "Player Information: Cahill, Allison," Boston Renegades, accessed 4 July 2020, https://www.bostonrenegadesfootball.org/player/cahill-allison/.

3. Jim Fenton, "Brockton's Chante Bonds Is a Hit in Football," *Brocton (MA) Enterprise*, 25 August 2018, https://www.enterprisenews.com/story/sports /2018/08/25/brockton-x2019-s-chante-bonds/10956666007/.

4. "2013 Boston Militia Team Summary for Weeks 1 through 11," Women's Football Alliance, Hosted Sports, 2013, https://www.hostedsports.com /hsi_stats.asp?league=wfa&season=2013.

5. Mark Staffieri, "Whitney Zelee Emerging as the Finest Running Back in All of Women's Football," *Bleacher Report*, 18 June 2013, https:// bleacherreport.com/articles/1675886.

6. Mark Staffieri, "Boston Militia Makes History as First Team to Capture Two WFA Titles," *Fourth and Feminine*, 10 September 2014, https:// fourthandfeminine.wordpress.com/2014/09/10/boston-militia-makes -history-as-first-team-to-capture-two-wfa-national-titles/.

7. Neal Rozendaal, "The Greatest Players in Women's Football History: Part 3," Neal Rozendaal website, 2017, http://nealrozendaal.com /womensfootball/greatest-players-history-2017-part-3/.

8. "Women's Football Alliance," Hosted Sports, accessed 11 July 2020, https://www.hostedsports.com/hsi_stats.asp?league=wfa&season=2013.

9. Neal Rozendaal, *The Women's Football Encyclopedia* (Rockville MD: Roze-hawk, 2016), 102.

10. Kathy Kuras, dir., *Open Field* (Crook and Nanny Productions and Vanguard Muse, 23 October 2020), https://www.imdb.com/title/tt12642316/.

11. New York Sharks, "Award-Winning Actress, Julie Bowen," Facebook, 25 July 2021, https://m.facebook.com/watch/?v=863503350931816&_rdr.

12. Gracie Watt, "Six Texas Films at Austin Film Festival You Won't Want to Miss," *Texas Lifestyle & Travel Magazine*, 22 October 2021, https:// texaslifestylemag.com/entertainment/six-texas-films-at-austin-film-festival -you-wont-want-to-miss/?fbclid=IwAR2_ofVOCe6L6xnKj93XHeWt _RRxlNtIMGLY9DXhKMKUU0E2IGfPPD2j1HU.

13. Russ Crawford, "Women's Football Arrives at Super Bowl LIII," *American Football International*, 6 February 2019, https://www .americanfootballinternational.com/women-athletes-gained-major -recognition-during-super-bowl-liii/.

14. Secret Deodorant, "Secret Super Bowl 2020 TV Commercial: The Secret Kicker Featuring Carli Lloyd, Crystal Dunn," YouTube, 4 February 2020, https://www.youtube.com/watch?v=so9yUfsFQSQ.

15. NFL, "NFL 100 Kickoff," Facebook, 15 August 2019, https://www.facebook.com/NFL/videos/887775208247004.

16. Steve Salzman conversation via text message, 26 July 2020.

17. Steve Dixon conversation via text message, 26 July 2020.

18. New England Patriots, "A story of passion, perseverance and proof that football is for everyone," Twitter, 1 July 2020, 10:46 a.m., https://twitter.com/Patriots/status/1278339178535817216.

19. Audrey Cleo Yap, "How ESPN Documentary 'Born to Play' Shows Football in Its 'Purest Form,'" *Variety*, 30 June 2020, https://variety.com/2020/tv/news/espn-born-to-play-football-documentary-clip-1234694760/#article-comments.

20. Stephen Shaefer, "ESPN Doc Tackles Renegades—Boston's Champ Women's Tackle Football Team," *Boston Herald*, 1 July 2020, https://www.bostonherald.com/2020/07/01/espn-doc-tackles-renegades-bostons-champ-womens-tackle-football-team/.

21. Steve Kopian, "Born to Play (2020) Hits ESPN Tonight and Is a Must See," *Unseen Films*, 1 July 2020, http://www.unseenfilms.net/2020/07/born-to-play-2020-hits-espn-tonight-and.html.

22. Gerrad Hall, "Women's Football Team Takes the Field in Rousing Doc *Born to Play*," *Entertainment Weekly*, 17 July 2020, https://ew.com/tv/born-to-play-sports-documentary-womens-football-boston-renegades/.

23. Russ Crawford, "ESPN's Born to Play a Groundbreaking Documentary on Women's Football," *American Football International*, 14 July 2020, https://www.americanfootballinternational.com/espns-born-to-play-a-groundbreaking-documentary-on-womens-football/.

24. Oscar Lopez, "Gridiron Beauties," Facebook search results for *Born to Play*, 12 February 2020, https://www.facebook.com/page/156585881051771/search/?q=born%20to%20play; Michael Burmy, "Hometown Women's Football," Facebook search results for *Born to Play*, Wyn Flato, 17 July 2020, https://www.facebook.com/groups/1191151254247248/search?q=born%20to%20play.

25. Women's Sports Foundation, "I feel like they were the purest form of the sport," Twitter, 17 July 2020, 11:26 a.m., https://twitter.com/WomensSportsFdn/status/1284162611282575361.

26. ESPN, "Seven Straight Titles," Twitter, 4 July 2020, 11:39 a.m., https://twitter.com/espn/status/1279454785649938434.

27. Russ Crawford, "Women's Football Alliance Crowns Three National Champions," *American Football International*, 27 July 2021, https://www

.americanfootballinternational.com/womens-football-alliance-crowns
-3-national-champions/.

28. "WFA Champions to Be Honored Yearly in Pro Football Hall of Fame,"
WFA, 26 August 2021, https://wfaprofootball.com/wfa-mvps-to-be
-honored-in-pro-football-hall-of-fame/.

29. "WFA Signs Television Network Deal with ESPN," WFA, 11 January 2020,
https://wfaprofootball.com/wfa-signs-television-network-deal-with-espn
/?fbclid=IwAR3eM3TGz9ezTOh7697gVXvbZN2yx5o18syFoF3r1JgBcpc
-Ci4UJ-bsxdc.

30. Andra Douglas, *Black and Blue: Love, Sports, and the Art of Empowerment*
(New York: BookBaby, 2019), 81.

# Index